First Edition

50
Fabulous
Places
To Retire In America

By Lee & Saralee Rosenberg

THE CAREER PRESS
180 FIFTH AVE.,
PO BOX 34
HAWTHORNE, NJ 07507
1-800-CAREER-1
201-427-0229 (OUTSIDE U.S.)
FAX: 201-427-2037

50 FABULOUS PLACES TO RETIRE IN AMERICA

ISBN 0-934829-29-2, $14.95

To the best of the authors' knowledge, the information provided in this book was the most current and accurate available at the time of printing. The material is for reference purposes only and is subject to change. Readers should confirm the latest information with the appropriate sources indicated.

Copies of this book may be ordered by mail or phone directly from the publisher. To order by mail, please include price as noted above, $2.50 handling per order, plus $1.00 for each book ordered. (New Jersey residents please add 7% sales tax.) Send to: The Career Press Inc., 180 Fifth Avenue., PO Box 34, Hawthorne, NJ 07507.

Or call Toll-Free 1-800-CAREER-1 to order using your VISA or Mastercard or for further information on all titles published or distributed by Career Press.

Attention: Schools, Organizations, Corporations

This book is available at quantity discounts for bulk purchases for educational, business or sales promotional use. Please contact: Ms. Gretchen Fry, Director-Special Markets, Career Press, 180 Fifth Ave., Hawthorne, NJ 07507
or call 1-800-CAREER-1

Acknowledgements

Compiling a book that incorporates more than 10,000 pieces of information cannot be accomplished without the help of a great many people.

The first word would never have appeared without the tireless efforts of our research team: Barbara Aymong Knab, Elizabeth Campisi, Debbie Hamilton, Donna Henderson, Stacy Mandel, and Judy Orner (the "Backup Genius"). We feared epitaphs that read, "died on hold," but their perseverance was unyielding.

We are grateful to the hard-working staffs at the chambers of commerce, local realty boards and real estate agencies who gave of their time and expertise. Without their honest assessments and insights, our area profiles would be hollow.

We are especially grateful to the Coldwell Banker agents who responded to our barrage of questions with genuine ease and interest. They are, without a doubt, the top relocation specialists in the country.

A special thanks goes to the numerous organizations that willingly provided important data: AARP (national and state/area offices), ACCRA (American Chamber of Commerce Researchers Association), area agencies on aging, the Household Goods Carriers Bureau (thank you, Joe Habib), the Joint Commission on Accreditation of Healthcare Organizations, the National Association of Realtors, the U.S. Census Bureau and the United States Conference of Mayors.

We are especially pleased with the spirited cooperation of The Weather Channel, the 24-hour all-weather satellite network. With the help of Director of Meteorology Bill Campbell, we were able to rely on the most extensive, accurate climatological data for all 50 areas. The Weather Channel is truly a great American resource.

Our initial research was enhanced by Dr. Charles F. Longino, Wake Forest University Professor of Sociology, who is certifiably the most knowledgeable person in the country about retirees and relocation. His generosity with information and support of our concept were inspiring.

Our editor, Betsy Sheldon, was also there with an encouraging word (editors are trained to keep it short). Her vision and latitude contributed immensely to a final product of which we can all be proud. Ellen Scher, our fearless production designer, did a masterful job putting this manuscript to bed (which is where she deservedly headed when it was all over).

Finally, we are eternally grateful to our families for their support and help. The mothers, Rita Rosenberg and Doris Hymen, made phone calls and compiled facts. Freda Rosenberg sweated over a hot keyboard to enter data. And the children, Zack, Alex and Taryn, mustered up enough patience and love to last a lifetime.

To Zachary, Alexandra and Taryn

Every accomplishment, great or small, starts with two words. "I'll try."

Table of Contents

Fast Facts

About the Authors   **256**

Introduction

Pick a day, any day. If the statistics are right, 5,960 Americans are going to celebrate their 65th birthday. In recent past, this milestone officially marked the start of a person's "Declaration of Independence." Today, however, more than 60 percent of men this age have already retired. In fact, more than half of the retired workers who applied for Social Security benefits last year were 62. And in a brand-new study of adults working for large companies, an overwhelming 90 percent said they planned to retire before turning 65.

Aside from the "freedom years" starting sooner, retirement itself is a whole new ballgame. Today's older Americans are more likely to have the combined good fortune of wealth, health and longer life expectancies than any previous generation. They are typically educated, still married, and, for the first time, have pensions, investments and equity to provide financial security.

The most dramatic change among retirees is that many are relocating to other parts of the country. Unlike their parents and grandparents who spent their last years living in or near their childrens' homes, the U.S. Census Bureau reports that more than a half-million adults 55 and over move out-of-state every year.

Companies who market their products and services to this fast-growing segment of the population refer to independent seniors as the "Go-Goers," the "Equity Immigrants" and "ACES" (Active College Educated Seniors). Whatever the label, their destinations have been predictable. The majority have headed to one of 10 popular retirement states, including Florida, California, Arizona, Texas, North Carolina and Georgia.

Another major change is that relocating upon retirement was traditionally a privilege of the rich. Now it's the middle class who doesn't summer where it winters. For those on a fixed income, moving to an area where the living costs and taxes are manageable is the best strategy for financial survival.

There are other benefits to relocating. Many say they want a more temperate climate. Others expressed a need to leave urban blight, with its increasing crime, pollution and congestion. Still others cited rising property taxes and utility costs as their reasons. And naturally, some were anxious to get away from *all* of the above.

Regardless of the reasons, there was an almost universal agreement on what a retirement spot should have: four mild seasons, great scenery, affordable living costs, abundant culture and recreation, low crime, low taxes, and enough activities to entice the kids to visit.

Alas, that was our mission in researching fabulous places to retire. To find areas from coast to coast that could give people all that and more. Most people would be happy to find just one place that fit the bill. We found 50!

How we arrived at 50 fabulous places

The task of narrowing our list was a tremendous challenge when you consider that there are hundreds, if not thousands, of desirable areas across the country. No doubt there is relief among the residents of the areas we didn't include (the attitude is "Close the doors after I get in.").

We began our search by talking to people. Countless numbers of people. Representatives of AARP state and regional offices, state realtor associations, local realtors, chamber of commerce executives, long-distance movers, directors at the U.S. Census who track geographic mobility, and their counterparts at the U.S. Department of Agriculture who study rural retirement counties.

In every case, we asked the same questions. "Where are retirees moving to, and why?"

We also spoke to an infinite number of retirees. Those who were considering a relocation, those who had already experienced one and especially those who had moved and were in the process of doing it again. We asked about the areas they were most enamored of and what was wrong with the places they were leaving.

Finally a pattern began to emerge. Predictably, we heard about the three S's of relocation: St. Petersburg, Scottsdale and San Diego. And about the latest "hot spots": Las Vegas, Santa Fe, and Naples. Then we started hearing of unfamiliar places—or what we referred to as the "you're kidding?" names: Sequim (Wash.), Clayton (Ga.), Coeur d'Alene (Idaho), Lincoln City (Ore.), and Duck (N.C.).

To a list of more than 100 locations, we applied our checklist of "must haves." No area could be considered unless it offered 15 important characteristics (they are of equal importance and are thus presented in random order):

1. Great scenic beauty
2. Three to four seasons of glorious weather
3. A diversified housing market with wide ranges of affordability
4. An overall reduced tax burden compared to the major metropolitan areas where retirees are migrating from
5. Affordable living costs
6. A fast-growing area, improved services, more housing, shopping, jobs, etc.
7. An abundance of culture, recreation and annual events
8. Access to quality medical care, as well as reasonable health care costs
9. A thriving economy that offers solid job and business opportunities (approximately 25% of retirees go back to work)
10. Proximity to major highways and airports to make vacation travel and trips back home convenient
11. Availability of continuing education and volunteer programs
12. Ample attractions and events to entertain visiting family and friends
13. Availability of quality services for seniors, including those that offer social, physical and emotional support.
14. An area where residents feel safe because of low crime rates and/or excellent police and fire protection
15. A warm, friendly community where newcomers are welcome

We did allow for a few exceptions. Maui and Palm Springs are two of the country's most expensive areas to live in, but also some of the most beautiful and fantasy-filled. If you can afford them, count your blessings. Door County, Wis., and Sullivan County, N.Y., can get blustery cold, but we had to consider the hearty ones who thrive on invigorating climates. San Diego and San Antonio are big cities with their share of crime, but their climates and amenities are so extraordinary, they couldn't be eliminated.

Then there were the cities that quickly disappeared from our list, much to our surprise. Take Orlando, for instance (please). We can't tell you how many people expressed an interest in this city. It certainly is one of the fastest-growing in the country, but upon further investigation we found nagging problems. The heat and humidity in this inland city could be insufferable, not just during the summer but year-round. Also, the housing market is so overbuilt that if you were unhappy and wanted to sell the prospects would be dismal. Most troubling is that the area is so transient and there is virtually no sense of community.

OK, so on to the 50 that made it. We found fabulous college towns (Bloomington, Ind.), military towns (Colorado Springs), state capitals (Carson City, Nev.), golf capitals (Hilton Head Island, S.C.), ski capitals (Santa Fe, we kid you not). Why we'll even tell you about a place where you can golf and ski on the same day (Clayton, Ga.)! You'll be able to check out big cities and tiny towns. We've also covered the bases with climate. What's your pleasure? Tropical, semi-tropical, desert, semi-arid, four mild seasons?

If you've been dreaming of a particular retirement lifestyle, but aren't sure where it exists, we'll help you find the best place. This invariably raises the most asked question. Which place *is* the best?

We don't have a clue. What we do know is that our fabulous 50 have enough outstanding attributes to be worthy of your consideration! With all due respect to the popular guides that rank and rate an assortment of lifestyle factors, throw in a year's supply of statistics and then assign each area a final score, we frankly never understood how that was valuable. Fort Myers may emerge as the number-one choice, but if you would be miserable in a place that had 12 months of summer, would it be your first choice? We think not.

That's why we won't inundate you with numbers. Instead, we give you relevant facts, inside information and a feel for what it's like to *live* in each area. For example, our profiles won't bore you with the numbers of hospitals in the community; we identify them and describe the level of available care. We won't bombard you with FBI crime statistics, we'll tell you if a community is a safe place to live and why. We've also laid out the profiles in such a way that you can read them in their entirety or "cherry pick" by subjects of interest (climate, recreation, etc.). Now you can be your own judge!

Before you start your shopping expedition, however, we urge you to first read the chapters, "50 Fabulous Ways to Get Ready for Retirement," and "How to Hold On to Your Possessions and Your Sanity." These common sense "short courses" offer hundreds of great ideas to save you headaches, heartache and money!

Perhaps the most important chapter is the one that will turn this book into an incredible investment. "Sending Your Money Out to Work So You Don't Have To" suggests sophisticated strategies for preserving your assets and managing your retirement income.

Finally, as we interviewed people across the country, we kept heaping certain pieces of advice for fellow seniors who were contemplating a move. We thought it would be invaluable to share their first-hand experience.

10 tips from the front line

1. The best substitute for living somewhere is reading the local newspaper. Subscribe to the Sunday edition for even a month, and learn about real estate, jobs and business opportunities, entertainment, local issues, etc. The cost is nominal (averages $8-$12/mo.) and for your convenience, we've included the address and phone of the major paper serving each area.

2. Take some of the guesswork out of estimating utility costs by calling the gas and electric companies with addresses of homes you are considering. They can tell you how much the previous owners paid in the past year (average highs and lows). Although your usage habits will probably differ, you'll have a sense if the home is well-insulated, what months run highest, etc.

3. Unless you are very familiar with an area, rent before buying. Taking time to get to know a town, meet people and see it from every angle is vitally important. This is particularly true in areas where houses and condominiums have been on the market for a long time. If you buy a place and discover that the area is not right for you, your options will be limited.

4. If you plan to live in an area year-round, visit during as many seasons as possible. Find out which seasons you can tolerate and which you can't. The time to discover your endurance level is *before* you move.

5. When contacting a real estate agency, ask to work with a relocation specialist. This trained professional, who works almost exclusively with out-of-town buyers, is well-equipped to understand your special needs.

6. Join AARP's national organization ($5/yr.) and benefit from its services, discounts, and excellent magazine, *Modern Maturity*. Write to AARP Membership, P.O. Box 199, Long Beach, CA 90801. For information on local chapters, send a stamped, self-addressed business-size envelope to: AARP Chapter Records Office, 601 E St., NW, Washington, DC 20049 (202-434-2277).

7. If you plan to visit several areas at one time, be sure to record your impressions as you go. Take notes, pictures, videos, brochures, etc. Anything you can do to jog your memory will be a help.

8. When you visit an area, don't limit yourself to real estate. Stop by church or synagogue, senior centers, country clubs, and conduct your own personal interviews. Talk to people who live there and see if you feel comfortable.

9. Many people told us that husbands adjusted faster to their new surroundings than their wives. Women tended to miss family, friends and familiar routines more. Men, on the other hand, woke up every day and couldn't wait to go fishing, play golf, or engage in other outside interests. Anticipating an adjustment period may help you cope.

10. Finally, if you think that your retirement destination is going to be your final resting place, think again. At some point you could decide you need a change of scenery. Medical needs may arise that force your hand. Or you'll discover, for example, that living in a restricted retirement community depresses you. Whatever the reason, we learned that it was very common for retirees to move two to three times.

You are about to embark on one of life's most fascinating journeys. Our hope is that **50 Fabulous Places To Retire In America** will be the vessel that takes you to your greatest destination ever. In the meantime, take heart in one other wonderful discovery we've made along the way.

The grass *is* greener on the other side!

## Chapter 1

50 Fabulous Ways to Get Ready for Retirement

Remember taking the family on a long road trip? When you were finally within a few miles of your destination, nothing could have stopped you from driving Indy 500-style to the finish line. You simply couldn't wait to arrive. It's the same with approaching retirement. Once the "freedom years" are within reach, whether it's next month, next year or even five years from now, you start sounding like the kids. "Are we there yet?"

And why not? Typical retirees have devoted an average of 90,000 hours of their lives to earning a living, and an even greater amount of time to raising a family. Retirement is finally the chance to change gears. Some may be looking forward to slowing the pace while others will feel like horses at the starting gate. At the sound of the gun they'll be off and running, enjoying hobbies, socializing, traveling, pursuing new interests, starting a business—the choices are endless.

Regardless of the retirement fantasy you envision, it should embody a lifetime of dreams. The purpose of this chapter is to get you to focus on important lifestyle issues that can prevent it from turning into a nightmare!

As a certified financial planner specializing in retirement planning for more than 15 years, I can tell you that entering the "golden years" is not as easy as it looks. One man recently told me he needed to find a way to spend all his time without spending all his money. His wife confided that for her, retirement meant half the bank account but twice the husband. "When does the fun start," she asked?

There seems to be this almost universal perception that once the stress of working and raising a family is gone, life is bliss. And it is certainly possible provided you make a commitment to *plan ahead!*

Just as with a vacation, a dinner party or a night on the town, a successful retirement is only as good as the preparations behind it. Furthermore, your generation's "retirement class" has been given the gift of longevity. According to all the latest mortality tables, a 20- to 30-year life expectancy is not unthinkable. With practically a third of your life ahead of you, the only prudent course of action is to leave as little to chance as possible.

A recent study by the Teachers Insurance and Annuity Association found that 92 percent of the respondents said they were satisfied with their retirement. But those who had planned ahead were the most fulfilled and the most financially secure.

In the next chapter we'll discuss the most effective retirement financial planning strategies. But before deciding on the kind of lifestyle you can afford, you've got to decide on the kind of lifestyle you want!

Instructions: Here is a checklist of 50 important lifestyle questions to ponder and discuss. The best way we know how to avoid headaches and heartaches is to: 1) anticipate your needs; 2) focus on your likes and dislikes; and 3) prepare for a transition period. Just remember: The more honest your answers, the easier it will be to develop a game plan for *where* and *how* you want to live.

Decisions, decisions

1. Timing is everything. Have you decided exactly when you'll retire? Will you and your spouse be retiring at the same time? If not, have you considered how the one whose retirement begins first will handle free time while the other still works?

2. If it ain't broke. Are you the type of person who finds it difficult to make changes? If so, can you ease into retirement? Some experts suggest semi-retirement to see how you handle more leisure time and less structure.

3. When the snowman cometh. Are you planning to relocate permanently or will you be only heading south at the first sign of frost?

4. As time goes by. Ideally, how would you like to spend your day? Will you be happy without a daily regimen or do you absolutely need structure? What sort of activities, hobbies, recreation or volunteer work will fill your day?

5. Social hour. Do you currently have an active social life or are you more the homebody type? Are you prepared for the fact that this might change when you first relocate? Thing may be a little dull until you make friends. Conversely, you may find that new neighbors are more "neighborly" than you're used to.

6. Minding your own business. Do you plan to start or buy an existing business, invest in a franchise, or become a consultant? If so, are you considering areas where the business climate is favorable to such a venture?

7. Work, work, work. Will you be counting on a part-time job to supplement your income? Are you looking at areas where the local economy has a good employment picture? (College towns are often poor choices for senior employment opportunities because competition from students is fierce.)

8. Ready or not. When you leave your job, will you feel let down and lost? Some people so enjoy the friendships, the decision making, the deal making, the travel and other aspects that nothing else can fill the void. If that's your feeling, are you really ready to retire?

9. The "B" word. If you'll be living on a fixed income, are you prepared to set up a budget? Now's the time to establish your financial priorities (controlling credit card spending) and identify what you're willing to cut out.

10. Dream a little dream. Is there something you have waited your whole life to do? From taking a world tour to buying a cabin in the woods, consider how you can turn your fondest dreams into reality in your retirement years.

11. Common bonds. Do you and your spouse currently have mutual interests or are you accustomed to doing your own thing? When you relocate, is there something you can do together that will make retirement more enjoyable?

12. Lines of communication. Are you and your spouse discussing your retirement honestly and openly? If there is strong disagreement about how and where to live, are you working out compromises?

Location, location, location

13. Weather or not. What type of climate do you prefer? Do you need a change of seasons or could you be happy with 12 months of summer?

14. A month in the country. What does your ideal retirement spot look like? Is it a tropical paradise? Woodsy? A quiet, rural area? A small town? A college town? A suburb? A medium-sized city? A large metropolitan area? If your retirement hot spot is a dramatic departure from your current environment, is your spouse as comfortable with the idea as you are?

15. By the sea, by the sea. How do you feel about living on or near water? Would you consider an inland area? If so, what's the farthest you'd want to be from the ocean, lakes, etc.?

16. All together now. Does the idea of living in a restricted retirement community such as Sun City and Leisure Village appeal to you? Or, would you prefer a heterogeneous community with working people and young families?

17. Off the beaten path. If you've always dreamt of retiring to a secluded location, are you making contingency plans for medical emergencies or if the roads are impassable due to inclement weather?

18. Those who pray together. Are you looking at areas where there are others of your religious background? Joining a house of worship is a wonderful way to meet people and to get involved in the community.

19. That's what friends are for. If you currently depend on family and friends to help you with shopping and errands, are you looking at areas that have good public transportation or where stores and services are within walking distance?

Housing options

20. Dream house. What kind of home would best suit your needs? A brand-new house, a smaller, older home, a high-rise condo, a townhouse, a garden apartment, a mobile home, etc.? How much maintenance (inside and outside) can you handle?

21. No man is an island. If you've been living in a private home, are you now considering a retirement community or development? Will you be able to adjust to a communal environment if it means less privacy, decisions by committee and rules and regulations?

22. To buy or not to buy. If you don't know that much about the area you choose to move to, have you considered renting an apartment or home for six months? That decision could be a lifesaver if you realize later on that you'd be happier in the next development, the next town or the next state.

23. Breakfast on the greens. If you are looking for a retirement community, a housing development or other park-like setting, which amenities are the most important? Golf and tennis on premises? A clubhouse? Shopping and restaurants? Medical facilities? Canals for docking? All of the above?

24. To sell or not to sell. Have you decided to sell your home so you can make a permanent relocation or do you plan to come back for part of the year? If you are unable to sell, will you try to rent so your move is not delayed? Have you spoken with a certified financial planner or an accountant to learn about the laws and tax breaks concerning rental property?

25. Man's best friend. If your pets are coming with you, have you checked with the condo development, apartment management, etc., to see if they're allowed?

26. Drive time. Are you looking at an area that is so close to shopping and services that you might only need one car? How is public transportation and service to the airports? Getting rid of an older car can be a considerable savings (no gas, repairs or insurance). If you absolutely don't need to be a two-car family, simplify your life.

The leisure life

27. Leisure suits you fine. How do you currently spend your free time? Entertaining? Babysitting the grandkids? How will you fill the void if your favorite pastimes are back home?

28. What's your hobby? Do you enjoy any hobbies? With more free time, would you increase your involvement and/or pursue something new? If you've never been a hobbyist, is there something you've wanted to try?

29. Build a better mousetrap. Are you looking forward to trying new things, improving your skills, learning computers, etc.? A great retirement is one that combines old interests with new loves. If retirement changes nothing in your life, how can you expect to avoid boredom?

30. Get smart. Does the idea of taking college courses or continuing education programs interest you? Would it be important for you to live close to a local college or university?

31. Tennis anyone? If you or your spouse are an avid golfer, tennis player, skier, boater, fisherman, etc. are you considering areas that offer enough activities for both of you?

32. Forget Uncle Sam, the community wants you. Do you see yourself doing volunteer work? Are there opportunities in your prospective community for you to get involved—helping the needy, raising funds, etc?

33. Try it, you'll like it. If you've never done volunteer work before, are you good at working with children, the elderly, the physically impaired? Are you a someone who prefers to be in front of people or behind the scenes? What would make volunteering worthwhile for you?

34. It's show time. Are you a theater, opera or dance buff? Could you live in an area that did not have ongoing cultural events or would it be OK to drive an hour to take in a show when the urge hit? If showbiz is your calling, have you checked out the local theater groups?

35. On the road again. Have you been waiting for your retirement to travel, take long vacations, join elderhostels, etc?. Are you looking at areas that are in close proximity to major highways and airports? Do many airlines serve the area?

36. Join the club. Do you plan to become active in clubs, organizations, civic groups, etc? If you are typically not a joiner, how do you plan to meet people in the community? At a minimum we urge you to join AARP. It's the best $5 you'll ever invest in your retirement lifestyle.

37. Hey, sports fans. If you're a real sports nut, could you live in an area that did not have professional teams? What's the farthest you'd want to live from a city that had major league baseball, professional football, etc.?

38. On your mark. When it comes to physical recreation, do you enjoy competing at a sport, participating in classes or being on a team? Have you checked out the availability of public and private clubs, recreation centers and other places to play?

Family and friends

39. You've got to have friends. Are you planning to follow friends to a retirement spot? If not, could you adjust to living without a close social circle at first? Are you the type who's comfortable to break the ice?

40. Younger generations. If you live near your children now, will you be able to adjust to long separations? How do they feel about your relocating? Will your new home be big enough to accommodate them when they visit?

41. Siblings and other friends. See above.

42. Home for the holidays. Whether it's Christmas, Rosh Hashanah, Thanksgiving or another important holiday to you and your family, you'll want to decide whether you'll head back to relatives or whether you'll start a different tradition in your new location.

43. Going through customs. What customs do you have emotional ties to? Sunday Dinner with the kids? Weekly card games? Monthly camping trips? Annual picnics? Which will you be able to continue, and what new traditions can you start to help ease the longing?

44. Extending yourself. If your extended family is rather large, have you thought about how you'll split your time when it comes to visiting children, step-children and grandchildren, etc. What arrangements will you make for them to visit you?

45. The family plan. Are one or both of your parents living? Have you asked them to relocate with you? Have you checked on the availability and quality of housing for the elderly, nursing homes, medical facilities and programs?

46. Suddenly single. How would you handle the loss of your spouse? Would living thousands of miles away from family make it difficult to cope?

The healthy life

47. For the health of it. Do you have certain physical conditions that will determine the kind of lifestyle you can enjoy? Is there a special climate that would be more favorable for you? Will you need to be within driving distance to a certain type of medical facility?

48. Let's get physical. Are you physically fit or have years of being sedentary left you feeling sluggish? With more free time, will you change your ways?

49. Food for thought. Have you changed your dietary habits to compensate for a slower metabolism and greater risk of disease? Are you overweight by more than 20 pounds? Are you considering areas where the climate would enable you to incorporate physical activity into your daily regimen? (Our physical decline as we get older is often caused by lack of exercise, poor eating habits and boredom.)

50. What's up, doc? Have you asked your family, friends and your doctors if they can refer you to physicians in your new town? Although most places have a physician's referral service, it's always better to start out with personal recommendations.

As you can see, many of these lifestyle issues have little to do with where you live. Whether you stay in your current home, move to the next town or halfway across the country, a successful retirement depends a great deal on emotional preparation.

And as for deciding where to move, *the real key to finding a fabulous place to retire in America is simply to listen to what's already in your heads and in your hearts.*

## Chapter 2

Sending Your Money Out to Work So You Don't Have To

Unless you are a recent lottery winner or have the privilege of using Rockefeller as a surname, a successful retirement in the United States will depend an awful lot on your *financial* state. Forget about whether your belongings will arrive in one piece, you should be wondering if your *money* is in good enough shape to make the move!

I know what you're thinking. Many of the retirement locations you are considering have lower taxes, reasonable housing prices, etc. While that can be a big help in sustaining a comfortable lifestyle, not one of the 50 areas we looked at is called Shangri-la. In fact, moving to a place with lower living costs is only the first step towards financial security.

What many people are beginning to realize is that unlike any previous generation, today's retirees are facing a double-edged sword. On one hand, life expectancy has never been greater. The problem is that in these uncertain economic times, many people now fear that they will outlive their money!

According to IRS mortality tables, men who are 65 today are expected to live for another 15.6 years, women for another 19.3 years. Further, there is a 50 percent chance that either you or your spouse will live to age 90.

But not only is retiring different today insofar as prolonged life is concerned, lifestyles are vastly different as well. Older Americans lead active, full lives. They travel, begin new careers and start businesses. All it takes is money.

That's why it has never been more important to insure *in advance* that your finances are ready to work at full capacity. With the prospect of a long, fulfilling retirement, it would be a shame if your money didn't work as hard for you as you did for it!

Surprisingly, over the years I've heard many intelligent people make light of this discussion. They anticipate that the profits on the sale of their home, their Social Security benefits, savings and investments will provide adequate income throughout their retirement years.

They also assume that with a lower cost of living, a decreased tax burden and the need to support only two people, their lives will be free of financial worries. I'm always hopeful they're right. Unfortunately, as a certified financial planner in private practice for more than 15 years, I've seen a lot of people guess wrong.

In many cases, retirees discover that their retirement nest egg is eroding faster than a locomotive. Others watch as maintenance costs and property taxes go up like clockwork every year. But the worst scenario is when certain medical conditions affect one or both spouses and health care costs deplete their savings. The bottom line is that the living is easy, but the payments are hard!

You don't have to have these problems

I know this sounds discouraging at a time when you are so excited about your new lifestyle. But by focusing on the most common and costly mistakes retirees make when managing their financial affairs, you should be able to avoid them. Furthermore, with such a wide variety of sophisticated planning tools and investment vehicles, it has never been easier for retirees to live on their assets.

What can you do to insure a secure, comfortable and happy retirement? The most important step is putting your "financial" house in order.

The pre-retirement checklist

There are 15 ways to prepare financially for your retirement. Please review these and place a big "X" by all those that require *immediate* attention.

Your Pre-Retirement Checklist

_____   Do you know the size of your retirement nest egg?

_____   Have you contacted your employer(s) regarding the amount vested in your pension plan(s)? Have you decided how the funds will be disbursed?

_____   Have you contacted Social Security to determine your estimated retirement benefits? Have you informed them that you are ready to receive benefits?

_____   Are you making arrangements to move some of your liquid and equity assets into income-producing vehicles?

_____   Are you aware of the most current tax laws and how they will affect your retirement income?

_____   Have you estimated your living expenses after retirement?

_____   Are you aware of how much it costs you to live now?

_____   Are you cutting back on your living expenses now so that you don't carry unnecessary debts into retirement?

_____   If you plan to work after retirement, are you aware of the income limitations established by Social Security (this is for people who plan to collect benefits *and* work)?

_____   Will your mortgage be paid off when you retire?

_____   Have you reviewed your insurance policies to determine which policies can be restructured or canceled?

_____   Do you have a will and an understanding of the laws pertaining to inheritances, taxes and probate?

_____   Does your spouse, or children, relatives or close friend know where important records are kept?

_____   Do you know where you want to live after retirement?

_____   Have you discussed your retirement needs with a certified financial planner?

Taking inventory of your assets

Although every single item on this list is important, if you do nothing else after reading this chapter, I hope that you'll take an inventory of your assets and analyze what portion of those can be turned into income.

You see, during your working years, your investment strategy was dedicated to accumulating assets that had a high degree of appreciation. In theory you had the opportunity to take advantage of both your earnings, (which presumably increased over the years) as well as a growing portfolio. The former covered your living expenses, the latter was earmarked for future needs: college educations, weddings, retirement, etc.

Once retirement is upon you, there is no biweekly paycheck. There is no annual raise or the option to wait out an investment for many years. Now is the time to find a way to replace your earnings and your assets with monthly income. Alas, that is where your portfolio comes in. Some portion of it must be converted to income, with the balance left to appreciate as a continued hedge against inflation.

In this chapter, I'll help you find out how much you'll have to live on each year, how much to reinvest, save, etc. Armed with that information, you and your financial advisors can develop the best strategy for insuring that your money stands the test of time. And ultimately you'll be able to decide the kind of retirement lifestyle you can afford.

How *will* you support yourselves? For the average retiree, the investment portfolio represents the largest portion of your income. Total sources include:

Source of Income	% of Total Income
Pensions, Annuities,Gifts, Dividends, Interest and other Investments	52.0%
Social Security	27.0%
Sale of Assets, Home Equity, Personal Savings	10.5%
Earnings (Part-time work)	7.4%
Supplemental Security Income and Public Assistance	1.9%
Other	2.0%

Establishing your net worth

While it's helpful to know your sources of retirement income, it's even more important to know the size of your retirement nest egg. The first thing to look at is the value of your combined assets. This would include your home, your investments, your pension(s), savings, etc. At the same time, you have to assess your liabilities, such as mortgages, installment loans, etc. When you subtract what you owe from what you own, this is your net worth. Net worth, in essence, is a like-it-or-not snapshot of your personal wealth.

Here's how to prepare your personal Net Worth Statement.

Cash reserve assets

Add up your cash or near-cash resources such as checking accounts, savings accounts and money market funds. These are your "liquid" assets because they can be "liquidated" quickly without penalties.

It's also possible to include the cash value of a life insurance policy as well as a bank Certificate of Deposit (CD). These vehicles are liquid to the extent that it's possible to tap into them in an emergency. However, doing so may result in penalties for early withdrawal, or in the case of borrowing from the cash value of a life insurance policy, trigger interest charges on the value of the loan.

In my opinion, between 15 percent and 20 percent of your total assets should be liquid and there should be enough ready cash to cover your living expenses for a minimum of three months, preferably six.

Equity/retirement assets

Generally, the most valuable asset in your portfolio is the equity in your home. But ideally, you will also have a combination of other investment assets including stocks and options, mutual funds, taxable and tax-free bonds, T-Bills, annuities, investment property (not your residence) and/or equity in a business.

Retirement assets include IRA/Keogh Plans, 401Ks, vested pension plans, employee savings and stock option programs. In tandem, these should represent 50 percent to 60 percent of your total assets.

Keep in mind that if you do sell off investment assets, it will more than likely trigger tax liabilities and possibly penalties for early withdrawal.

To establish the values of these assets, ask your insurance agent, stockbroker, realtor and certified financial planner for assistance. You can also refer to recent price quotes in the newspaper. Although establishing values for real estate limited partnerships and vacation timeshares is complicated, for the purpose of this exercise, it's acceptable to place the value at the price you paid.

Finally, to determine the value of your 401K or other company benefit prgrams, ask your employee benefits department to provide the calculations.

As for *personal property,* clothing, furs and jewels, cars, furniture, etc., appraise value by estimating how much money the item would generate if it were sold today (only if you intend to liquidate).

Liabilities

This represents the outstanding balances on your mortgage(s), cars, installment loans, credit cards, etc. It also includes your projected state and federal tax bill. Normally, your liabilities should represent no more than 30 percent to 50 percent of your total assets. In retirement, however, I urge clients to carry as light a load as possible with respect to debts. They add significantly to monthly living expenses at a time when income may be fixed and limited.

In addition, the interest on car loans, credit cards, and installment loans is no longer deductible. Furthermore, with banks charging 18% interest (in Florida, it can be up to 21%), but only paying out 6%-7% on savings, it doesn't take an accountant to tell you that installment debt is a raw deal.

If you do not have a current net worth statement, please fill out the form on the next page. If you need help, consult your financial planner and/or accountant.

ASSETS

CASH RESERVE ASSETS

Checking Accounts/Cash $ _____

Savings Accounts   _____

Money Market Funds   _____

Certificates of Deposit   _____

Life Insurance (Cash Value)   _____

EQUITY/RETIREMENT ASSETS

Time Deposits (T-bills)   _____

Stocks and Options

Retirement Savings (IRAs/Keoghs)   _____

Annuities (Surrender Value)   _____

Pensions (Vested Interest)   _____

Profit Sharing Plans   _____

Collectibles   _____

House (Market Value)   _____

Other Real Estate/Limited Partnerships   _____

Business Interests   _____

Personal Property (Auto, Jewels, etc.)   _____

Loans Owed You   _____

Other Assets   _____

TOTAL ASSETS   _____

LIABILITIES

Mortgage or Rent (Balance Due) $ _____

Auto Loan (Balance Due)   _____

Credit Cards   _____

Installment Loans   _____

Annual Tax Bill   _____

Business Debts   _____

Student Loans   _____

Brokerage Margin Loans   _____

Home Equity Loans/2nd or 3rd Mortgages   _____

TOTAL LIABILITIES   _____

TOTAL NET WORTH   _____

Living on your assets

Once you've compiled a list and the value of your assets, it's imperative to examine which ones can be converted into cash and/or income-producing investments. In essence, we want to figure out where you can generate more than 50 percent of your annual "salary."

One possibility is to look at any non-performing stocks that don't pay dividends. It can be advantageous for retirees to sell them off and purchase income-bearing government security mutual funds. These pay a predictable monthly income.

Other strategies involve selling off investment property (very long-term assets) to buy bonds or dividend-paying stocks. Or, when a CD paying 6 percent comes due, roll it over into bonds or income mutual funds paying 8 percent or more.

After you've established your sources of income, it's equally important to monitor your investments on an annual basis. Because it is inevitable that living costs will increase every year, you need to know that after taxes and inflation, the rate of return of your investments is breaking even, at a minimum. Obviously the best-case scenario is when your return exceeds inflation. Either way, you need to know if your assets are being preserved to the greatest extent possible. We'll discuss a very simple way to track investments later in this chapter.

Social Security benefits

After you've identified the assets that are income-producing, the next step is to gather the facts on your Social Security benefits. Contact your local Social Security office or call their toll-free number for details on estimated benefits owed to you and your spouse.

To request your Personal Earnings and Benefits Estimated Statement (Form #SSA-7004), call 1-800-234-5772. There's no lage requirement to review your file.

The Personal Earnings Statement shows annual income for every year you worked, Social Security taxes paid in and number of quarters that have been credited to you and/or your spouse's accounts.

The issue of "quarters" is an important one because meeting the minimum number is the basis on which you are deemed eligible to receive benefits at all.

When you receive the information, review it carefully. Do not assume the records are correct. I, personally, know of many people who have discovered major discrepancies in their files.

Pension plans

The last step in sizing up your retirement assets is getting a copy of the Summary Plan for your company's pension program. Read the document carefully (have your financial planner or the benefits manager of your personnel department review it, too) and find out your current status as well as an estimate of what will be paid out to you at retirement. By law, you are entitled to review this report once a year.

Although every pension plan is different, be aware that the one thing they have in common is they are designed to insulate your employer from serious losses. In other words, when employees leave or are laid off before certain minimum commitments have been met (i.e., number of years of service), it's the employee who loses out, not the company.

In fact, one of the biggest mistakes people make is assuming they are entitled to a certain amount, only to discover that certain vesting requirements were not met. Or that the plan was designed to prevent them from withdrawing before a certain time...or at all.

If you have a Keogh plan (401K), a profit-sharing program or other retirement funds set up, work with your financial planner or accountant to establish their current values.

Regardless of the type of retirement fund you have, the single biggest consideration before disbursement is the tax ax. While I believe that most taxpayers are honest and would rather give than deceive, I also know that none of us wants to pay one more penny in taxes than we absolutely have to.

Never is this more true than when a taxpayer retires and has to make decisions about allocating the funds sitting in a pension plan. It's no wonder that when clients come in, they throw their retirement plans at me as if the documents were hot potatoes. Instinctively they know that they're holding on to the largest financial decision they'll ever make.

It's a shame that after 30 to 40 years of labor and toil, we're deathly afraid of how much money we've accumulated. But the fear is justified. Thousands of taxpayers every year make strategic errors in removing and disbursing retirement funds.

How to handle the biggest paycheck you ever saw

The first thing to be aware of is that a pension check represents both your earnings over the past decades and the compounded interest on those earnings. This income has been flourishing without any income tax impeding its growth.

With the imminent threat of income tax once you withdraw the funds, the question is this: Do you have your company make out a single check for the entire "lump sum?" Or, do you elect to annuitize your pension benefits? This means that you would keep your money in the company pension plan in exchange for having them mail you a check for a set amount each month.

In many cases, an employee doesn't get to decide because the company forces retiring employees to take an annuity pay out. However, if you are given a choice between taking a lump sum or annuitizing your pension benefits, you should be aware of the pros and cons of each.

Annuities vs. lump sum payments

The single biggest advantage of having your pension funds annuitized is that your company is responsible for guaranteeing that you receive a set amount of money every month. Annuities are a sure thing, no matter the state of the economy, market conditions or even if your employer goes out of business.

When your pension funds are annuitized, you have several options for withdrawing the funds starting at age 59 1/2. Basically you can choose to either receive the maximum annual payout, which results in leaving nothing for a beneficiary at your death, or, you can name a beneficiary, which guarantees a monthly income for him/her upon your death. Providing for a beneficiary reduces the amount of your monthly check.

Here is a description of the most widely used options:

- **Maximum benefit.** Opting for the maximum monthly allowance means you agree that upon your death, payments to your beneficiary will not continue regardless if you received one payment or 100 payments. By law, though, your spouse has to consent in writing.

- **Lifetime payments to a beneficiary.** Should you choose to name a lifetime beneficiary, one who receives payments after your death, there are four ways your beneficiary may receive benefits: 1) the same monthly allowance you did for life 2) three-fourths of your monthly allowance for life 3) half of your monthly allowance for life or 4) a quarter of your monthly allowance for life.

Once the beneficiary is named and once your retirement starts, you cannot change the beneficiary. That is because the age and sex of your beneficiary will determine the monthly allowance. Further, the more your beneficiary is scheduled to receive after your death, the less you will receive each month while you are still alive.

- **Guaranteed payments for certain periods.** Age and sex are not a factor in determining the amount of the monthly payment. Instead, the actuaries work out a formula that determines the exact amount you can receive each month based on the length of the guarantee.

Why annuitized benefits can be a disadvantage

When you annuitize your pension benefits, you must realize it's an irrevocable decision. Once you retire, you immediately start to receive checks. So even if a better investment opportunity comes along five years from now, you cannot buy into it using your pension benefits. Not having access to the principal also means you can't benefit from certain favorable tax advantages, you can't control how the assets are invested, nor can you pass the assets to your heirs. For some people this is a deterrent.

The benefits of a lump sum distribution

The biggest reason that a lump sum distribution is so advantageous is that it gives you the flexibility to reinvest the money as you see fit. It also allows you to take advantage of certain tax breaks, have access to the money and incorporate the remaining funds into an estate plan. You can even buy an annuity from an insurance company at a later date, should you decide it is advantageous.

Conversely, the downside of a lump sum is that it can give you a false sense of security. People see a huge number in their bank account and think they're rich. Suddenly the "greed" factor sets in and they start considering some tempting but risky options. But what happens if you guess wrong? Your life savings is history.

What to do with a lump sum distribution

Recently, a client retired from his position as vice-president at a company he joined in 1963. On his last day, the head of the benefits department handed him a check for $327,899.05. He was so nervous just holding it, he called his wife to drive him home. She was so nervous having the check in the car, she hit a parked car on the way there.

"It didn't matter that I'd earned that money over 25 years, I felt like I'd just won the lottery," he said. "It just plain scared me."

It's understandable, and the very reason people should defer to the expertise of a certified financial planner (CFP). Let them help you decide which of the options for lump sum distributions is most viable for you.

Forward tax-averaging

The first option is called forward averaging, or five-year and 10-year averaging. In this case, you eliminate an annual tax burden by making a one-time upfront settlement with the IRS.

For example, if your pension benefits totaled $100,000 and you chose 10-year forward averaging, you would be taxed as if you had earned $10,000 a year over a 10-year period. The tax would be paid up front. The same concept applies to five-year forward averaging. Either way, the IRS taxes you at a reduced rate (in most cases) because they are getting the use of your tax dollars in advance. Once you are paid up, your pension money is free and clear.

Generally 10-year averaging is slightly more favorable than 5-year averaging in reducing your tax liability. For example, on a $200,000 lump sum, you could save close to $7,500 more in taxes with 10-year averaging than with 5-year averaging. However, once the distribution is $473,700 or more, there is no difference between 5-year and 10-year averaging.

The following chart further illustrates the difference in tax savings.

5-Year vs. 10-Year Forward Averaging

Lump-Sum Distribution	5-Year Avg. One Time Tax Liability	10-Year Avg. One Time Tax Liability
$50,000	$6,900	$5,874
$100,000	$16,398	$14,471
$200,000	$44,398	$36,922
$473,700	$132,636	$132,736

*The figures above are based on a 28-percent federal tax bracket.

Who is eligible to forward average?

Only those who meet certain requirements can forward average. To be eligible for 5-year forward averaging, you must: 1) have participated in your company pension plan for at least five years; 2) taken the distribution in a lump sum; and 3) meet the following age requirements:

	Reached Age 50 Prior to Jan. 1, 1986 (Born prior to 1936)	Age 59 1/2 or Older But Didn't Reach 50 Prior to 1/1/86	Not Yet 59 1/2
Eligible for 5-Year Forward Averaging	Yes	Yes	No
Eligible for Either 5- or 10-Year Averaging	Yes	No	No

The benefits of averaging

If you are considering forward averaging, here are the major benefits:

- **One time tax.** Lump sum distributions can be sizeable amounts repre-
  senting an enormous tax obligation (particularly when calculated at the
  rate of ordinary income). With forward averaging, you pay the tax once
  and the money is free and clear.

- **It's less of a bite.** Not only is the tax bite a one-time obligation, the bottom
  line is you'll probably end up paying much less that one time than if you
  had paid taxes on the same lump sum (at a rate of 28%) over five or 10
  years.

- **Freedom of choice.** Once you pay the IRS, the money is yours to do as you
  see fit. You can reinvest it, pass it on to your heirs, buy a home, etc.

IRA rollovers

IRA rollovers are a second option for disbursing a lump sum distribution. You literally roll over your pension benefits from one tax-advantaged pension into another. Your money goes from a company-managed pension into a personally managed pension, or Individual Retirement Account (IRA).

All of the money that your employer contributed to your pension is eligible for the rollover. However, any after-tax dollars that you contributed are not. In addition, it is not permissible to combine a rollover with forward averaging.

After you receive your benefit check, which is written in a lump sum amount, you have 60 days to open an IRA account. By meeting this requirement, you will not incur any current taxes on that money.

As far as investment flexibility is concerned, you can opt for any instrument that regular IRAs invest in: stocks, bonds, mutual funds, etc.

Similar to other IRAs, the funds are not taxed until they are withdrawn, which is possible starting at age 59 1/2. Should you withdraw prior to that, there could be a penalty in addition to the amount withdrawn being taxed as ordinary income.

Keep in mind that, with an IRA rollover, you have the flexibility to draw your income or defer it so that it grows, tax-free, until you're 70. At that point you must begin withdrawing funds and paying taxes on the amount withdrawn each year. This is called taking the maximum tax deferral. The thinking is that your earned income at this age will be less and subsequently the tax bite smaller.

Portability

A typical concern among pre-retirees is whether you're allowed to have more than one IRA. The answer is yes. You can have as many as you can afford, and, it's also perfectly legal to roll over your pension benefits into an already established IRA account.

However, if you ever intend to go back to work and participate in a company pension plan, or hope to start a business where you would establish a new pension plan, it would be very important to establish a separate IRA account for your original pension funds.

Keep in mind that once your pension funds are commingled with a personal IRA, the one you contributed to with after-tax dollars, you can never move the pension benefit portion back into a new company pension plan.

Important considerations

In weighing the pros and cons of all of the options we've discussed, it's easy to lose perspective and only consider the tax implications. However, there are issues to consider other than how to keep Uncle Sam away from your pension.

What about your lifestyle? How do you want to live? What about your medical care needs? What about helping your children while you're alive and leaving a legacy when you die? What about the desire to invest or pursue a new career? Perhaps you've always wanted to open a small business.

Staying liquid

For example, to what extent will you need this money to have liquidity? If you don't have savings and money market accounts or other cash investments, then annuitizing your pension could be quite harmful. What if, one day, you absolutely needed cash to meet an emergency? If all of your money is still tied up in your company pension plan, you'll be out of luck.

Major investments

Or, what if you want to buy a new home or business, or invest in real estate? This will require a lot of money, ruling out both an IRA rollover and an annuity.

Depending on how much you had accumulated in pension benefits, it might be possible to take a partial distribution and still have enough in the lump sum to accomplish your goals. Before making a final decision about disbursing your pension benefits, you must take these other important factors into consideration.

How far will your retirement dollars go?

After you've created a net worth statement and added your Social Security and pension benefits to the mix, you'll finally know the size of your nest egg.

But the next pressing matter is figuring out how long these funds can be expected to last. Refer to the chart below to calculate the number of years you'll have funds to draw from, depending on the growth rate of your investments and the rate of withdrawals.

Number of Years Your Retirement Dollars Will Last

Annual Rate of Withdrawal	Expected Rate of Return on Investments			
	7%	8%	9%	10%
7%	*	*	*	*
8%	30	*	*	*
9%	22	29	*	*
10%	17	20	27	*

* Capital will never be depleted

Explanation: If you withdrew 10% of your retirement nest egg every year, and it averaged an annual growth rate of 8%, your money would last approximately 20 years.

Another way to get a fix on the strength of your retirement account is by looking at the total amount of funds you're starting with. Refer to the next chart to see how many years the money will last if you take out a certain dollar amount each month for a given number of years.

How Much Money Can You Withdraw?

Size of Nest Egg	If you withdraw this amount each month for the following number of years, you'll have a "0" balance.					If you withdraw this amount each month, you won't be touching the nest egg at all.
	10 yrs.	15 yrs.	20 yrs.	25 yrs.	30 yrs.	35 yrs.
$15,000	$174/mo.	$134	$118	$106	$99	$59
$25,000	290	224	193	176	166	118
$50,000	580	448	386	352	332	285
$80,000	928	718	620	564	532	467
$100,000	1,160	896	772	704	668	585

Note: These figures are based on 7% net annual growth (after taxes).

The effects of inflation on retirement dollars

Anytime I've showed this chart to clients, the first thing they want to know is what will happen to their money when inflation is entered into the equation. It's an excellent question. Certainly, economic fluctuations of any sort will affect finances, but inflation is a particularly cruel adversary.

Consider that if the long-term inflation rate is 6 percent, living costs will double approximately every 12 years. Another indicator of inflation's harm is purchasing power. To give you a sense of that, take a look at what things cost 20 years ago, 10 years ago and today. Can you imagine what the following items will cost in the year 2000?

Average Prices	1970	1980	TODAY
Postage Stamp	.06	.15	.29
Loaf of Bread	.23	.43	.68
Automobile	$3400	$6,910	$13,000
House	$25,600	$64,000	$99,468

Now let's take a look at the impact inflation will have on your monthly retirement income.

6% Annual Inflation Rate

Monthly Income: $1,000	Today	5 yrs.	10 yrs.	15 yrs.	20 yrs.	25 yrs.
How Much You'll Need To Have Same Purchasing Power	$1,000	$1,338	$1,791	$2,397	$3,207	$4,292
What $1,000 Will Be Worth	$1,000	$747	$558	$417	$312	$233

Explanation: If the annual rate of inflation is 6%, in 10 years you will need $1,791 to buy what $1,000 bought today. The reason: in 10 years, $1,000 will only be worth $558.

How do you protect your retirement nest egg? As we said earlier, it is imperative to monitor your investments and analyze the net rate of return (after taxes and inflation). You must be aware how they're faring. In today's market, for example, most savings vehicles are not keeping pace with inflation. Thus, if you've got considerable funds tied up in money markets, the most prudent course is to convert a portion of those funds into equity investments, such as balanced mutual funds. These consistently out perform inflation.

Another way to keep pace with inflation is to insure that you draw from your interest earnings only as much as you need. You want the opportunity to reinvest any excess so that your principal has an opportunity for continued growth. This is why many people defer their IRA investments for later years. It gives them the opportunity to reinvest the interest so the original amount compounds annually. It's a great way to give yourself a raise. And without a raise, as the inflation tables reveal, you'll have a difficult time making ends meet down the road.

With respect to other income, such as Social Security, while it's true that checks will increase according to COLA's (Cost of Living Adjustments), it's unlikely that there will ever be a large jump in benefits from one year to the next. It's also unlikely that your other retirement funds will be tied to any kind of inflation index at all. Only a few of the original pension plans were designed to keep pace with annual living cost increases.

Finally, if you are considering holding on to your house as a hedge against inflation, perhaps you should reconsider. While houses will presumably escalate in value, gone are the days where prices jumped by double digits as they did during the 1970s and 80s. More likely, values will only increase 2 percent to 5 percent a year. You won't lose anything by keeping the house, but you need to consider an older home's increased maintenance expenses as well as rising property taxes. These costs will go up every year, potentially offsetting any gains.

How much will you need to live on at retirement?

Once you understand the impact of inflation on your living costs, you can see why it is so important to figure out how much your expenses will be at retirement. That is the only way you can determine how to budget accordingly so that your nest egg supports a comfortable lifestyle for as long as possible.

You may be wondering how you can anticipate your living expenses in retirement when you've never been retired before. It's a reasonable question. One way is to identify your current living expenses and then determine which ones can be cut back or eliminated when your lifestyle changes.

If you don't know what your new rent or mortgage payments (and subsequent property taxes) will be when you relocate, fill in the rest of the blanks in the form below. Then, if have a sense of your monthly income, just work backwards and calculate how much money you'll have left to budget for housing.

CURRENT MONTHLY LIVING EXPENSES

Rent or Mortgage Payments $ _____
Real Estate Taxes
Vacation Home Mortgage/Taxes
Home Equity Loan
Savings Plan Contributions
Income taxes
Food
Clothing & Uniforms
Utilities
Dining Out
Furniture/Electronics
Vacations/Recreation
Entertainment
Car Payments
Autos: Gas & Repairs
Financial & Legal Services
Medical Care/Medications
College Tuition/Loans
Life & Disability Insurance
Car Insurance
Health Insurance
Property & Casualty Insurance
Pet Care
Birthday & Holiday Gifts
Housekeeping
Commutation: Tolls, Trains, etc.)
Cable TV
Household Maintenance
Telephone Bills
Religious Institutions
Books, Magazines & Papers
Clubs, Sports & Hobbies
Dues: Unions & Others
Alimony/Child Support
Parental Support/Nursing Home
Other

TOTAL ANNUAL LIVING EXPENSES $ _____

With respect to living costs, the traditional rule of thumb is that upon retirement, you should be able to live on 50 percent of your current gross income, or 70 percent of your take-home pay. This takes into consideration that you have eliminated work-related expenses (commutation costs, lunches, a business wardrobe, etc.) as well as heavy real estate and income tax burdens. Another major expense eliminated is paying in to Social Security.

For some retirees, these savings are offset by the increases now spent on vacations, hobbies and recreation.

Investing for income

Thus far we've made some major inroads in terms of establishing the size of your retirement nest egg. Now we must look at strategies for allowing it to flourish while you live off your assets.This is called investing for income.

With more than half of your retirement income dependent upon investments, we'll review the most important rules for retirees. Then, I'll tell you how to structure your portfolio so that it works to its maximum potential. Finally, I'll share my own personal method for keeping track of income so that you know where you stand at all times.

There's just one caveat. While it's essential to be an informed investor, please don't take it to mean that you should handle the execution on your own. Something as critical as preserving your estate is best handled by a certified financial planner.

Think of it as having an operation. Would you read about the procedure and then do the surgery yourself? Of course not. You would go to the experts and let them do their job. The same is true with handling your retirement planning.

Let's get back to investing. The two disciplines that should be central to any investor's decisions, but are especially crucial to a retiree's portfolio are: 1) *diversification* and 2) *risk tolerance*. Without an understanding of the role they play in investment strategies, it's impossible to execute a sound game plan.

Diversification

Who doesn't like a sure thing? That's the thinking of people who put money into one investment that consistently performs well. But with the unpredictable world we live in, sure things have gone the way of nickel candy bars. No single investment, no matter how tried and true, offers all the answers. For every advantage there's a disadvantage.

And what happens when that investment suddenly stops generating the same return? It's hell to pay. The crippling stock market crash of October, 1987, was just one reminder that "too many eggs in one basket" can be disastrous, especially when you are counting implicitly on your investments to produce income.

Let's pretend that in September, 1987, the largest segment of your portfolio was tied up in stocks, about $200,000 sitting in your favorite blue-chips. A month after the crash, the market was down by 22 percent. That would have left you with a net loss of $44,000, or a balance of $156,000. Three to six months later there was even further erosion. In a very short time, you lost a year's worth of income.

Now let's take your know-it-all brother-in-law who believed in putting his eggs in more than one basket. He also had a $200,000 portfolio but it was divided equally among blue-chip stocks, U.S. Treasury Bonds and a money market account. A month after the crash, he had only suffered a 6-percent loss even though stocks had plummeted by 22 percent. That's because bonds rallied and money market funds remained stable. His portfolio still had $184,000 and was continuing to hold its own several months later.

This is just one example of why the backbone of any sound financial plan is "asset allocation," or just good old fashioned diversification.

A well-balanced portfolio has a mix of liquid accounts for emergencies, Treasury Bills and CDs as a safety net, stocks for growth and as a hedge against inflation, municipal bonds for tax-free income, real estate and, yes, even a small amount of oil and gas, precious metals, or collectibles for long-term growth and appreciation.

This "balancing" act helps insure that your assets will be better insulated when any particular category is weathering a storm. Then continued diversification within those categories, as well as continued monitoring, will further shelter you from downward trends in a particular investment.

Finally, the more diversified you are, the more confident you can be if you decide to take some risks within an investment category. At least you know that whatever the outcome, the majority of your portfolio is still intact.

Risk tolerance

Interestingly, when it comes to tolerating risks, most people react emotionally rather than intellectually. It's like the guy who can't wait for his turn on the roller coaster and then begs to get off the first time it plunges. If he would just stay calm and hold on tight, he'd enjoy the ride when it climbed back up again.

Even though it is *common knowledge* that investments are like roller coasters and either rise, coast, or plunge, it's not always *common practice* to hang on for the whole ride. Nobody wants to lose, they only want to win.

Here's an example. If you had a 100-percent chance of winning $3,000 or an 80-percent chance of winning $4,000, which would you choose? Most people opt for the sure thing. They'd prefer to win $3,000 instead of $4,000 if it meant they could eliminate the risk. And yet, the alternative choice would be a better risk because it is generally preferable to gamble on a gain.

Here is another example of detrimental common thinking. Remember in the '80s when many investors were in love with junk bonds? The 15 percent yields were irresistible and people willingly gambled their principals for that high a return. Did they expect that the bonds would default? Of course not, but it happened. The result was not only a loss of dividends, but the entire loss of principal as well. The lesson here: Gambling on a risk is not prudent investing.

Unfortunately, human nature being what it is, most people hate to lose money more than they like to make it. In other words, they worry more about the return *of* their money than they do *on* their money.

This attitude results in some bad judgment calls, the most common of which is pulling out before an investment has a fair amount of time to perform.

Investments that can pass your safety inspection

Before we explore the most beneficial investment vehicles for retirees, it's important to have a basis for evaluating and assessing them. We've already discussed how critical it is to measure your risks carefully and to maintain the most diversified portfolio possible. But after that, how can you be sure that you're making the right decisions?

There are numerous factors that should be taken into consideration as well as questions that must be addressed. The first is that your after-tax return at least equals the inflation rate. If an investment can't meet that minimum goal, you're wasting your time and your money. Other considerations include:

- **Yields.** What are the anticipated returns and what guarantees are built in for the future? To what extent will the yield be reduced by commissions, service charges and fees? What is the annual tax liability?
- **Safety.** Is the principal safe? What kind of market conditions will cause the values to decline? Can you bail out before the losses are substantial?
- **Liquidity.** Will you have immediate access to your money or will you be locked in? For how long? What are the penalties for early withdrawal? How easy is it to get to your money? Are phone and wire transfers available? Will you have check writing privileges? Any limitations?
- **Insurance.** Is either your yield or your principal guaranteed? What about FDIC or MBIA insured?
- **Terms.** How long are you committed for? Will you have any problems holding on for that amount of time, and if not, can you live with the penalty for early withdrawal? Are you clear on all the terms and conditions?
- **Inflation.** Is this investment expected to at least keep pace with inflation? What is the anticipated rate of return annually and over the lifetime of the investment?

Insofar as viable investment options for retirees, combinations of the following should provide financial security:

- **Bank instruments:** Passbook savings, money market accounts, certificates of deposit
- **Government securities:** U.S. Treasury bills (T-bills), U.S. Treasury bonds and notes, Government mutual funds
- **Equities:** Mutual funds, stocks (blue chip, growth & income, balanced)
- **Debt instruments:** Corporate bonds, Bond Funds
- **Tax-advantaged investments:** Municipal bonds
- **Insurance products:** annuities, single pay life insurance (variable single pay)
- **Income-producing real estate investments:** real estate limited partnerships, REITs (real estate investment trusts), direct ownership

Structuring your portfolio so you can live on your assets

We've just gone over the most important principles of investing diversification and risk tolerance and we've reviewed the most common and desirable investment vehicles for retirees. Now it's time to look into structuring your portfolio so that you have the proper *balance* of investments.

What's the point of selecting the right investment vehicles if they're not working in tandem to give you the highest possible return and the greatest protection against inflation and taxes?

The basic structure of a sound portfolio looks like an Egyptian pyramid.

Pyramid power

The image of the great pyramids has been likened to the ultimate "towers of power." With an unwavering base, they are pillars of strength that can support the weight of whatever has been thrust upon them.

As a financial planner, I have always believed that a model portfolio should also have the strength of a pyramid. It should be constructed in such a way that risks and rewards are completely balanced from top to bottom. The soundest, safest investments support the hierarchy while those that can potentially reap the greatest rewards but also have the greatest risks are positioned at the top.

Here is what the ideal investment pyramid looks like at retirement:

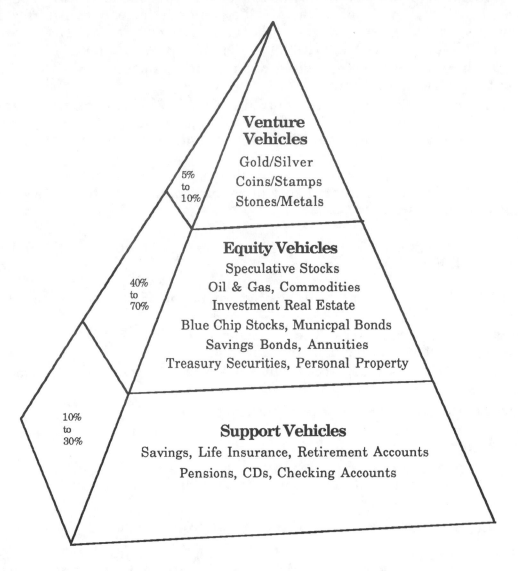

Pyramid power at retirement

In financial terms, the investments at the bottom represent your principal. They are safe but cannot be expected to do combat with inflation because their yields are low. The riskier investments at the top represent your capital, which can be reduced or lost altogether through faulty decisions or a downturn in the economy. Conversely, the risk investments have the potential to generate strong returns that will create growth while holding inflation and overtaxation in abeyance. You'll see, however, that those that have the greatest level of "chance" are squeezed in at the apex, indicating that they should be given the least amount of power.

Every portfolio needs the combined strengths of risks and rewards.

Turn the pyramid upside down

Once your investment pyramid is in place, ready to support your retirement, I'm going to suggest that you do something interesting. Turn the pyramid upside down. That's right, your "Pyramid Power" is now going to be called your "Funnel Force."

By turning your investments upside down, your riskiest investments will now appear at the bottom of the funnel, and will then be the first ones to be liquidated during your retirement. Your principal investments, those that are safest, are at the top and will be the last to go.

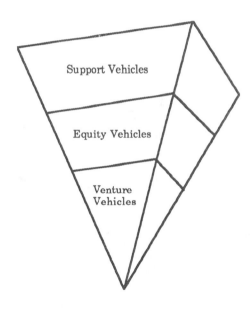

The reason it helps to think of your investments sitting in a funnel is that it is a device that allows you to control the flow of something. In this case, you'll be able to control the flow of funds simply by opening and closing the valve at the bottom as needed. Ultimately you'll be able to regulate the rate at which your investments are discharged.

What happens to the funds that come through the funnel? They will get poured into a Master Account, which is an interest-bearing checking account. Now you can monitor all your income. Let me explain.

Tracking your income

Once you retire, keeping track of what's coming in and going out is very difficult because your source of income will be coming from so many different places and at all different times.

While Social Security is mailed on the first week of the month, it's a relatively small amount. You'll probably be counting more on your investment income.

Unfortunately there is no such thing as a pay day for stocks. When a dividend comes due, you get a check. Will it come in again next quarter? Who knows?

Because the level of financial activity will be at an all-time high and the uncertainty as to when the money will arrive is so great, I have devised a strategy for staying on top of your financial affairs. I call it the Master Account and it is the companion to your Funnel Force. The Master Account is a very simple idea, and it works, no matter how little or how much money comes in every month.

To start a Master Account, open an interest-bearing checking account. Use it to deposit every single check you get, whether from Social Security, tenants, pensions, CDs, annuities or the lottery. Think of this account as the "Ellis Island" for your money. Nothing gets through the gates until it's been signed in and admitted through the system. How it gets dispersed is another discussion, but before anything else happens, the money has to sit in the Master Account.

From there, you can funnel money into a separate checking account that you use to pay certain bills, or you can dump the surplus into a savings account or, when there's enough left over, reinvest.

To better illustrate how the Master Account works, the diagram below provides an example.

Master Account

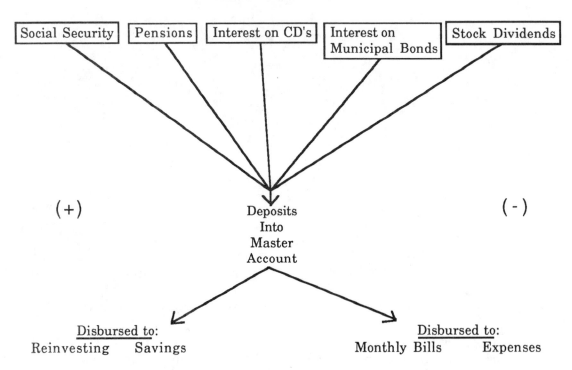

Benefits of a master account

The best reason to set up a Master Account is so that you'll know the total amount of income earned each month as well as how much is available to pay expenses.

Another advantage is that because some checks will be small, by pooling your resources in one account, there will be a lump sum large enough to pay bills, reinvest, etc. In effect, it will serve the same purpose as depositing a monthly paycheck.

The other important benefit is that you'll receive a monthly bank statement, which will give you an accurate reading of where your finances stand. With all of your deposits and debits listed in one place, you'll know immediately how much of a surplus you have, or conversely that your debits are exceeding your deposits. Then it becomes your "damage control" statement your warning to reexamine your budget and cut back.

If you don't start out with a Master Account, your income will be so scattered it will result in mass confusion and sometimes the inability to take care of certain large obligations.

The bottom line

From my many years of experience working with retirees, I know that their single biggest fear is running out of money. They are deeply concerned about illness, death, loneliness, separation and other emotionally charged issues too, but that is nothing compared to the anxiety of becoming dependent on family, friends or the government for financial survival.

With the proper amount of planning, investing and budgeting, this fear can be eased. The key is to make a commitment to knowing what you have to start with, putting the money in safe places where it can grow and provide income, and monitoring it closely so that you can control the reins.

Then, and only then, can you live on your you-know-what. Your assets, of course. Or as a client so aptly put it, "The key to a decent retirement is having enough money to live on, but not too much money to worry about!"

## Chapter 3

How to Hold On to Your Possessions and Your Sanity

"Moving 101"

How can a civilization that invented microwave ovens, fax machines and computers not have a clue how to make moving a snap? Nothing would be better than relocating without packing up a household of goods and trucking them cross-country. Unfortunately, the only way to get there is the old-fashioned way, using men and their machines. To help you fly through the ordeal with the greatest of ease, we've put together a short course called "Moving 101." Anyone who reads is an automatic "A" student.

In addition, be sure to send away for a very important free booklet from the Interstate Commerce Commission, the government agency that oversees long-distance movers. It's a consumer guide called "When You Move: Your Rights and Responsibilities." Write to the ICC at 12th & Constitution Ave., Washington, D.C. 20423.

What does it cost to move?

Moving to the next town can be a costly proposition; moving cross-country will certainly give one pause. It's why the first question a mover is asked is "What's this gonna cost?" The trouble is that it's like asking the price of a new car. Do you want a luxury sedan or a mini-van? What about options? The questions continue until the salesperson arrives at a number, and then the negotiating begins. So it goes with moving.

The best way to get a fix on moving costs is to be aware of all the charges that can be factored into your estimate. The three most important variables include:

1. Distance. Movers must first determine the approximate mileage between your new and old homes. This is accomplished by mapping out the shortest distance between points A and points B on *highways that are useable for truck travel.* Obviously, the longer the haul, the more costly the move.

2. Weight. As prices are based on every 100 pounds moved, it's best to ask at least three movers to "guess-timate" the size of your shipment. Don't be surprised by wide variations as each mover refers to its own "Table of Weights" when developing an estimate.

3. Time of year. All movers reduce their prices, but how extensively depends upon the time of year. Reserving a carrier between May 15 and September 30 (when 50 percent of all moves take place) almost guarantees that discounts will not be as deep. In fact, you can count on paying a 10-percent premium for moving during busy season. What's more, service is often slower because of peak demand.

Taking distance, weight and time of year into consideration, the average residential move weighs 5,251 pounds, travels 1,217 miles and costs the shipper a total of $2,384 ($45.41 per 100 pounds). Here is a breakout of costs:

Service	Avg. cost	% of total cost
Basic transportation	$1,806	76.0%
Additional Transport & Liability Insurance	$353	14.8%
Packing Services	$225	9.5%

(Source: Household Goods Carriers Bureau, 1989)

The following section will give you a brief overview of these services and introduce you to others that can be factored into your estimate. As you'll see, hiring a long-distance mover is much like dining at a restaurant where everything on the menu is *à la carte*. And similar to good waiters, movers like to make tempting, but costly, suggestions. The key to negotiating a fair price is being aware of the different ways they earn their keep.

Basic transportation

Basic transportation includes use of the mover's truck, use of labor to move goods out of your house, load them on to the truck, drive to your destination, and reassemble everything in your new home.

Additional transportation

If your move originates and/or terminates in a high-density area, there will be additional transportation charges (ATCs). In congested locations, movers will face traffic jams, construction delays, inaccessible entrances, etc. To compensate for lost time, expect to pay from 40 cents to $3 more per 100 pounds.

Liability insurance

By law, every interstate moving company must assume some liability against damage or loss when agreeing to move your household goods. Unfortunately, the liability they assume is at a minimum, compelling the shipper to purchase additional coverage. And even with that, the mover is protected from you almost as much as the other way around. In other words, the coverage actually limits the mover's liability if they lose or damage your shipment.

The good news is that full replacement value insurance, the maximum protection you can buy, is relatively inexpensive and worth every penny.

However, before you purchase any insurance from the mover, *check your homeowners policy*. It's possible your belongings are already covered during a move, alleviating the need for additional coverage.

If you do buy liability insurance from the mover, know your rights. By law, the mover must provide you with a copy of your policy (or a formal receipt) at the time of purchase. Without proper documentation, they can be held fully liable for any claim that is a result of their negligence.

Here are the four types of available coverage:

Released value protection: This protection allows you to "release" your goods to the mover without making a declaration as to their value. If there is loss or damage, the mover's only obligation is to pay you up to 60 cents per pound per article. In other words, weight is the only consideration when calculating a reimbursement.

For example, if the mover breaks a 7-pound lamp, it won't matter if it was a priceless heirloom or a gift from your Savings and Loan, the maximum you would receive is $4.20. The mover does not charge for released value protection, but you know what they say about getting what you pay for.

Minimum declaration: Making a minimum declaration means that you believe your total shipment is valued at $1.25 per pound. If your goods weigh a total of 5,251 pounds (the average weight of an interstate move), the mover would be liable for losses or damage up to $6,563. The cost of this "added protection" averages $5 for every $1,000 in liability.

The major difference between this protection and "released value" coverage is that the reimbursement is based on the depreciated value of the item. To settle the claim, the mover refers to a depreciation schedule for thousands of household items.

Now, if the mover breaks your favorite lamp, you'll be reimbursed based on the age of the item. A three-year-old lamp that originally cost $145 might entitle you to $75. *Keep in mind that all of this is contingent on proving the mover's negligence.*

Lump sum declaration: If you determine that your shipment is valued at more than $1.25 per lb. you can declare a specific dollar value, or a "lump sum declaration." In other words, you can declare that your 5,251 lb. shipment is actually worth $10,000. The mover will charge you the same $5 per $1,000 of declared value, you'll just pay proportionately more.

When trying to determine how much to declare, consider the fact that today's household contents are worth $3.25 per pound, on average.

Full value protection: Full value protection or replacement cost coverage is exactly as the name implies. You'll receive full replacement value if, because of the mover's negligence, items are damaged or lost and cannot be totally restored. The cost of replacement coverage averages $8.50 per $1,000 of valuation, but can be less if you agree to take a deductible. As with any insurance policy, the higher the deductible, the lower the premium.

Full value protection is the absolute maximum protection you can buy and the only coverage we recommend. Common sense tells you that 99 percent of the contents in your home were never built to be moved cross country. The industry reports that 25 percent of all residential moves result in claims for losses or damages, so good liability coverage is critical.

Packing services

There are two types of services to consider. The first is *purchasing* packing materials—dishpacks, wardrobes, cartons, etc. Say what you will about movers, they have sturdier boxes than the local liquor store. For your fragile and valuable items, they are worth the money.

The second packing service is *labor*. You can opt to have the mover either pack up your old residence and/or unpack your cartons at your new home.

We believe there are two very important reasons to having the movers do your packing: time and money. You can avoid weeks and possibly months of standing, bending, folding, and rolling valuable breakables into newspaper when the movers are in charge.

Secondly, if the mover does the packing and there is damage, they can't blame you. Otherwise, when the boxes are marked "PBO" (packed by owner), it allows the mover to argue that damages were the result of a bad packing job (and they may be right).

The cost for packing services will vary according to your home county's current labor rates. As the chart on page 38 indicates, packing should represent approximately 10 percent of your total costs. Again, it is well worth the money!

Note: Movers will try to talk you into packing the house on moving day. Start a day or two before. Moving day is hectic and when the men are rushed, it could lead to added losses and damages.

More extras that add to the cost

In addition to all of the cost factors we've just mentioned, there are numerous others that may be included in your estimate. Here is a brief rundown:

New York to Florida: With many more people moving south than north, some movers charge an extra 50 cents per 100 pounds to compensate for an almost certain empty van on the return trip.

Apartment buildings: As many retirees move into high-rise condos, it's important to know that movers get added compensation for dealing with elevators, stairs, and long carries (when the apartment is far from the stairs or elevators and/or the goods must be brought to a loading dock, etc.) In theory these efforts are time-consuming and tiresome, which is how they justify charging 75 cents to $1.20 per 100 pounds for every 50 feet they have to go after the first 75 feet. If the mover is *forced* to use an elevator, you'll pay $1.20 to $1.45 per 100 pounds because elevators are restrictive and slow.

Storage: Unfortunately, storage can be a necessary evil even with the most advance planning. Often, people are forced to move from their home or apartment before their new home is ready for occupancy. In other instances, unexpected delays because of illness or travel arrangements prevent people from meeting the van when it arrives. If so, the mover has the right to place the entire shipment in storage. It happens more often than you think, so build storage costs, even for a few days, into your moving budget.

The average cost to store a 5,000-pound shipment for one week at a local storage warehouse can run $250 to $350 or more, depending on the part of the country (assume everything costs more in the East). It is generally more costly to store your goods in the mover's warehouse than a local storage facility.

Space reservations: If you want to move on a specific date, you can reserve space in the van. If moving during May to September, there may be a charge.

Expedited service: If you absolutely have to be at your new home by a certain date, the mover can speed up the amount of time it takes to make the trip. Ordering an expedited service is costly, but possible.

Exclusive use of a vehicle: If you do not want your shipment commingled with other shipments for fear of delays or problems associated with sharing space, you can request that your shipment be the only one on the van.

Guaranteed service on or between agreed dates: If you need to know the exact day the mover will show up on either end, you can arrange for guaranteed service, which provides that your shipment be picked up, transported and delivered on agreed-upon dates. If the mover fails to deliver as scheduled, you'll be entitled to compensation.

How to keep moving costs way down

If you are like most, after reading the numerous expenses incurred in a move, you are probably planning the biggest garage sale of your life! And no doubt you should. By now you've realized that you can control two of the three factors that drive costs through the roof: time of year and weight. Remember, the real expense is in *what* and *when* you move, not *where* you move.

Since you'll be paying for every 100 pounds shipped, refer to this proven method for moving the minimum. It calls for giving as many items as possible one of the following designations:

Sell it, donate it, toss it, give it away...

Here's how this works:

Furniture. If it's old and you're tired of it, if it's not going to match your new decor, if it won't fit in the new rooms, it makes more sense to replace than to move. **Tools.** If you're moving from a house to a condo, you probably won't have the need or the storage space. **Books.** Just hang on to your most treasured favorites. Inquire about the cost of mailing them or shipping UPS instead of moving them in the van. **Plants.** Without oxygen and water, how would you look after five days? Besides, they require a certificate of inspection from your county Department of Agriculture and in some states, such as Florida, plants *are* subject to inspection upon arrival. It's better to start over. **Clothes.** If there's no longer a need for a winter wardrobe, leave it behind for winter visits. If you know you won't wear it again, it should never see the inside of the van. **Records.** 100 record albums weigh 50 pounds. Purge your collection of the ones you no longer listen to. **Toys and hobby equipment.** Stop saving for the grandkids. If they want their parent's toys, give them a deal and a deadline. "Pick them up by midnight tomorrow and they're yours free of charge. Miss the deadline and *Toys for Tots* will be ever grateful." **Miscellaneous (junk).** Every home has its own special assortment. You know where it's hiding. Is it worth several hundred dollars to have it follow you? **Rugs.** Unless they are valuable or match your new decor, clean them and find a new owner. **Artwork.** Take only what you absolutely love, has value as an investment or has such sentimental value it won't feel like home without it. **Musical instruments.** If the musicians in your home are no longer active, let them part company with their instruments. Pianos and organs are extremely expensive to move and require special handling and tuning after a move. **Chandeliers, ceiling fans, etc.** The movers add on special handling charges for these, the electrician will charge you to disconnect and dismantle. It could be cheaper to buy new. **Appliances.** If any one your major appliances are like you, on the brink of retiring, don't take them. Measure your new place to make sure the refrigerator's not too tall, the washer and dryer fit in the laundry area, etc. Any major appliances you move (TV antennas, air conditioners, washers and dryers) will need special disconnections and installations in addition to the cost of moving them. **Fireplace equipment.** If you're moving to a warm climate, it's unlikely you'll have a fireplace. Give the people who bought your place a "housewarming" present. **Flagpoles, basketball backboards, sleds and other bulky items.** By now you've got the hang of this exercise.

The time to do all this contemplating of what goes and what stays is before you get your moving estimates. Estimates are a waste of time until you know what is an accurate reflection of the move itself.

Getting estimates

Movers will provide two types of estimates, binding and non-binding. A non-binding estimate allows the mover to give you a best guess as to the cost of your move, but does not bind him to that price. Ultimately, you could pay more and in some cases, less. This is because the final cost will be based on actual, not estimated weight.

If, for example, you are quoted $2,800 but are getting rid of furniture, books, etc., up until moving day, you could end up paying $2,400. Conversely, if you told the mover not to include two beds and your lawn furniture in the estimate and later change your mind, your final bill could be more than $3,000.

One would think that the problem with non-binding estimates is that movers might "lowball" a bid to get the job. Yet a recent ICC Study found that long-distance movers overestimated prices as often as they underestimated them. Human error is most often the reason.

With a binding estimate, the mover sizes up the job and commits to a final price based on the *estimated* weight of your shipment. Keep in mind that if the mover is going to have to live or die by this price, he's going to build enough profit into it to cover himself for certain contingencies. That could mean paying a higher amount than is necessary.

Another possible drawback with binding estimates is lack of flexibility. For example, if you told the mover not to include the cost of shipping your piano because you were certain you could sell it, you'll need to get another estimate if that plan fails. Without a second estimate, the mover is not obligated to take the piano because according to your contract, he's not going to be paid to do so. In addition, there might not be room on the van because only a certain amount of space was allocated for you. That's a last minute hassle you don't need.

Most people opt for non-binding estimates because they feel they're only going to pay for what they actually ship. Regardless of which type you settle on, the estimate must be put in writing in the order for service (initial commitment) and the bill of lading (final contract).

Hiring a mover

Given the number of personal circumstances that could affect your move, coupled with the different services you can opt for, it's vitally important to shop the competition. Prices will vary greatly, particularly in the off season.

It's also possible that some movers will offer discounts to seniors, veterans and members of organizations, such as AARP or Lions Club.

However, and this is a big however, by no means is the cheapest quote neces-sarily the best quote. Movers that "lowball" their estimates have to save money somewhere and often that somewhere is in their service. "Buying" a mover is like making any other major purchase. Bargain hard but make your final decision based on price as well as other important criteria. This includes:

Personal Recommendations. Do you know anyone who used the mover and was pleased with the service? **Overall Treatment.** How were your questions and concerns addressed when you spoke with representatives of the moving company on the phone and in person? **Overall Appearances.** An industry spokesman highly recommended that you make an on-site inspection of the mover's offices and warehouse to confirm that it's a legitimate, well-run operation. **Better Busi-ness Bureau Reports**—It never hurts to check with your local BBB to see if there are complaints on file against the mover.

Independents vs. nationally known carriers?

Most people prefer to buy brand names because a recognized company stands behind the product. It's no different with movers. When a truck is pulling off with your valuable possessions, there's a certain comfort level in choosing an Allied or United Van Lines over Joe's Fast Moving Company. Also, if there are problems with an agent affiliated with a nationally known company, at least there's a home office to intervene, if necessary.

More importantly, "common carrier" agents are under contract to meet cer-tain performance requirements. They are not intentionally going to make mis-takes or jeopardize their standing.

On the down side, common carriers may not have as much price flexibility because they split their profits more ways than do independent movers.

As for the independents, many have excellent reputations and can provide very personalized service. In addition, they may be more affordable. The tradeoff is that should you have problems, resolving them with a "one-boss" organization may be very frustrating.

Should you decide to work with a local independent mover, an on-site inspec-tion is very important. In addition, you'll want proof that the firm is authorized by the Interstate Commerce Commission to move goods out of state. If it's not licensed, your liability coverage is null and void.

Keep in mind that neither the size of the moving company nor claims that it is "bonded", "certified," or "insured" are any guarantee of reliability. However, if you see that the mover has a CMC designation, for Certified Moving Consultant, you know that at least they passed arduous tests and comply with the highest stan-dards set by the industry.

Are your cars moving with you?

At some point in the planning stages of a move, it occurs to people that their cars may be moving with them. It would very convenient to load them onto the van, but at a cost of more than $40 per 100 pounds, it's doubtful there would be any takers. That's why many people drive their own cars. It also gives them space for special belongings they don't want the movers to haul. Others sell their cars and buys new ones as retirement gifts.

If neither of these options are workable, a good alternative is to use an auto transport company. One such firm, Auto Driveaway, will arrange for your cars to be driven to your destination anywhere in the country. Based in Chicago and operating 90 offices in all 50 states, this ICC-licensed firm moves more than 50,000 cars a year.

Let's say you need to get your car from Long Island to Delray Beach on a particular date. The firm will match your request with a licensed driver who is over 21 and who has requested to drive a car from the New York area to a destination close to Delray.

Next, Auto Driveaway will check references as well as conduct a computer search to examine the person's driving record in all 50 states. If the driver passes muster, he or she will be photographed and finger-printed. The driver will then post a cash deposit, which is returned if the car arrives undamaged and on schedule. Incidentally, drivers are required to cover 400 miles a day.

As the car owner, you must guarantee that the car is no more than five years old and mechanically able to make the trip.

Auto Driveaway's standard or "casual" service is based on the mileage between the originating and destination states. For a drive from New York to Florida, the cost is $250 plus the first tank of gas. If your car is needed immediately, a paid employee can drive to your destination. The cost for "Professional Expedited Service" is based on exact mileage. For example, a trip from New York City to Ft. Lauderdale (1,267 miles) would cost $750 plus the first tank of gas. Ideally, reservations should be made two to three weeks in advance. For more information, call 1-800-346-2277.

Note: If your car is leased, check with the leasing company to find out where you can turn in the car at the end of your lease.

Tips for a smooth moving day

Here are some important suggestions for orchestrating an uneventful but speedy moving day.

- Read the bill of lading (your contract) carefully before you sign it. Keep it on your possession until your shipment is delivered, charges are paid, and all claims are settled. It is your only proof that the mover is working for you.

- Make sure the bill of lading confirms the proper liability coverage you purchased when signing the order for service.

- Join the movers as they take inventory, the process of inspecting each item being shipped. Watch to see which items they designate as scratched, dented, etc. If you disagree, argue your case right there. Once the items are on the van is no time to discover the condition report is not an accurate reflection.

- If you got a non-binding estimate and are concerned that it may be way off, you can observe the official weighing of the van by going to the scales with the mover immediately before and after the shipment has been loaded. This will confirm or deny your suspicions.

- Make sure you have worked out payment arrangements with the mover in advance. Unloading day is the wrong time to find out that your certified check is unacceptable. You can even look into charging your move (many of the bigger carriers now except MasterCard and Visa).

- If your estimate was non-binding, there's always a chance that the final cost will be higher. *By law, you are only obligated to pay the estimate plus 10 percent of the remaining balance at the time of delivery.* You can usually request 15 to 30 days to pay off the balance.

- Before unloading gets into full swing, take your copy of the inventory sheets and check the condition of the items as they're pulled off the van. If you see damage, or notice something is missing, alert the mover and ask him to mark it on both your copy and the mover's copy of the inventory. This is called "taking exceptions."

Filing claims against the mover

If you can believe it, most moves are disaster-free. And the vast majority of claims only involve losses or damages of $100 or less. Nonetheless, submitting claims can be a painful process. If breakage is involved, movers will generally argue that items were improperly packed (and in a lot of cases they are right). The burden of proof is your responsibility.

Remember, too, that the actual reimbursement depends on the type of liability coverage you bought. Still, there's no need to panic if you have a legitimate claim. Follow this checklist for getting through the process:

10 steps for handling claims

1. It's not necessary to unpack and inspect all the cartons before signing the inventory sheet, but you should indicate any obvious damage to the carton's exteriors.

2. Concealed damage discovered at a later time can be reported. Because you'll have to offer some proof of the mover's negligence, leave the damaged items in the carton until the claims adjustor inspects the damage, or the claim can be denied.

3. Claims for loss and damage can legally be filed within nine months of delivery, but don't delay. The longer you wait, the easier it will be for the mover to claim the damage occurred after the move.

4. Movers must acknowledge claims within 30 days and settle them within 120 days.

5. Claim forms must be submitted with the bill of lading, so be sure to keep it in a safe place.

6. All claims must be submitted in writing, but first find out if there is a special hotline number for instructions on filing claims.

7. Don't be afraid to be overly detailed in your claim report. Settlements are often delayed because more information was needed.

8. List lost and damaged items separately, along with estimates for repairs or replacement. You may be asked to justify a replacement cost. If you no longer have a receipt, check mail order catalogs or store ads for similar values.

9. If you incurred any hotel or other living expenses caused by the mover's delays or losses, add that to the claim forms.

10. Finally, understand that the actual dollar amount you receive from the mover will be determined by the representative who does the claim inspection. In anticipation of getting the kind of adjuster who assumes your furniture was shabby to begin with, it's helpful to know that you can take your case to arbitration (at no cost to you) if you are unhappy with a settlement.

Wrapping it all up

Retiring and relocating will be one of the most highly emotional times in the lives of you and your spouse. It is a time of beginnings and endings. Of intense feelings and infinite details. It's not necessarily a time when clear thinking is an easy achievement. That's why you should be kind to yourselves by organizing a smooth, uneventful and perfectly boring move. There will be enough excitement without it!

Arizona	1. Prescott
	2. Scottsdale
	3. Tucson
Arkansas	4. Fayetteville
	5. Hot Springs Village
California	6. Palm Springs
	7. San Diego
Colorado	8. Colorado Springs
	9. Fort Collins
Florida	10. Boca Raton
	11. Daytona Beach
	12. Fort Myers
	13. Gainesville
	14. Melbourne
	15. Naples
	16. St. Petersburg
	17. Sarasota
	18. Winter Haven
Georgia	19. Brunswick
	20. Clayton
Hawaii	21. Maui
Idaho	22. Coeur d'Alene
Indiana	23. Bloomington
Massachusetts	24. Cape Cod
Nevada	25. Carson City
	26. Las Vegas
New Jersey	27. Ocean County
New Mexico	28. Las Cruces
	29. Santa Fe
New York	30. Sullivan County
N. Carolina	31. Asheville
	32. Brevard
	33. Chapel Hill
	34. Outer Banks
Oregon	35. Eugene
	36. Lincoln City
	37. Medford
S. Carolina	38. Charleston
	39. Hilton Head Island
	40. Myrtle Beach
Texas	41. Austin
	42. Brownsville
	43. Kerrville
	44. San Antonio
Utah	45. St. George
Virginia	46. Charlottesville
	47. Hampton
Washington	48. Olympia
	49. Sequim
Wisconsin	50. Door County

50 Fabulous Pl.

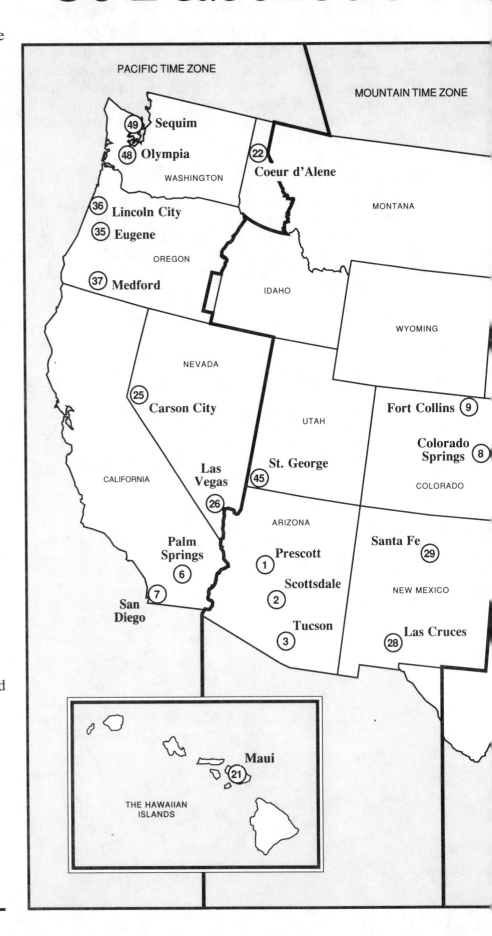

ces To Retire In America

CENTRAL TIME ZONE

EASTERN TIME ZONE

NORTH DAKOTA

SOUTH DAKOTA

MINNESOTA

WISCONSIN

MAINE

VERMONT

NEW YORK

NEW HAMPSHIRE

MASSACHUSETTS

Cape Cod

24

MICHIGAN

Door County

50

CONNECTICUT

RHODE ISLAND

Sullivan County

30

NEBRASKA

IOWA

PENNSYLVANIA

Ocean County

27

NEW JERSEY

KANSAS

ILLINOIS

INDIANA

OHIO

MARYLAND

DELAWARE

WEST VIRGINIA

Bloomington

23

MISSOURI

Charlottesville

46

Hampton

47

VIRGINIA

KENTUCKY

Chapel Hill

33

Outer Banks

34

OKLAHOMA

Fayetteville

4

TENNESSEE

Asheville

31

NORTH CAROLINA

ARKANSAS

Brevard

32

5

Clayton

20

SOUTH CAROLINA

Myrtle Beach

40

Hot Springs Village

GEORGIA

Charleston

38

TEXAS

ALABAMA

Hilton Head Island

39

MISSISSIPPI

Brunswick

19

LOUISIANA

Gainesville

13

Austin

41

Daytona Beach

11

Kerrville

43

Winter Haven

18

Melbourne

14

San Antonio

44

St. Petersburg

16

Sarasota

17

FLORIDA

Fort Myers

12

Boca Raton

10

Naples

15

Brownsville

42

How to Use
the Area Profiles

Area profiles are presented in alphabetical order by state, then city (from Arizona to Wisconsin). The handy cross-reference below will help you locate them in alphabetical order by city.

Each profile examines 17 categories of interest and more than 40 different factors within those categories. The easy-to-use format allows you to read the entire summary, or quickly refer to the topics of greatest interest, such as recreation, climate or income tax rates.

If one particular factor is foremost in your selection of a retirement location—size, housing cost or climate—then flip to the handy "Fast Facts" section on pages 252 to 255. This chart lists all 50 locations with key facts and best reasons to move there. Shop for exactly what you want, or use for a quick comparison.

The following glossary explains some terms that may be unfamiliar to you.

ACCRA: We referred to the latest American Chamber of Commerce Researchers Association report, comparing living-cost differences in 291 urban areas. The figures reflect expenses for a household with two adults (one a salaried execcutive) and two children, but what's most relevant is how much more or less they spent to purchase the same products and services in that city vs. another.

Climate: The Weather Channel, the 24-hour all-weather satellite network, was our exclusive source of climatological data. They want to remind you that everything in a community is subject to change except the weather. The four seasons will prevail from year to year so be sure you're looking at areas where the climate suits you.

There are other factors to consider: Those with heart trouble or arteriosclerosis respond well to mild climates while arthritics respond best to warm weather. Hay fever sufferers get relief from dry climates. **Elevation:** The higher the elevation, the thinner the air and the more difficult it can be to breathe. Those with heart conditions or respiratory problems should take caution. Also, for every 1,000 ft. of increased altitude, the temperature is decreased by an average of 3.5 F. **Relative Humidity,** when combined with high temperatures, is the single most common climactic condition to put stress on the human body. For example, if the temperature is 88 and the relative humidity is 78%, it will feel like 106. It can cause fatigue, accelerated heart rates and also raise blood pressure. In the most serious cases, heatstroke and sunstroke are possible. Remember that humidity is only a concern when the air temperature is high. (Anyone with a medical condition should consult with a doctor when considering relocation, though.)

JCAH: The Joint Commission on Accreditation of Healthcare Organizations is a private, nonprofit group that sets the standards for health care facilities and evaluates their performance before rendering an accreditation. You can be sure that hospitals achieving this designation offer a high quality of patient care.

Median Housing Price: Similar to a highway median that divides traffic down the middle, a median price indicates that half the houses in the market are selling for less than the median, half are selling for more. It's a good way to gauge affordability. Average prices, however, are a more accurate reflection of what people are paying and generally run higher.

RSVP: Retired Seniors Volunteer Program is the largest volunteer network in the U.S. Its goal is to give adults 50 and older an opportunity to use lifetime skills to enrich the community. **SCORE:** Senior Corps of Retired Excecutives is a national volunteer program made up of former business owners and corporate executives who share their expertise by way of free consultations to small business owners in their community.

SAGE: Senior Achievement Through Growth and Education is a special program available at many colleges and universities that offers courses of interest to people 55 and older.

Utility Costs: The average monthly bills for gas and electric service provided are an excellent way to compare costs between locations. They're not necessarily a way to predict actual charges as bills will vary substantially based on square footage of a home, number of people, number of appliances, personal habits, unusually hot or cold weather, method of heating/cooling, etc.

1. Prescott, Arizona

Area Snapshot

Nickname: "Everybody's Home Town"
County: Yavapai
Area code: 602   **Zip code:** 83601
Local population: 30,000   **County:** 55,000
% of population 65+: 35%
U.S. region: Central Arizona
Closest metro areas: Phoenix, 90 miles
Nearby areas to consider: Prescott Valley, Chino Valley
Median housing price: $125,000
Best reasons to retire here: Very liveable climate (4 distinct seasons), pleasant small town qualities, spectacular scenery, great outdoor recreation, low property taxes, their own retirement college.

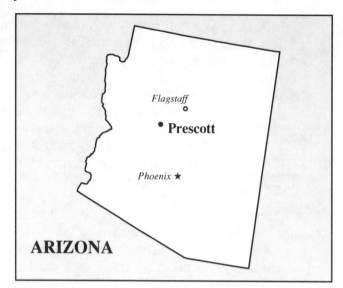

Fabulous Features

Noted retirement writer Peter Dickinson says Prescott (pronounced "press-kit") has the most liveable climate in the country. He would know. He lives there along with 30,000 other devoted residents. Located in the heart of central Arizona, you'll enjoy four mild seasons which literally blow hot and cold but always sunny. The summers bring dry, warm desert air, the winters see invigorating mountain chills and an average 25 inches of snow. Prescott is one of Arizona's best-kept secrets and house-rich Californians who have been migrating for years would like to keep it that way. The charm of Prescott is that it's small and friendly but packed to the city limits with great services, recreation and a well-blended population. In fact, over 1,200 seniors are students at the local community college. They're such an important faction, a special Retirement College was created to encourage their involvement. And when they speak of a "high" quality of life, they're not kidding. Prescott is a mile high in elevation. The views don't get any better than this. With a backdrop of snow-covered mountains, rolling hills and Ponderosa Pines as far as the eye can see, the state has lovingly coined Prescott "Arizona's Christmas City." For residents, living here is such a great gift, it's Christmas in July, too.

Possible drawbacks: Make note of the elevation. At 5,000 feet up (1 mile), the thin air can cause breathing problems for some people. Those with heart conditions would be advised to check with their physicians before retiring here.•Shopping is limited, with major discount stores and malls an hour's drive away. Ditto with big-name entertainment and culture. Now, however, two malls are under construction which will be easier on folks.

"You can quote me on that"

"We're from Oklahoma and this area was perfect for us. First of all, we didn't have to worry about tornadoes anymore. The climate is great all year. The winters aren't harsh and the summers aren't miserable. The size of the town was also important. The population isn't overwhelming. We like the pace, too. People have time to be friendly. They're not always in a hurry. I do wish I didn't have to drive so far to go fishing, but you can't have everything."—Mr. L.B.

Climate

Elevation: 5,082'	Avg. High/ Low	Average Inches		Avg. # Days Precip.	Avg. % Humidity
		Rain	Snow		
Jan.	59/26	1.4	-	5	55
April	78/40	.5	-	6	35
July	95/66	2	-	10	40
Oct.	80/45	1	-	4	40
YEAR	77/43	13	32	-	-
# days 32° or below: 131			# days 90° or above: 47		

Let the Good Times Roll

Recreation: Outdoor recreational opportunities abound. There are 900 acres of city parks and 20 state and national parks in the area. Prescott National Forest has 20 different recreational areas including Acker Park, Badger Park, Groom Creek Horse Camp, Lynx and Watson Lakes, and Thumb Butte Park (ideal for fishing, picnicking, hiking, camping, tennis, and boating). But you can be happy if you do nothing more than enjoy the spectacular mountain scenery. Prescott is situated in the hub of the drive to the Grand Canyon, known as Grand Canyon Scenic Circle. For the sports-minded, there are two 18-hole golf courses, pools, tennis and racquetball, softball fields (it's the softball capital of the world, with international tournaments every year). Horseback riding and fabulous cross-country skiing are popular and rock-climbing on 7,600 ft. Granite Mountains attracts climbers from all parts.

Culture: Prescott has six museums and galleries: The Bead Museum, Mountain Artists Guild, Prescott Fine Arts Association, The Phippen Museum of Western Art, Sharlot Hall Museum, and The Smoki Museum which displays Indian artifacts; The Yavapai Symphony Association presents symphonies and pop concerts and professional opera. The Friends in Concert Association, with the Community College, present chamber music and recitals by renowned artists. The Prescott Fine Arts Association also offers theater productions (a fine gallery as well); Elks Opera House performs symphony concerts and opera. Prescott Department of Parks and Recreation also provides many recreational activities including square dances, community concerts, and arts and crafts classes.

Annual events: Phippen Western Art show (May); All Indian Pow Wow and Market (June); Tucson Territorial Days (June); Governor's Cup Antique Car Show and Rallye (fall): Starts in Prescott and ends in Grand Canyon; Copper State Fly In (fall): Airplane show and events. New home of the state event. World's Oldest Rodeo and Frontier Days (July 4th) Arizona's Christmas City (parade, elegant ball and holiday festivities).

Local Real Estate

Real estate sales have been brisk with homes selling at 95 percent of asking prices. People want in and homes are not out of line, so hard-core negotiating seems out of place. Mobile home developments are popular. But gorgeous new custom homes in subdivisions are attracting retirees as well. For real country living, the Williamson Valley Road area is worth looking at. The fruit trees, large acreage and older homes are quite charming.

Median price for single family home: $125,000. New homes start at $150,000; resales: $110,000.

Median price for 2BR condo: $80,000

Rental housing market: Apartments and condominiums are in good supply. 2BR units rent for $400 and up. Single family homes are in short supply, with owners asking up to $850/month for a 3BR.

Common housing styles & features: The look is uniquely Southwestern (hope you like the color red). Special features include large, open floor plans; great rooms instead of separate living and family rooms; large bedrooms and bathrooms; den or Arizona room sometimes used instead of a third bedroom.

Amenities in condo developments: pools, golf courses, hiking/biking trails.

Nearby areas to consider: Prescott Valley and Chino Valley. **Unique features of these areas:** Prescott Valley (12 miles away) is more rural, with larger lots and more acreage available. The land is grassy and flat. Real estate is less costly, with the median price for homes at $60,000. Chino Valley (12 miles from Prescott) is also more rural with many properties suitable for stables and riding. Housing prices are in the $65,000-$70,000 range.

What Things Cost

Overall living costs are 9.5% above average, primarily because real estate is more costly here. It rates about 37% above the national average. Lower utilities and property taxes help offset the fixed living expenses.

Gas company: Southern Union Gas *(445-2210)*. The average monthly bill is $35-$48.

Electric company: Arizona Public Service Co. *(776-3668)*. With electric heat in the winter, avg. bill is $130; Summer/air conditioning costs about $55/mo. (prices are based on 1,500 sq. ft., 2BR condo).

Phone company: U.S. West Communications *(445-1862)*. Basic budget service is $8.45/month with additional charges per call; unlimited local calling $15.90 a month including touch-tone.

Car registration/license: Driver's license: $7 (for four years); auto tags: minimum fee $23.50 based on the factory list price and age of the vehicle. Price can go as high as $1,200. Registration fee: $8.25; Emissions test fee: $1.50.

The Tax Ax

Sales tax: 6% (currently a 1% tax on food but that may be eliminated).

State income tax: Arizona taxes 8% of gross adjusted income for federal income reported, less the federal income taxes paid.

Retirement income: Residents 65 and older get a $1,500 exemption.

Property taxes & tax breaks: Property tax is assessed at 10% of market value. (usually about 8/10 of 1% of assessed value). For example, a $100,000 home would run $800.

Medical Care

Major hospitals/regional medical centers: **Yavapai Regional Medical Center** is the fully accredited facility in the area, and thanks to its recent expansion and renovation, it now boasts state-of-the-art medical care. Services include: cardiac care and rehabilitation, radiology, EKG, mobil MRI diagnostic imagery, nuclear medicine, outpatient oncology, home health care, a hospice, and a family resource center. The **Department of Veterans Affairs** also has a major facility at Prescott with a very good outpatient surgical center. There is also a private **Outpatient Surgical Center** as an alternative to ambulatory surgery.

Emergency medical services (EMS): The Prescott Fire Department has four stations and 10 licensed paramedics, 53 full-time employees and 12 reserves. Average response time: 4.5 minutes. The Central Yavapai Fire District serves 146 miles, two-seven stations, 46 full-time firefighters and 35 reserves, three ambulances.

Physician's referral: Yavapai Medical Center *445-2700*.

Continuing Education

Yavapai Community College's retirement college has more than 1,200 senior students (anyone 55 and older can enroll). Those 62 and older are entitled to a reduced tuition ($17 a credit hour). College alumni pay $27/hour. Standard tuition is $44. You can sign up for any of their more than 200 courses (the same ones offered to undergraduates) on a pass/fail basis *(445-7300 ext. 2051)*. Prescott College has adult degree programs and adult education classes, as does the Department of Parks and Recreation.

Services for Seniors

Prescott has an unbelievable number of programs and services for a community this size. The Adult Center is the gathering place for recreational and social activities and many organizations (including **AARP**). The **County Health Department** provides home nursing services on a sliding-fee basis. Volunteerism is very strong, with both an **RSVP** chapter and a Volunteer Center in town. The **Central Arizona Seniors Association** (CASA), sponsors wonderful outings and social activities. Yavapai has a special lifeline service, which is a personal emergency response system ($17.50/month). Call the Adult Center and AARP for more information *(778-3000)*.

Crime & Safety

The police are genuinely committed to making sure that Prescott residents are not prisoners in their own homes. Crime rates are very low and solid prevention programs may be part of the reason. Block Watch, Sexual Assault Seminars (for all ages) and DARE (Drug Abuse Resistance Education) are well-supported.

Earning a Living

Current business climate: Tourism is the number-one industry and population growth is on the upswing. The town has been growing at rate of 5% to 6% a year for the past decade, and most are optimistic that businesses will fare well.

Help in starting a business: Yavapai Community College has a very active Small Business Development Center which offers free consultations and business planning for entrepreneurs. *(445-7300).*

The job market: Part-time work is available, particularly during the tourist season. Even professionals, such as engineers and attorneys are able to drum up consulting jobs. Seniors are a valued commodity here, which is evidenced by the strength of the SCORE chapter.

When the Kids Come to Visit

Grand Canyon (only 125 miles and worth every one to get there); Prescott Animal Park; Prescott National Forest (1 million acres preserved) with vast recreational facilities including a set up for campers with horses; Granite Mountain and Basin (gorgeous scenery on the way to the Basin Recreation Area); Smoki Museum; Granite Dells (a scenic drive to the famous formation "point of rocks").

Getting Around Town

Roads & interstates: US 89; US 69; I-17; I-10
Airports & airlines: Prescott Municipal Airport: commuter airline service to Phoenix and Las Vegas.
Public transportation: Prescott Whipple State and Transit is a private bus company. Two routes cover the shopping area and hospital. A day pass is $3 (monthly, $24). No senior discounts are available.
Managing without a car: Difficult.

What Residents Already Know

Prescott is a summer haven for asthma and allergy sufferers. With a climate that vacillates between desert heat and cool mountain air and tall Ponderosa pines that block out the pollen, your allergy pills can stay in the medicine chest.•Everybody looks young in this town. Many of the retirees are in their 50s and early 60s and are extremely conscious about their health. The motto is "In Prescott, you're only as old as you think!" The President's Council on Fitness should film a commercial here.

For More Information

Chamber Of Commerce Office:
Prescott Chamber of Commerce
117 Goodwin Street
P.O. Box 1147
Prescott, 86302
445-2000

Newspaper:
The Courier
147 North Cortez Street
Prescott, 86301
445-3333

Realtor:
Bob Polacek, Judy Jensen
Realty World/
Mountain Air Realty, Inc.
303 East Gurley Street
Prescott, 86301
455-2715

2. Scottsdale, Arizona

Area Snapshot

Nickname: "Arizona's Playground"
County: Maricopa
Area code: 602   **Zip code:** 85251-85268
Local population: 135,000   **County:** 2.1 million
% of population 50+: 40%
U.S. region: Central Arizona
Closest metro areas: Phoenix, 20 miles; Tucson, 125 miles
Nearby areas to consider: Mesa, Tempe
Median housing price: $112,500
Best reasons to retire here: Excellent medical, desert climate, large retirement population, wonderful recreation and services, real estate in all price ranges.

Fabulous Features

They call it "America's Playground" but it is more like the world's best "Sleep Away Camp for Grown Ups" (with much nicer cabins). The list of activities, programs and places to play are endless. And with a good 40 percent of the community involved in the pursuit of a great day, you really do feel like your part of large scale operation—Operation Retirement! Scottsdale's casual chic ambience sets the stage. It's the nostalgic Old West with the upscale, cosmopolitan New West. Outdoor recreation abounds with 125 golf courses, Championship Tennis, access to some of the country's best sightseeing, loads of culture (Arizona State in Tempe contributes) and food is cheap because of some of the fiercest supermarket competition you've ever seen. Shopping is paradise (they even have a Fifth Ave.), not to mention the more than 200 restaurants. Year-round climate is warm to very hot, (average is 70, but June-August stay in the 90s). The saving grace is dry air and low humidity. Scottsdale prides itself on excellent medical facilities including the new $50 million Mayo Clinic. With such a heavy concentration of seniors in the city, retirees have a lot of economic and social clout. This results is an abundance of organizations, services, and activities serving their needs. *USA Today* ranked Scottsdale as one of the top 25 retirement spots in the country. One retiree told us, "It's not like Florida. You don't hear of hordes of people trying it and moving out. Unless they just can't bear the heat, most everyone stays."

Possible drawbacks: The highway system is terribly outmoded and not directly accessible to the city. Public transportation, while good in the center city, wanes in the outlying areas.•We hear the state Welfare/Medicaid system is a mess (slow and unresponsive).•Then there's the climate. Everyone advises making several visit during different times of the year to check your tolerance.

"You can quote me on that"

"We absolutely love it here. It's upscale, the services are excellent and the local government is very responsive to our needs. We all vote and they know it. Yes it's hot, but without the humidity most days it's very comfortable. Believe me, a 100° day in Scottsdale is still much nicer than a humid 80° day in Chicago."—H. L.

Climate

Elevation: 1,129'	Avg. High/ Low	Avg. Rainfall (Inches)	Avg. # Days Precip.	Avg. % Humidity
Jan.	65/38	.71	4	40
April	84/52	.32	2	20
July	105/78	.75	4	24
Oct.	88/57	.46	3	26
YEAR	85/57	7	-	-
# days 32° or below: 13		# days 90° or above: 164		

Let the Good Times Roll

Recreation: The Indian Bend Wash Greenbelt (a 7.5-mile-long flood-control project) offers a network of parks, lakes and golf courses, and is considered the "recreational pulse" of Scottsdale, there are 29 golf courses in the Scottsdale area and 125 in the metro area, including the Tournament Players Club of Scottsdale (permanent home of the PGA Phoenix Open, open to the public); The city offers 19 public and plenty of private tennis courses (World Championship Tennis has numerous tournaments). And Cactus Park offers a 50-meter heated pool, weight room, dance studio, picnic ramadas (sun shelter) and jogging/bike paths. Visit Horseworld, with 9 show arenas, a grand prix field, polo fields and a marketplace bazaar. A new Arts Pavilion/ Amphitheater is under construction. Other activities include: desert jeep excursions, river rafting, hot air balloons, backpacking and cross country skiing. Major League Baseball Spring Training (The Giants, Padres, Cubs, Oakland As, Brewers, Mariners and Cleveland Indians all play in the Phoenix Metro area) and Cactus Baseball League as well as the NBA's Phoenix Suns (Scottsdale).

Culture: Scottsdale is one of the art centers of the Southwest, with more than 120 galleries. Scottsdale Gallery Association sponsors the Thursday Evening Art Walk, year-round; Scottsdale Center For The Arts (the Scottsdale Symphony Orchestra, theater productions, etc.); Arizona State University offers the Kerr Cultural Center (great jazz fests); the Gammage Center for the Performing Arts; and the Lyceum Theater.

Annual events: Phoenix PGA Open (Jan.); Sunkist Fiesta Football Bowl/Parade (Dec.); All Arabian Horse Show (Feb.); Scottsdale Air Fair and All Indian Pow Wow (April); Scottsdale Festival Of The Arts (May); Wrangler Jeans Rodeo Showdown (Oct.).

Local Real Estate

Scottsdale's planned communities have every conceivable amenity you could ask for—from horse trails to championship golf to country clubhouses. In recent past there has been a tremendous surge in activity and sales. Prices remain stable, however, with the average home selling for $145,000 (combined new and resale). New homes in the northern section average $175,000. Average lot size is 80 x 140. In some of the more established areas, older townhouse condos (1,300 sq. ft. 3BR 2 1/2 bath, 2 levels) sell for $58,000. Taxes would be about $600/yr. The homes in south Scottsdale average $150,000, but go as high as $500,000. McCormick Ranch, which has shopping, two golf courses and man-made lakes, beautiful new homes start at $65,000 and go up to $600,000. Most of the developments are within 15 minutes of the big malls.

Median price for single family home: $112,500.

Median price for 2BR condo: $55,000 (up to $200,000).

Rental housing market: The rental market is generally good, although between October-April, anything and everything gets snatched up. A 3BR house runs $700+/mo; 2BR apt. $500-$800/mo.

Common housing styles & features: Most homes are framed stucco or block stucco with tiled roofs. Interiors include vaulted ceilings, gourmet kitchens and large master bedroom suites. Patio homes are very popular (larger than condos with some land but not as costly as single family homes). Both ranches and two-story homes are available.

Amenities in condo developments: Pool, spa, tennis courts, security, golf communities.

Nearby areas to consider: Mesa, Tempe.

Unique features: Tempe is the home of Arizona State University and offers good services and shopping on a smaller scale. Home prices are lower (starting at $60,000) with the average cost $139,000. Mesa is further out and offers similar values.

What Things Cost

Living costs in the Phoenix Metro area are about 3% above the national average. Health care is about 12% above, but utilities and homes are 2%-6% below. Property taxes are also very low. (Food and restaurants offer real savings as well).

Gas company: Southwest Gas Corp. *(894-6674)*. Avg. summer bill: $15; winter months $42-$50.

Electric company: Arizona Public Service Company *(371-7171)* and Salt River Project *(236-8888)*. Avg. bill: $80/mo. winter; $130-$140 summer (2BR condo).

Phone company: U.S. West Communications *(490-2355)*. Basic monthly service is $18 including touchtone service.

Car registration/license: Driver's license: $7 (4 years); Auto tags: minimum fee $23.50 based on the factory list price and vehicle age. Price can go as high as $1,200. Registration fee: $8.25; emissions test fee: $1.50.

The Tax Ax

Sales tax: 6.7%. (Prescriptions/food exempt).

State income tax: Arizona taxes 8% of gross adjusted income for federal income reported, less federal income taxes paid.

Retirement income: $1,500 exemption for those seniors 65+.

Property taxes & tax breaks: Property taxes are based on $9.42 for every $100 of assessed valuation (10% of the market value, which is the lowest rate in the valley). A homestead protection measure protects against foreclosure for up to $100,000 of the value of the house. Taxes on a $100,000 home run $942/yr. Contact the Maricopa Tax Assessors office for more information *(262-3406)*.

Medical Care

Major hospitals/regional medical centers: Scottsdale Memorial Hospital Mayo Clinic is an internationally known diagnostic, research and outpatient center. The $50 million facility opened in 1987 (there are only two others in the world *(391-8000)*; **Scottsdale**

Memorial Hospital (2 locations) has a new cardiovascular center with open heart surgery; extensive private nursing and home health care services; a skilled nursing facility for patients who need a few extra recovery days). Several specialized facilities include the Headache/Stress Center; Scottsdale Cardiovascular Center; and Camelback Behavioral Services (Psychiatric).

Emergency medical services (EMS): Scottsdale contracts with Rural Metro to provide fire and EMS services. Many city workers are also cross-trained to provide emergency services. Eight paramedic teams and ambulances operate within city limits. Average response time: 4.8 min.

Physician's referral: Memorial Hospital *941-4882*.

Continuing Education

Scottsdale Community College has developed a tremendous Continuing Education program offering classes on business, Medicare, photography, self-hypnosis, and the popular "Do Something For Yourself." Fees range from $20-$75 and seniors 62+, can get 50% off certain courses *(423-6000)*.

Services for Seniors

The Scottsdale Senior Center offers extensive recreation, classes, health screenings, support group meetings and serves as a central meeting zone for many of Scottsdale's Senior Clubs. Its social services division offers everything from legal assistance to "pets-on-wheels" (bringing pets to nursing homes) to "waste not" programs from participating restaurants (food to the needy). The Scottsdale **RSVP** matches seniors with volunteer needs, runs a 50+ employment program, and even loans out free medical equipment. The city sponsors Senior Tennis, lap swimming and water aerobics, Senior Softball Leagues (Scottsdale hosted the World Series of Senior Softball), Senior Olympics, Senior Boxing and Senior Slim and Trim classes. Arizona Senior World is an excellent monthly newspaper to keep track of issues and events *(438-1566)*; Information on **AARP** Chapter #1457 is available *(994-2375)*.

Crime & Safety

Crime is low considering how quickly the area has grown, although the burglary rate has risen. It has spurred action among the Neighborhood Watch programs. Overall, seniors we spoke to felt that the area was very safe. One problem mentioned was telephone fraud. Seniors are often targets of phony land deals, free vacation offers, etc. The police department's Senior Citizen Crime Prevention and Crime Intervention programs have been working to reverse the trend.

Earning a Living

Current business climate: The prospects are excellent because of the continued population boom and the high level of disposable income.
Help in starting a business: The Scottsdale Chamber has an outstanding program to develop small business. Its 36-person staff provides personal consultants to entrepreneurs and can even negotiate financial incentives with the city (free service). It also conducts seminars and distribute handbooks on better business strategies. The local SCORE chapter runs seminars, helps with business plans and loan applications *(379-3843)*.
The job market: The part-time job market has traditionally been good. With the vast number of retail and service outlets, the opportunities are there. The Scottsdale Senior Center has an excellent job placement program.

When the Kids Come to Visit

Phoenix Zoo; Grand Canyon National Park and Monument; Jerome "ghost town"; Painted Desert (high desert region with spectacular scenery); Petrified Forest; Roosevelt Dam (forms Lake Roosevelt, a scenic spot along the Apache trail); Sedona (located in Red Rock Country and one of the most unique, scenic towns in the world); McCormick Railroad Park (steam and diesel railroads, 5 ramadas, shops featuring railroad memorabilia and a restored carousel).

Getting Around Town

Roads & interstates: I-17 (20 min. west); I-10. No highways directly intersect with the city. **Airports & airlines:** Sky Harbor International Airport (25 minutes from downtown) is served by Southwest, Midway, TWA, United, USAir, American, America West, Continental, Delta, and Northwest. **Public transportation:** "Scottsdale Connection" runs 2 north/south routes and 4 east/west routes (half price for seniors is 40¢ one-way or $14/mo.) Operates daily except Sunday. The trolleys run every 15 minutes October-May to major shopping and resorts. Dial-A-Ride offers door-to-door bus service for the handicapped and seniors 65+. **Managing without a car:** It's possible.

What Residents Already Know

This is one of the cleanest cities in the country. The streets are spotless and the neighborhoods impeccably maintained.•The $130 million Galleria shopping mall just opened and credit cards are flying.

For More Information

Chamber Of Commerce Office:
Scottsdale Chamber of Commerce
7333 Scottsdale Mall
Scottsdale, 85251-4489
945-8981

Tempe Chamber of Commerce
60 E. 5th St.
Tempe, 85281
967-7891

Newspapers:
The Arizona Republic/
Phoenix Gazette
P.O. Box 1950
Phoenix, 85001
800-331-9303

Tempe Daily News/Tribune
51 W. 3rd St. #106
Tempe, 85281
898-5680

Realtors:
Abe Stolberg
Coldwell Banker
8201 N. Hayden Rd.
Scottsdale, 85251
991-3100

Fred Pulve
Arizona 1 Realty
7502 E. Monterey Way
Scottsdale, 85251
941-4410

3. Tucson, Arizona

Area Snapshot

Nickname: "The Old Pueblo"
County: Pima
Area code: 602   **Zip code:** 85702
Local population: 405,700   **County:** 678,300
% of population 65+: 12.5%
U.S. region: Southern Arizona
Closest metro areas: Phoenix, 116 miles
Nearby areas to consider: Saddlebrook, Green Valley
Median housing price: $100,000
Best reasons to retire here: Large college town, abundant culture and recreation, affordable housing, rejuvenating desert climate, excellent medical care.

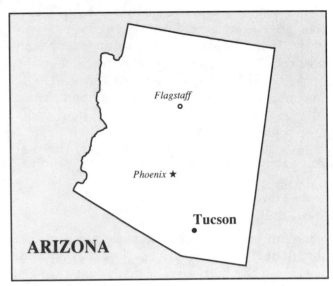

Fabulous Features

If someone were to go to the drawing board to create a most hospitable retirement area from scratch, they would need to look no further than Tucson. Tucson is a tough act to follow. Every aspect of the quality of life here has been thought through. From the luxurious housing developments to the outstanding cultural and recreational activities. For good measure putting the dynamic University of Arizona in the center of town has served to bring youth, vitality and intellectual growth to the community. And then there's the climate. For some, the dry, sunny weather with low humidity is a gift. January has the greatest changes, ranging from 38 to 64. July is the hottest, ranging from 73 to 98, with cool evenings. Tucson is a city rich in history and beauty, exemplified by the young and old who meld their interests and their concerns for one another. When you learn of the in-depth programs and services designed specifically for seniors, you understand that this is not just rhetoric. The health and wellness programs and facilities are some of the most innovative we've seen. And it's not just offered by one hospital. They're all involved. The educational outlets such as SAGE (Senior Achievement & Growth through Education) stimulate a comaraderie and purpose that is unmatched. The extensive volunteer network and referral system says loud and clear, this community cares.

Possible drawbacks: It's a large city, with the metro area covering almost 500 square miles. There is a nice community feeling, but this is by no means a small town life.•Traffic is a serious problem. The solution lies in rebuilding the road system, which older voters keep nixing.•Also, it's *hot*. Yes, the humidity is low, but you don't get the same relief you would in northern Arizona. But for retirees seeking refuge from bitter northern winters, Tucson offers respite from the cold.

"You can quote me on that"

"Tucson offers so much to retirees. It's a big city but it only works to your advantage. The University brings so much to town that wouldn't be here otherwise, and the weather is great. I've lived here for 45 years and while prices have gone up, I still feel it's an affordable place to live. And now that I'm the right age, I can take advantage of many discounts from the stores and restaurants. I highly recommend that active people who want to be busy all the time spend some time in Tucson. You'll see what everyone raves about."—A.S.

Climate

Elevation: 2,647'	Avg. High/ Low	Average Inches		Avg. # Days Precip.	Avg. % Humidity
		Rain	Snow		
Jan.	64/38	.74	-	4	50
April	81/50	.34	-	2	30
July	98/74	2.4	-	10	40
Oct.	84/56	.66	-	3	40
YEAR	82/54	11	1.4	-	-
# days 32° or below: 20			# days 90° or above: 146		

Let the Good Times Roll

Recreation: Surrounding state parks and national monuments are some of the most beautiful in the country. You'll love Gates Pass, with panoramic views, Madera Canyon, with hiking trails and picnic grounds, Catalina Park, Agua Caliente Park, Tohono Chul Park, and Mt. Lemmon in the Santa Catalinas, with year-round fishing, camping and picnicking. It is also the southernmost ski area in the continental U.S. Tucson has more than 100 parks, 28 golf courses and 300 tennis facilities. Swimming pools, jogging tracks, bike paths, roller-skating, horseback riding and miniature golf is also available. A favorite swimming hole is the clear pool at Seven Falls in Sabino Canyon. NCAA sports at the University of Arizona; Houston Astros AAA farm team, Tucson Toros; Cleveland Indians Spring Training Camp; greyhound racing; rodeo's PGA Tournament Players Association; LPGA open; and Pima County Polo Club.

Culture: Tucson is one of 14 cities in the U.S. that has a professional resident theater, opera, symphony and dance company. The designated Arts District is home to the Temple of Music and Art, the Tucson Convention Center, Leo Rich Theater and the Music Hall. The Arizona Theater Company, and the state's only opera, Arizona Opera Company, earn national recognition. Don't miss the Tucson Ballet Company and the Southern Arizona Light Opera Company. Museums: Tucson Museum of Art, The Center for Creative Photography and the University Museum of Art.

Annual events: Fiesta de los Vaceros Rodeo (February); Annual Poetry Festival; Street Fair (Dec.); Mariachi Conference (April); Tucson Meet Yourself (Oct.); Copper Bowl: NCAA football on New Year's Eve.

Local Real Estate

Land and housing prices are the lowest they've been in a decade.
Median price for single family home: $100,000. New: $125,000-$200,000. Resales: $90,000.
Median price for 2BR condo/townhouse: $72,500.
Rental housing market: Rentals are scarce. $650-$800/mo. for 3BR. 2BR apts.: $250 and up.
Common housing styles & features: Classic Southwestern design.
Amenities in condo developments: Pools, tennis, full amenities (may have to pay an extra maintenance fee of about $60/month).
Nearby areas to consider: Del Webb's Sun City Tucson, Fairfield's San Ignaio Hills, Saddle-Brooke Country Club. **Unique features of these areas:** Del Webb's is a growing retirement community with single-family patio homes, pools, recreation area, tennis courts and golf courses. Range from $79,900 to $200,000. Golf villas for guests available on a weekly basis. 2,500 units planned, 600 in existence. In Green Valley, Fairfield's San Ignacio Hills is a smaller retirement community similar to Sun City. It has its own newspaper and radio station, medical and dental offices, clinics and shopping centers. Prices range from $80,000-$200,000. Planned 900 units. SaddleBrooke Country Club is almost as big as Sun City, with 2,000 units planned. It has just completed a $4 million club house.

What Things Cost

ACCRA (1st quarter, 1991), reports the cost of living in Tucson is average compared to 290 other urban areas. Utilities are almost 15% lower than average, but health care and transportation are 13% and 20% higher respectively. Housing costs are 8% below average. Almost all businesses in Tucson offer seniors at least a 10% discount.
Gas company: Southwest Gas (889-1888). A 2BR house with gas water/heater/stove/ costs avg. $15-$20 in peak heat. The balance of the year, avg. $35-$40/mo.

Electric company: Tucson Electric Power Company *(623-7711)*. A 2BR house with air conditioning/electric heat averages $135/mo.
Phone company: U.S. West Communications *(670-2355)*. Basic budget service is $8.45/mo. with additional charges per call; unlimited local calling $15.90/mo. including touchtone.
Car registration/license: Driver's license: $7 (4 years); auto tags: minimum fee $23.50 based on the factory list price and age of the vehicle. Price as high as $1,200. Registration fee: $8.25; Emissions test fee: $1.50.

The Tax Ax

Sales tax: 7% (prescription drugs, food exempt).
State income tax: Arizona taxes 8% of gross adjusted income of federal income reported less the federal income taxes paid.
Retirement income: Residents 65+ get $1,500 exemption.
Property taxes & tax breaks: Property taxes in this town are best understood by tax assessors. The average person will struggle, but as best we can tell each type of property is assigned a primary value. The value of private homes is 10%. A secondary value is also determined and multiplied by the current millage rates. For example, a home valued at $100,000 might have a millage rate of 1.165 on the primary value and 3.4206 on the secondary value. The combined amounts are your tax bill. Contact the Pima County Tax Assessor's office and ask for anyone but Linda *(740-8630)*.

Medical Care

Major hospitals & regional medical centers: Nationally renowned facilities mean excellent medical care here. The city has a total of 15 hospitals. The major centers are **University Medical Center**, the teaching hospital for the University of Arizona, known for cancer, heart disease and respiratory illness research, and for heart transplants. It also has an excellent trauma team. The **Tucson Medical Center** was the former Desert San Tuberculosis Sanitarium (people originally came to the area to recover), also known for arthritis and allergy clinics. **St. Joseph's Hospital** is known for the Arizona Lions Eye Bank (a low-vision clinic),

the Southern Arizona Bone Bank and comprehensive cardiac care program. **Tucson General Hospital** has a well-respected alcohol and chemical abuse program. **Emergency medical services (EMS):** Tucson Fire Department has 400 paid firefighters, all certified EMTs. Average response time: under 4 min. **Physician's referral:** *252-2844*.

Continuing Education

Elderhostel/Eldercollege: At the University of Arizona, seniors from around the world take classes in Southwestern culture, archaeology, desert wildlife and more. **OASIS** (Older Adult and Information System): nonprofit organization offers free courses in pottery, creative writing, and exercising. **Pima Community College:** Non-credit courses geared to seniors (55+) include archaeology, writing and photography. It also offers organized tours of Mexico and other areas. PCC also has a Senior Option Program that allows seniors the opportunity to enroll in credit courses on a non-credit, seat-available basis. **SAGE:** sponsored by University of Arizona's Extended University, offers opportunities to learn and teach. Primary focus is higher education in a social setting.

Services for Seniors

Local hospitals sponsor a number of excellent wellness programs. Services available include lectures, health screenings, insurance claim processing, physician's referral services, discounts, planned activities such as mall walking and arthritic aquatics, day trips and free counseling. The Pima Council on Aging produces a monthly newsletter and a weekly radio show. The Gray Panthers are also very active. Tucson's 5 YMCAs run senior fitness programs and have special clubs for older members. OASIS Volunteers in Action helps out with Young Audiences of Southern Arizona and United Way Loaned Executives.

Crime & Safety

The most prevalent crimes in Tucson are thefts and burglaries. Much of the assaults are student-related in this college town. A bigger problem for seniors are cons and fraudulent schemes. The police department offers awareness programs. Their crime prevention division also offers a free home security survey. Seniors we spoke to expressed no fears about safety. They travel freely day or night and know the areas to avoid.

Earning a Living

Current business climate: Tucson expects continued growth through the end of the decade with a projected population of a half million. Currently the area welcomes 2,000 new residents a month. Tucson is one of the fastest developing high tech/manufacturing centers, doubling jobs since 1976. But the focus for innovation has been in small business development—98% of county businesses have 4 or fewer employees. Technically, Tucson has yet to experience a no-growth period. However, the current business climate was described as "challenging" by the Chamber of Commerce. **Help in starting a business:** Contact the Chamber of Commerce for resources to contact *(792-2250)*. **The job market:** The outlook for seniors is good, with numerous resources to help with placement and training. Retiree Skills, Inc. is a placement service to find temp work if you're 50+. It matches seniors to available jobs through a computerized data bank.

When the Kids Come to Visit

Arizona-Sonora Desert Museum (rated as one of the top 10 zoos in the country) combines zoo, botanical gardens and Museum of Natural History. Reid Park Zoo has lions, tigers and bears in natural environments. Famous for its giant anteater breeding program. Tucson Botanical Gardens: collection of native plants. Gives classes, has special events and meetings. Old Tucson: western theme park that has also been used for movie locations. Nicknamed "100 years from town." Also offers stagecoach rides and reenactment of gunfights. Air Museum: over 135 aircraft on display. Sabino Canyon: located in the Coronado National Forest, offers picnic sites hiking, and great scenery.

Getting Around Town

Roads & interstates: US-10 and US-19. **Airports & airlines:** Tucson International Airport is served by Aero California, America West, American, Continental, Delta, TWA, United and USAir. **Public transportation:** Tucson's local transit system was recently ranked first for a city this size. Bus routes span the entire city. Seniors pay a reduced fare of 25¢. **Managing without a car:** It's possible.

What Residents Already Know

One of every five Arizonans is 55+, giving their unified voice tremendous political clout. The Tucson Electric Power Company recently proposed a restructuring plan that would give back a 60% stake in the financially plagued utility. The city is in desperate need of an improved highway system, but older residents continually vote it down. Newcomers stand out—they're the ones who mispronounce all the Spanish and Mexican street names.

For More Information

Chamber Of Commerce Office:
Tucson Metropolitan Chamber
of Commerce
P.O. Box 991
Tucson, 85702
792-2250

Newspapers:
Arizona Daily Star
4850 South Park Ave.
Tucson, 85714
573-4420

Tucson Citizen
P.O. Box 26767
Tucson, 85126
573-4400

Realtors:
Sallie Smith, CRS
First American Realty
8830 Speedway
Tucson, 85710
296-5491

Vicki L. Cox
Vicki L. Cox Associates
3415 E. Golder Ranch Road
Tucson, 85737
791-7861

4. Fayetteville, Arkansas

Area Snapshot

Nickname: "Land of Opportunity" or the "Natural State"
County: Washington
Area code: 501   **Zip code:** 72703
Local population: 42,000   **County:** 109,000
% of population 65+: 12%
U.S. region: The Ozarks (North West Arkansas)
Closest metro areas: Little Rock, 192 miles
Nearby areas to consider: Roger, Bella Vista
Median housing price: $72,000
Best reasons to retire here: Clean environment, low crime, gorgeous Ozark scenery, great college town, very affordable living costs, fabulous outdoor recreation.

Fabulous Features

This place looks like God's country, if ever any place did. It's impossible not to be inspired by the rolling hills, national parks, forests, crystal-clear lakes, breathtaking mountains and clean air. The unspoiled natural beauty and temperate year-round climate allow for superb outdoor living. And as home to the University of Arkansas, the cultural and educational offerings are equally impressive. Residents are anxiously awaiting the magnificent new performing arts center which will open in 1992. The Walton Arts Center will be Northwest Arkansas' first permanent home for theater, dance and visual arts. For many reasons, Fayetteville has long been the darling of the press. "Money" magazine, "USA Today," "Inc." magazine, "Places Rated"—they all consistently give it high ratings as a retirement location. The appeal is understandable. This is the financial and business hub of the Ozarks, it offers the region's top medical facilities, the economy is thriving, real estate is affordable, the University contributes to the vitality, and you won't find people constantly griping about the weather. In fact, you won't find them griping about much at all.

Possible drawbacks: Just as you get used to things being a certain way, here comes new communities, new roads, new people. Also, Fayetteville is not "condo country." Land is plentiful and cheap and everybody wants a piece of it. If you want home ownership without the maintenance, there are condo communities, but they're hardly on every block.

"You can quote me on that"

"We're from California and when our daughter applied to school here we said, "Why in the heck would you want to go to Arkansas?" But after we visited, we were hooked. All we talked about was retiring to the Ozarks and that's what we did. We love the slow pace, the weather and, compared to California, we're living like kings on a mountain."—Mrs. F.G.

"I used to come here on business trips over the years and I'd look forward to it more and more each time. One time my wife came with me and said, "We're not leaving until we buy some property." I thought she'd hate a small town, but we've been here for six months and it's even better than we expected. There's a lot to do and no pressure if you just feel like keeping to yourself. My son just visited with his new wife and I heard her whisper to him, "I like it here." If they came it would make my day."—Mr. A.L.

Climate

Elevation: 1,257'	Avg. High/ Low	Average Inches		Avg. # Days Precip.	Avg. % Humidity
		Rain	Snow		
Jan.	48/26	2.7	-	9	74
April	70/47	4.9	-	11	65
July	89/70	3.8	-	10	66
Oct.	75/49	3.5	-	8	66
YEAR	70/47	48	12	-	-
# days 32° or below: 97			# days 90° or above: 78		

Let the Good Times Roll

Recreation: The Ozark National Forest is an ideal camping spot (it's as popular as some of the hotels). Beaver Lake stretches over 500 miles of shoreline, making it the perfect spot for boating, fishing and water sports galore. Lake Fayetteville Park and Lake Wedington offer nature trails, picnic pavilions and swimming. Devils Den State Park and Boston Mountains are two ideal choices for camping, hiking, and fishing (great rustic cabins and campsites). In town, there are more than 25 city parks to enjoy.

Culture: Fayetteville is a historical landmark, having been the site of the largest Civil War Battlefield west of the Mississippi. Preserved homes and other remains from the mid-1800s dot the landscape: The Walker-Stone House, the Old Post Office, and the Confederate Cemetery, just to name a few. But that's history as they say. Now the fuss in Fayetteville is over the future: The Walton Arts Center (opening in September 1992), will present three theaters, a visual arts gallery, a learning center and vast cultural offerings to the area. For seniors, the center will offer life enrichment programs (creative art classes, dance, and more).

Annual events: Hogeye Marathon (April); Music Festival of Arkansas (June); Ozark Native Arts & Crafts Fair (September); Rodeo of the Ozarks (July); Arkansas Apple Festival (October); Fayetteville Autumnfest (October).

Local Real Estate

Home sales have remained strong because of the tremendous population growth, particularly in the retirement market. The inventory in all price ranges is vast, and homes are appreciating at about two to three percent a year. New construction is available even in the $50,000 range, with most new homes priced in the mid $70s. That buys a 3BR, 2BA ranch on a 110 x 110 lot in a subdivision. Many retirees are buying at Carly Meadows near Beaver Lake.

Median price for single family home: $72,000

Median price for 2BR condo: They're scarce, with most of them available as rentals only.

Rental housing market: With a 15,000-strong student body, there is a lot of competition for rental units and the inventory is scarce. Apartments and condos are slightly easier to find. Long-term house rentals are impossible. If you do find one, expect to pay $600-$700 a month.

Common housing styles & features: Ranch styles with split-floor plans (the master bedroom at one end and two bedrooms on other) is very popular. You'll also see a lot of "New Victorian" construction and "New Country" wrap around porches.

Amenities in condo developments: The "planned unit" developments are generally small 2BR, 2BA, sometimes with a pool. Paradise Valley is a popular golf course community

Nearby areas to consider: Rogers, Bella Vista.

Unique features of these areas: Rogers offers a lot of lakefront property. Bella Vista is where the golf course communities are.

What Things Cost

Retirees on a fixed income, take note. Overall living costs are ten percent below the national average, with housing being almost twenty percent below and health care thirty percent below. Taxes are within reason as well.

Gas company: Arkansas Western Gas Company *(521-5400)*. Average monthly bill is $80. During summer months, it may be as low as mid $20s, Winter months, on the other hand, may be as high as $120. New customers pay a $50 deposit and a $10 connection fee.

Electric company: Southwestern Electric Power Company (SWEPCO) *(521-3000)*. Deposit is based on average two month billing in the past for that location. Average monthly bill is $85 for all electric and $52 for partial (use gas also).

Water/sewer: City Water Department (521-7700). A $25 deposit is required.

Phone company: Southwestern Bell Telephone Company (442-9800). Basic service is $11.17 month, plus local calls or $17.96 month with unlimited local calls. $45 installation new or moved charge. The average monthly bill $20.

Car registration/license: Rates vary based on the size of the vehicle. These rates represent the most expensive: Tags & title: $35.25; registration: $30 (or less); license: $14.25 (good for four years). Written test required: $5.

The Tax Ax

The per capita tax burden in Arkansas is approximately one-third less than the national average. Compare that to Wisconsin (32% higher than average) and to Michigan (24% higher), and Arkansas is very inviting.

Sales tax: 6% (pay 1% more for restaurants and hotels).

State income tax: If your adjusted gross income is between $15,000 to $25,000, the tax rate is 6%; if your income is $25,000 and over, the tax rate is 7%.

Retirement income: First $6,000 of either public or private pensions are exempt. A personal tax credit of $40 per person is allowed if you are 65 or older.

Property taxes & tax breaks: Taxes are based on 20% of the assessed value. The current millage rate is .0456. Estimated property taxes on a $80,000 home would run $730 a year. There are no homestead exemptions.

Medical Care

Major hospitals/regional medical centers: Washington Regional Medical Center (JCAH-accredited), is a not-for-profit acute medical center and teaching hospital. Specialties include 24-hour emergency/trauma, hospice care, radiology, renal dialysis, and general surgery (including one-day procedures). The hospital also offers a center for exercise.

Fayetteville City Hospital is the area's main geriatric center and source for home health care.

Emergency medical services (EMS): Fayetteville has eleven ambulances, 35 certified EMT

specialists. Average response time is less than six minutes.

Physician's referral: Northwest Arkansas *800-422-0322*.

Continuing Education

The University of Arkansas offers free tuition to any senior resident who is interested in taking courses (575-5451).

Services for Seniors

The Community Adult Center is the focal point for programs and services for seniors. Open year-round, the center encourages older residents to take advantage of special classes, one-day excursions, exercise programs and more.

Crime & Safety

The crime rate in Fayetteville is extremely low, even with the presence of a major university. The police attribute the nominal crime activity to the lack of a major interstate running through town. Gas station hold-ups and bank robberies are difficult to carry off when there's no fast getaway. There are also 21 active Neighborhood Watch Groups in the area, accounting for the low number of break-ins. Sadly, the most common crime is domestic violence.

Earning a Living

Current business climate: Fayetteville is a thriving business center, as it is headquarters to the ever-expanding Tyson Foods and Wal-Mart. Campbell Soup, IBM, and Proctor & Gamble are here, contributing to a low unemployment rate and an economic oasis of sorts. And yet there is a strong need for small-service businesses—anything that caters to homeowners (cleaning, lawn service, etc.).

Help in starting a business: Contact the Chamber for information on required licenses, local business leaders and recommended locations (521-1710).

The job market: Jobs are available, particularly part-time work. The University, the industries, the retail and restaurant trade and the hospitals are good places to start. Several temporary agencies may be able to help.

When the Kids Come to Visit

The Fayetteville Youth Center (gym, indoor pool, game rooms, and other activities); Air Museum at Drake Airport; University Museum features the history of Arkansas, dinosaurs, Indian artifacts, and a glass collection; Eureka Springs: great Victorian homes, hotels, museums, shopping, crafts and entertainment (country music shows); Farmers Market (May-October) spreads over three counties and sells local produce, flowers, and crafts. Other attractions include the Carry Nation Home, Thorncrown Chapel, Pivot Rock and Natural Dam, Quigley Castle, Castle at Inspiration Point, Cosmic Cavern, Onyx Cave and Blue Spring. Horseback riding, hiking trails, and miniature golf are available.

Getting Around Town

Roads & interstates: US Highway 71, US Highway 471, and Scenic Highway 12 (for leisurely drives through beautiful Ozark country, attractions, resorts).

Airports & airlines: Drake Field Airport is serviced by American Eagle, Air Midwest, Atlantic Southeast and Republic Express Airlines. Frequent daily flights link the city with major airports.

Public transportation: Jefferson Bus Lines is the local service.

Managing without a car: The University transit system provides transportation for the elderly and handicapped, but for the most part, a car is essential.

What Residents Already Know

Where's the traffic? That's what newcomers ask. There isn't any and, in fact, you get so spoiled that if you have to sit at more than one traffic light in a row you get impatient. There are no flatlands in these parts. Rolling hills, lakes and streams, and the famous Ozark Mountains keep the views from ever getting stale.

For More Information

Chamber Of Commerce Office:
Fayetteville Chamber
P.O. Box 4216
Fayetteville, 72702-4216
521-1710

Newspaper:
Northwest Arkansas Times
212 North East Avenue
Fayetteville, 72701
442-6242

Realtor:
Mary Bassett
Dykes Bassett Mix & Assoc. Inc.
3263 North College
Fayetteville, 72703
521-5600

5. Hot Springs Village, Arkansas

Area Snapshot

Nickname: "The Other Hot Springs"
County: Garland
Area code: 501   **Zip code:** 71909
Local population: 8,500   **County:** 74,000
% of population 65+: 60%
U.S. region: West Central Arkansas (the Ouachita Mountain Region)
Closest metro areas: Hot Springs, 22 miles; Little Rock, 65 miles
Median housing price: $90,000
Best reasons to retire here: Four glorious seasons, rock bottom taxes, vast recreation, large retirement population, private community, breathtaking views.

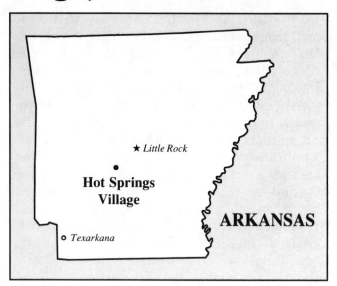

Fabulous Features

We've had an opportunity to learn about planned communities all over the country and Hot Springs Village is one of the most extraordinary we've come across. Situated on 30,000 acres in the heart of the Ouachita mountains and Diamond Lakes region, there is none more beautiful or enticing than this Cooper Community (Arkansas' #1 home builder). Every last detail has been thought through—from the five championship golf courses to the Coronado Natatorium and Fitness Center (it's a veritable showplace), to the lavish lakefront homes to the magnificent grounds (25% of the Village will remain green). Every home faces trees, lakes or is on the fairway with prices ranging from $40,000 to $300,000. The whole state of Arkansas is one of the least expensive places to live in the country. An independent survey of 135 retirement spots showed Hot Springs lower than 85% of the others. Property taxes for a $100,000 home average $500 a year, not a month. The amenities are endless—six private man-made lakes (including 950-acre Lake Balboa where the fish are so big, people don't have to lie about their catches), tennis, 120 clubs and organizations, shopping, a large community center, two pools and more. What's the cost for these privileges? $23 a month for everything! Outside the Village, you're in the heart of one of the most spectacular mountain and lake-filled regions in the U.S. Unending culture and attractions are 15 minutes away in Hot Springs as are the natural hot springs mineral baths—one of nature's most healing powers for 4,000 years. Everyone shared the same story. Friends and family thought they were crazy to come to Arkansas. But guess who had the last laugh? The residents at Hot Springs Village.

Possible drawbacks: This Village is not recommended for people who get "antsy." It is very quiet, the pace is slow and it can take the average person a year to adjust. There seem to be three big reasons people leave: 1) there isn't enough hustle/bustle 2) they miss their families and 3) they require a level of care not available here.

"You can quote me on that"

"If you're a golfer, you're going to love Hot Springs Village. I think the greens fees are 1/10th of what I paid in Austin. The biggest surprise was how many unbelievable amenities you get for $23 a month. Plus we like the security of a closed community. Every owner has a vested interest and it's safe. I leave my clubs and cart in the driveway and never think twice about it."—J.B.

Climate

Elevation: 558'	Avg. High/ Low	Average Inches		Avg. # Days Precip.	Avg. % Humidity
		Rain	Snow		
Jan.	53/30	4.8	-	9	75
April	73/50	5.2	-	11	67
July	93/70	4	-	9	68
Oct.	77/50	3.2	-	7	68
YEAR	73/49	52	5	-	-
# days 32° or below: 66			# days 90° or above: 78		

Let the Good Times Roll

Recreation: Welcome to the neighborhood, indeed! Hot Springs Village offers unbelievable recreational amenities. There are five 18-hole championship golf courses ($3 greens fees for owners), driving ranges, and putting greens open all year. For an annual fee of $350, you can have unlimited usage. There are six man-made lakes (we bet they're the cleanest ones you've ever seen) for fishing, boating, water skiing, scuba diving, and sailing. And you can choose from eleven tennis courts with a full-time professional staff (daily fee, or a $100 annual fee). Other recreational options? Two pools (one indoor, heated). Fourteen miles of trails for hiking and jogging. And the icing on the cake (fat-free of course), is the Coronado Natatorium Fitness Center, featuring nautilus equipment, sauna, classes and professional staff. Don't forget that there's a magnificent playground right outside the Village, too—the grand Ouachita Mountains, the Diamond Lakes region and the natural hot springs mineral baths.

Culture: Hot Springs and Little Rock are both less than an hour away, and offer a wonderful opportunity to enjoy museums, galleries, theater, and ballet. Little Rock has the Arkansas Symphony Orchestra, The Ballet Arkansas, and frequent Broadway productions. Hot Springs features the Mid American Museum (largest in the state), the Ponce de Leon Auditorium for symphonies, ballet and other performing arts. The Hot Springs Arts Center and the Gallery Walks will impress even the most discriminating (the art community is truly flourishing).

Annual events: Arkansas Derby Festival (April); Racing Festival of the South (April); Good Ole Summertime Arts & Crafts (July); Arkansas Oktoberfest; 10K Run (November).

Local Real Estate

Every single home in the Village has barriers between the lots to assure that no owner has to look out at another home. You either see trees, a lake or a golf course rather than someone else's backyard barbeque.

Median price for single family home: $90,000 (but many homes start at $40,000). Larger homes on the lake sell in the $200,000-$300,000 range.

Median price for 2BR condo: $60,000

Rental housing market: 2BR apartment: $500; 3BR house: $650-$750.

Common housing styles & features: The most popular is the Madrid, a 3BR, 2BA house, with an extra-large living room and an 18 square foot deck. The original homes were all ranch styles, but with the hilly terrain, two-story homes are now just as popular. Lot sizes average 80 x 150.

Amenities in condo developments: Townhouses are the most popular style. All owners have access to the common property and amenities.

Nearby areas to consider: Not one person could think of another location in the vicinity to recommend.

What Things Cost

The whole Hot Springs area enjoys one of the lowest costs of living in the country. In an independent survey of 130 retirement locations, 85 percent of the other locations cost more insofar as utilities, real estate, taxes, and other fixed expenses.

Electric company: Arkansas Power & Light *(321-8500)*. The average monthly bill is $85-$90 (10¢ per kwh).

Phone company: Southwestern Bell *(624-8800)*. Basic monthly service is $20; installations start at $50. Deposits are usually not required.

Water/sewer: Average bill is $18/mo.

Car registration/license: Rates vary by size of vehicle. These rates represent the most expensive: Tags & title: $35.25; registration: $30 (or less); license: $14.25 for four years. A written test is required: $5.

The Tax Ax

The per capita tax burden in Arkansas is approximately 1/3 less than the national average. Compare that to Wisconsin (32% higher than average) and to Michigan (24% higher), and Arkansas becomes a very inviting retirement option.

Sales tax: 5% (1% accommodations tax for hotels, motels and restaurants in Hot Springs; prescriptions and eyeglasses are exempt from any sales tax).

State income tax: If adjusted gross income is between $15,000 to $25,000, the tax rate is 6%.; $25,000 and over is 7%.

Retirement income: First $6,000 of either public or private pensions are exempt. A personal tax credit of $40 per person is allowed if you're 65 or older.

Property taxes & tax breaks: Property taxes are based on 20% of market value multiplied by the current millage rates. There are two school districts in the Village, spanning two counties but in either case the tax estimate on a $100,000 home is $500 a year.

Medical Care

Major hospitals/regional medical centers: St. Joseph Regional Health Center in Hot Springs is the closest full-service hospital, and is relocating to a brand-new facility in early 1992. It specializes in open heart surgery, coronary care, neurology, the latest available cancer treatment and home health care. The hospital also has a Home Health Care Agency and Diagnostic Center in the Village (come in for a free blood pressure check). **Leo N. Levi Arthritis Hospital** offers comprehensive care of arthritis and related problems *(624-1281)*.

Emergency medical services (EMS): Cedar Mountain Ambulance Service will respond to all emergency calls in less than six minutes *(922-2634)*.

Physician's referral: St. Joseph's *622-1000*.

Continuing Education

Garland County Community College (located in Mid America Park, Hot Springs) allows seniors to enroll tuition-free, provided they've been a resident for six or more months. Enrollment is on a seat-available basis. All lab fees and books are extra *(767-9371)*.

Services for Seniors

There are 120 different clubs and organizations to join in Hot Springs Village, from philanthropic to civic to recreational to religious. The Turtles is a fitness club for seniors that meets every morning. There is also one retirement home (Good Samaritan). Many of the clubs sponsor programs, classes and activities for seniors.

Crime & Safety

In this self-contained village where residents and tourists don't want any trouble, there is none. The local police and fire departments and the 24-hour security guards see to it. In fact, after twenty years, there was finally a bank robbery. Everyone feels it was an inside job because there are hundreds of dead-end streets in the Village. A stranger could never have escaped. Crime in Hot Springs, however, is another story entirely, and one of the reasons Hot Springs Village is infinitely a more desirable place to live.

Earning a Living

Current business climate: Commercial development has been flat and business owners question the growth potential. The jury is still out on whether more new businesses are needed, although Cooper Communities certainly welcomes the opportunity to talk.

Help in starting a business: Cooper Development's Commercial Leasing Department *(922-3225)*. SCORE has a local chapter in the Village *(922-1443)*.

The job market: It's extremely limited. Better prospects for part-time employment are in Hot Springs.

When the Kids Come to Visit

An incredible number of sites and attractions will keep visitors busy in the Hot Springs area. In addition to the fabulous natural surroundings, you can take in Magic Spring (amusement park, concerts). Mid America Museum is a very special "hands-on" center). Duck Tours features amphibious vehicles that tour the city then plunge into Lake Hamilton for a cruise; Hot Springs Mountain Tower glass elevator ride takes you up 1,200 feet for a breathtaking view of Hot Springs National Park. Also check out Castleberry Riding Stables; National Park Aquarium; Tiny Town (exciting indoor, mechanical displays); Mule Line (mule drawn trolley rides); Arkansas Alligator Farm & Petting Zoo; the I.Q. Zoo (zoo-educated animals); Hot Springs Diamonds: mining for diamonds and gem stones at the Crater of Diamonds State Park.

Getting Around Town

Roads & interstates: State 70: 15 mi. south; State 7: adjacent to Village; I-30: 30 mi. east.

Airports & airlines: Little Rock Regional Airport is served by Delta, American, TWA, United, USAir and others.
Public transportation: No local transit available.
Managing without a car: You definitely need a car.

What Residents Already Know

The fish out of 950-acre Lake Balboa are so big, nobody ever has to lie.•There is so little that goes wrong in the Village that the paper is hard up for news. Fender benders make the front page.•Property owners will challenge you to find purer drinking water anywhere else in the country.

For More Information

Chamber of Commerce Office:
The Greater Hot Springs Chamber
P.O. Box 6090
Hot Springs, 71902
321-1700

Hot Springs Village
Property Owner's Association
P.O. Box 1600
Hot Springs, 71902
922-0200

Newspapers:
The Arkansas Gazette
314 Ouachita Ave., Suite 310
Hot Springs, 71909
624-0564

La Villa News
Bldg. 9, Suite 2, De Soto Ctr.
Hot Springs Village, 71909
624-6157

Realtor:
Mike Campbell or Glenn Hoiney
Coldwell Banker
Big Red Realty, Inc.
Star Rt. 10, Box 369
Hot Springs Village, 71909
922-0444

6. *Palm Springs, California*

Area Snapshot

Nickname: "The Valley of Contentment"
County: Riverside
Area code: 619   **Zip code:** 92260-2
Local population: 40,600   **County:** 1,100,000
% of population 55+: 25%
U.S. region: South Central Calif.; The Coachella Valley
Closest metro areas: Los Angeles, 115 mi.; San Diego, 137 mi.
Nearby areas to consider: Palm Desert, Hemet
Median housing price: $150,000
Best reasons to retire here: Country club living, dry, desert climate, world-class golf, tennis, and shopping, awesome mountains and canyons as a backdrop, excellent medical services.

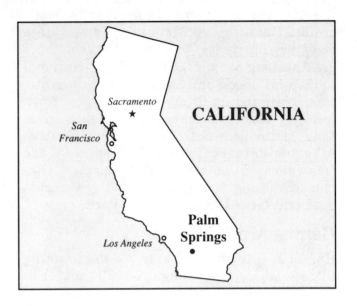

Fabulous Features

"In places" for the monied, leisure crowd change with the winds. But this small desert oasis is still considered to be among the most auspicious retreats. Whether you're stepping onto the fairway at PGA West ("Best 18 holes in Southern California" says *Fore* magazine) or swimming in a hot mineral pool with hidden "rainbow" jets, everything you see and do in Palm Springs comes with a first-class ticket. Situated in the heart of the low-lying Colorado desert, you'll relish the dry, mountain air and average daily temperatures in the 70s and 80s. Daytime humidity is low, the winters are short and mild, and it can rain more in Florida in one day than it does here in a year. The housing market is surprisingly diversified and relatively affordable. Even though it's the desert, Palm Springs is in the best shape for water supply than just about anywhere else in the state. They're saying, "What drought?" That's because of plentiful underground water sources and a well-planned system good for the next 40 years. Palm Springs not only has access to water, they have access to outstanding medical care. The facilities, services and programs are so impressive they could be models for other cities. If you can afford it, Mayor Sonny Bono's town is a retiree's paradise.

Possible drawbacks: The summer months are a good time to head home. Even with low humidity, it's hot (although the evenings can be very cool and pleasant).•In Palm Springs, the living is easy, but the expenses are high. Food, restaurants, shopping, recreation, real estate and taxes, are 20% to 50% higher than the national average.•And speaking of taxes, California is not a "Be Kind to Taxpayers" state. If you make this your permanent legal residence, be prepared to ante up. On average, you'll pay two times more in total taxes than you would in Florida.

"You can quote me on that"

"The first time we came here on vacation, we drove in at night and were immediately taken with the clean air, the beautiful mountains and the skyline. We bought a home and, honestly, our lifestyle is paradise. We're very big tennis players, we get into tournaments and it's great. Palm Springs has really fulfilled our dreams of what our retirement should be like."—B.D.

Climate

Elevation: 482'	Avg. High/ Low	Avg. Rainfall (Inches)	Avg. # Days Precip.	Avg. % Humidity
Jan.	70/35	.5	5	45
April	85/52	.5	3	30
July	105/70	trace	1	35
Oct.	90/53	.5	2	40
YEAR	87/54	5.0	-	-
# days 32° or below: 0		# days 90° or above: 122		

Let the Good Times Roll

Recreation: If you're into golf and tennis, you've come to the right place. There are more than 600 tennis courts in town and more than 100 public and private golf courses (an equal number of national tournaments and invitationals). The courses, some of the best maintained, most challenging and prestigious places to play, include PGA West, O'Donnell Golf Club and Desert Dunes. Palm Springs is considered the "Winter Polo Capital." The Empire Club (the largest polo club in the U.S.) and the Eldorado Polo and Equestrian Center attract international players as well as the "mink and manure" crowd. With more than 7,500 pools in Palm Springs alone, cooling off is a breeze. Get ready to check out Japan's top major league players in intensive training at Don Drysdale's Winter Baseball camp. The California Angels go through spring training here as well.

Culture: The "stars" come out at night to enjoy Palm Spring's cultural happenings. Some of the more renowned events take place at the beautiful new McCallum Theater for the Performing Arts in the Bob Hope Cultural Center. For museum lovers, the Palm Springs Desert Museum and the Living Desert (a 1,200-acre animal park and botanical garden) will enlighten and entertain. The Living Desert is host to outdoor jazz concerts. The College of Desert Palms offers numerous plays and concerts. There are also more than 20 art galleries to explore.

Annual events: Adidas Invitational Tennis Tournament, Bob Hope Desert Classic, Don Drysdale Hall-of-Fame Golf Classic, Palm Springs International Film Festival (Jan.); Sinatra Celebrity Invitational (Feb.); Newsweek Champions Cup, Hyatt Grand Champions, Nabisco Dinah Shore LPGA Major Tournament (March); Tram Road Challenge, Tour of Palm Springs Bicycle Race and Senior Olympics (Oct.); Stouffer Esmeralda Balloon and Polo Festival (Dec.).

Local Real Estate

New construction is somewhat limited; most sales are for existing properties. The most affordable homes are small ones near the expressway ranging from $130,000-$160,000. Moving up a bit, $250,000 will buy a 3BR/2BA home in a "spotty" neighborhood. Movie Colony, Old Las Palmas or Canyon homes are $350,000 and up. South Palm Springs has new homes for $450,000 and up.

Median price for single family home: $150,000

Median price for 2BR condo: Prices start at $65,000, but the average is closer to $125,000 and up.

Rental housing market: Rentals are readily available. Rent control helps prices remain affordable. Avg. rent for is $800-$1,200/mo. for a small house. Townhouses and condos rent for $700/mo.

Common housing styles & features: There is absolutely nothing common about the houses here. Seeing is believing.

Amenities in condo developments: Pools, clubhouse, spas, golf, tennis, all appliances and maintenance.

Nearby areas to consider: Palm Desert, Rancho Mirage, Indio and Hemet. **Unique features of these areas:** Palm Desert (pop. 19,000) is 13 miles east of Palm Springs. It's near Palm Springs, but offers a lot in its own right as well. Hotels, golf and tennis and other recreation are widely available. Median price is $126,000 (north) and $180,000 (south). Hemet is a lovely area that has fast become a desirable retirement community. It's located between Palm Springs and Los Angeles, allowing for the best of all worlds. The small town (pop. 14,000) offers affordable housing and lots of recreation. Pacific Adult Communities has built a beautiful retirement development (age-restricted) with single-family homes starting at $100,000 *(800-343-2670)*. Going from west to east, the communities are newer and more affordable. In Cathedral City, average housing prices are $117,000. Rancho Mirage has homes starting in the high $200,000s. And Indian Wells is the poshest area with homes starting at a half-million.

What Things Cost

Residents will argue that you get what you pay for, but for the record, housing is 46% above the national average, health care 29% higher, and goods and services about 10% higher. Overall costs are 19% above average (ACCRA, 1st Quarter, 1991).

Gas company: Southern California Gas (In Calif.: *800-292-0713*). Avg. apartments run $40 a month. Houses run $80/mo. Deposit may be required.

Electric company: Southern California Edison *(324-8500)*. Depending on the size of your home you could pay $300-$1,000/mo. With constant 100° days, summer months run higher.

Phone company: GTE (In California: *800-482-6711*). $46 start-up service charge; $10.20/mo unlimited local calling.

Water: Desert Water Agency *(323-4971)*. Avg. monthly bill is $60. Connection charges based on size of meter and type of service.

Car registration/license: You have 10 days to apply for a license and 20 days to register your car once residency is established. There is an average fee of $35 plus 2% of the appraised value of the car, in addition to a 2.2% surcharge on that amount. A California driver's license can be switched from an out-of-state one for $10. All cars must be inspected for smog. DMV *(327-1521)*.

The Tax Ax

Sales tax: 7.75% (includes city, county, mass transit, and earthquake relief taxes). **State income tax:** It's a graduated tax, up to a maximum of 9.3%. California residents are taxed on earned and unearned income. Personal exemptions for seniors amount to $55 a year per person. **Retirement income:** Not only does California tax the pensions and IRAs of even former residents if they earned the money in that state, it also grabs a piece of the pensions that new residents earned in other states

(although they do get credit for taxes paid to the home state). **Property taxes & tax breaks:** Property taxes are established under Proposition 13 as 1% of the purchase price plus limited locally approved bonds. The total rarely exceeds 1.25%. The current local average is 1.11%. Call the County Assessor's office for more information *(323-8536)*.

Medical Care

There is a current labor shortage in hospitals but that appears to be the only deficiency in this highly respected medical community. We were impressed with the listings of support groups, health care organizations, classes and programs available to the community. Call *Palm Springs Life* magazine and ask for a copy of the Desert Medical Directory for complete listings *(325-2333)*. **Major hospitals/ regional medical centers: Desert Hospital** has the largest emergency care facility in the Coachella valley. It also offers comprehensive acute care, general surgery, and rehabilitation. In the middle of a $62 million expansion, it will provide state-of-the-art emergency and cancer care by the end of 1993. It offers Health Key Plus 50 and other outreach programs. **Eisenhower Medical Center** (Rancho Mirage), specializes in cardiology and cancer care and is also home to the **Betty Ford Center**, the **Dolores Hope Outpatient Center, Desert Orthopedic Centers** and an **Immediate Care Center**. Other hospitals include: **John F. Kennedy Memorial Hospital** (Indio), and **The Heart Institute of the Desert** (Rancho Mirage). **Emergency medical services (EMS):** The police or fire department will respond within 3-5 minutes with a paramedic to administer emergency procedures. Springs Ambulance (private) handles emergency transports. They are required to respond within 10 minutes but average 6-8 minutes. A Medivac or air ambulance to Los Angeles can arrive in less than 35 minutes. **Physician's referral:** Desert Hospital's Medical Directory *323-6100*.

Continuing Education

College of the Desert offers classes for credit and non-credit, along with special community service programs *(346-8041)*. California State

University, San Bernadino Annex has a program where seniors take classes for $10 a semester on a space-available basis *(341-2883)*.

Services for Seniors

The Palm Springs Mizell Senior Center is a full-service operation that has thought of everything. Don't expect Bob Hope to drop by, but you will find fitness classes, bridge games, referral services, cultural events, and an excellent newsletter. If you stop in and apply, you can get a discount card for participating stores and restaurants. Don't be embarrassed, everyone loves a bargain. Call *(323-5689)*. Pick up a copy of *Senior Lifestyle Magazine* for an interesting read *(341-9404)*.

Crime & Safety

Budget cuts have eliminated Neighborhood Watch programs; this affects second home owners with vacant houses. Property crime is the most pervasive. California has passed a law increasing the severity of the penalty for people convicted of crimes against seniors.

Earning a Living

Current business climate: Palms Springs is a major hotel, convention, retail and financial center. Steady traffic is not the norm (big hotels use airline-like tactics to fill rooms in the summer). Yet, with over 2 million tourists a year, business is thriving. **Help in starting a business:** Chamber of Commerce *(325-1577)* or SCORE *(320-6682)*. **The job market:** With the huge retail and service sector, part-time work is available in season. There are also labor shortages in health care.

When the Kids Come to Visit

Palm Springs Aerial Tramway: (8,500 feet up Mount San Jacinto) you'll pass through five different climate zones and a 40° change from the base to the top; Mount San Jacinto State Park (13,000-acre island with 54 miles of trails); Hot Air Ballooning; Disneyland and Sea World (90 miles); Oasis Waterpark.

Getting Around Town

Roads & interstates: Interstate 10 (west to LA, east to Phoenix), Highway 74, California 111. **Airports & airlines:** Palm Springs Regional Airport is served by America West, Delta (winter), Skywest with Delta Connection, TWA, United, United Express, and USAir. **Public transportation:** Sunline system has service to Coachella Valley communities. **Managing without a car:** Rent one, lease one, or hire one with a driver. But this is California, don't go anywhere without wheels.

What Residents Already Know

Forget "Dallas" and "Miami Vice." The latest city series being produced is in Palm Springs. "P.S. I Luv U" stars Connie Sellecca and Greg Evigan and everyone is hoping it boosts tourism as much as it did for other city shows. Not coincidentally, "P.S." is Palm Springs' unofficial nickname.

For More Information

Chamber Of Commerce Office:
Palm Springs Chamber of Commerce
190 West Amado Road
Palm Springs, 92262
325-1577

Palm Desert Chamber
of Commerce
72-990 Highway 111
Palm Desert, 92260
346-6111

Newspaper:
Desert Sun (Daily except Sunday)
611 S, Palm Canyon Dr.
P.O. Box 190
Palm Springs, 92263
322-8889

Realtors:
Paul Shepard
Paul Shepard Associates
1111 Tahquitz Canyon Suite 120
Palm Springs, 92262
322-7285

Jeff Hayes
**Coldwell Banker/
Sky Ridge Realty**
74-850 Highway 111
Indian Wells, 92210
773-2131

7. San Diego, California

Area Snapshot

Nickname: "America's Finest City"
County: San Diego
Area code: 619   **Zip codes:** 92101, 02, 03, 08, 12, 17
Population: 1.2 million
% of population 65+: 20%
U.S. region: Southern California (bordering Mexico)
Closest metro area: Los Angeles, 125 miles
Nearby areas to consider: Coronado, La Jolla, Rancho Bernardo
Median housing price: $186,600
Best reasons to retire here: Ideal climate, excellent health care and seniors services, some of the most enjoyable recreation and culture in the country.

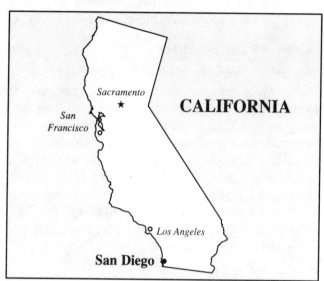

Fabulous Features

With 12 months of glorious weather, San Diego's retirees keep their rockers in permanent storage. They're out every day of the year taking in world-renowned attractions, golf, tennis and boating, professional football and baseball, 70 miles of sun-drenched beaches and intriguing galleries and museums. The great restaurants (a lot of them are reasonably priced), the great shopping, and the great people add to their enjoyment. And what's the city's universal cheer? "The sun's out!" It's sunny, it's mild, and the constant sea breezes prove it doesn't get any better than this for year-round living. And despite those who complain about the lack of variety, there is a subtle change of seasons. Spring is foggy, fall is rainy, and winter brings hot dry wind from the desert. You can even see snow on the Cuyamacas mountains. San Diego is also known for its highly rated medical facilities where more than 25 hospitals offer some of the best health and rehabilitative care in the country (Places Rated says it's #1 in this category). Senior services are so extensive we couldn't think of one they didn't already offer. It's no wonder that San Diego was recently ranked as the 4th best city for quality-of-life (University of Pennsylvania, Wharton School of Business, survey of 130 cities, March/April, 1991.)

Possible drawbacks: Unless you're coming to the area with deep pockets, San Diego may be a better vacation destination than a place to retire. According to Chamber of Commerce data, it's one of the 10 most expensive U.S. cities in which to live. While mild climates allow people to lead healthier lifestyles, real estate, taxes, and health care will take a giant bite out of a fixed income. Also, San Diego is a big city, complete with its share of urban problems, including air quality and drug-related crime.

"You can quote me on that"

"I moved here from Connecticut because I was disgusted with the freezing rain and New England winters. I adore San Diego. I don't live in a retirement community, but there are retirees all around. Nobody is from here originally so it's easy to adjust. I also love that the food tastes fresher. It's a treat to eat an orange that's just been picked. And the restaurants are cheaper, too. When you smile at someone, they not only smile back, they look you in the eye."— Mrs. B. C., Poway   (Note: We agree with Mrs. C. Each person we spoke to was nicer than the next. One woman told us that when the weather is this nice, there's nothing to be grouchy about.)

Climate

Elevation: 30'	Avg. High/ Low	Avg. Rainfall (Inches)	Avg. # Days Precip.	Avg. % Humidity
Jan.	65/46	1.9	7	65
April	68/54	.8	5	70
July	75/64	.1	1	70
Oct.	74/58	.3	2	70
YEAR	70/55	9.5	-	-
# days 32° or below: 1		# days 90° or above: 8		

Let the Good Times Roll

Recreation: Imagine starting the day walking along a stretch of Pacific Ocean beach, then meeting friends for parasailing on the San Diego Bay, or heading over to the mountains and Lake Cuyamaca for a picnic lunch and a few games of tennis. There are more than 70 public and private golf courses (more than any other U.S. county), 1,200 tennis courts, and every water sport you can think of: deep-sea fishing, boating, and snorkeling. La Jolla Underwater Park is one of the West Coast's most exciting treasures. Another treasure is the Mission Bay Aquatic Park with fabulous waterskiing, boating and swimming. If you can do it outdoors, you can do it in San Diego! The San Diego Padres, the Chargers, the Hawks and the Sockers (eight-time World Soccer League Champs) give the home town something to cheer about. Golfers look forward to the annual Andy Williams PGA Open. The city also hosts a collegiate football tournament, the Sea World Holiday Bowl. Cross the Mexican border and check out a bullfight or horserace.

Culture: The legendary San Diego Zoo is in the heart of downtown's Balboa Park. It has 1,800 acres of wildlife preserves, 750 species, art galleries, a theater and an open-air monorail. The San Diego Opera, Symphony and Theater attract audiences from around the world, as do the galleries and museums. The Aerospace, Natural History and Scripps Aquarium museums will fascinate you. A senior citizen ID card qualifies you for special discounts at virtually every major attraction and event, including the bus and trolley.

Annual events: Del Mar National Horse Show, Flower Show, Gem Diego, Art Alive (Spring); Corpus Christi Fiesta (June); Admission Day (September); Christmas on the Prado.

Local Real Estate

Land is at a big premium in California, contributing to the high price of homes. Yet 25% of retirees relocating here opt for a grand style house rather than a smaller condominium. Planned communities are popular because of the extensive amenities and low maintenance. **Median price for single family home:** $186,600 (New homes are running about 20% higher than resales). **Median price for 2BR condo:** $117,000. **Rental housing market:** 2BR apartments rent from $880-$1,000. **Common housing styles & features:** The older homes are Southern California bungalows. Newer homes are varied, from Cape Cod to Mediterranean Style. **Amenities in condo developments:** Many developments are age-restricted (55) and revolve around special interests (the ocean, golf, etc.). **Nearby areas to consider:** Coronado, La Jolla, and Rancho Bernardo. **Unique features of these areas:** Coronado Island (25,000) is a peninsula off San Diego Bay (a ferry and 2-mile toll bridge connects it to the city); It's a beautiful resort area with a small-town feel. Wealthy retirees love Coronado Cays, with boat slips at your door step. Single-family homes start at $150,000 and go into the millions. Styles range from old Victorians to California bungalows. La Jolla (32,000), "the jewel" of San Diego's coastal communities, offers homes from small bungalows to million dollar estates. Ideal for the country club set. It's also the home of UCSD. Rancho Bernardo is a planned community with both condos and single family homes—60% of the owners are retirees. Great golfing is the big draw.

What Things Cost

According to ACCRA (1st quarter, 1991), overall living costs are 31% above the national average. Compared to 290 other urban areas, housing costs rated 111% over the national average. Comparing median home prices across the U.S., San Diego is in the top 5 at $186,600). Health care costs were 35% above average, and transportation 28% above. Only utilities were below average (30%).

Water: San Diego Water Dept. *(533-4100)*. Within city only. Bimonthly minimum: $47.58 plus extra usage. Summer most costly.

Electric/gas company: San Diego Gas and Electric *(239-7511)*. Avg.: $78.86/mo. Deposit waived by attending Energy Education class and/or having good history. Otherwise it's twice avg. monthly bill.

Phone company: Pacific Bell *(339-5888)*. Avg. mo. charge is $11.85.

Car registration/license: You have 10 days to apply for a license, 20 days to register once residency is established. Avg. fee of $35 plus 2% of appraised car value, as well as a 2.2% surcharge. A California driver's license can be switched from out-of-state for $10. All cars must be inspected for smog. DMV *(565-6691)*.

The Tax Ax

Sales tax: 8.25% (prescription drugs are exempt). **State income tax:** It's a graduated tax, up to 9.3%. Residents are taxed on earned and unearned income. Personal exemptions for seniors amount to $58 a year per person (we're serious). **Retirement income:** Not only does California tax the pensions and IRAs of even former residents if they earned the money in that state, it also grabs a piece of the pensions that new residents earned in other states (although the taxpayer does get a credit for taxes paid to the home state). **Property taxes & tax breaks:** Property taxes are established under Proposition 13 as 1% of the purchase price plus (limited) locally approved bonds. In San Diego, the rate varies between 1-2% of the assessed value (avg. between purchase price and values of comparable homes in the area). It's possible that a home sold for $200,000 could have an assessed value of $250,000. At a rate of 1.5%, property taxes would be $3,750/yr. Call the County Assessor's office for more information *(236-3771)*.

Medical Care

San Diego is known for the best emergency/trauma system in the country. Its other strength is research. UCSD Medical and Scripps are responsible for some of the latest discoveries and techniques now used worldwide. With two new HMOs, seniors have access to some of the finest medical care in the country. **Major hospitals/regional medical centers: University of California San Diego Medical Center** *(543-6222)* offers the latest available procedures for cardiac and cancer care. It's also known internationally for its major organ transplants and emergency/trauma center. **Scripps Memorial Hospitals** are part of the world-famous Scripps Institutions of Medicine and Science. In addition to its full medical and surgical services, The La Jolla facility has the Stevens Cancer Center, the Cardiovascular Institute and the Whittier Institute for Diabetes. Currently there are three hospitals and, by 1992, there will be five *(457-4123)*. **Mercy Hospital** and **Alvarado Hospital** are known for cardiac and cancer care. Contact the Seniors Services office to learn about medical plans and discounts *(260-7310)*. **Emergency medical services (EMS):** The fire department's 42 stations have EMTs and paramedics who handle the first response. Avg. response time: 4 1/2 min. A private service handles emergency transports. Response time: 5 1/2 min. **Physician's referral:** San Diego County Medical Society *565-8888*; Doctor's Service Bureau *565-8772*; Dental: *223-5391*.

Continuing Education

UCSD (La Jolla campus) offers the Institute for Continued Learning, a program for those 55+. Guest speakers form their own classes, topics chosen by members *(534-3409)*. San Diego State University's College of Extended Studies has developed two programs for seniors: Educational Growth Opportunities and Retired Adults Classes cost $12-$20 for 8-week course *(594-5821)*. Classes also held in Rancho Bernardo. More than 200 classes offered each year.

Services for Seniors

San Diego has more than 120 social clubs and social service organizations for seniors. The **Area Agency on Aging** *(236-5212)* and the

Senior Information and Reference Service coordinate most, including legal services, transportation, employment assistance, etc. Send your SASE to the Senior Information and Reference Service, 202 "C" Street, San Diego, 92101 *(236-5765)*. Southwestern Bell publishes the San Diego Silver Pages, for seniors (60+). Pick up a free copy at any recreation center, senior center or library. General information on services for seniors *(236-6905)*.

Crime & Safety

Rancho Bernardo has the lowest crime rate in the city. Other "safe" neighborhoods include San Pasquale, Miramar, La Playa, Harbor, and Pomerado. Residents are vigilant about their Neighborhood Watch programs. The annual "Light the Night" march raises money for crime prevention programs, which target LA gangs and night crimes. Overall, people spoke of feeling safe. The SDPD recently received a $24 million budget increase.

Earning a Living

Current business climate: Unstoppable growth (between 1989 and 1990, the population grew by 92,000), has not protected San Diego from the recession. Boutiques and other non-essential businesses go in and out while service businesses, restaurants and many retailers do well. In fact, the service sector has overtaken the government as the driving force of the economy. **Help in starting a business:** The Chamber of Commerce has two Small Business Development Centers that provide assistance with business plans, financing, and other needs *(450-1518)*. **The job market:**

Wages and salaries are embarrassingly low considering the high cost of living. Job competition is fierce for whatever is available and there are many qualified people taking menial jobs until things open up.

When the Kids Come to Visit

San Diego Zoo, Sea World of California, Wild Animal Park, Old Town, California Missions, Belmont Park, The Children's Museum, The Malibu Grand Prix, Reuben H. Fleet Space Theater and Science Center; Whale Watching Trips (Dec.-Feb.).

Getting Around Town

Roads and interstates: I-8, I-15, I-5. **Airports and airlines:** Lindbergh Field is served by American, TWA, United Delta and most major carriers. **Public transportation:** San Diego Transit, San Diego Trolley (light rail system), Wheels (seniors and disabled), and the Ferry to Coronado. **Managing without a car:** Excellent city bus and trolley service: seniors buy unlimited monthly passes for $11. Many developments and neighborhoods are walking distance to shopping and services. A car is often the safest way to travel (at night).

What Residents Already Know

"June Gloom" is the not-so-sunny kickoff to San Diego summers. It's pretty grey for a few weeks, but it sure keeps the temperatures down. • Who lives in San Diego? According to a young woman priced out of the market they're either "newly wed or nearly dead." Admittedly the retirement population is pervasive. Ain't that great?

For More Information

Chamber Of Commerce Office:
San Diego Area Chamber
of Commerce
110 West C Street, Suite 1600
San Diego, 92101
232-0124

Coronado Chamber of Commerce
720 Orange Avenue, P.O. Box 396
Coronado, 92118, 435-9260

Newspaper:
San Diego Union
Union Tribune Publishing Co.
P.O. Box 191
San Diego, 92112
299-4141

Realtor:
Bill Opie
Opie & Abbott/Re-Max
16/66 Bernardo Center Drive
San Diego, 92128
487-6743

8. Colorado Springs, Colorado

Area Snapshot

Nickname: "America's Choice City"
County: El Paso
Area code: 719   **Zip code:** 80901-80903
Local population: 290,000   **County:** 408,000
% of population 65+: 12.5%
U.S. region: Pikes Peak/Rocky Mountain area (central Colorado)
Closest metro areas: Denver, 68 miles
Nearby areas to consider: Woodland Park, Monument Area
Median housing price: $90,000
Best reasons to retire here: Mild, dry year-round climate, gorgeous scenery, exciting recreation, very affordable, appealing to retired military.

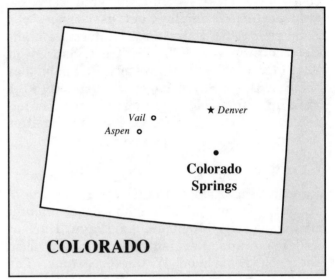

Fabulous Features

Considering the high elevation (6,000 ft.), Colorado Springs has a surprisingly pleasant and mild year-round climate. The winters are long but sunny, and whatever snow accumulates melts quickly. The rest of the year is warm (never hot) and is often humidity-free. With the dry air, it's an ideal place for many allergy and asthma sufferers. Aside from the great climate, people are attracted to the low living costs, which run eight percent below the national average. Housing is new and affordable, taxes are reasonable, and crime is not much of an issue here. The scenery is breathtaking (the Pikes Peak region inspired the lyrics to "America the Beautiful"), the town is often uncongested, and getting around is easy. Medical facilities are adequate (two hospitals are accredited) and both have added cancer research facilities. Colorado Springs is home to three major military installations and a brand-new Space Station, all of which represents about 20-30% of the town's economic base. Colorado Springs also attracts loads of retired military personnel. The universal rejoinder to the question "Why do you live here?" is "Because we want to!"

Possible drawbacks: One doesn't have to be from a military family to enjoy this town, but it helps. Also, with such strong military ties, the local economy is affected by "Star Wars" cuts. If you're politically to the left, prepare for the conservative mindset.

"You can quote me on that"

"We'd been growing tired of California's living costs and taxes. When we came here for an army reunion, we loved the climate and the town, so we packed up and moved here. We're very happy and don't really know anyone who doesn't like it. My advice is don't put off the decision to move. If it's the right place you'll kick yourself for not coming sooner."—L.K.

"We lived in Santa Cruz but knew we couldn't afford to retire in California. Housing and taxes would kill us. We used to live in Boulder and knew this area and are very happy we came. It's an ideal-sized community, the weather is pleasant, and the costs of things are within reason. There's a large military presence here but it doesn't affect us any."—K.F.

Climate

Elevation: 6,211'	Avg. High/ Low	Average Inches		Avg. # Days Precip.	Avg. % Humidity
		Rain	Snow		
Jan.	41/16	-	4.6	5	60
April	59/33	.98	7.1	7	55
July	84/57	3.1	-	14	55
Oct.	64/37	.71	3.1	5	50
YEAR	61/35	13	41	-	-
# days 32° or below: 161			# days 90° or above: 19		

Let the Good Times Roll

Pikes Peak country is heaven on earth for golfers, skiers, hikers and lovers of the great outdoors. If golf is your bag, you'll be impressed with the caliber of courses in the area, some of which have achieved national prominence. The Broadmoor Golf Club (part of the famous 5-star resort hotel) hosts the annual World Senior Tournament and both Ladies and Mens Invitational (In 1995, they'll also host the Ladies U.S. Open). For cross-country, downhill and powder skiing, there are 20 ski resorts within a three-hour drive including some of the world's most famous: Breckenridge, Vail, Steamboat Springs, Aspen and Telluride. For those who are so inclined, six months out of the year it's possible to shoot the front nine in the morning and schuss the slopes that afternoon. With one of the most extensive park systems in the country and endless miles of national forest, you can also hike, camp, and horseback ride to your heart's delight. Hunting, fishing, rock climbing and river rafting round out the menu of outdoor activity.

Culture: Residents are most proud of the Pikes Peak Center, a performing arts arena that attracts Broadway touring shows, The Colorado Springs Symphony, The Colorado opera festival and local theater productions. Music and dance are also alive with the city's own dance troupe, concert band, chorales and the Air Force Academy Band. The Fine Arts Center hosts year-round art exhibits.

Annual events: U.S. Space Symposium (exhibits and lectures open to the public); Pikes Peak Auto Hill Climb (world racers meet Pikes Peak); Pikes Peak or Bust Rodeo (largest professional rodeo in the state); Southwest Colorfest (events to highlight fall colors); Festival of Lights Christmas Parade.

Local Real Estate

It's been a buyer's market for several years so the housing values are excellent. Most retirees opt for single-family homes. Condo/townhouse developments are available but less in demand. Nearly every house has a basement (25% have sloping lots and have walkout basements) and is constructed for severe winters (they rarely occur, so heating bills are reasonable).

Median price for single family home: $90,000
Median price for 2BR condo: $60,000
Rental housing market: Apartment rentals $400-$450; Single family homes $600/mo.
Common housing styles & features: Open construction styles are the most popular type homes in Colorado Springs. It's all to take advantage the endless sunshine, the gorgeous mountain views and the wonderfully clean air. The exteriors benefit from the natural terrain as well, with many homes featuring rock and stained wood siding.
Nearby areas to consider: Woodland Park (25 mi. west), The Monument Area/Woodmoor Area (17 mi. north). **Unique features of these areas:** Woodland Park is true mountain country (it's up another 2,500 feet) so the summers are extra cool. Contemporary construction is most common, with homes in the same or slightly higher price range than Colorado Springs. Retirees love the Woodmoor section in the Monument area because of the country club settings and private golf course. Houses start at $130,000 and can easily go for more than $200,000.

What Things Cost

Everyone agrees that living costs are very reasonable but seeing is believing. Utilities costs are 30% below national average, making it among the lowest in the country. Food is 9% below and housing 11%. below average. Overall living costs were 8% below average.
Utility company: (gas, electric, water and sewer). Colorado Springs Department of Public Utilities *(636-5401)*. Avg. gas bill is $34.92

(Jan. is highest at $71.52). Deposits are not required with good credit ratings. Electric rates: Avg. bill is $31.56 (Jan. is highest at $41.88). Water: Avg. bill is. $27/mo in the city and $39 in the suburbs.

Phone company: Mountain Bell *(636-6020)*. Basic service is $15/mo.

Car registration/license: Registration and title is $5.50; Plates vary by make and value of car. A 1991 auto valued at $12,000-$15,000 pays $250-$300.; Drivers license is $15 for 5 yrs.

The Tax Ax

Sales tax: 6.5% (food is exempt).

State income tax: 5% of federal taxable income.

Retirement income: For persons 55 and older, the first $20,000 of retirement or pension income is exempt from state income tax. There is no estate tax above the federal credit or an inheritance tax.

Property taxes & tax breaks: Averages 1% of market value, reassessed every 10 years or upon sale of the home. There is no homestead exemption.

Medical Care

Major hospitals/regional medical centers: **Memorial Hospital** (JCAH-accredited) has a burn unit and specializes in intensive coronary care, cancer care, complete rehabilitation services and radiology. **Penrose Community Hospital** (JCAH-accredited) has coronary and cardiopulmonary care as well. Another facility, **St. Francis Hospital**, offers laser eye surgery and other progressive procedures. The closest regional teaching hospitals are the **University Hospitals** in Denver (68 mi.). As for military hospitals, the **Air Force Academy Hospital** and the **U.S. Army Community Hospital** (Fort Carson) are full-service facilities.

Emergency medical services (EMS): There are 10 advanced life support vehicles and 36 paramedics. Firemen are also cross-trained as Emergency Medical Technicians. Avg. response time is 4-6 minutes. St. Francis Hospital operates a "Flight For Life" Emergency Transport System. **Physician's referral:** El Paso Medical Society *591-2424*; Health Link *474-5959*; Dental: *473-3168*.

Continuing Education

Pikes Peak Community College allows seniors 60+ to register for $11 and take as many courses as they want (must be a state resident). **The University of Colorado** campus (UCCS) gives seniors a 50% discount on courses if they don't take them for credit. Golf Acres Senior Center has a "Listening In Program" where they can arrange for seniors (must be 62+) to enroll for free at any local campus *(578-6808)*.

Services for Seniors

The **Pikes Peak Area Agency on Aging** publishes a directory of services and referral information for seniors *(471-2096)*. In addition, there are a number of organizations and facilities that enhance the quality of life. The **Colorado Springs Senior Center** offers a variety of health, fitness and enrichment programs. **Silver Key Senior Services** is a private business that assists with everything from home care to filling out forms *(632-1521)*. The Pikes Peak Area Agency on Aging runs a discount program with merchants, parks and recreation and medical services. Anyone 60+ can get a free ID card. For **AARP** membership information, contact Wayne Bricker *(632-9422)*. The **Senior Beacon** is a monthly newspaper with loads of information on local activities and events, especially on travel. It's free at certain locations *(599-3696)*. The **Senior Spotlight** covers local and national news (free).

Crime & Safety

Crime is down for the fifth year in a row, bucking national trends of rampant increases. To help seniors who are victims (car accidents, property crime), the police department has a Senior Victims Assistance Team. It's made up of trained volunteers who assist with the paper work, trauma counseling and other support. Interestingly, there's a special statute in Colorado that increases the severity of the penalty if you're found guilty of committing a crime against persons 55 and older. Too bad they have these laws where they're least needed. **Advice from the police:** Speak to one of the department's Crime

Prevention officer for suggestions on personal safety.

Earning a Living

Current business climate: Having a strong military presence is a double-edged sword for local business. The bad news is that area defense contractors are laying off people (it's all those spending cuts) and jobs are already scarce. The good news is that with other military installations closing all over the country, Colorado Springs is receiving hundreds of new personnel, which can help stimulate the economy.

The job market: Jobs have been hard to come by for several years and wages were never anything to brag about anyway. There is also a high rate of underemployment (highly qualified people doing menial labor). What minimum wage jobs are available are often taken by military dependents who are stationed there for a short time.

When the Kids Come to Visit

The Air Force Acadamy is one of Colorado's most popular tourist attraction; Pikes Peak and Pike National Forest (have you ever seen a 14,000 ft. mountain?), Cheyenne Mountain Zoo, U.S. Olympic Headquarters and Training Center, Will Rogers Shrine, Garden of the Gods (940-acre site of 300-million-year-old rock formations) and the U.S. Space Foundation.

Getting Around Town

Roads and interstates: I-25 (to Denver), US Highways 85, 87

Airports & airlines: Colorado Springs Municipal Airport (with both military and civilian aircraft, one of the largest municipal airports in the U.S.) served by American Airlines, TWA, Continental, America West and Aspen Airways. Denver Stapleton Airport is served by all major carriers.

Public transportation: Springs Transit (city bus system) charges 25¢ a ride for Seniors with a 60+ card. On Friday's, they also do grocery runs. A local private car service, Silver Key Senior Services, specializes in transporting seniors to doctors and hospitals, shopping, weekend outings, etc. *(633-2611).*

Managing without a car: It's no problem because of excellent public and private transportation services.

What Residents Already Know

The downtown is so quiet, drivers never have to get out of second gear.•Lots of retirees start out wanting rural acreage, but after one winter in the "boonies" they can't wait to find a home more convenient to town. In the higher elevations, the winters are more severe and the roads often impassible.•This is a great place for your children and grandkids to move with you. They have an outstanding local school system (*Parenting* magazine named it one of 10 best "family" cities in the U.S.).

For More Information

Chamber Of Commerce Office:

Colorado Springs Chamber
of Commerce
P.O. Drawer B
Colorado Springs, 80901
635-1551

Newspaper:

Gazette Telegraph
30 S. Prospect St.
Colorado Springs, 80903
632-5511

Realtor:

Mr. John Flynn
**The Performance Group/
Metro Brokers**
5520 N. Union Blvd.
Colorado Springs, 80918
800-451-7217

9. Ft. Collins, Colorado

Area Snapshot

Nickname: "Poster City, U.S.A."
County: Larimer
Area code: 303   **Zip code:** 80524
Local population: 93,600   **County:** 194,200
% of population 65+: 7.7% (and growing)
U.S. region: Rocky Mountains
Closest metro areas: Denver, 66 miles; Cheyenne, Wyo., 45 miles
Nearby areas to consider: Adriel Hills, Oakridge Village
Median housing price: $80,000
Best reasons to retire here: Spectacular scenery, outstanding services and programs, phenomenal recreation and culture, low living costs, dry mountain climate (the "banana belt of Colorado").

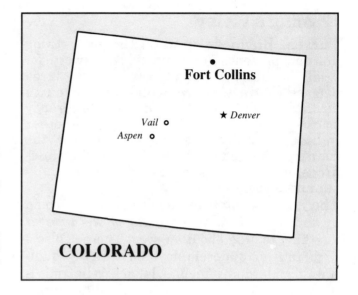

Fabulous Features

If ever there was a user-friendly city, Ft. Collins is it! It's as though the town fathers sat down and said, "What can we do to enhance the quality of life?" For one thing they made sure that every residential area was within walking distance to a beautiful park as well as shopping. All that planning worked. *Newsweek* magazine just ranked it as the 19th best place to live in the U.S. and it's easy to understand why. For a city this size, the amount of recreational, cultural and educational opportunities is remarkable. The Poudre River's "Gold Medal Trout Route," the canyons and reservoirs for hiking, biking and mountain climbing and the fabulous cross-country skiing are just the start of outdoor living. Thanks to Colorado State University and a culturally minded community, the performing arts, galleries and musical events are everyday occurrences. Vistas of the majestic terrain, vertical cliffs, waterfalls, and sparkling blue lakes provide daily doses of inspiration. This is a semi-arid region, with only 14 inches of rainfall a year. In fact, dry air dominates in all four seasons. And while Canadian air masses make the winters cold, the snow melts in a few days. The sun shines close to 300 days a year. Property taxes are an affordable 1% of purchase prices and patio homes (private houses with all maintained services) are ideal for retirees who stay for six months, or travel a lot. If you want to live in a city that's as inviting as a picture postcard, discover Ft. Collins.

Possible drawbacks: Land development has virtually come to a grinding halt because the banks aren't financing builders as they did in the past. One realtor predicted that within a few years, you won't be able to buy a hovel. •"Small town, small minds," say some. Long-time residents with old-fashioned attitudes as well as some special interest groups (the "No-Growthers") are often pitted against the city council, the chamber and citizens who have high hopes for Ft. Collins' future.

"You can quote me on that"

"My children live in other parts of the country and have asked me to move, but there's no way I'd leave Ft. Collins. I love being close to the Rocky Mountains and being part of a small community. I know lots of people now and they're like family. What's special about this place is that seniors don't feel discriminated. And there are more activities for us than in any other place I can think of."—Mrs. M.N.

Climate

Elevation: 5,033'	Avg. High/ Low	Average Inches		Avg. # Days Precip.	Avg. % Humidity
		Rain	Snow		
Jan.	41/16	-	7	6	59
April	58/32	1	9	10	58
July	86/57	1.8	-	10	49
Oct.	65/35	.7	4	5	55
YEAR	62/35	10	56	-	-
# days 32° or below: 169			# days 90° or above: 22		

Let the Good Times Roll

Recreation: Ft. Collins is the land of enchantment for outdoor enthusiasts. Horsetooth Reservoir offers fishing, waterskiing, boating, swimming, rock climbing, camping and hiking. Horsetooth Mountain Park (adjacent to the reservoir) boasts 25 miles of spectacular hiking trails and cross-country skiing. Poudre River Canyon is great for fishing, hiking and relaxing. The Rawah Wilderness area near the top of the canyon offers tranquil mountain lakes and unsurpassed hiking and backpacking. Snowmobiles and cross-country skiers make use of the trails surrounding Cameron Pass during winter. Lory State Park offers hiking, horseback riding and overnight camping (with a permit). And then there's the granddaddy of 'em all—the Rocky Mountain National Park and Estes Park (one hour) are prime locations for unbelievable skiing, camping, climbing, bird watching. In the summer, take a trip over Trail Ridge Road, the world's highest continuous paved road. At CSU's Learning Center, view the golden eagles and other wildlife while strolling through two miles of nature trails.

Culture: Who needs New York when Ft. Collins has its own Lincoln Center, a city-owned performing and visual arts auditorium and meeting facility? It sponsors wonderful series as well as the Fort Collins Symphony, the Larimer Chorale and the Open Stage Theater. Rotating art shows run in four exhibition spaces, The Intimate Gallery, Lobby Gallery, Walkaway Gallery and Sculpture Garden. One West Contemporary Arts Center offers three galleries, an art school and library. Ft. Collins Museum displays Pre-Columbian and Plains Indians artifacts and exhibits of Ft. Collins' roots. Old Town District, in the heart of Ft. Collins, has been restored to an attractive entertainment and shopping plaza. At Christmas, it lights up like a fairyland. Other times it's home to concerts under the stars, magicians and more. The Avery House is a Victorian landmark house constructed of native Colorado sandstone and built by Franklin and Sara Avery. Blackwood Gallery is the studio and home of nationally known watercolorist Susan Blackwood. In fact, the number of art galleries for a city this size is remarkable.

Annual events: Biennial International Poster Exhibit featuring original posters created by international artists (Sept.): Poudre Valley Art League Show, an art show featuring 600 original works by western artists (April); Rendezvous—Ft. Collins Museum, a recreation of the region's fur trading era (June); Skookum Day—Ft. Collins Museum, historical reenactments (July): New West Fest (Aug.); Historic Homes Tour (Sept.); Fort Collins Annual Balloon Fest (Sept.); The Great Christmas Hall (Nov.).

Local Real Estate

It's very much a seller's market now, with California's "equity immigrants" coming in and buying everything. Realtors tell of taking two and three contracts on a single home.

Median price for single family home: $80,000. New 2BR patio homes sell for $80,000-$125,000.

Median price for 2BR condo: $70,000. Condos are available starting at $50,000, but there are very few for sale on the market.

Rental housing market: Some agencies have closed down their rental departments. College students take over the apartment complexes and single-family homes are hardly available because purchase prices are low.

Common housing styles & features: Retirees are gravitating to patio homes—one- or two-story duplexes with 2BR, a sunroom, beautiful backyards and 2-car garages. And all exterior maintenance is done through homeowner's associations.

Amenities in condo developments: pools, exterior maintenance maintained.

Nearby areas to consider: Adriel Hills, Oakridge Village. **Unique features of these areas:** Adriel Hills is a condo and townhouse community on a golf course that's also within walking distance to the Ft. Collins Country Club. Retirees are buying homes from $60,000-$160,000. Oakridge Village is a new patio home community that borders a golf course. Prices range from $90,000-$130,000.

What Things Cost

Overall living costs are 14% below the national average, with housing 23% below and utilities 36% below. Health care costs are approx. 3% below. No category was above the national avg.
Gas company: Public Service Company of Colorado *(482-5922)*. Avg. bill: $40/mo. (High months: $80, low months: $18). No deposit required for new residents.
Electric company: Electric Utilities Dept. *(221-6785)*. Avg. bills for all electric homes are $75-$100/mo.. No deposit for new residents.
Phone company: U.S. West Communications *(679-7000)*. Basic service: $18.50/mo. for unlimited local calls.
Car registration/license: Registration and title: $5.50; Plates vary by make and value of car. A 1991 auto valued at $12,000-$15,000 pays $250-$300; Driver's license: $15 for 5 yrs.

The Tax Ax

Sales tax: 6.5% (food is exempt). **State income tax:** 5% of federal taxable income. **Retirement income:** For persons 55+, the first $20,000 of retirement or pension income is exempt from state income tax. There is no estate tax above the federal credit nor an inheritance tax.
Property taxes & tax breaks: The rule of thumb is that property taxes are 1% of the purchase price. There are no homestead exemptions. Tax Assessor's office *(498-7050)*.

Medical Care

Major hospitals/regional medical centers: Poudre Valley Hospital (JCAH-accredited) is known for their Neuroscience Intensive Care Unit and a Chronic Wound Care Center. The North Colorado Kidney Center operates a dialysis unit as well. Specializations include coronary care (open heart surgery), rheumatology and oncology. It has state-of-the-art imaging facilities. The Aspen Club for seniors assists with admissions paperwork and other need and its Lifeline Alert program provides a necklace or bracelet that can be activated to immediately notify a list of possible responders (neighbor, emergency room, etc.) Cost is $15/mo.
Emergency medical services (EMS): Ft. Collins has a high-performance emergency command center with a network of paramedics, firefighters who are EMT-D (defibrillation trained). Response time: less than 8 minutes.
Physician's referral: Larimer County Medical Society *490-4105*. Dental: *493-1200*.

Continuing Education

Colorado State University has a wonderful series called "55 and Better," offering topical one-day seminars on everything from IRAs to Native American Indians. Classes are $15. Seniors can also enroll in credit or non-credit classes for half the tuition, which is $50/credit *(491-5288)*. Elderhostel programs are at Pengrey Park in the mountains *(881-2150)*. Fort Range Community College does not offer specific classes for seniors but allows those 62+ to enroll in either credit or non-credit courses for half the regular tuition, $52/credit, with most courses 2-5 credits *(226-2500)*.

Services for Seniors

The Senior Center has a monthly newspaper that keeps more than 1,000 members apprised of classes, activities and services. Programs include: a current events forum, card groups, Senior Games, quilting and trips. A Medicare counseling group and the local **RSVP** chapter meet at the center. Try "Seniors Helping Seniors," where people trade services (fill out income taxes in exchange for handyman jobs, etc). Plans call for a new facility to be built by 1994 *(221-6644)*. Local **AARP** chapter president, Vernon McHone *(482-4256)*.

Crime & Safety

The Ft. Collins Police Dept. is very proactive. All officers participate in crime prevention programs (more than 60) including home security surveys, fraud prevention seminars, "Operation Identification," and Neighborhood Watch. Crime is very low, with domestic violence, criminal mischief and bar fights requiring the most attention. Overall, residents walk anywhere without fear.

Earning a Living

Current business climate: There are currently 5,200 active businesses in the area, but only 30 employ more than 140 people (Kodak, Hewlett Packard). An average of 60 new businesses open a month, but of those, only half survive the first five years.

Help in starting a business: Contact Melanie Hein at the Chamber's Center for Business Assistance for outstanding no- or low-cost services that provides materials, training and counseling on a confidential basis to any small business owner (482-3746). The local SCORE chapter can also advise on business conditions, site locations and other aspects (484-1406).

The job market: Unemployment has been a level 3.6% for years, indicating the job market is tight. With competition from several nearby universities, part-time work can be difficult to get. Contact the county's Senior Employment division for assistance (223-2470 ext. 203).

When the Kids Come to Visit

The Farm of Lee Martinez Park is an original dairy farm with goats and a museum (March-Oct.); Swetsville Zoo (free) includes Sculpture Park featuring Harry the Hitchhiker and Dino the Brontosaurus plus 70 other sculptures, a miniature live steam railroad and a display of antique tractors, engines, old farming equipment. Anheuser-Busch Brewery offers free tours and a close-up look at the beautiful Clydesdale horses. The Collins Trolley runs on weekends/holidays to commemorate of one the finest trolley systems in the U.S. (and the last to survive in Colorado). Ft. Collins has the new Edora Pool and Ice Center (EPIC).

Getting Around Town

Roads & interstates: I-125, US Highway 87. **Airports & airlines:** Denver Stapleton International Airport (65 mi. south). Airport Express provides shuttle service (482-0805). Most major carriers serve the Denver airport (more than 900 daily flights). **Public transportation:** Ft. Collins Transfort is the city bus service. Nine routes, to the hospital, shopping and residential areas, run Mon.-Sat. Seniors pay 25¢ one-way or buy an annual pass for $15. SAINT (Senior Alternatives in Transportation) is a volunteer program where people drive seniors (60+) to the doctor, shopping, etc. (221-6621). **Managing without a car:** Between the bus service and volunteer programs, it's possible to manage without a car. Most residential sections are near shopping and services.

What Residents Already Know

Denver is building a gorgeous new airport (opening in 1993) that will be a boon to Ft. Collin's high-tech manufacturers and residents alike, provided the state funds a new highway (the E-470) that will bypass Denver, making the trip from Ft. Collins a dream drive. It's a long shot, but the fight's not over.

For More Information

Chamber Of Commerce Office:
Ft. Collins Area Chamber
of Commerce
P.O. Drawer D
Fort Collins, 80522-0460
482-3746

Newspaper:
Fort Collins Colorodoan
1212 Riverside Avenue
Fort Collins, 80524
493-6397

Realtors:
Arthur Williams
Moore Realty, Inc.
3665 JFK Parkway, Bldg. 1
Fort Collins, 80525
226-5511

Judy Bogaard
Coldwell Banker/Everitt Realty
2900 S. College Ave.
Fort Collins, 80525
223-6500

10. Boca Raton, Florida

Area Snapshot

Nickname: "Silicon Beach"
County: Palm Beach
Area code: 407   **Zip code:** 33444
Local population: 74,000   **County:** 875,000
% of population 50+: 42.4%
U.S. region: East Coast Florida (between Palm Beach and Ft. Lauderdale).
Closest metro areas: Ft. Lauderdale, 44 miles; Miami, 67 miles
Nearby areas to consider: Palm Beach Gardens, Jupiter
Median housing price: $106,400
Best reasons to retire here: Exclusive communities, great recreation and culture, low crime, waterfront living, lush scenery.

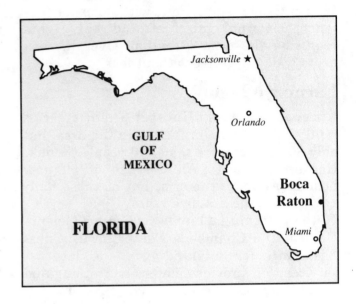

Fabulous Features

Landing in Boca for your retirement is as satisfying as landing on Boardwalk and Park Place after you've just bought them from your opponent! You've arrived, and the good life is waiting. The championship golf courses, the exclusive country clubs, the fabulous shopping (the new Mizner Park downtown is a potpourri of boutiques, eateries, and entertainment) and the glorious year-round weather (how does a balmy 75 degrees sound?) would make anyone's day. The awe-inspiring homes and, no less impressive, the Atlantic Ocean are the finishing touches for a first-class lifestyle. Your neighbors may be some of the most accomplished business, political and professional leaders in the world because Boca has success written all over it. Of greatest fame are the extraordinary communities where people can hang their hats (and their furs and their Rolls Royces), including the exquisite Bocaire Country Club and the famous Polo Club (Chris Evert's home base), to name a few. Even the smaller, less costly townhouse condos and homes are as pretty as a picture. Everything looks appetizing in this delectable, fun city. A retired business owner from New Jersey told us that he was having the time of his life in Boca. And yet in the year since he'd arrived, he hadn't taken advantage of the culture and recreation. "It's like the Statue of Liberty. I'm just glad it's there."

Possible drawbacks: If you plan to summer where you winter, make sure you can stand the heat. The high temperatures and humidity are intense.•When you live in an area that attracts millions of tourists each year, all of whom drive, be prepared for more traffic, longer lines, and other annoyances associated with company you didn't invite.•The prevailing attitude here is if you don't like the place, it must be *you*. Defending Boca is an automatic reflex. If you are going to be critical, do the honorable thing and whisper.

"You can quote me on that"

"To me, Boca is a dream retirement spot. There's nothing dilapidated or depressing about the area. From one end of the city to the other, it's new and beautiful. And there's everything you could possibly want or imagine for shopping, golf and tennis, restaurants, doctors, the beaches. The communities are fabulous, too. You don't have to drive to your country club, it's just down the block."—Mr. E.T.

Climate

Elevation: 19'	Avg. High/ Low	Avg. Rainfall (Inches)	Avg. # Days Precip.	Avg. % Humidity
Jan.	75/56	2.6	7	78
April	83/65	3.5	7	72
July	90/74	6.5	15	79
Oct.	84/70	8.7	13	80
YEAR	83/66	62	-	-
# days 32° or below: 3		# days 90° or above: 92		

Let the Good Times Roll

Recreation: Every day is Sunday in Boca. The sports and recreational activities are vast as well as first-rate. In addition to all the private country clubs and communities, the public parks and beaches are equally impressive. Enjoy two miles of gorgeous beaches, over 30 parks and picnic grounds, tennis courts, jogging trails, boating, fishing (saltwater and freshwater), water skiing, snorkeling, surfing, scuba diving and windsurfing. The Mission Bay Aquatic Training Center, the largest in the world, offers hundreds of programs for swimmers of all ages. And for the sports-minded, come watch the Senior League Players (former Major Leaguers), the Atlanta Braves and Montreal Expos spring training, and the Camel Grand Prix in Palm Beach. Tennis fans will be impressed with the complex at Patch Reef Park—the 1990 Facility of the Year (U.S. Professional Tennis Association). Polo at the Royal Palm Polo Sports Club is an award-winning excitement, too, with international championship action (January-April). **Culture:** This area has so much culture, there's an "800" number for upcoming events. Organizations that bring a myriad of enjoyment to the community include the Boca Symphonic Pops, Boca Raton Museum of Art, The Philharmonic Orchestra, the Florida Academy of Dramatic Arts, regional theater, and for the outdoor enthusiast, the Gumbo Limbo Nature Center, an exciting outdoor classroom with 20 acres of boardwalk, observation tower and trails. Call 800-ARTSLINE for more information.

Annual events: South Florida Fair (Jan.); Mardi Gras (Feb.); Meet Me Downtown PGA Seniors Golf (April); Camel Grand Prix (April); Florida Music Festival (July); Boca Festival Days (Aug.); Oktoberfest; Florida Heritage Fest (Nov.).

Local Real Estate

Boca has been a buyer's market since 1983 when the building boom created infinitely more supply than even the huge demand called for. The market remains active, but few of the developments are completely sold out. There are no new major communities being built. Palm Beach County's zoning laws are prohibiting the development of remaining farmland.

Median price for single family home: $106,400, but the figures don't tell the whole story. Fourteen of Florida's most exclusive developments are in Boca. Yes, there are single story plain janes, but the real story is with the sprawling multi-level showplaces with sculpted lakes, poolside docks and riding stables. The average listing for a single family home with sizzle is $378,200.

Median price for 2BR condo: $165,000

Rental housing market: Rentals, especially condos, are readily available at any time of year. Average is $1,830/mo. (condos are less).

Common housing styles & features: Most favored exteriors are Mediterranean, California contemporaries and even Victorians and Tudors. Florida's native flora create beautiful entries, private gardens and distinctive landscape designs. The interiors are awesome expanses of bright, white and light.

Amenities in condo developments: Aside from tennis and pools, most offer security, exercise rooms, spas and courtesy buses to shopping.

Nearby areas to consider: Palm Beach Gardens, Jupiter. **Unique features of these areas:** As a premier planned community, Palm Beach Gardens' country club environment offers gorgeous homes situated on lakes and waterways. It's the home of the PGA and championship golf courses, and is a mix of young families and retirees. Jupiter, at the tip of Palm Beach County, is one of its fastest-growing communities. The array of homes and condos in all price ranges affords retirees the best of available resources without congestion and high costs.

What Things Cost

Gas company: Most residents use all electric.
Electric company: Florida Power & Light *(395-8700)*. Average bill for a 3,000 sq. ft. home is $150-$200/month. Summers can range from $250-$300/month. Depends on pool pumps, air conditioning, etc.
Water/sewer: City of Boca Raton Utilities Dept. *(393-7750)*. Avg. bill is $32/mo. for 3BA home, plus a 8.5% utility tax.
Phone company: Southern Bell Telephone *(800-753-0710)* in Florida. Basic monthly service is $13.55. Installations start at $44.50. Deposit is generally not required.
Car registration/license: New residents must obtain a Florida driver's license within 30 days of establishing residency. Title fees: new vehicles: $29.25; used: $33.25. Initial registration: (cars and trucks): $100. New Residents Impact Fee: $295 (One-time charge applies to each vehicle previously titled outside of Florida). Driver's license: (good for 6 years). New residents: $20/yr. License tags (1 yr): Vehicles up to 2,499 lbs.: $34.60; vehicles 2,500 to 3,499 lbs.: $42.60; vehicles 3,500 lbs. and over: $52.60.

The Tax Ax

Sales tax: 6% (prescription drugs and food exempt except prepared or restaurant foods).
State income tax: None.
Retirement income: Florida ranks first among 10 popular retirement states for taking the smallest tax bite from retirees. There's no income tax, no death or estate taxes (over and above federal credit) and property taxes are still lower than the northeastern cities where many people migrate from. **Property taxes & tax breaks:** Florida offers a $25,000 homestead exemption for permanent residents whose principal home is in Florida. Property taxes are based on millage rates. To estimate, deduct $25,000 from the appraised value of the home (provided you own and reside in the house by Dec. 31), multiply the balance times the millage rate and divide by 1,000. Millage rates in Boca are 21.2362 per $1,000 of valuation. A home appraised at $300,000 would be $5,840/yr. Tax appraiser: *(276-1250)*.

Medical Care

Boca residents used to have to travel to take advantage of top medical treatment. Now with two accredited, full-service facilities, the latest available technology and services are here, including emergency and trauma centers.
Major hospitals/regional medical centers: **Boca Raton Community Hospital** offers cancer care, rehabilitative therapy, and new Imaging Center (outpatient diagnostic radiology). The state has approved the creation of an open-heart surgical center. **West Boca Medical Center's** 400 physicians cover every specialty. Florida Laser Center is the area's first multi-disciplinary program to provide alternatives to invasive surgery.
Emergency medical services (EMS): Boca's six fire stations are equipped with a Mobile Intensive Unit for advanced life support. Certified paramedics and firefighters (all EMT trained) are the first response team, with an average response time of 6-8 minutes.
Physician's referral: West Boca Medical Center *488-8175*; Palm Beach County Medical Society *433-3944*.

Continuing Education

Florida Atlantic University offers continuing education classes including antiques and collectibles, interior design, computer courses and languages. There are no senior discounts *(367-3000)*. College of Boca Raton has a fabulous Institute for Learning in Retirement offering peer-taught courses. Classes run from October-December and January-May. A $30 membership fee entitles you to take as many classes as you want *(994-0770)*. Palm Beach Community College has the largest selection of classes including People's Law School and Computers for Mature Learners (hands-on seminar). Nominal fees vary *(338-2200)*.

Services for Seniors

Contact Better Living For Seniors for in-depth information and referrals on programs and activities for elderly parents or an ill loved one *(335-4191)*. The Mae Volen Senior Center offers 25 different services to low-income residents but is also an excellent resource for learning about transportation, health screenings and other needs *(395-8920)*. The Adolph and Rose Levis Jewish Community Center runs a Senior Adult Walking Course *(395-5546)*. For **AARP** membership, contact Robert Deas, District 26 in Coconut Creek *(426-3566)*.

Crime & Safety

Security guards, gates and alarms are the city's most visible mascots. Everyone has something to protect, and yet according to the police, 50% of the reported burglaries last year were "no force." This means people had not locked their doors. So much for expensive precautions. Neighborhood Watch Programs are probably responsible for the surprisingly low rate of crime. Violent crime is statistically minor.

Earning a Living

Current business climate: While a Boca business address is one of the most prestigious in the world, it does not preempt owners from their fair share of high commercial rents, fierce competition and basic survival tactics. In this extremely expensive and competitive environment, success in the service sector requires more commitment than a 3-day a week hobby.
Help in starting a business: Contact the Chamber of Commerce for information on necessary operating licenses, taxes and other help *(395-4433)*. **The job market:** Part-time work in retail, restaurant and service businesses is always available, but with Florida's notoriously low wages, one has to be in it for fun and employee discounts rather than the paychecks.

When the Kids Come to Visit

Singing Pines; Children's Science Explorium; Animal Kingdom, Dreher Park Zoo; Nine Country Safari (West Palm Beach); and, of course, the beach.

Getting Around Town

Roads & interstates: Florida Turnpike, I-95, A1A, US 1, US 441.
Airports & airlines: West Palm Beach International Airport, Ft. Lauderdale Airport and Miami Airport serve the area. Virtually every carrier serves the area.
Public transportation: Contran bus service allows seniors to travel for half price (40¢). But the big news is the Tri-Rail shuttle: commuter service between West Palm Beach and Miami during the business week.
Managing without a car: With the help of friends, it's possible. Many developments offer courtesy bus service.

What Residents Already Know

Every charitable organization in the world has a presence and a fundraising mission here. The American Cancer Society and American Heart Association raised over $1 million in Palm Beach County. United Way raised over $2 million.

For More Information

Chamber Of Commerce Office:
Boca Raton Chamber of Commerce
1800 North Dixie Highway
Boca Raton, 33432
395-4433

Newspaper:
The Boca Raton News
33 S.E. Third Street
Boca Raton, 33432
368-9400

Realtor:
Bill Doherty
ERA Gator Realty
23048 Sandalfoot Plaza Drive
Boca Raton, 33428
488-6228

11. Daytona Beach, Florida

Area Snapshot

Nickname: "The World's Most Famous Beach"
County: Volusia
Area code: 904 **Zip code:** 32115-32118
Local population: 62,000 **County:** 370,900
% of population 65+: 23.1%
U.S. region: East Central Coastal Florida (on the Atlantic Ocean).
Closest metro areas: Orlando, 54 mi.; Jacksonville, 89 mi.; Gainesville, 98 mi.
Nearby areas to consider: Ormond Beach, Ormond-By-The-Sea, Ponce Inlet
Median housing price: $86,000
Best reasons to retire here: Casual lifestyle on the ocean, close proximity to Florida's best attractions, very affordable housing and living costs.

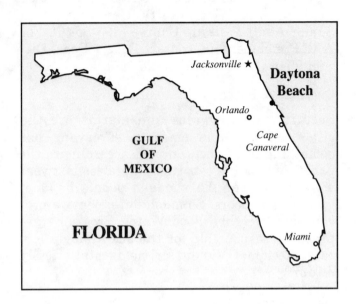

Fabulous Features

Every spring, news reports would have one think that Daytona is nothing more than a place for tourists to converge. But retirees who thrive on outdoor recreation and year-round strolls on the beach will convince you it's not just a nice place to visit, it's a fabulous place to settle. Today's Daytona is a young (and young at heart) person's city with excellent restaurants, shopping and activities. Residents also look forward to the world-famous Daytona 500 and other annual racing events. More importantly, living costs are low, the housing market is diversified and affordable, the temperatures vary by season (expect some downright chilly evenings in the winter) and there's an abundance of culture and continuing education programs. Seniors especially love the Elderhostel at Stetson College in nearby DeLand. The twin counties of Volusia and Flagler have seen a tremendous surge in population (110% increase in the past five years),

primarily because of excellent real estate buys and proximity to the ocean and beaches. But between 1980 and 1989, the area also experienced a near 40% increase in residents 65 and older. An easy-going lifestyle that revolves around special events, interesting activities and endless sunshine (no less than 347 days a year) explains the phenomenal appeal.

Possible drawbacks: While some residents swear by Daytona, others swear at it. With each spring come the crowds; with each summer comes the intense heat. Daytona is simply a poor choice for anyone not interested in a "fun-in-the-sun" lifestyle. It's also a difficult place to find good-paying jobs and business opportunities. Wages are some of the lowest in the state and competition is fierce, particularly in the lucrative service sector. On the other hand, one never has to be concerned that the kids won't come for a visit. There is always something fun to do in Daytona!

"You can quote me on that"

"We're from Ohio, but so are half the other people down here. Daytona is a wonderful place to retire. Everyone is so friendly and you can be busy, busy, busy every day. We're beach people, so we couldn't have picked a better place. Plus we think it's very affordable."—Mrs. R.R., Ormond Beach

Climate

Elevation: 40'	Avg. High/ Low	Avg. Rainfall (Inches)	Avg. # Days Precip.	Avg. % Humidity
Jan.	69/48	2.1	7	78
April	80/59	2.4	6	72
July	90/72	6.7	14	80
Oct.	81/65	5.5	10	80
YEAR	80/61	50	-	77
# days 32° or below: 6		# days 90° or above: 63		

Let the Good Times Roll

Recreation: The Daytona area is a peninsula resting on 47 miles of gorgeous Atlantic Ocean beaches, lakes and rivers with access to the Intercoastal Waterway. Add the new 500-slip marina, and Daytona is a boater's delight! National and state parks: Canaveral National Seashore, Bulow State Park (Ormond Beach), Hontoon Island State Park (DeLand). County parks: 30, many with boat launching areas, ballfields, trails, camping facilities and fishing. City parks: 70 in Volusia County. Golf courses: Daytona Beach Golf & Country Club has a 36-hole course; 17 public and private courses. Tennis courts: 70 hard-surface courts. Marinas: 18. Fishing: Deep-sea, pier, surf, river, and freshwater fishing. Jai alai and greyhound racing: year-round races with pari-mutuel wagering.

Culture: Galleries, museums, dance companies, theater, the symphony and concerts. The Ocean Center: A new $40 million sports and entertainment complex hosts the London Symphony, Ringling Brothers and more. Museum of Arts & Sciences: Permanent fine arts and sculpture exhibits, planetarium, etc.; 11 other galleries and museums. Casements Cultural Arts Center (Ormond Beach): The former Rockefeller residence sponsors lectures, dance performances and well-known artists. Daytona Beach Symphony: Orchestral performances Oct.-April. Theater: 6 local repertory groups. Dance: The Daytona Beach Civic Ballet and International Folk Dancing schedule performances year-round.

Annual events: Speed Weeks (Feb.): 7 different world-class auto races, ending with the famed Daytona 500 NASCAR Winston Cup. Pro-Am Motorcycle Races (Oct.): Over 1,300 entries in this 3-hour endurance contest. Daytona Greek Festival (Nov.): Dancing, music, exotic dishes. Halifax Art Festival (Nov.).

Local Real Estate

Median price for single family home: $86,000. Comparable houses in Orlando or Miami would run $25,000-$30,000 more.

Median price for 2BR condo: A new oceanfront 2BR/2BA starts at $109,000; $140,000 for better views. Resales on the ocean start at $115,000 and anything inland starts in the low $70s.

Rental housing market: 3BR house $650/mo., 2BR apt. $450/mo. In season, a furnished condo on the ocean can run $1,200 a month.

Common housing styles & features: Most 3BR homes are contemporary split plan ranches (master BR on one side, guest on the other).

Amenities in condo developments: Most have underground parking, security, pools, tennis courts, health and fitness rooms.

Nearby communities to consider: Ormond Beach, Port Orange, Ormand By-The-Sea, Ponce Inlet, Daytona Beach Shores. **Unique features of these areas: Ormond Beach** (pop. 29,700) is a quiet, residential community away from the tourists. Young professionals reside here as well. It offers affordable older homes, vacation cottages and exclusive developments. The older homes are small, low-maintenance styles priced from $50,000-$80,000. **Ormond by-the-Sea** (pop. 12,000) is a beautiful township, also on the beach side of the Daytona Peninsula (it's the northernmost point in Volusia). It offers affordable small houses and condos no more than 3 blocks from the ocean. **Ponce Inlet** (pop. 2,000) is a tiny township across the bay with luxurious highrise condos. One exit and entrance and virtually nothing in the way of hotels, shopping or services. Residents drive 5 miles to get to civilization. 2BR/2BA condos range from $100,000-$350,000.

What Things Cost

Of Florida's 67 counties, Volusia was ranked 27th (1 being most costly) for overall living expenses, according to the 1990 Florida Price Level Index. They run 5.5% below the average county, and 9% below in health, recreation and personal services. Real estate prices are stable with low property taxes.

Gas company: People's Gas *(253-5635)*. Avg. monthly bill: $35-$40. Summer averages $22. Winter averages $44-$56.

Electric company: Florida Power & Light *(252-1541)*. Avg. monthly bill: $79.

Water/sewer: Hook-ups are $98 (refundable after account is closed/paid in full).

Phone company: Southern Bell Telephone *(780-2355)*. Basic monthly service: $18-$20 (for customers with own phones). Includes unlimited local calling and touchtone service.

Car registration/license: Title fees: New vehicles: $29.25; used: $33.25. Initial registration: $100. New residents impact fee: $295 (One-time charge for each vehicle previously titled outside of Florida) Driver's license (good for 6 yrs.): New residents: $20 annual. License tags (1 yr.): Vehicles up to 2,499 lbs.: $34.60; 2,500-3,499 lbs.: $42.60; 3,500 lbs. and over: $52.60.

The Tax Ax

Sales tax: 6% (prescription drugs/food exempt except prepared/restaurant foods).

State income tax: None.

Retirement income: Florida ranks first among ten popular retirement states for smallest tax bite. No income tax or death taxes.

Property taxes: Property taxes are based on millage rates. To estimate annual property taxes in Florida, deduct $25,000 from the appraised value of the home (provided you own and reside in the house by Dec. 31), multiply the balance times the millage rate and divide by 1,000. For more information, call the tax appraisers office *(254-4601)*. Using 1990 rates, property taxes for the following areas with houses appraised at $90,000 would cost as follows: Daytona Beach, $1,460; Ponce Inlet, $1,396; Ormond Beach, $1,422; Ormond-by-the-Sea, $1,183.

Medical Care

Major hospitals/regional medical centers: 7 hospitals serve the county. The Joint Accredited facilities all have 24-hr. emergency care as well as therapeutic and diagnostic services. **Halifax Medical Center:** A Level II trauma center with multi-specialty coverage, same-day surgery, regional oncology center, mobile breast screening. **Humana Hospital:** Same-day surgery, pulmonary rehabilitation, angioplasty. **Fish Memorial** (Deland): Outpatient eye center, hospital-based home health care, nuclear medicine, radiology. **West Volusia Memorial** (Deland): Home health services, primary clinics. **Memorial Hospital** (Ormond Beach): excellent reputation for cardiac care. For diagnostic analysis, the new Mayo Clinic in Jacksonville is less than 100 miles away.

Emergency Medical Services (EMS): 11 emergency vehicles (county), 15 ambulances, 56 paramedics, 48 med. technicians, 7 EMS stations. Response time within city limits: 4.6 minutes. County-wide: 6.7 minutes.

Physician's referral: Halifax Medical Center has a Physicians's referral service *254-4000*.

Continuing Education

Daytona Beach Community College shares a new $4 million campus with the U. of Central Florida. Seniors are offered "Lifelong Learning": 40 different subjects. Registration is $10 per semester (subsidized). Subjects include ballroom dancing, and "Writing Your Own Life Story." Also have 100 "Self-Supporting" classes. Classes run 1 week to entire semesters. Cost avgs. $15 a class, held at New Smyrna, DeLand and Palm Coast campuses. Dept. of Continuing Ed. *(255-8131)*. **Stetson College** (Deland): Elderhostel program 9 months a year. 5-day packages include 3 courses, meals and activities. Registration is $260 per person for classes, activities and accommodations and $130 for commuters *(822-7500)*.

Services for Seniors

Volusia County Council on Aging offers numerous free services including a Senior Employment Referral Service, **RSVP** (Retired Seniors Volunteer Program), transportation arrangements and **Meals on Wheels** *(253-4700)*. **AARP:** For membership information in Daytona Beach *(258-6963)*.

Crime & Safety

Crime was down 11% in 1990 due to an outstanding Neighborhood Watch Dept. (voted #1 in Florida by the State Attorney General's office). There are 22 active Neighborhood Watch Programs in the city. The Beach Patrol has more than 1,000 volunteers, including hundreds of seniors. "They are the eyes and ears of this community and the reason that crime is down," said Sgt. Tillard of the DBPD. **Most common crime against seniors:** "Push ins"—people who claim to be from the gas company but are burglars. Sgt. Tillard says, "Everyone whose job requires entering a home carries a City I.D. card. If people would just verify that, it would save a lot of grief."

Earning a Living

Current business climate: Small businesses are having a rough go of it unless they cater to tourists or are in durable medical goods and health care services. Competition is heavy. Daytona is one of the fastest-growing areas in the state. With more people needing services, the cycle will eventually shift. **Programs to help you get started:** For seniors who want to start or expand a business, Stetson College (DeLand) runs a Small Business Development Center, providing free counseling and seminars (*734-1066*). Former executives can provide counseling by calling SCORE (Service Corp. of Retired Executives), (*255-6889*). **The job market:** Wages/salaries are ridiculously low. Avg. household incomes are $14,000.

When the Kids Come to Visit

Cypress Gardens: 100 mi., Florida's Silver Springs: 70 mi., Kennedy Space Center: 56 mi., Marineland: 45 mi., Sea World: 65 mi., St. Augustine: 53 mi., Walt Disney World/EPCOT: 67 mi., Wet 'N Wild: 63 mi.

Getting Around Town

Roads & interstates: State: A1A; US: Rt. 1; Interstates: 95, 4. **Airports & airlines:** Daytona Beach Regional Airport: Delta, USAir, Continental, American, United. Daily nonstops to Atlanta, Newark, Orlando, Charlotte, Washington, DC. Orlando International Airport: TWA, USAir, Continental, Delta, Northwest and Piedmont. ComAir operates 25 daily flights between Orlando and Daytona. **Public transportation:** VOTRAN (Volusia County Transportation): Seventeen bus routes daily except Sunday. One-way for seniors is 30¢. Trolley service along A1A daily except Sunday. Daytona-Orlando Transit Service operates bus service to Daytona and Orlando airports, Disney World, etc. Cost for seniors is $21 one-way/$37 round-trip. (*Outside Florida: 1-800-231-1965*). **Managing without a car:** Many seniors rely on public transportation without a problem. Shopping is walking distance everywhere.

What Residents Already Know

Voters are approving millions of dollars of general obligation bonds to insure development of infrastructures.•In the meantime, water shortages cause heated debates as each community tries to insure adequate supply.•Daytona is proud to be the new home of the LPGA. They're working hard to include the city in the '92-'93 tour.

For More Information

Chamber Of Commerce Offices:

Daytona Beach & Halifax Area
P.O. Box 2775
Daytona Beach, 32115
255-0981

Ormond Beach Chamber
P.O. Box 874
Ormond Beach, 32074
677-3454

Newspapers:

The Daytona Beach News-Journal
911 6 Street
Daytona Beach, 32015
252-1511

The Ormond Beach Observer
P.O. Box 695
Ormond Beach, 32175
673-5577

Realtors:

Deenya Sorenson, **Adams, Cameron & Co.** 3929 S. Nova Rd. Port Orange, 32127 (761-6100)

Douglas & JoAnne Gavic, **Emerson Realty**, 322 Silver Beach, Daytona Beach 32118 (258-0555)

Karen Harden, **ERA/Hudson Realty**, 1546 Ocean Shore Blvd., Ormond Beach, 32074, (441-1400)

12. Fort Myers, Florida

Area Snapshot

Nickname: "The City of Palms"
County: Lee
Area code: 813   **Zip code:** 33901-21
Local population: 40,000   **County:** 324,000
% of population 50+: 42%
U.S. region: South west Florida (on the Gulf of Mexico)
Closest metro areas: Naples, 30 mi; Sarasota, 70 mi; Tampa, 120 mi.
Nearby areas to consider: Cape Coral, Sanibel Island
Median housing price: $82,500
Best reasons to retire here: Gorgeous beaches and barrier islands, diversified real estate market, subtropical climate, casual living.

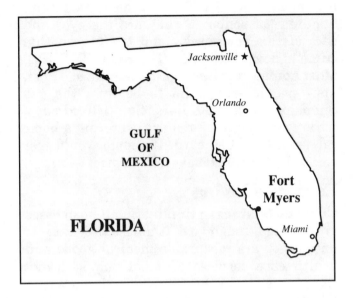

Fabulous Features

Thomas Edison made more than one great discovery when he settled in Fort Myers back in 1855. It was a bright idea to live on the dazzling Gulf of Mexico and it still is. For decades, Midwesterners have also migrated to Florida's west coast. During snowbird season, there are so many Ohio license plates it's easy to be temporarily confused as to where you are. Now it seems the state's best-kept secret is out of the bag. This area is seeing unparalleled growth, ironically because people are fleeing the congested east coast (including diehard New Yorkers). Fort Myers and its barrier islands (Captiva, Sanibel) along with the resort town of Cape Coral offer beauty, charm, sophistication, upscale living and some of the most splendid waterfront properties in the Southwest. Golf and tennis are played 365 days a year and the atmosphere is informal. Housing is very beautiful and diversified, with ample opportunities to spend in the $200,000-$400,000 range. Regardless of where and how you live, everyone has a love affair with the quartz sand beaches. In fact, newcomers often ask, "Are the beaches always so beautiful?" The answer? Only 99% of the time. As for the climate, you can set your watch by the lightning and thunder every late afternoon between May and September. But other than the brief downpours, the subtropical climate brings sunny and hot weather year-round (the average daily temperature is 75 degrees). Come and sea.

Possible drawbacks: "U-er's" are ex-residents who make a quick U-turn to Georgia or the Carolinas after living here for a short time. What's the fuss? The high humidity, the increasing cost of homes and the population boom. Land values have soared because of scarcity; waterfront property that cost $200,000 two years ago, is now $350,000-$400,000. Property taxes are up as well. The summer heat and humidity is another complaint. Still, Fort Myers is paradise to most.

"You can quote me on that"

"We moved from Iowa and honestly, we feel like we're on vacation every day and we've been here for three years already. The area has grown so much since, but for us, the pace is still slow. Our routine is wonderful and it wouldn't change no matter how many people moved in."—Mrs. P.L. S., Cape Coral

Climate

Elevation: 13'	Avg. High/ Low	Avg. Rainfall (Inches)	Avg. # Days Precip.	Avg. % Humidity
Jan.	75/52	1.6	5	81
April	85/62	2	5	72
July	91/72	8.9	15	80
Oct.	85/68	4.4	8	82
YEAR	84/64	54	-	-
# days 32° or below: 3		# days 90° or above: 123		

Let the Good Times Roll

Recreation: The expansive shoreline is all the invitation you need to enjoy water recreation year-round. Between the Gulf of Mexico, the Caloosahatchee River and Pine Island Sound, you can enjoy swimming, boating and everything under the sea. Tarpon fishing is best from Boca Grande and Pine Island. If shelling is more your style, welcome to the world's "Seashell Capital" (don't forget to bring a bag to collect sand dollars). Back on shore are some lovely parks and nature walks including Lakes Park (great paddleboating) and the Everglades Wonder Garden (exotic and native wildlife). And each winter, it's time to "batter up" with the Minnesota Twins (their new spring training stadium is a beaut) and the Sun Sox, a senior league. Get into the swing of things at the more than 25 private and public courses in the area, and don't assume that Florida's flat topography will bore you. Famous golf architects like Fazio and Hills have built enough double doglegs and Cape Cod bunkers to challenge the pros.

Culture: From Bach to rock, the Barbara B. Mann Performing Arts Hall of the University of South Florida brings year-round shows, concerts and other entertainment. It's also the home of the Southwest Florida Symphony Orchestra. The Nature Center and Planetarium and the Fort Myers Historical Museum are other noteworthy offerings. The Lee County Alliance of Arts brings numerous events to town.

Annual events: Edison Festival of Light (Feb.); Pine Island Seafood Festival (March); Munich in Cape Coral (Oct.); Taste of the Town (Nov.).

Local Real Estate

According to "Florida Trend" Magazine, Fort Myers has the sixth best housing market in the state in terms of land values and opportunities for buying waterfront property. With the widening of State Road 78, the focus is on Pine Island Sound where land is still available at down-to-earth prices. In town, the Iona/McGregor subdivisions, near the beach, are making lots of waves. But taxes are rising faster than the tide, forcing many retirees to look for more affordable homes inland.

Median price for single family home: $82,500. Resales for under $150,000 go like hotcakes because there aren't enough of them. Waterfront homes sell for $350,000-$400,000.

Median price for 2BR condo: $70,000-$80,000 for small townhouses and villas. Golf course communities start at around $100,000.

Rental housing market: The rental market is very strong, with many retirees staying in condos for months at a time. Reflections, Windows, Vernadas and Iona Lakes are popular locations. Rentals start at $500/mo, but there is more available at $700-$850/mo. Don't forget there's a 9% bed tax for rentals for less than 6 months.

Common housing styles & features: Concrete block with stucco overlay. Some are framed. Newer homes all have vaulted ceilings, carports or garages and beautiful landscaping. Ranch style split plans are popular.

Amenities in condo developments: Clubhouses, pools.

Nearby areas to consider: Cape Coral, Sanibel Island. **Unique features of these areas:** Cape Coral, across the river, has traditionally been an affordable retirement haven, with housing prices in the $50s and $60s. The homes are smaller and older. The area offers ample shopping and services and gorgeous waterfront views. Sanibel Island is the other side of the coin, with exclusive estates and waterfront properties commanding $400,000 and up (and worth every penny). This picturesque community is the ultimate in gulf front living.

What Things Cost

Lee County's overall living costs are considered average for Florida.

Gas company: No natural gas.

Electric company: Florida Power & Light *(332-2627)*. Avg. is 78.78/mo. with summer months possibly doubling.

Water/sewer: Lee County Utilities *(335-2800)*. Avg. bill is $30.73. Refundable connection fee: $30.

Phone company: United Telephone *(335-8201)*. Basic monthly service runs $9.45. Installations start at $50 plus labor.

Car registration/license: New residents must obtain a Florida driver's license within 30 days. Title fees: new vehicles: $29.25; used: $33.25. Initial registration: (cars and trucks): $100. New residents impact fee: $295 (One-time charge applies to vehicle previously titled outside of Florida). Driver's license: (6 years): $20 annual. License tags (1 yr): Vehicles up to 2,499 lbs.: $34.60; vehicles 2,500 to 3,499 lbs.: $42.60; vehicles 3,500 lbs. and over: $52.60.

The Tax Ax

Sales tax: 6% (Prescription drugs and food exempt except prepared/restaurant foods).

State income tax: None.

Retirement income: Florida ranks first among 10 popular retirement states for taking the smallest tax bite from retirees. There's no income tax, no death or estate taxes (over and above federal credit) and property taxes are still lower than the northeastern cities where many people migrate from.

Property taxes & tax breaks: Florida offers a $25,000 homestead exemption for permanent residents whose principal home is in Florida. Property taxes are based on millage rates. To estimate annual property taxes in Florida, deduct $25,000 from the appraised value of the home (provided you own and reside in the house by Dec. 31), multiply the balance times the millage rate and divide by 1,000. Average millage rates in Fort Myers are 20.1668 per $1,000 of valuation. A home appraised at $200,000 would run $3,529/yr. Tax appraiser's office *(335-2294)*.

Medical Care

Major hospitals/regional medical centers: The Gulf Coast Hospital, opened in 1990, offers a full range of services, and deep discounts to seniors. It features a plan that entitles Medicare patients to waive their deductible and out-of-pocket expenses for inpatient care. For those with commercial insurance, substantial discounts are offered on inpatient and outpatient care. The hospital also offers monthly, "Dining with the Doctor," a healthy meal and discussion. "Alive 55" teaches safe driving techniques. JCAH-accredited **Southset Florida Regional Medical Center** specializes in open heart surgery, kidney transplants and oncology. For seniors, there's "A Walk for Your Heart," program five days a week. **Lee Memorial**, also JCAH-accredited, specializes in cancer and coronary care. Its free Older Adult Share Club provides health screenings, seminars and other services. **Cape Coral Hospital** (JCAH-accredited) has all private rooms and free transportation to and from day surgery and radiology treatments. It offers a diabetes center, rehabilitative care, general surgical, a lifeline emergency response system and classes and support groups. **Emergency medical services (EMS):** Lee County offers basic and advanced life support vehicles with telemetry and certified EMTs and paramedics. Avg. response time is 4 minutes. **Physician's referral:** SW Florida Regional *939-8414*; Lee Memorial *334-5900*; Gulf Memorial *768-8400*; Cape Coral *574-0309*.

Continuing Education

Edison Community College has a Lifelong Learning Center with courses such as "Cautious Investing." The fees are only $1 for every two-hour course *(489-9220)*. Adult and Community Education offers everything including "zero-scaping" (landscaping design to help the water shortages). Residents pay 50¢ per hour and classes run 2-3 hours one evening for seven weeks *(334-7172)*.

Services for Seniors

Age Link is a solid source of information and referrals *(337-1179)*. The North Fort Myers Senior Center offers bridge and bingo, swimming, dances and more. Membership is $12/yr. *(997-7133)*. Senior News is a monthly newsletter with the latest events and services. Available free at the library and other distribution centers. **AARP** meets the fourth Monday of the month at the Redeemer Lutheran Church (2800 Broadway).

Crime & Safety

The biggest headaches are break-ins (attributed to transients who come to the resorts and restaurants for work) and drug abuse in certain sections of town. For the most part, the area is quite safe and many people told us that they read about crime in the paper but sometimes feel it's happening elsewhere. They have the highest accolades for law enforcement in both the city and county.

Earning a Living

Current business climate: Over the next two years, Lee County expects to get more new residents than any other county in Southwest Florida. That holds a lot of promise for real estate and the retail and service sector. **Help in starting a business:** The Small Business Development Center will offer guidance with loan applications, licensing, marketing and other start-up matters *(481-2131).* **The job market:** The job prospects are fairly good, with tourist-related work available most of the year. There are job placement programs for seniors through the Senior Job Bank *(278-7140 ext. 30)* and Hire a Senior *(959-5872).*

When the Kids Come to Visit

Thomas A. Edison Home: Burroughs Home; Henry Ford Home; Fort Myers Historical Museum; Nature Center of Lee County/Planetarium; Greyhound Racing; Shell Factory; Waltzing Waters; J. "Ding" Darling Wildlife Refuge; Everglades Wonder Gardens; Wooten's Everglade Air Boat Tours.

Getting Around Town

Roads & interstates: I-75 merges with Alligator Alley, US 41, State Road 31, Highway 80. **Airports & airlines:** Southwest Florida Regional Airport is served by 15 major airlines including Delta, American, United and USAir. **Public transportation:** Lee County Transit seniors with a Medicare card a fare of 35¢. Or they can purchase an unlimited pass for $15/month. **Managing without a car:** It would be difficult.

What Residents Already Know

It's nice to be at one with mother nature, but don't feed the animals. Wild raccoons openly beg food in picnic areas and will bite if irritated or startled. Also, the coral snakes (poisonous) and king snakes (harmless) look a lot alike with alternating rings of coral, black and gold. Remember this rhyme: "Head of red, go ahead; head of black, stay back!" Speaking of snakes, some newcomers from a certain part of the East (no names mentioned) will offer a realtor money under the table to grab a property at a certain price. Things don't work that way down here.

For More Information

Chamber Of Commerce Office:
The Chamber of Southwest Florida
819 College Parkway, #306
Fort Myers, 33919-5121
433-3321

Newspaper:
Fort Myers News-Press
2442 Anderson Avenue
Fort Myers, 33902
335-0200

Realtors:
Lois A. Tous
Priscilla Murphy Realty
6360 Presidential Court #5
Fort Myers, 33919
482-5112

Barbara Cummings
Claude Allen Realty, Inc.
1500 Colonial Boulevard
Fort Myers, 33907
936-4621

13. Gainesville, Florida

Area Snapshot

Nickname: "The Tree City"
County: Alachua
Area code: 904   **Zip code:** 32601-32611
Local population: 90,000   **County:** 181,600
% of population 65+: 15.3%
U.S. region: North Central Florida
Closest metro areas: Jacksonville, 68 miles
Nearby areas to consider: High Springs, Newberry, Archer
Median housing price: $68,800
Best reasons to retire here: Picturesque college town, cosmopolitan but small, noticeable change of seasons, affordable, so much to do, excellent medical care.

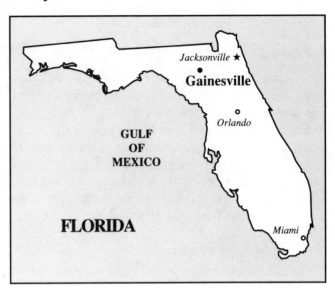

Fabulous Features

Gainesville is a gracious, tree-lined college town complete with beautiful old homes, countryside and rolling hills (yes, even in Florida). But people are enamored with this town, even moreso because it offers southern warmth and hospitality as well as a cosmopolitan lifestyle. And Gainesville boasts an intellectual and cultural climate that is lacking in many other parts of the state. Add to that the youth and vitality from the University of Florida, and one can understand how Gainesville is often compared to the beautiful town of Ann Arbor (a fine compliment). In fact, it's not surprising that in a recent study of the quality of life in 130 cities, Gainesville was ranked third. There's ample year-round recreation, housing is affordable, the health care facilities are top-notch and getting around is easy. For retirees, beautiful communities abound and yet there is a consensus that seniors are a welcome part of the population mix. Another special aspect is the change of seasons. The fall foliage is breathtaking and although the summers are scorchers, the evenings cool off considerably. Retirees we spoke to said they especially appreciated the slower pace, the lack of congestion and the fact that complete wilderness was 30 minutes away. With access to nature's lakes and bounty, Gainesville residents claim that they live in Florida's *real* magic kingdom.

Possible drawbacks: The cost of living is slightly higher than other areas in Florida, however, it is still very affordable. The summers are hot and humid—it's a great time to plan your vacations. As with many college towns, competition for part-time jobs is fierce and the rental market is tight. Finally, the recent campus murders have given this town an undeserved black eye. It would be a shame for people to reconsider this area because of these tragic, but "it could happen anywhere" events. In fact, overall, the crime rate in 1990 had decreased.

"You can quote me on that"

"We lived in several overseas locations and chose Gainesville because of the University. We're very happy here. The people are nice and easy going. Gainesville is hospitable but sophisticated. Just watch out for the summers. It gets very, very hot."—G.B.

Climate

Elevation: 165'	Avg. High/ Low	Avg. Rainfall (Inches)	Avg. # Days Precip.	Avg. % Humidity
Jan.	71/46	2.5	7	78
April	81/57	3.2	7	70
July	92/73	7.0	18	78
Oct.	83/62	4.3	8	77
YEAR	81/59	51	-	-
# days 32° or below: 18		# days 90° or above: 91		

Let the Good Times Roll

Recreation: Gainesville has 30 parks, many with tennis courts and pools. The Ironwood Golf Course (public) is an 18-hole, par 72 championship course. The area also boasts beautiful nature parks including Biven's Arm Nature Park (a wildlife nature center), Morningside Nature Center (a 280-acre wildlife sanctuary), Devil's Millhopper State Park and Paine's Prairie State Preserve (a wildlife sanctuary with museum, campground, and observation tower). There's also the Kanapaha Botanical Gardens and Lake Alice, infamous for its large, alligator population. There are more than a dozen lakes for freshwater and saltwater fishing. Don't forget, Gainesville is home of the University Gators, recognized as a powerhouse college football team that competes in the Southeastern Conference. They draw sellout crowds. The residents also love to watch their gymnastics, swimming, basketball and teams. The city hosts several sporting events, including the Florida Relays, the Gator Nationals Drag Racing Championship, jai alai, and greyhound racing.

Culture: Gainesville has so much to offer culture enthusiasts. It has its own professional dance company, Dance Alive, as well as a Chamber Orchestra. Theater and opera buffs can go to the Hippodrome theater and the Gainesville Community Playhouse. The university and Santa Fe College add to the enjoyment by bringing a variety of events to town. The university's natural history museum is ranked among the top 10 in the U.S. Their art museum and galleries also have an excellent reputation.

Annual Events: Gainesville has two annual arts and crafts festivals that attract more than 100,000 people. The Friends of the Library sponsor two book sale festivals, which are also very popular (April, Nov.) Residents also look forward to Senior Games, similar to an Olympics, which offers competition in golf, tennis and other sports.

Local Real Estate

Median price for single family home: $68,800
Median price for 2BR condo: $50,000-$70,000
Rental housing market: During the academic year, rental housing is hard to come by. When available, the prices are 3BR house: $600/mo. (difficult to find); 2BR apt.: $375/mo; 1BR apt.: $225- 275/mo. (utilities extra).
Common housing styles & features: Single story, 3BR/2BA, one-car garage or carport. Old homes are electric; new homes have gas.
Amenities in condo developments: Mid-priced units include pool and racquetball. Higher priced unit offer tennis.
Nearby communities to consider: Newberry, High Springs and Archer. **Unique features of these areas:** These communities are small and country-like within 15 minutes of the city. Housing is less expensive and acreage is greater ($50,000 can buy 2-7 acres). Also look at any area west of Gainesville. Everything there is up and coming.

What Things Cost

Overall, they're 5% over the national avg. primarily due to utilities (20% over the avg.). However, food, housing and health care costs are quite affordable compared to other counties in and out of Florida.
Gas & electric: Gainesville Regional Utilities *(334-3434)*. Average monthly gas bill is $25. If gas heat, it can avg. $85. Other monthly charges include water waste: $11-14; Storm water runoff: $3.75; Water: $6-12; Refuse: $11.75. Average monthly bill for all electric is $45-$90, with severe months (Aug., Jan.) ranging from $75-$190. There's a $10 service charge to turn on electric service and a 10% utility tax.
Phone company: Southern Bell *(800-753-2909 outside Florida)*. Basic service: $13.30/mo.

Connection charge for new home: $79, homes with existing service: $44. Deposits vary ($65-$75) depending on payment history.

Car registration/license: Title fees: new vehicles: $29.25; used: $33.25. Initial registration (cars and trucks): $100. New Residents Impact Fee: $295 (This one-time charge applies to each vehicle previously titled outside of Florida). Driver's license (good for 6 years): New residents: $20 annual. License tags (1 yr): Vehicles up to 2,499 lbs.: $34.60; vehicles 2,500-3,499 lbs.: $42.60; vehicles 3,500 lbs.+: $52.60.

The Tax Ax

Sales tax: 6% (Prescription drugs and food exempt except prepared/restaurant foods).
State income tax: None.
Retirement income: Florida ranks first among 10 popular retirement states for taking the smallest tax bite from retirees. There are no income taxes, no death taxes and low property taxes.
Property taxes & tax breaks: Florida offers a $25,000 homestead exemption for permanent residents whose principal home is in Florida. Property taxes are based on millage rates. To estimate annual property taxes in Florida, deduct $25,000 from the appraised value of the home (provided you own and reside in the house by Dec. 31), multiply the balance times the millage rate and divide by 1,000. Millage rate of 28.5 per $1,000 of assessed value. Using 1990 rates, property taxes for houses appraised at $68,000 would be $1,225. Tax appraiser *(374-5230)*.

Medical Care

Everyone we interviewed raved about the hospitals and local health care.

Major hospitals/regional medical centers: The following are all JCAH-accredited. **Shands Hospital** (at University of Florida), is a world-class teaching hospital with outstanding technical facilities as well as cardiovascular, neurology and cancer diagnosis and treatment. It also has a renowned diabetes center and gerontological care. **Alachua General Hospital** has an excellent reputation covering more than 40 specialties. **North Florida Reg-**

ional Medical Center is an innovator with the first cardiac, back and pulmonary rehab centers (and wellness center) in North Florida. **Veteran's Administration Hospital** offers a special nursing home care unit.
Emergency medical services (EMS): Calling 911 dispatches a fire engine, as firefighters are fully trained emergency medical technicians. 90% of the calls are answered within 4 min., transport by ambulance within 7 minutes.
Physician's referral: Alachua City Medical Society *376-0715*. Hospitals offer referrals.

Continuing Education

Santa Fe Community College, in conjunction with the Alachua county School Board, offers courses to seniors on a space-available basis. Fees are often waived. Courses range from German to golf and are offered at various locations. **University of Florida**: Senior registration with a fee waiver for non-credit courses is done on a seat available basis (lab fees/books are extra). Participants must be 60+ and have lived in Florida for a year.

Services for Seniors

Gainesville abounds in support groups—such as caregiver, living with cancer, alcohol abuse and bereavement. A senior help line is available *(800-262-2243)*.
Special outreach programs: RSVP (Retirees Senior Volunteer Program) coordinates seniors to help with everything from drug abuse to child advocacy. Meetings held with police for awareness of local developments *(373-7814)*. **SPICE** (Special Program Interagency Council for Elderly) meets monthly to address concerns. Thelma Boltin Recreation Center offers free activities from crafts to dancing. **AARP:** Contact Paul Urone *(375-0223)* for membership.

Crime & Safety

Crime rates are slightly higher than comparable-sized cities in Florida, but on par with other college towns. However, most seniors felt the police were doing an excellent job and did not view crime as a threat. They said 90% of property crimes are drug-related. Crimes against persons are negligible. In fact, many seniors said they still don't bother to lock doors. **Advice from the police:** They're very community-oriented and encourage seniors to get active in RSVP, which educates them about scams and other crimes. They also ask that you get involved in your Neighborhood Crime Watch program.

Earning a Living

Current business climate: Eighteen months ago things looked pretty sour for retailers and service businesses. However, as in the past, this area has been one of the first to pull out a recession and the outlook is more promising.
Programs to help you get started: GAIN (Gainesville Innovation Network) has volunteers that nurture fledgling businesses by providing expertise and help locate financial support *(466-4387)*. There is also a Small Business Development Center that provides free consulting, and a local SCORE chapter.
The job market: If you are going to work in the university, medical or consulting fields, the employment picture is good. However, for minimum-wage jobs you'll compete with students.

When the Kids Come to Visit

Morningside Nature Center (an 1880s working farm where kids can do chores, feed the animals). In addition to Gainesville's own parks and lakes, it is a short drive from Florida's biggest attractions: Silver Springs (45 mi.), Sea World (110 mi.), Busch Gardens (130 mi.), Disney World (135 mi.)

Getting Around Town

Roads & interstates: I-75, US 441; and State 26.
Airports & airlines: Gainesville Regional Airport—COMAIR, Delta, US Air, USAir Express and Atlantic South East. Jacksonville International Airport (68 mi.), American, Continental, Delta, United, US Air, PAN AM and TWA. **Public transportation:** The RTS (Regional Transit System) offers scheduled bus service but because Gainesville is so spread out, it doesn't cover the whole city. **Managing without a car:** Public transportation is not adequate enough in most areas so a car is essential.

What Residents Already Know

The city of Gainesville owns the utility company and has been able to siphon $17 million in profits to help fund city government. • If you're a health care worker, job security is solid. The medical employee payroll has jumped by 10.5% in the last year alone. • In a recent poll 59% of residents said they favored restrictions on economic growth to help curb pollution, traffic and water shortages. • As for safety, the northwest, southwest and central parts of town offer the nicest, safest neighborhoods. They're away from the university but close to shopping.

For More Information

Chamber Of Commerce Office:

Gainesville Chamber
of Commerce
300 E. University Ave.
Gainesville, 32606
336-7100

Newspaper:

Gainesville Sun
2700 So. W. 13th Street
Gainesville, 32607
374-5000

Realtor:

Mr. Joe Johnson
Bosshardt Elwood Realty
3620 NW 43rd St.
Gainesville, 32606
371-6100

14. Melbourne, Florida

Area Snapshot

Nickname: "The Harbor City"
County: Brevard (South)
Area code: 407   **Zip code:** 32901
Local population: 60,000   **County:** 415,000
% of population 65+: 14%
U.S. region: Florida's Space Coast
Closest metro areas: Orlando, 67 mi.; West Palm Beach, 105 mi.
Nearby areas to consider: Palm Bay, Indiatlantic Beach, Melbourne Beach
Median housing price: $71,300
Best reasons to retire here: Well-managed small city, not a big tourist haven, low living costs, Florida's high-tech capital, casual lifestyle on the Atlantic, great family town.

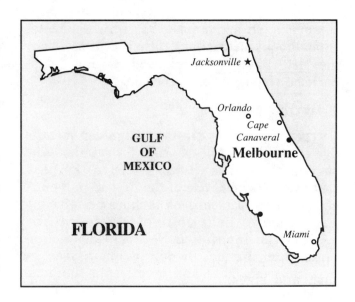

Fabulous Features

Keep your eye on the sky! Melbourne is 40 miles south of Cape Canaveral! It's also 40 miles north of Vero Beach and 60 miles east of Disney World. You could say it's at the epi-center of excitement in Florida. The wonderful thing about Melbourne is that it's a small urban city without the typical urban problems. Crime is decreasing, bucking all the national trends. It's not overly crowded. The services and infrastructure have grown with the population (too often the people come before the amenities) and for its size, it offers an abundance of programs and activities. The regional medical facilities are quite good and with the influx of high tech/space coast personnel, the population is well-educated and cosmopolitan (this is no podunk town). The population is not inundated with elderly. It's a family town, where retirees are a welcome part of the mix and are evenly distributed geographically (there's no "ghetto mentality").

Housing is extremely reasonable, there are plenty of retirement communities for those who are so inclined and taxes are proportionately low. Although the relative humidity averages 77% a year (we're talking lots of air conditioning) the average year-round temperature is a comfortable 72. The ocean breezes bring very comfortable evenings and in the winter months, you might just grab for a sweater.

Possible drawbacks: People who leave are generally the ones who came from big cities and miss the razzle dazzle. Melbourne is still relatively small and for some, it's too restrictive.•Health care is good but limited. There is only one acute care hospital in the area and Medicare assignment is not as widely accepted as it is in Florida's large retirement communities.•Rain gear is mandatory, given the 56 inches of annual precipitation.

"You can quote me on that"

"When we first retired to Florida, my wife insisted on being close to her sister in Ft. Lauderdale. I wanted to come here because it was less crowded and it didn't cost so much. A year later she finally agreed with me. We even got her sister to move with us and we all love it. It's fun here. Everything is easy to get to and you don't feel like you have to wait in line all the time."—D.V.

Climate

Elevation: 33'	Avg. High/ Low	Avg. Rainfall (Inches)	Avg. # Days Precip.	Avg. % Humidity
Jan.	73/55	2.1	6	80
April	82/60	3.5	7	72
July	90/73	7.0	16	80
Oct.	85/69	7.0	13	82
YEAR	82/64	56	-	-
# days 32° or below: 3		# days 90° or above: 78		

Let the Good Times Roll

Recreation: Any place that starts out with 33 miles of uncrowded beachfront has got to be special. But that's just where the fun begins. There's every type of fishing (deep-sea, pier, surf, and river), canoeing, boating, surfing, scuba diving, water and jet skiing—you can even do something as conventional as swim. Scuba diving at Sebastian Inlet (578 acres of state park) between Melbourne and Vero Beach is very exciting. Hunting in the woodlands is permitted. There are also 40 public parks, bike paths along many streets and thoroughfares, nine private and municipal golf courses, 63 public tennis courts, 60 private tennis courts, 2 yacht clubs and 15 marinas. If you're the type to enjoy the wildlife (and we don't mean loud parties) you'll love the Botanical Gardens, Merritt Island National Wildlife Refuge and Turkey Creek Sanctuary. In fact, this area boasts 40% of Florida's sanctuary's with over 3,000 species to observe.

Culture: Music: Brevard Performing Arts Center (the new $12.5 million center on the campus of Brevard Community College) is where the Brevard Symphony Orchestra performs), Melbourne Chamber Music Society; Space Coast Philharmonic; Theater: Indian River Players; Ensemble Theater; Brevard Civic Opera. Museums: South Brevard Historical Museum; Space Coast Science Center; Brevard Art Center and Museum.

Annual events: Senior Games hosted by Melbourne Leisure Service (Oct.); Melbourne Oktoberfest (Oct.); Senior Golf Championship (Nov.); Eggstravaganza: Annual Spring Festival (Mar.); Melbourne Arts Festival (Apr.); The Pineapple 10,000 meter run (May).

Local Real Estate

The real estate market has been up for grabs and although it's a buyer's market, there have been some very encouraging signs of life recently. Home prices range from $45,000 to $150,000. In the $60,000 range, you can buy a lovely 3BR, 2BA on the beach side. Choose from oceanfront condos, horse farms and estates, to traditional single family homes. Melbourne has traditionally been a strong market for second home buyers as well (there are many snowbirds).

Median price for single family home: $71,300. Average prices range from $95,000-$105,000 new, and $77,000 for existing.

Median price for 2BR condo: $71,000 to $120,000 (waterfront); $45,000.00 + (inland).

Rental housing market: House (1,600-1,800 sq. ft.): $750; 2BR apt.: starts at $400/mo. (if you can actually find something this low, grab it).

Common housing styles & features: One-story ranch style with garage or carport, CAC. As in most parts of Florida, there are no basements.

Amenities in condo developments: Tennis courts, swimming pools, CAC, some saunas and exercise rooms. The higher-priced units have their own washer/dryers; others have laundry rooms.

Nearby areas to consider: Palm Bay, Indiatlantic Beach, Melbourne Beach.

Unique features of these areas: Palm Bay is one of the fastest growing cities in the state, with 56,000 people. Indiatlantic and Melbourne Beach are small, quiet coastal towns with great views, great golf and great beach living. These are very popular areas for snowbirds. Housing prices are pretty much the same as in Melbourne.

What Things Cost

The U.S. Department of Labor shows that living costs are the lowest of all the high-tech regions in the country, and if housing prices are any indication, prices are as low as they go in today's economy. Compared to other Florida counties, the latest index shows Brevard county being dead center.

Gas company: City Gas Company of Florida (636-4644). Avg. mo. bill is $6 plus 63¢ per thermostat; the highest consumption is in Dec./Jan. First bill averages $43 (includes turn-on fee and processing). $30 deposit may be required. **Electric company:** Florida Power and Light Company *(631-2000).* Avg. monthly bill: $85-$90. Deposit is $160 (based on 2 month avg.) Initial service charge: $16. **Phone company:** Southern Bell *(780-2355).* Basic monthly service runs $13 + tax. Installation starts at $44.50 for existing home, $79 for new. No deposit required with good credit.

Car registration/license: New residents must obtain a Florida driver's license within 30 days of establishing residency. All applicants must take a written and vision test. Title fees: new vehicles: $29.25; used: $33.25. Initial registration (cars and trucks): $100. New residents impact fee: $295 (This one-time charge applies to each vehicle previously titled outside of Florida). Driver's license (good for 6 years): New residents: $20 annual. License tags (1 yr): vehicles up to 2,499 lbs.: $34.60; vehicles 2,500 to 3,499 lbs.: $42.60; vehicles 3,500 lbs. and over: $52.60.

The Tax Ax

Local sales tax: 6% (Prescription drugs and food exempt except prepared and restaurant foods). **State income tax:** None. **Retirement income:** Florida ranks first among 10 popular retirement states for taking the smallest tax bite from retirees. There's no income tax, no state tax on social security, no death taxes, and low property taxes. **Property tax & tax breaks:** Florida offers a $25,000 homestead exemption for permanent residents whose principal home is in Florida. Property taxes are based on millage rates. To estimate annual property taxes in Florida, deduct $25,000 from the appraised value of the home (provided you own and reside in the house by Dec. 31), multiply the balance times the millage rate and divide by 1,000. Current property taxes are assessed at 18.6358 per $1,000 valuation. Thus, a home valued at $100,000 would run $1,397/yr.

Medical Care

Major hospitals/regional medical centers: Holmes Regional Medical Center is an accred-ited hospital and the only general acute care facility in the area. A 60-bed satellite hospital is under construction for residents of Palm Bay. It is the regional center for cardiac and cancer care. It also provides home health care, hospice care and wellness programs. Helicopter transportation to Orlando or Gainesville is available for organ transplants and burn victims. With only one hospital, many snowbirds schedule surgery at home and come back to Melbourne's warm climate for recuperation. **Emergency medical services (EMS):** 4 rescue vehicles are on 24-hr. standby. Response time is 2-3 minutes. **Physician's referral:** *676-7263;* Dental: *453-8551.*

Continuing Education

Brevard Community College *(254-0305)* offers a wonderful continuing education program for seniors, with a bargain enrollment of $2. Interesting classes include "The Law and You," "Trusts, Wills and Estate Planning," "Sign Language," and "Investing in the Stock Market." In addition, special classes are offered on home health care for the Elderly (registration fee of $25 plus $80 paid to the American Red Cross). Rollins College Continuing Education at Winter Park *(646-2604)* has a line up of fascinating courses on antiques, art history, ESP and awareness, creative writing, etc. Enrollment ranges from $75 to $125. Frequent lunch symposiums cost $20.

Services for Seniors

The South Brevard Senior Association *(723-5983)* runs numerous programs and activities and is an excellent resource for community information. Media: Two publications offered to seniors include "50 Plus" (free at the seniors centers or by subscription) and "Golden Years Senior News" (monthly publication distributed free at newsstands or by subscription *(725-4888).* **AARP:** There are five local chapters in Brevard county, including Melbourne. Contact Thomas King *(984-2921).*

Crime & Safety

The Melbourne Police Department was happy to announce a 5% cut in crime over the previous year. Still, the area's growth has brought with it a need for awareness. Programs on crime prevention include Neighborhood Watch, home security surveys and lectures on personal safety and residential security. A new program on crime prevention for seniors is in the works.

Earning a Living

Current business climate: Thanks to the 11 Fortune 500 companies that have moved into the area, Melbourne is now sixth in the nation in business and income growth. The broad diversity of companies along with one of the most educated work forces in the state has paved the way for dynamic business development in all sectors. Local prognosticators say that the timing is right for entrepreneurs, or "the sky's the limit."

Help in starting a business: Contact the Melbourne/Palm Bay Area Development Council's business assistance line with questions *(800-342-0771)*.

The job market: The Space Coast Private Industry Council offers a job placement program for seniors called Title I Older Worker (JTPA), which provides on-the-job training and matches workers to jobs *(452-0150)*.

When the Kids Come to Visit

Cape Canaveral and Kennedy Space Center: 40 miles; Orlando-Disney World and EPCOT Center: 60 miles; Space Coast Science Center (a "touch and feel" museum); U.S. Astronaut Hall of Fame (Titusville); Sebastian Inlet Recreational State Park.

Getting Around Town

Roads & interstates: I-95, US-1, US-192, State Highway A1A, Beeline Expressway

Airports & airlines: Melbourne Regional Airport is served by 7 major carriers, including, American, Continental, Delta, USAir, and Comair. Orlando International Airport is a 1 hr., 15-minute drive.

Public transportation: Space Coast Area Transit and Coastal Transportation. Space Coast Area Transit offers door-to-door service to seniors from 8:45 to 2 p.m. (50¢ one-way). With recent budget cuts, they are now limiting local destinations. Some buses run free trips to the libraries, hospital, and shopping centers and Brevard Community College. Coastal Transportation has a pick-up and return service for seniors ($1 one way).

Managing without a car: It's actually doable.

What Residents Already Know

On a clear day, you can stand in your backyard and watch a launch from Kennedy Space Center. You won't ever forget it. • Forget the Ninja Turtles. The largest sea turtle nesting area in the U.S. is at Sebastian Inlet. From May to August, they come ashore and lay eggs.

For More Information

Chamber Of Commerce Office:
Greater South Brevard Area
Chamber
1005 East Strawbridge Avenue
Melbourne, 32901
728-7321

Newspapers:
Florida Today
P.O. Box 363000
Melbourne, 32936
259-5000

Orlando Sentinel
737 Apollo Blvd.
Melbourne, 32901
453-5500

Realtor:
Ms. Donna Buchanan
Melbourne Realty, Inc.
212 W. New Haven Ave.
Melbourne, 32901
800-749-3421

15. Naples, Florida

Area Snapshot

Nickname: "Seashell Shangri-La"
County: Collier
Area code: 813   **Zip code:** 33940-3799
Local population: 21,000   **County:** 145,000
% of population 65+: 35.6%
U.S. region: Southwest Florida
Closest metro areas: Fort Myers, 30 miles
Nearby areas to consider: Pelican Bay
Median housing price: $137,500
Best reasons to retire here: Small, exclusive community, one of the fastest growing metro areas in the country, a subtropical climate, excellent medical care, amenities galore, picture-perfect beaches.

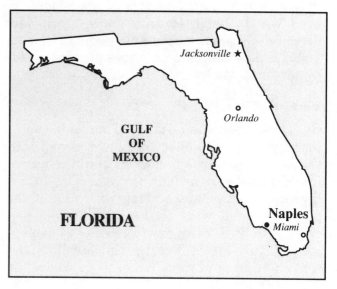

Fabulous Features

Naples sits due south of an imaginary border line that marks the beginning of the Florida's subtropical climate. The winters are delightfully warm and the summers are hot, yet many days are cooler than expected. The average daily temperature is 75, with "tropicooling" gulf breezes. Some say that Naples is the West Coast's Palm Beach, but residents beg to differ. Naples is a haven for Midwestern entrepreneurs, executives and conservative types with old money. There's very little flash and glitz, and an air of sophistication and charm pervades. In Naples, one finds high-class shopping, exclusive country clubs, posh dining and ultra luxurious homes and condos. Rentals are costly and limited. It's got some of the most gorgeous beaches in the world, truly outstanding health care and highbrow cultural events. Naples is a very hot area now (Collier County is one of the fastest growing in the country) because people think it's undiscovered territory. Natives will tell you the "nouveaus" are coming late to the party.

Possible drawbacks: Naples is a small town with limited opportunities. Without a steady circle of friends to invent activities and functions, Naples is awfully quiet (particularly at night). Also, there is no public transportation and real estate is among the highest in the state. As they say of menus without prices, if you have to ask the cost, you probably can't afford to be here.

"You can quote me on that"

"My husband and I drove all over the West coast of Florida looking for a quiet, beautiful retreat. We fell in love with Naples right away. We love the climate, the beaches, and our condominium is gorgeous. I wake up every morning, walk out on the terrace overlooking the Gulf and can't believe what a dream-come-true this place is. As soon as my husband found some golfing buddies, he felt the same way."—S.S.

"We moved to Naples almost 15 years ago from Chicago. It was a quiet, charming community. Now there are so many people here and it's so congested in season, we're saddened by what's become of our home. Don't send anyone else here. Send them to the East Coast."—L.M.

Climate

Elevation: 13'	Avg. High/Low	Avg. Rainfall (Inches)	Avg. # Days Precip.	Avg. % Humidity
Jan.	75/52	1.6	5	81
April	85/62	2	5	72
July	91/74	8.9	18	80
Oct.	85/68	4.2	8	82
YEAR	84/64	54	-	-
# days 32° or below: 3		# days 90° or above: 123		

Let the Good Times Roll

Recreation: Here's your chance to enjoy year-round golf on the Gulf. Some of the most exclusive private golf communities and clubs in Florida are here in Naples—more than 35 different courses to check out (more per capita than anywhere else in the world). There's only 7 miles of beaches, but they're 7 of the most gorgeous sugar sand (quartz) miles you've ever laid eyes on (renown for shelling, sailing, fishing, boating and enjoying). The tennis is terrific at the Naples Bath & Tennis Club, the World Tennis Center and at city parks. You can really go overboard with backwater fishing. Take a trip to the Everglades National Park and the 10,000 Islands for a day of memorable catches, or stay right in town at the Naples Pier (1,000 ft. into the Gulf). If it can be done outdoors, it can be done in Naples—in style!

Culture: Philharmonic Center for the Arts in Pelican Bay (a new $19 million dollar concert hall for the Naples/Marco Philharmonic and other celebrated performers); Naples Theater Ensemble, (professional productions year round); Naples Concert Band at Cambier Park; Naples Art Association, some of the state's most unique art galleries, including the Naples Art Gallery (the foyer alone is worth the trip).

Annual events: The Aetna Challenge: Southwest Florida's only Senior PGA Tour (Feb.); Swamp Buggy Races (March, Oct.); Super Jazz Under the Stars (Summer); Great Dock Canoe Races (Spring); Windsurfers Regatta (Oct.); Naples Arts Festival (Spring); The Goodland Mullet and Everglades Seafood Festival (Summer).

Local Real Estate

Naples real estate offerings are some of the most luxurious in the state. The private golf communities are especially prestigious, with championship courses, breathtaking homes on the fairway and every amenity you could ask for. Homes and villas range in price from $200,000-$600,000. The oceanfront property is also spectacular, and compared to Florida's east coast, you don't have to spend a million to buy something palatial (a mere 3/4 of a million will do the job).

Median price for single family home: $137,500 (represents the low end of the spectrum.) Avg. prices start at $175,000 and span into 7 figures. Homes sell for approx. 94% of asking prices.

Median price for a 2BR condo: Prices range from $60,000 to $300,000 and up.

Rental housing market: House (1,600-1,800 sq. ft.) $1,000/mo. and up, 2BR apt.: $500-$1,200/ mo. The rental market is very tight unless you're in the high end category.

Common housing styles & features: The architecture in Naples is modern, mostly 1-story (although 2-story homes are cropping up) with distinctive interiors and fabulous landscape design. Elaborate master suites are in great demand.

Amenities in condo developments: Many are turnkey units (furnished, maintenance-free) with golf and tennis, clubhouse, pools and total amenities.

Nearby community to consider: Pelican Bay (in Naples). **Unique features of this area:** Pelican Bay (a Westinghouse community) is a private, environmentally protected community offering some of the most breathtaking views in Naples. It has golfing, fabulous beachfront properties, restaurants and parks, and com-plete privacy. Homes: $425,000; condos: $225,000-$375,000. Beachfront runs higher—3BR/2.5BA: $425,000; condos range from $225,000 to $375,000.

What Things Cost

According to the Florida Price Level Index (1990), Collier County is ranked overall as the 4th most expensive in Florida (behind Broward, Dade and Monroe/Key West), yet housing is ranked only 1% above average compared to the other counties. If not for Naples, Collier County would probably fare better, because according to the Florida Realtor's Association, the only other place in Florida where it costs more to buy a house, on average, is Key West.

Gas company: There is no natural gas service. Heat is mostly electric.

Electric company: Florida Power & Light *(262-1322)*. Avg. monthly bill is $75.46. There is an initial connection fee of $16.

Phone company: United Telephone Systems *(800-335-3111)*. Basic monthly service runs $11.05 to 13.70/mo. Installation start at $50. Deposit may not be required.

Car registration/license: New residents must obtain a Florida driver's license within 30 days of establishing residency. Title fees: new vehicles, $29.25; used, $33.25. Initial registration (cars and trucks): $100. New residents impact fee: $295 (This one-time charge applies to each vehicle previously titled outside of Florida). Driver's license: (good for 6 years): New residents: $20 annual. License tags (1 yr): Vehicles up to 2,499 lbs.: $34.60; vehicles 2,500 to 3,499 lbs.: $42.60; vehicles 3,500 lbs. and over: $52.60.

The Tax Ax

Sales tax: 6% (Prescription drugs/food exempt except prepared/restaurant foods)

State income tax: None.

Retirement income: Florida ranks first among 10 popular retirement states for taking the smallest tax bite from retirees. There's no income tax, no death taxes and low property taxes.

Property taxes & tax breaks: Florida offers a $25,000 homestead exemption for permanent residents whose principal home is in Florida. Property taxes are based on millage rates. To estimate annual property taxes in Florida, deduct $25,000 from the appraised value of the home (provided you own and reside in the house by Dec. 31), multiply the balance times the millage rate and divide by 1,000. Millage rates in Naples have more than 200 variations. For specific neighborhood rates, call the tax appraiser's office *(774-8999)*. It's estimated

that a home valued at $230,000 would pay $2,974 (at a millage rate of 14.506).

Medical Care

It's comforting when there is a universal agreement among residents that the quality of medical care is superb. Everyone we spoke to raved about the modern facilities, how kind the nursing staffs are and the top caliber of available physicians living in the area. One woman summed it up: "I have never wanted to be sick anywhere, but if I was going to need a doctor's care or surgery, God help me to be in this town when it happens." **Major hospitals/regional medical centers: Naples Community Hospital** is an outstanding private, accredited facility for acute care and emergencies. It handles cardiac catheterization, open heart surgery, and burn victims. The hospital is not a single building; it encompasses a wellness center, a health resource center, exercise facilities, and a day surgery facility. In addition, the **Beatrice Branch Briggs Senior Evaluation Center** is located on the hospital grounds. Seniors can come down and have their questions answered, or they can call for a phone consults. There's even an excellent library with books explaining various conditions and diseases in laymen's terms *(262-4221)*. **North Collier Hospital** is a satellite facility of Naples Community Hospital. Everyone who sees it swears it looks more like a hotel than a hospital, with its luxurious ambience and bright skylights. **Emergency medical services (EMS):** 8 EMS stations in the county with 9 road vehicles on road and 1 helicopter. Response time is 6 minutes (15 minutes in outlying areas). **Physician's referral:** *262-4221*; Dental: *597-4944*.

Continuing Education

Edison Community College *(489-9235)* offers a Lifelong Learning Program where interesting two-hour classes, such as financial planning and massage therapy, cost $1 (state residents only). Classes in the continuing education program include creative writing and introduction to computers. Enrollment is $18-$20. The Collier County Public Schools also offer adult education on money management, mythology, computers, etc. *(643-2700)*. Enrollment is $5 to $18.

Services for Seniors

The **Collier County Council on Aging**, a non-profit organization, meets throughout the year and serves as a wonderful resource for retired residents. They publish a biannual Directory of Community Services, which helps familiarize you with available programs and offerings *(263-2601)*. **AARP:** The local AARP chapter can be reached at *(775-3193)*.

Crime & Safety

The Naples Police Department has programs on crime prevention including classes on recognizing consumer fraud and medicare scams, free home security and burglar alarm analysis. In addition, it runs a volunteer program in which seniors living alone are called daily to check on their well being. According to the Department and statewide statistics, Collier County and Naples has one of the lowest crime rates in the state. This is attributed to the fact that the tightly knit community is off the beaten path, discouraging the wrong kind of people from "just driving through town."

Earning a Living

Current business climate: Naples is one of the fastest growing metro areas in the country, and yet it's not been spared the "now you see it, now you don't" phenomenon that has plagued the retail and service sectors throughout the state. Shops and restaurants open and close at an alarming rate. Still, with the tremendous growth, everyone is betting that as potential goes, Naples is the place to be. **Help in starting a business:** Contact the Economic Development Council *(263-8989)* to learn about financial incentives for new businesses. **The job market:** Part-time, minimum wage jobs are more readily available during the tourist season (hotels, restaurants and boutiques hire extra employees). But frankly, the retirees who settle here aren't looking for employment opportunities.

When the Kids Come to Visit

Everglades National Park; Jungle Larry's Zoological Park; Collier Automotive Museum; Teddy Bear Museum; Indian Villages and Exhibits at Fort Myers.

Getting Around Town

Roads & interstates: I-75 (Alligator Alley); US-41 (Tamiami Trail).
Airports & airlines: South Florida Regional Airport at Fort Myers (45 min.) served by Delta and most other major carriers. The Naples Airport offers shuttles to Orlando and Tampa for connecting flights.
Public transportation: There is *no* local bus service. Regularly scheduled trolley service brings people to the Olde Marine Marketplace and Tin City (wonderful shopping and restaurants on the bayfront).
Managing without a car: Don't try it.

What Residents Already Know

Never head out to the beach unless you bring a bucket. You never know when you'll come across a shark's eye, a moon snail or a calico scallop (seashells, of course). If you want to fit in immediately upon arrival, just complain about all the newcomers ruining the peace and serenity of Naples.

For More Information

Chamber Of Commerce Office:
Naples Area Chamber of Commerce
3620 Tamiami Trail North
Naples, 33940-3799
262-6141

Newspaper:
Naples Daily News
1075 Central Ave.
Naples, 33940
262-3161

Realtor:
Ms. Jean Cardin
Coldwell Banker
4700 Tamiami Trail
Naples, 33940
261-1551

16. St. Petersburg, Florida

Area Snapshot

Nickname: "The Sunshine City"
County: Pinellas
Area code: 813   **Zip code:** 33700-99
Local population: 250,000   **County:** 839,891
% of population 65+: 26%
U.S. region: Florida West Coast (Central)
Closest metro areas: Tampa, 10 miles; Orlando, 103 miles
Nearby areas to consider: Tierra Verde, Clearwater
Median housing price: $69,000
Best reasons to retire here: Year-round sunshine, outdoor recreation, affordable housing/taxes, city-wide programs and services, world's biggest day camp for seniors.

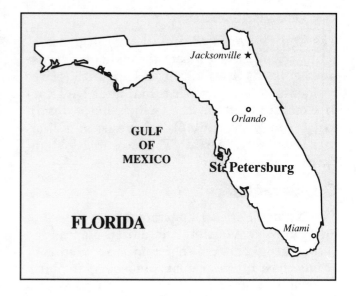

Fabulous Features

While some retirement locales are suddenly hot then not, St. Petersburg is one of the country's few havens that has never lost its appeal. Located in the heart of the Tampa Bay region and boasting more than 300 miles of magnificent shoreline, this famous Florida city is 100 percent committed to the well-being of its senior population. Yet, people are surprised to find out the median age here is actually 42, not 72. The thriving business community and commercial vitality has done away with the "old" image. In the past few years the downtown has been revitalized, resulting in what *Time* magazine's architect critic called the most beautiful urban waterfront in the country. The only thing that has gone unchanged is the year-round sunshine. On average, it disappears only 4 days a year, while the annual temperature hovers around 73. There's golf and tennis, water sports, beaches, professional sporting events, annual festivals, and more. For an outdoor city, the level of indoor activities is no less impressive with education programs at Eckerd College, first-rate museums, and more than 5,000 civic clubs and organizations. Many of the city's programs are used as models for other communities. Today's St. Pete is a far cry from its former status as "God's waiting room." People come here to live, not die.

Possible drawbacks: St. Petersburg is a big city, and with big cities come urban problems. Drug-related crime, although hardly on par with New York and Los Angeles, is a staple item in the paper. Property taxes are on the rise, medical costs are catching up with Florida's east coast and if there's not a crowd at an event, people think they've got the wrong time and date.

"You can quote me on that"

"We retired to Pompano Beach in 1984 and thought we were happy. Then we came to visit friends in St. Pete and couldn't believe how much nicer they had it. It was cheaper to live and not so crowded. We moved here a year later and have never looked back."—Mrs. S.L.

"What's not to like? The whole city caters to us. I think they must do more for senior citizens here than anywhere else in the world. I take classes at Eckerd College and I just heard my new teacher is going to be James Michener. This is unbelievable."—A.B.

Climate

Elevation: 25'	Avg. High/ Low	Avg. Rainfall (Inches)	Avg. # Days Precip.	Avg. % Humidity
Jan.	71/60	2.3	6	80
April	82/72	2.1	5	72
July	90/82	8.4	16	80
Oct.	84/75	2.5	7	79
YEAR	82/72	49	-	-
# days 32° or below: 6		# days 90° or above: 85		

Let the Good Times Roll

Recreation: St. Petersburg is synonymous with beaches and parks. Boyd Hill Nature Park is a 216-acre preserve with nature trails off of Lake Maggiore for walks, night hikes and photography. Straub Park, on the waterfront features sports, health exhibits, concerts, big name entertainers and festivals. The tarpon are biting at Ft. DeSoto Park where five islands join to form a beautiful county park. It's also a bird, plant and animal sanctuary with campgrounds. Golfers have their choice of many private clubs, and two municipal courses, Mangrove Bay (an 18-hole championship course) and Twin Brooks (a par 54, 18-hole course) hold up to scrutiny as well.

Culture: The gorgeous new Bay Front Center is a 2,000-seat arena that presents broadway shows, the ballet, opera, and more. St. Petersburg Museum of Fine Arts contains an eclectic grouping of modern and traditional paintings, and sculpture. The internationally acclaimed Salvador Dali Museum houses the world's largest collection of the surrealist's paintings. The Florida Sun Coast Dome is the giant new stadium and arena for sporting events, concerts and more. The most incredible news is the city's purchase of The Coliseum Ballroom (remember it in "Cocoon?") featuring weekly ballroom dances, and more. The Pier, a newly renovated city landmark, offers food and festivals galore!

Annual events: The city is host to more than 400 events a year, including: International Folk Fair: food fests, song and dance (Feb.); Festival of States: concerts, sporting events, car shows, exhibitions, etc. (Spring); Demen's Landing Park: setting for the American Stage Company's annual "Shakespeare in the Park." Good Life Celebration (for seniors 55 +): 10 days of parties and competitions; Artworks: festival of sights, sounds images celebrating the arts community (May); Sun Coast Tarpon Round-up: the largest "single fish" sport fishing event in the nation. (May-July).

Local Real Estate

Still a buyer's market, St. Pete has a glut of almost 8,000 low- to medium-priced homes. Waterfront on Snell Isle and the northeast section of town are two bright spots for sellers. **Median price for single family home:** $69,000. New homes range $80,000-$120,000. Resales in the 50s, but most avg. $75,000.
Median price for 2BR condo: $60,000-$70,000
Rental housing market: Available in virtually every type community within the area. 2BR, 2BA, 1,200+ sq. ft.: $675-$950/mo.; 3BR, 2BA, 1,600 square feet will be $725-$1,100/mo. Premium prices for waterfront.
Common housing styles & features: Virtually all homes are ranch style; most are tiled roofs with Florida rooms and lanais. Avg. lot size is 75 x 100. Restored 2BR bungalows downtown are very affordable. A beautiful community with full amenities is the Pasadena Golf and Country Club.
Amenities in condo developments: Many have club rooms, activities, pools, tennis courts, golf courses and beach front. Sun City Center (45 min. east) is a self-contained planned community with every conceivable facility and service (medical, shopping, golf, etc.) Condos average $85,000 (homes sell for $135,000).
Nearby areas to consider: Clearwater, Tierra Verde. **Unique features:** Clearwater (18 mi.) is a lovely year-round resort community with many services and activities. Housing ranges from waterfront condos to southern-style ranches to cottages. Prices are comparable to St. Petersburg. Tierra Verde is an exclusive residential island off St. Petersburg Beach. Prices range from $350,000-$800,000. 2BR condos start at $150,000.

What Things Cost

Overall living costs are average for Florida. Utilities are 14% above while housing is 7%

below. Health care is 7% above. Much is available for free, and eating out is still the number-one inexpensive pastime.

Gas company: Peoples Gas System *(895-3621)*. Avg. for 2-person household: $20-$60/mo. Oct.-Jan. avg.: $50-$100/mo.. $10 charge for reading meter with existing gas on; $25 charge for gas to be turned on and meter read. Deposits not required.

Electric company: Florida Power Corp. *(895-8711)*. Avg.: $80-$150/mo. for 2-person household. Dec./Jan. avg.: $150/mo. $140 deposit waived with utility reference letter.

Phone company: GTE General Telephone *(800-282-2525 in Florida only)*. Local basic service: $11.63/mo. Installations start at $53.25.

Car registration/license: New residents must obtain a Florida driver's license within 30 days. Title Fees: new: $29.25; used: $33.25. Initial registration: (cars/trucks): $100. New residents impact fee: $295 (One-time charge applies to vehicles previously titled outside Florida). Driver's license (6 yrs.): new residents: $20/yr.. License tags (1 yr.): Vehicles up to 2,499 lbs.: $34.60; 2,500 to 3,499 lbs.: $42.60; 3,500 lbs. and over: $52.60.

The Tax Ax

Sales tax: 6% (Prescription drugs and food exempt except prepared/restaurant foods). **State income tax:** None. **Retirement income:** Florida ranks first among 10 popular retirement states for taking the smallest tax bite from retirees. There's no income tax, no state tax on, no death taxes and low property taxes. **Property taxes & tax breaks:** Florida offers a $25,000 homestead exemption for permanent residents whose principal home is Florida. Property taxes are based on millage rates. Deduct $25,000 from the appraised value of the home (provided you own and reside in the house by Dec. 31), multiply the balance times the millage rate and divide by 1,000. In St. Petersburg, the rule of thumb is that property taxes range from just under 1% of assessed value. Tax Assessor *(892-7652)*.

Medical Care

Major hospitals & regional medical centers: There are 22 hospitals in Pinellas county.

Bayfront Medical Center specializes in cancer, cardiac care, and rehabilitation (head injuries, physical therapy), It also has a Level-I emergency/trauma center with helicopter service, an imaging center and a Center for Women's Health. **St. Anthony's General** specializes in gerontology, cardiac and cancer care, orthopedics, and laser surgery. **Bay Pines Veterans Administration Medical Center** (the largest in the city) has all major specialties. **Palms of Pasadena Hospital** has an excellent laser center and numerous senior services. All of the above are JCAH-accredited. **Emergency medical services (EMS):** The fire department oversees 11 paramedic units and serves as the first response team. Response time: 4 1/2 min. Medical transport is handled by Medic One and Life Fleet. **Physician's referral:** Pinellas County Medical Society *541-1159*.

Continuing Education

Eckerd College is recognized as one of the five most innovative liberal arts colleges in the U.S. Its outstanding programs for seniors draw retired professionals into the classroom to share lifetime experiences. The Program for Experienced Learners (PEL) offers a fully accredited degree completion program specifically designed for adult learners *(867-1166 ext. 226)*. St. Petersburg Jr. College is rated one of the nations top 10 junior colleges. Adult Education Program entitles seniors to enroll free in classes with openings *(341-3600)*. University of South Florida (St. Petersburg campus) is internationally renowned for its coastal and offshore research areas. Seniors take classes for free on a space-available basis. The St. Pete campus has the largest senior enrollment in the country *(893-9142)*. Ambassador Program is to orient new residents *(442-1171)*.

Services for Seniors

The St. Petersburg Office on Aging serves as a bridge between the community and older citizens, monitoring hundreds of services and programs *(893-7102)*. Its Sunshine Center provides social, recreational and educational programs including seminars, political forums, musical entertainment, travelogues, fitness, painting, etc. *(893-7101)*. Four other senior centers are located throughout the city.

Crime & Safety

There are scores of senior citizens crime prevention groups. Common-sense procedures are reviewed to avoid the most common crimes—cons, purse snatchings, etc. Neighborhood Watch programs are effective (burglaries are down). However, there has been an increase in drug-related crimes such as drive-by shootings, armed robberies, etc. For the most part, both the perpetrators and the victims of serious crimes are products of the drug culture.

Earning a Living

Current business climate: Tourism is the number-one industry but there's added diversification with high-tech, light industry and service-related trade. With the huge population boom, the area is primed for new businesses.

Help in starting a business: Contact the Small Business Development Center at the University of South Florida (Tampa campus) for help *(974-4274)*. The city's Economic Development Office has a funding agency as well as a Retention Program for existing small business *(893-7788)*.

The job market: The city offers Workforce 2000, training and placement program specifically for seniors (55+) who want to get into today's job market *(545-4511)*. The outlook is good, with unemployment at 4.9% (well under the national average). Municipal job openings *(893-7033)*. Job Service of Florida *(893-2255)*.

When the Kids Come to Visit

Great Explorations: Hands-on museum, Halloween House of Horrors and a baseball exhibit. Endless attractions are within driving distance: Disney World, Epcot Center, MGM Studios (Orlando); Busch Gardens, Sea World (Tampa); and the Ringling Museum (Sarasota).

Getting Around Town

Roads & interstates: I-275 ties St. Petersburg to Tampa, I-4 West to the Atlantic coast, heading toward Orlando, southbound I-275 provides direct link to Sarasota and southern part of state. **Airports & airlines:** Tampa International Airport (20 min.) is served by 22 national and international carriers. **Public transportation:** Pinellas Suncoast Transit Authority has scheduled service throughout the city daily. Senior fares are 40¢ + 5¢ for transfers (with a Medicaid card or PSTA card). A monthly pass is $35. **Managing without a car:** It's very easy.

What Residents Already Know

Once you live here, you'll understand the bumper stickers that reads, "Pray for me. I drive US-19."•The *St. Petersburg Times* is consistently ranked as one of the top 10 newspapers in the country.•The city is most proud of the wealth of new research institutes including the U.S. Geology Survey which moved from Woods Hole, Mass.

For Your Information

Chamber Of Commerce Office:
St. Petersburg Chamber
of Commerce
P.O. Box 1371
St. Petersburg, 33731
821-4069

Newspaper:
St. Petersburg Times
P.O. Box 1121
St. Petersburg, 33731
893-8111

Realtors:
Stacey Dixon and
Katherine McClain
Marie Powell and Assoc.
7601 9th St. North
St. Petersburg, 33702
800-352-7325 ext. 390

Joe Delk
Marie Powell and Assoc.
3325 66th St. North
St. Petersburg, 33710
381-2345

17. Sarasota, Florida

Area Snapshot

Nickname: "The Culture Coast"
County: Sarasota
Area code: 813   **Zip code:** 34233
Local population: 52,288   **County:** 261,400
% of population 65+: 31.8%
U.S. region: Florida West Coast
Closest metro areas: Tampa, 50 miles, Fort Myers, 70 miles
Nearby areas to consider: Long Boat Key, Bradenton
Median housing price: $92,075
Best reasons to retire here: Gorgeous Gulf Coast city, impressive cultural offerings, exciting real estate, subtropical climate, large retirement area.

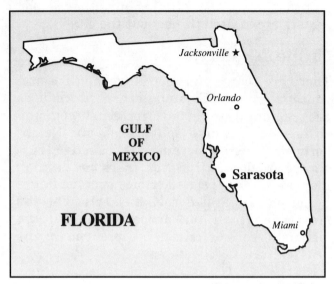

Fabulous Features

There is no place like Sarasota for a comfortable, classy, action-packed retirement. The city has planned well for the immense growth and there's always something new coming in or going on. Everything you could ask for in outdoor recreation, culture, and a high-quality of life is at your doorstep (or at least within a 15-minute drive). Unlike Naples, which practically votes you into residency, Sarasota has a compatible mix of wealthy (and very wealthy) with middle class folks, all of whom can take advantage of the beauty and the ambience. For a small town, the biggest surprise is the quantity and quality of culture. Patrons of the arts are unabashed in their praise for the theater, symphony, opera, dance, and performing arts. The variety in the housing market is also astounding, offering magnificent luxury homes, large and small condo developments, old tree-lined neighborhoods, new golf course communities. You name it and it's here in every price range. And then there is Sarasota's other coveted prizes: the beaches, (you could live here for 20 years and never tire of strolling on Siesta Key), and the downtown waterfront area. Complete with dazzling skyscrapers, gourmet restaurants and fashionable St. Armand's Circle, this town makes you wonder if there is any other town this size that has this much to share. For the answer, just ask the more than 7,000 people who move down every year. Sarasota is a city you don't dare to compare.

Possible drawbacks: Sarasota's subtropical climate means extreme summer heat and humidity and almost 23 inches of rainfall. • Non-stop flights from the New York area and other eastern cities are very limited. • Snowbird season brings flocks of traffic, although new roads have eased much of the congestion.

"You can quote me on that"

"When we decided to move from Indiana, we drove all over Florida looking for we didn't know what. Until we stopped here. We looked at each other and said this it. When we found out there was a temple and an active Jewish community, we couldn't get here fast enough. That was 10 years ago and we love it as much now as we did then. Maybe more. We walk on the beach, play tennis, try new restaurants with friends. The area is so beautiful and has so much to offer we feel very fortunate to make this our home."—Mr and Mrs. H.H.

Climate

Elevation: 25'	Avg. High/ Low	Avg. Rainfall (Inches)	Avg. # Days Precip.	Avg. % Humidity
Jan.	71/60	2.3	6	80
April	82/72	2.1	5	72
July	90/82	8.4	16	80
Oct.	84/75	2.5	7	79
YEAR	82/72	49	-	-
# days 32° or below: 6		# days 90° or above: 85		

Let the Good Times Roll

Recreation: The 35 miles of beautiful beaches are perfect for snorkeling, fishing, sailing, waterskiing and motor boating. Golf was introduced to the U.S. in Sarasota, so it's only fitting there are close to 3 dozen courses, including the 36-hole Tournament Players Club. Myakka and Oscar Scherer State Parks are perfect for walks in the wetlands. Jogging trails and public tennis courts are everywhere. For more than 25 years, the Chicago White Sox have gone through Spring Training here. The new Ed Smith Stadium is fabulous (the Sarasota White Sox play April through August).

Culture: The County Arts Council offers a 24-hr. hotline *(359-ARTS)*. Check out: The Ringling Museum of Art (10,000-piece collection making it the state's most distinguished art museum); Van Wezel Performing Arts Hall (dance companies, Broadway shows, international celebrities, orchestras); The Asolo Performing Arts Center ($10 million film and theater facility); The Florida Studio Theater; The Florida Symphonic Band; The Sarasota Opera; The Players Theater of Sarasota; Florida West Coast Symphony; The Sarasota Ballet.

Annual events: Chrysler Cup; PGA Seniors Tour (February); Suncoast Offshore Grand Prix: national powerboat race to benefit handicapped children (July 4); French Foreign Film Festival (November); Ringling Medieval Fair (March); Ringling Brothers perform new acts (November-January); Royal Lippizan Stallions (Austria's famous performers are here January-March).

Local Real Estate

Even though residents recently rejected a building moratorium, new construction has slowed anyway. But with demand still brisk, the result is fast-rising property values and taxes. The prediction is that in a few years inventory will be tight and prices will soar. Some are comparing the future to Carmel, California (which is what the "growthbusters" are hoping for).

Median price for single family home: $92,075. On the mainland prices start at $80,000 and average $125,000 (primarily the north side). On the south side, prices average in the $150s. New construction goes up to $200,000.

Median price for 2BR condo: $80,000. The range is $50,000-$175,000 (more for golf course communities).

Rental housing market: The rental market is very tight, with less than a 4% occupancy rate. In season, there's virtually nothing. 3BR/2BA house (1,600-1,800 sq. ft.): $600-$1,000/mo.; 2BR apt.: $500-$800/mo. On Longboat, a 2BR condo will rent for $3,000+.

Common housing styles & features: New construction is contemporary, mediterranean and lavish: Screened-in lanai's, screened-in pools off expansive kitchens, master suites, one-story split plans and two-car garages are very popular.

Amenities in condo developments: pools, clubhouses, tennis, golf courses, biking/hiking trails, etc.

Nearby areas to consider: Long Boat Key (Sarasota and Manatee County), Bradenton (Manatee County). **Unique features of these areas:** Bradenton (40,000), in the shadow of Sarasota and Tampa, is finally coming into its own. It's the commercial and economic hub of the county and offers a lot of waterfront property. It's a fast-growing city of both retirees and Tampa Bay commuters. The median home price is $86,000, and you get more property. Long Boat Key is a gorgeous resort/retirement island, one of the most exclusive areas on the gulf. New 2BR condo units are selling for $380,000+. On the north end, waterfront is more than $400,000. There are resales for half that, but they're smaller, older and on a lower floor. Condo rentals run $3,000-$4,000 a month, and if you don't plan 6 months ahead, you're out of luck.

What Things Cost

Overall living costs are approximately 3% below the national average and about 2% above other Florida counties. Housing and health care are about 10%-15% below.

Gas company: People's Gas Co. *(366-4277)*. Average bill: $18/mo., highest consumption in Jan./Feb. Avg. annual bill: $160. Deposit of $25 or two months of service is required (whichever is greater).

Electric company: Florida Power & Light *(379-1424)*. Avg. bill: $80/mo. but Aug./Sept. can be close to twice that. No deposit with good credit. Social Security recipients have until the 6th of the month to pay, to allow for receipt of their check.

Water/sewer: City of Sarasota *(954-4197)*. Base charge: $28.35 (includes garbage pick up). $90 deposit may be required. Connect fee is $20.

Phone company: General Telephone *(800-458-1216)*. Basic monthly service: $10.45. Installation starts at $53.25 (for touchtone).

Car registration/license: New residents must obtain a Florida driver's license within 30 days of residency. Title fees: new: $29.25; used: $33.25. Initial registration: (cars and trucks): $100. New residents impact fee: $295 (one-time charge for each vehicle previously titled outside Fla.). Driver's license (6 years): new residents: $20 annual. License tags (1 yr): Vehicles up to 2,499 lbs.: $34.60; 2,500 to 3,499 lbs.: $42.60; 3,500 lbs. and over: $52.60.

The Tax Ax

Sales tax: 6% (Prescription drugs and food exempt except prepared/restaurant foods). **State income tax:** None. **Retirement income:** Florida ranks first among 10 popular retirement states for taking the smallest tax bite from retirees. There's no income tax, no state tax on social security, no death taxes and low property taxes. **Property taxes & tax breaks:** Florida offers a $25,000 homestead exemption for permanent residents whose principal home is Florida. Property taxes are based on millage rates. To estimate annual property taxes, deduct $25,000 from the appraised value

of the home (provided you own and reside in the house by Dec. 31), multiply the balance times the millage rate and divide by 1,000. Current property taxes in the city are assessed at 21.042 per $1,000 of appraised value (the county rate is only 14.524). Contact the property appraisers office *(951-5650)*.

Medical Care

Major hospitals/regional medical centers: Doctor's Hospital (private). **Sarasota Memorial Hospital** (JCAH-accredited) is the largest general hospital. Specializations include: open heart surgery, laser surgery, cancer care and leading-edge technology for various treatments. For seniors these are "Successful Aging" education courses and a senior care membership program. Support groups for handling bereavement, caregiving, mastectomies and more are offered. Ask about Newcomer Care *(953-1962)* and Senior Care *(953-1999)*. **The Heart Center of Sarasota** (HCA) offers comprehensive cardiovascular health care services including more than 10 procedures. **Emergency medical services (EMS):** 5 advanced life support vehicles, 2 reserve units, boats and a helicopter comprise the Sarasota EMS team. Response time within city: under 4 min. **Physician's referral:** Sarasota Memorial Hospital *957-7777*.

Continuing Education

The University of South Florida at Sarasota offers courses on an audit basis free to seniors who have been residents for at least a year and have instructor's permission *(359-4220)*. Sarasota Institute of Lifetime Learning offers 50 seminars from January-March *(371-2408)*. Manatee Community College offers classes with fees range between $21-$165 *(755-1511)*.

Services for Seniors

With many different organizations and services, the city created an information and referral number called "First Call for Help." Ask about clubs, recreation, health care, social services and more *(366-5025)*. **AARP** has a local chapter *(346-0355)*. Memorial Hospital offers health maintenance and programs on weight control, smoking, CPR, etc. **Vial of Life** is a program sponsored by Florida Power & Light and the American Red Cross. A medical form is kept in a plastic vial on the outside of the refrigerator door and glove compartment of the car. If communication isn't possible, vital info is there *(365-4292)*.

Crime & Safety

On a per capita basis, the crime rates have always been below national averages. Several new community programs have reduced rates further, such as bike patrols downtown (officers ride mountain bikes), DARE: Drug Abuse Resistance Education (drug awareness program for kids), and street beats (same officers patrol a neighborhood every day). The result? Burglaries are down 16%, and more people are taking common-sense precautions. The one recent trouble spot has been gang-related auto theft, but the police say they've "arrested" much of that problem.

Earning a Living

Current business climate: Thanks to a growing population and high per capita income, businesses are thriving, particularly in retail, service and health care sectors. Area affluence has attracted banking and financial institutions (more than 150 branches and offices in the county). With the favorable tax structure and solid labor force, go, go, go. **Help in starting a business:** The Small Business Development Center at the University of South Florida will provide assistance with business plans, loan applications and marketing *(359-4292)*. **The job market:** Job Service of Florida can assist with placement for seniors *(365-0511)*. Part-time work is readily available.

When the Kids Come to Visit

What kid, or kid-at-heart, wouldn't like a town where the Ringling Brothers Circus made its winter home? The Ringling Circus Collection at the Ringling Museum of Art is a treasure trove from "The Greatest Show on Earth"; Also the Myakka Wildlife Tours; Bellm Cars and Music of Yesterday Museum; and Sarasota Jungle Gardens.

Getting Around Town

Roads & interstates: I-75, U.S.-41 (Tamiami Trail), U.S.-301. **Airports & airlines:** The $56 million expansion of the Sarasota-Bradenton Airport is complete and traveling here will spoil you for good. Parking, car rentals and arrivals/departures are very convenient. It is now served by Delta, Continental, Midway, American, USAir and other major carriers. **Public transportation:** SCAT (Sarasota County Area Transit) provides bus service along 14 routes. Seniors who carry a gold card can ride for 50¢. **Managing without a car:** The city is spread out so it would be hard without a car.

What Residents Already Know

Leadfoots beware. Every day is Sunday for Sarasota drivers.•The great debate here is not water shortages or building moratoriums, it's where to eat. It's hard enough trying to familiarize yourself with the hundreds of restaurants in town, but then you need a scorecard to keep track of all the openings and closings.

For More Information

Chamber Of Commerce Office:
Sarasota Chamber of Commerce
P.O. Box 308
Sarasota, 34230-0308
955-8187

Newspaper:
Sarasota Herald-Tribune
801 South Tamiami Trail
Sarasota, 34236
957-5171

Realtors:
Juanita S. Bryan
Stonewood Realty
4509 Bee Ridge Road, Suite D
Sarasota, 34233
379-9900

Linda Barrett
Michael Saunders & Co.
1801 Main St., Sarasota, 34236
951-6660

18. Winter Haven, Florida

Area Snapshot

Nickname: "The City of Lakes"
County: Polk
Area Code: 813   **Zip Code:** 33880
Local population: 25,000   **County:** 400,000
% of population 65+: 45.7%
U.S. region: Central Florida
Closest metro areas: Orlando, 50 miles; Tampa, 55 miles
Nearby area to consider: North Auberndale
Median housing price: $63,400
Best reasons to retire here: 100 lakes within the area, beautiful small city with active retirees, ample culture and recreation, centrally located to the best of Florida's attractions.

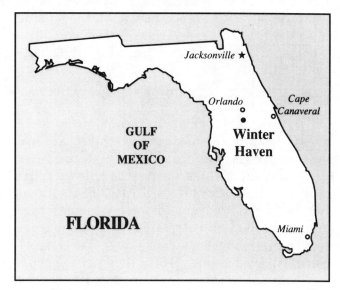

Fabulous Features

Winter Haven is a small, quiet retreat in the midst of some of the world's busiest and biggest attractions. Disney World, Sea World and Cypress Gardens are short drives, but they might as well be on the other side of the moon. "The City of Lakes" is a traditionally conservative, upscale community with active art and theater groups. Housing is very affordable and there's an abundance of golf courses, condo and townhouse communities. The developments are generally small providing ample opportunity to meet your former northern neighbors. The medical facilities are excellent and people gravitate here because of the gorgeous lakes and lush greenery. For frequent travelers, Winter Haven is just under an hour to either the Tampa or Orlando airports. Culture in this art-filled community abounds, as does year-round outdoor recreation (this is the water-skiing capital of the world). When you're ready for a change of pace, the local calendar of events is shockingly full. Spring and fall are quiet and pleasant; winters are short and sweet (people love to call north on New Year's Day and boast they just came out of the pool). The average daily temperature is 72. "Raindrops Keep Falling On My Head" is the region's theme song, with an average 50 inches of rain a year.

Possible drawbacks: There is no public transportation to speak of because with 14 lakes in the city, there's no straight path to anything.•The rental market is practically nonexistent. People buy homes and stay put. This is tough on northerners who want to come down for a few months and learn more about the area before they buy.•The summer heat and humidity can be oppressive. If you've got somewhere else to go, go.•Retirees tell us that it's not for everyone—only those who are looking for serene beauty, exciting activities, and a nice community happy to be your haven.

"You can quote me on that"

"I'm a retired Air Force Officer and, in my opinion, Winter Haven is a small town with all the advantages. There's access to some 100 lakes within a few minutes' drive. If you want to go where the action is, you're less than an hour's drive from Orlando and Tampa. It's the best of both worlds. You can be in the small town, without the hustle and bustle, but it's so close when you want it. I may be a little prejudiced, of course. I'm the mayor."—John Simmonds, Mayor of Winter Haven

Climate

Elevation: 238'	Avg. High/ Low	Avg. Rainfall (Inches)	Avg. # Days Precip.	Avg. % Humidity
Jan.	72/52	2.3	6	78
April	83/59	3.2	7	72
July	92/73	8.3	19	78
Oct.	85/66	3.9	9	79
YEAR	83/62	54	-	-
# days 32° or below: 5		# days 90° or above: 86		

Let the Good Times Roll

Recreation: With world-famous Cypress Gardens and the "Chain of Lakes" (14 natural lakes), Winter Haven is widely recognized as the water skiing capital of the world and a boater's paradise. Numerous public boat ramps are scattered along lake shores, many near beaches, fishing piers, recreational facilities and picnic grounds. Popular boating parks include Lake Shipp Park, Lake Maude Community Center, Lake Cannon Park and Saddlecreek Park. For golfers, six championship courses include Willow Brook (home of the Cypress Gardens Open Florida PGA Tour), Grenelefe Golf and Racquet Club (one of the state's top 20 courses with two par-72 courses), Lucerne Park Par Three Course, and the brand-new Baytree Golf Club (host of a celebrity golf tournament in Feb., 1992); Chain O'Lakes Stadium is the training camp for the Boston Red Sox. **Culture:** The beautiful lakes and gardens in Winter Haven have always attracted artists. The Chamber showcases all the local talent by putting their works on display. The annual Bach Festival (Mar.) features a chorus and orchestra that perform at area churches. Polk Community College's 500-seat auditorium provides an ideal setting for music, drama and dance performed by local and national talent, including the Concert Ballet Theater. The Imperial Symphony performs at Lakeland's Civic Center. Theater Winter Haven, a community theater group, puts on five large-scale productions a year and is considered the best community repertory group in the Southeast. **Annual events:** Citrus Festival (Feb.): par-ades, musical events and exhibits celebrate the harvest. Winterfest (Nov.-Dec.) has the Festival of Trees, Christmas Boat Parade, Holiday Homes Tour, Carols in the Park, Symphony and Jazz Concerts, plus many special performances. Winter Haven Hospital Spring Run and Tennis Tournament (March).

Local Real Estate

It's a buyer's market. With a huge inventory of homes and condominiums on the market and low interest rates, it's a great time to buy. However, as in many areas of the state, it can be difficult to sell. Move with caution.
Median price for single family home: $63,400.
Average price for 2BR condo: $80,000.
Rental housing market: Rentals are very hard to come by. The populations swells by 33% in season and, with a low inventory to begin with, the pickings get very slim, particularly for single-family homes. When they're available, houses rent from $350-$650/mo.
Common housing styles & features: Many homes are modest in size and price but are beautifully maintained, with close access to the lakes. Construction is cement block and stucco. Layouts are generally ranch-style with split-floor plans. Most are either 2-3BR with 2BA. Cypress Woods, with homes from $80,000-$150,000, is on a golf course. Homewood Drive has lovely single-family homes at $110,000. Overlook Estates and Eloise Point (exclusive homes start at $200,000) are new developments with full amenities.
Amenities in condo developments: All come with pools and lawn maintenance. Newer models have clubhouses and tennis courts.
Nearby area to consider: North Auburndale.
Unique features: North Auburndale (5 min. out of Winter Haven) is right off I-4 and offers convenient access to Orlando and Tampa. There's a lot of new construction and beautiful mobile-home parks attracting retirees. Sutton Place (single-family homes), and Auburn Woods (new patio homes) start in the low $70s.

What Things Cost

According to ACCRA (1st quarter, 1991) overall living costs in the Lakeland/Winter Haven area were 3.5% above the national average. Utilities appeared to be the culprit

(34.6% above the average). However, Winter Haven is serviced by Tampa Electric, which is much cheaper than Florida Power (which serves most of the region). Housing costs were 6% below the average. Compared to other Florida counties, Polk County living costs were 7.5% below the average, ranking it 43 out of the 67 counties (Florida Price Level Index, 1990).

Gas company: Central Florida Gas Corporation *(293-2125)*. Avg. bill for homes with gas range, furnace and water heater: $70-$80/mo. A $60 deposit may be required. Most older homes are all electric.

Electric company: Tampa Electric Company *(294-4171)*. Avg. bill for an 1,800 sq. ft. home (3BR, 2BA): $110/mo.

Phone company: General Telephone *(800-458-1216)*. Basic monthly service: $16 including touchtone, unlimited calls and long distance access. Connection charge: $48.25 per line. Deposit not generally required.

Car registration/license: New residents must obtain a Florida driver's license within 30 days of establishing residency. Title fees: new: $29.25; used: $33.25. Initial registration (cars and trucks): $100. New residents impact fee: $295 (One-time charge applies to each vehicle previously titled outside of Florida). Driver's license: (good for 6 years): new residents: $20 annual. License tags (1 yr): Vehicles up to 2,499 lbs.: $34.60; 2,500 to 3,499 lbs.: $42.60; 3,500 lbs. and over: $52.60.

The Tax Ax

Sales tax: 6% (Prescription drugs and food exempt except prepared/restaurant foods). **State income tax:** None. **Retirement income:** Florida ranks first among 10 popular retirement states for taking the smallest tax bite from retirees. There's no income tax or death or estate taxes (over and above federal credit), and property taxes are still lower than the northeastern cities where many people migrate from. **Property taxes & tax breaks:** Florida offers a $25,000 homestead exemption for permanent residents whose principal home is Florida. Property taxes are based on millage rates. Deduct $25,000 from the appraised value of the home (provided you own and reside in the house by Dec. 31),

multiply the balance times the millage rate and divide by 1000. In 1990, the average millage rate for Winter Haven was 21.384. Property taxes for a $70,000 home would be $976. County tax appraiser *(534-6000)*.

Medical Care

Major hospitals/regional medical centers: There are seven hospitals and 10 medical clinics in the county. The **Winter Haven Hospital** (JCAH-accredited) is a large, full-service facility with 24-hour emergency room service and all medical specialties (except open heart surgery). It has cardiac and respiratory rehabilitation, home health care, a hospice, and one of 10 spinal cord injury centers in the state. Its Regency Medical Center offers complete services for women, including same-day surgery. In addition, it offers support groups, health fairs and other community programs. **Emergency medical services (EMS):** There are 3 Advanced Life Support Units (sent out with an EMT and a paramedic) and 1 Basic Life Support Unit (sent with 2 EMTs). Avg. response time is less than 5 min. within city limits. **Physician's referral:** Winter Haven Hospital *293-1121*.

Continuing Education

The Florida Legislature recently prohibited community colleges from offering senior discounts. However, Polk County Community College (Winter Haven), has a Continuing Education program with more than 400 classes that are reasonably priced to begin with. Seniors are welcome to enroll in non-credit academic classes. Classes avg. $2 per contact hour *(297-1000)*. Other technical, vocational and state universities offer interesting courses as well, including Travis Vocational and the University of South Florida (Tampa).

Services for Seniors

The Winter Haven Senior Center offers extensive recreational activities including speaker forums, arts and crafts, card games, dances, and exercise classes. It's also the clearinghouse for referral services *(297-4024)*. Winter Haven's active **AARP** chapter is Florida's third largest chapter *(533-7075)*. Senior discounts are widely available. Look for businesses that have the "Golden Age" emblem on their windows.

Crime & Safety

The police and the county sheriff's department work together to develop crime-prevention programs. Neighborhood Watch is active as are crime-watch teams started by the mobile-home and condo associations. The "Residential Security Program" (police inspect your home and offer advice on improving security) is helpful to newcomers. The 55+ Senior Alert Program runs seminars on scams, safety tips, etc. Although considered a safe area, drug-related crime is a way of life for many Florida communities and burglaries have been on the rise.

Earning a Living

Current business climate: Citrus and tourism are the economic backbone of the region, and have remained healthy. New, small businesses contend with the seasonality of the area, but overall costs are reasonable. Commercial rents are lower than other parts of the state. Fine restaurants and high-quality women's apparel would be welcomed. **Help in starting a business:** Counselors from the University of South Florida's Small Business Center meet prospective or current business owners at the Chamber once a month. Schedule an appointment for assistance *(293-2138)*. **The job market:** Seniors make up a large portion of the part-time workers. Fast-food outlets, stores and supermarkets count on them to fill jobs. But keep in mind, the pay is almost always minimum-wage. Call Job Service of Florida *(294-2113)*.

When the Kids Come to Visit

The wonders of Busch Gardens, Walt Disney World, EPCOT Center, Sea World, Cypress Gardens, Kennedy Space Center, and Universal Studios are some of the country's greatest attractions. The newly renovated Winter Haven Mall puts on 40 major events including car shows, concerts, and fairs.

Getting Around Town

Roads & interstates: There is no direct access to an interstate. Highway 27 and I-4 are 10 miles out. Winter Haven is within short driving distances to both Orlando and Tampa. **Airports & airlines:** Tampa International and Orlando International (either one approx. 50 miles from Winter Haven) are served by all major carriers. **Public transportation:** None. **Managing without a car:** A car is essential.

What Residents Already Know

It's easy to tell when the tourists have arrived. That's when the car horns start blowing. Off season, residents don't beep the second the light turns green.•The Boston Red Sox are the beloved hometown team during spring training. The whole town wakes up and everyone heads over to Chain-O-Lakes Park to cheer them on, even former New Yorkers.

For More Information

Chamber Of Commerce Office:
Winter Haven Area Chamber
of Commerce
P.O. Drawer 1420
Winter Haven, 33822-1420
293-2138

Newspaper:
The Lakeland Ledger
455 Sixth St. N.W.
Winter Haven, 33881
293-9982

Realtors:
Norma Marcha
Century 21/Pyramid Realty
1478 6th St.
Winter Haven, 33881
299-2151

Betty Watson
David Watson Realty
1012 Ariana Blvd. (State Rd. 559)
Winter Haven, 33823
967-4496

19. Brunswick, Georgia

Area Snapshot

Nickname: "Gateway to the Golden Isles"
County: Glynn County
Area code: 912   **Zip code:** 31520
Local population: 18,000   **County:** 67,000
% of population 65+: 12.5%
U.S. region: Southeast Coast
Closest metro areas: Savannah, 50 mi.; Jacksonville, Fla., 60 mi.
Nearby areas to consider: St. Simons Island (The Golden Isles)
Median housing price: $140,000
Best reasons to retire here: Temperate climate most of the year, outstanding recreation, fabulous scenery and beaches, very safe, very mellow.

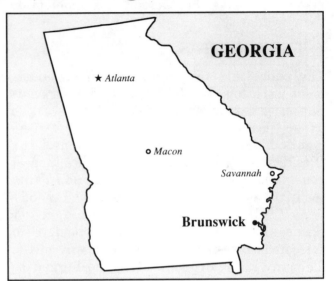

Fabulous Features

Welcome to the Colonial Coast of Georgia, a charming, historic district with natural beauty, sophistication and that famous southern hospitality. Brunswick is a "Georgia Main Street City"—one of 29 that has preserved its heritage, in spite of record population growth and business expansion. When newcomers ask about the climate, they're anxious to know if it's always so nice. The answer? Only about 90% of the time! The weather is a perfect mingling of temperate and subtropical, with the first three months of the year hovering in the mid-60s. The real estate market has much to offer in a variety of styles and prices— beautiful old homes in the historic district, oceanfront condominiums or gorgeous contemporary houses in the new subdivisions. Situated over the causeway are four glorious resort islands, one of which is an enchanting

place to reside. St. Simons Island (sun-drenched) offers a country club environment with all-you-could-ask-for amenities, swank golf courses, marinas, horse stables, fabulous shopping and dining and tennis year-round. It's all here but when the need or desire arises for a big city, Savannah and Jacksonville are only an hour by car. Brunswick is the home to many an active "loafer."

Possible drawbacks: Summers can be awfully hot and humid (although sea breezes cool things off a bit). Public transportation is nonexistant so a car is a must. Services for seniors are quite limited—the area is best for healthy, active, independent adults. Brunswick is so nice, don't be surprised if you encounter a high degree of unexpected company from up north.

"You can quote me on that"

"We're from Ocean City, Md., so we couldn't retire anywhere that didn't have beautiful beaches. We fell in love with St. Simons Island from the beginning. Its a nice, slow pace, the cost of living is reasonable and it's not at all pretentious. You need to come and experience it for a week and you'll see. We would never leave here."—J.S.

"We retired to Brunswick because my husband still had business in Miami and needed a place that was convenient to go back every few months. We love this place and wouldn't leave it for the world. The people smile and you're respected as a human being. It's very low key. Just check out all the different subdivisions and don't be in a hurry to make a decision. We'll wait for you."—T.C.

Climate

Elevation: 19'	Avg. High/ Low	Avg. Rainfall (Inches)	Avg. # Days Precip.	Avg. % Humidity
Jan.	65/45	2.5	8	75
April	77/56	3.3	7	70
July	92/72	7	12	79
Oct.	79/59	4	7	78
YEAR	78/58	50	-	-
# days 32° or below: 21		# days 90° or above: 82		

Let the Good Times Roll

Recreation: When they say "go fish" in the Golden Isles, they're not talking card games. They're talking freshwater fishing in Brunswick River and saltwater fishing in the Intercoastal Waterway. Blythe Island (1,000 acres of natural habitat) is another great fishing hole. It also has campgrounds for tents and RVs. Golfing is at Glynco Golf Course (greens fees are $10.60 for the day) and at numerous private courses. Play ball in the "50 and Better" softball league. Surf's up at neighboring resort areas, Sea Island, St. Simons Island and Jekyll Island. Rent a hoby cat or ride your bike along the magnificent stretch of beaches.

Culture: Brunswick's renovated opera house, the "Ritz," features four performances a year. Or take in a play at Summer Stock theater at the Island Players amphitheater on St. Simons. Coastal Center for the Arts offers year-round exhibits and is a showcase for local artists. The Left Bank Gallery on St. Simons is a favorite. Take in the symphony, the ballet and the theater by driving to Savannah (50 miles north).

Annual events: Brunswick Harbor Festival: arts & crafts, entertainment and great seafood (May); Beach Music Festival: musical entertainment, crafts and great food on Jekyll Island (August); Sunshine Festival and Brunswick Stew Competition: three days of music and fun and great Georgia cooks show off on St. Simons Island (July 4th); Sea Island Festival celebrates the African-American history of the Golden Isles with music and dance (August).

Local Real Estate

Brunswick is the commercial district for the area, with virtually all of the banking, industry and shopping. Homes in nicer neighborhoods range from $80,000 to 120,000. Homes on a marsh with views average $150,000 and for waterfront, expect to pay $200,000 to $250,000. Half the retirees relocate here permanently, the rest buy second homes and rent them off season.

Median price for single family homes: $140,000.

Median price for 2BR condos: $50,000

Rental housing market: House rentals range from $600-$1,100 a month. Condo rentals range from $475-$900 a month for a 2BR. Prices vary depending on whether the unit is furnished or unfurnished. Condos are in much greater supply than homes. Renting is a very popular option for people checking out the area.

Common housing styles & features: The tabby exterior is popular—a mixture of oyster shell with stucco (it's a traditional native building material). Many homes are designed for low maintenance in and out and to be energy efficient. Decks, screened porches and outdoor entertaining areas are common features. Homes with ocean, marsh or golf views are in great demand.

Amenities in condo developments: Most have pools and community associations to handle maintenance.

Nearby area to consider: St. Simons Island.

Unique features of this area: This is an exclusive resort hideaway seven miles from Brunswick (accessible only by a causeway). Houses range in price from $100,000 to $300,000 but can go up to the millions. Most homes have fireplaces and garages, but not basements. There is also a big second-home market here. Another big draw is the beaches, golf and tennis. People look so tan and healthy here you really can't tell the 45s from the 78s!

What Things Cost

There's a fair range of housing prices, but with the area attracting a large affluent group of retirees, most people don't seem concerned.

People come here, fall in love and write the checks as fast as they can.

Gas company: Georgia Natural Gas *(265-1020)*. Average monthly bill is $15-$20 (without gas heat); connection fee: $15. No deposit is required. February has the highest gas consumption.

Electric company: Georgia Power *(265-3440)*. Average monthly bill is $35-$65 (in summer). Deposit is usually not required. June through September have the highest consumption.

Phone company: Southern Bell *(800-356-3094)*. Basic Service is $15.82; Installation $42.50, ($110 for new homes not previously wired). No deposit is required with good credit history.

Car registration/license: How does $13 sound to get your Georgia license, plates, title and registration? That's all you pay. Just be sure to register within 30 days of establishing residency.

The Tax Ax

Sales tax: 6% (no exemptions).

State income tax: Income over $10,000 is taxed at a rate of 6% plus $340 (married filing jointly). If you use the standard deduction, you can increase your personal exemption from $3,000 to $3,700 ($700 increase is not an option if you itemize).

Retirement income: All income is taxable, including pensions and IRAs. However, residents 62 and older can apply a $10,000 exemption towards either earned or unearned income.

Property taxes & tax breaks: Property tax is based on 40% of fair market value minus a $2,000 homestead exemption. The current millage rate is .025 (25 mills). A home valued at $100,000 would pay approximately $980. A $150,000 home would run $1,436.

Medical Care

Major hospitals & regional medical centers: Southeast Georgia Regional Medical Center offers general surgery, a full range of therapeutic and diagnostic services for in/out patients. Also has a Diabetes Metabolic Center for screening, testing, and maintenace, a cardiac rehab center with cardiac catherization, and a breast imaging center staffed by women who provide self-exam training, medical tests and treatments. The hospital is also known for cancer care treatments, including the linear accelerator (replaces chemo and cobalt) and an excellent radiology/oncology department. A new total cancer care unit is in the works. When the need arises for open heart surgery or extremely critical cases, patients are sent to **St. Vincents Hospital** in Jacksonville. For expert diagnostic and clinical work, a satellite branch of the famed Mayo Clinic is open in Jacksonville as well.

Emergency medical services (EMS): The Fire Department is the first response team to provide first aid and life support until a county transport arrives (they're paid, not volunteer). Response time is under 5 minutes.

Physician's referral: *264-7077*.

Continuing Education

Brunswick College does not offer a specific program for seniors, but does allow seniors to enroll in courses on a non-credit basis *(264-7235)*. The Department of Parks and Recreation runs free or inexpensive classes on yoga, bridge, aerobics, etc. *(267-5770)*.

Services for Seniors

In addition to the Department of Aging's **Meals-on-Wheels** and other programs, there are local chapters of **RSVP** (Retired Senior Volunteers Program), **SCORE** (Senior Corp of Retired Executives) and **AARP** *(888-0077)*.

Crime & Safety

The crime rate in Brunswick is very low, with a fair share of burglaries but not much else. Many people told us it was one of the few places they'd ever lived where they felt safe to leave the windows and doors open.

Earning a Living

Current business climate: The business climate is good because the area is growing. New development is needed. There just doesn't seem to be enough upscale stores, department stores, or gourmet restaurants (particularly on St. Simons Island).

Help in starting a business: Small Business Developement Center *(264-7343)* can assist.

The job market: Part-time work is not readily available, find temporary jobs through Kelly. Department of Industry and Trade *(656-3586)*.

When the Kids Come to Visit

Mountasia Fantasy Golf (mini golf with waterfalls and underground caverns); Mary Miller Doll Museum (400 dolls from 90 countries, pre-Civil War to Cabbage Patch); Okeefenokee Swamp Park (guided boat trips, wildlife shows, canoeing); Blythe Island (1,000-acre island with campgrounds, fishing and boating); Summer Waves (exciting water park); Don't forget the gorgeous beaches.

Getting Around Town

Roads & interstates: I-95, US 17.

Airports & airlines: Savannah International Airport (50 mi.) Serviced by Delta, USAir, American; Glynco Jetport *(265-2070)* has commuter service via Atlantic Southeast. Jacksonville International Airport is 60 mi. south.

Public transportation: No mass transit.

Managing without a car: A car is a must.

What Residents Already Know

The climate is different every single day. It's not monotonous like Florida. • Lifestyles are low key and laid back. It's a cinch to pick out those who've just arrived. They get impatient at the bank and supermarket. • As soon as you unpack, check out Jekyll Island, the exclusive plaground for America's wealthiest families. The bike paths, dunes and uncrowded beaches will confirm your best suspicions. You've arrived!

For More Information

Chamber Of Commerce Office:
Brunswick-Golden Isles Chamber
of Commerce
4 Glynn Avenue
Brunswick, 31520
912-265-0620

Newspaper:
Brunswick News
(Daily except Sun.)
P.O. Box 1557
Brunswick, 31520
265-8320

Realtor:
Ms. Kathy Stratton
The Trupp-Hodnett Enterprises
520 Ocean Blvd.
St. Simons Island, 31522
800-627-6850

20. Clayton, Georgia

Area Snapshot

Nickname: "Where Spring Spends The Summer"
County: Rabun
Area code: 404   **Zip code:** 30525
Local population: 1,700   **County:** 11,600
% of population 65+: 18%
U.S. region: Blue Ridge Mountains (Northeast corner of Georgia)
Closest metro areas: Greenville, S.C., 83 mi; Asheville, N.C., 90 mi; Atlanta, 115 mi.
Nearby areas to consider: Habersham County, Union County
Median housing price: $75,000
Best reasons to retire here: Quiet, breathtaking scenery, year-round recreation, safe, affordable, cool mountain climate, friendly people.

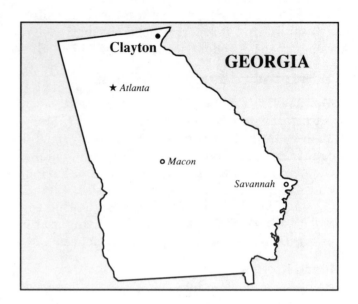

Fabulous Features

Clayton and surrounding Rabun county is, in a word, awesome. Once you lay eyes on the majestic peaks of the Blue Ridge Mountains, the glistening waterfalls, the crystal-clear Lake Burton, and four seasons of New England-style foliage, it's hard to justify city living. For the outdoor enthusiast, there is absolutely everything to do: white water rafting, mountain climbing, hunting, fishing and skiing (this is home of Sky Valley, the southermost ski resort in the U.S.). Golfers can even count on 253 playable days. The housing market offers a wide selection of styles and prices, health care is surprisingly good, crime is only something you read about and several major metro areas in both Carolinas are within a two-hour drive. But the icing on the cake is the weather. Rabun county has true mountain climate, with cool evenings and warm, sunny days. The daily temperatures throughout spring and summer range in the comfortable 70s with humidity so low, it's hard to measure. Winters are cool (mid 30s-40s) but rarely frigid. We spoke to a retired AT&T executive from Chester, N.J., who visited 45 retirement destinations before choosing Clayton. That was in 1985 and he and his wife and four dogs couldn't be happier. They wanted a small town with a big heart and they found it! You want to talk about the heartbeat of America? This is it!

Possible drawbacks: This is small-town living with its predictable shortcomings: limited culture and education (the nearest college is 35 miles), limited job opportunities, limited shopping, etc.•There is an average of 67 inches of rainfall every year, so there's no mistaking this place for Arizona.

"You can quote me on that"

"On a scale of one to ten, I rate Clayton a twelve! I visited over 45 places including Vermont, the Poconos, Colorado, upstate New York and both Carolinas. Clayton is fabulous because the area is multifaceted, it's serene and the people are friendly and honest. The air is clean and the vistas are magnificent. I had no trouble acclimating to a small town. I highly recommend that retirees leave big cities."—A.R.D.

"We moved to Clayton to be close to family. It's everything we expected it to be. We love the beauty and the slow pace. It helps to truly acquaint yourself with an area before deciding. Visit as many times as possible."—T.S.

Climate

Elevation: 1,925'	Avg. High/ Low	Average Inches		Avg. # Days Precip.	Avg. % Humidity
		Rain	Snow		
Jan.	51/32	5.6	3	14	70
April	69/44	5.5	trace	12	60
July	84/64	7.5	-	14	74
Oct.	69/46	4.8	-	8	70
YEAR	68/46	67	10	-	-
# days 32° or below: 82		# days 90° or above: 20			

Let the Good Times Roll

Recreation: The most popular activities are fishing, camping, whitewater rafting and hiking those beautiful Blue Ridge Mountains. Black Rock Mountain State Park (open year-round) is a place to head to do all of the above. There are RV campgrounds, tent sites, picnic areas, a beautiful lake and two back country trails. Moccasin Creek State Park (15 mi. west) is on the shore of Lake Burton and is another great spot for camping and fishing. Other campgrounds include Rabun Beach, Tallulah River and Tate Branch. Chattooga River is the hot spot for white water rafting and horseback riding. Sky Valley is one of the southernmost ski resorts in the U.S. It also offers golf, tennis, hunting, rock climbing and horseback riding. Boating enthusiasts head for Lake Burton and Lake Rabun. The Rabun County Country Club has a 9-hole course and is currently expanding. Rabun County is a hunter's paradise with three game management areas.

Culture: Residents enjoy summer stock theater at the Highlands Playhouse (22 mi.) and the Symphony, which brings classical music and brass ensembles to town every month. Many people also drive to Atlanta to take advantage of its vast offerings, such as the Atlanta Ballet (Atlantic Civic Center and the Robert Woodruff Memorial Arts Center). The Emory Museum of Art and Archaeology and the High Museum of Art have wonderful exhibits and programs year-round. Atlanta also offers The Atlanta Symphony and "legitimate" theater.

Annual events: Clayton's Arts & Crafts festivals are legend in these parts: Cabbage Festival: craft show, cabbage cook-off in Dillard (Sept); Rabun County Homemakers Festival: Crafts show at the Farmer's Market in Dillard (Aug.); Mountain Maffick Wiley: Major arts & crafts show (Spring) Hay-Day Festivals: costume parties, sidewalk sales, festivities (several times a year); Annual Christmas parade.

Local Real Estate

The market is slow and prices have dropped. It doesn't help that banks are getting tough with mortgage money. Retirees gravitate to homes priced between $40,000 to $150,000 and like the country club area, small cabins in the woods, or homes on the lake (these are the most expensive starting at $200,000 up to $1 million). As a resort community, Clayton is a big second home market. FYI: 75% of the county land is owned by the federal government and Georgia Power, so property is at a premium.

Median price for single family home: $75,000.

Average price for 2BR condo: Starts at $59,000.

Rental housing market: 3BR house: $300-$500 plus utilities; 2BR apt: $300-$325 (very few apts.).

Common housing styles & features: Very rustic, cedar, log, spruce, not too much brick. Most are 3BR/2BA.

Amenities in condo developments: Condos in the country club area start at $100,000 and offer golf, skiing, tennis, pools, etc.

Nearby areas to consider: Habersham County (Clarksville, Cornelia); Union County (Blairesville).

Unique features of these areas: Habersham County (23 mi. south) is at the foothills of the Blue Ridge Mountains. The terrain is flatter, housing costs are lower and, being in the valley, there's a warmer climate. Cornelia (15 mi. south of Clarksville) is mostly national forest but has beautiful, affordable homes and access to major shopping. Blairesville is very mountainous and cool. Golfers enjoy this area because of the terrain.

What Things Cost

Gas companies: No natural gas. Must purchase through local propane services: Tugalo

Gas *(782-4543)* and Farrell Gas *(782-4239)* sell liquid petroleum at an average of 90¢ per gallon. Service calls average $25. Average monthly bills are based on individual use.

Electric company: Georgia Power *(782-4236)*. Connection charge: $18. No deposit required. Average monthly bills: $60-$70. Summer months average bill can run $100 or more.

Phone company: Continental Telephone Systems *(647-5461)*. Basic monthly service: $18.70; connection charge: $30.

Car registration/license: Georgia residents pay a total of $13 to drive in this state. That includes your license, plates, title and registration. You must register within 30 days of establishing residency. The tax on vehicles is levied at time of purchase of tags, based on the Blue-book value of your car. Tag costs vary on vehicle weight.

The Tax Ax

Sales tax: 6% (everything is taxed: food, clothing, prescriptions, etc.).

State income tax: Income over $10,000 is taxed at a rate of 6% plus $340 (married filing jointly). If you use the standard deduction, you can increase your personal exemption from $3,000 to $3,700 ($700 increase is not an option if you itemize).

Retirement income: All income is taxable, including pensions and IRAs. However, residents 62 and older can apply a $10,000 exemption towards either earned or unearned income.

Property taxes & tax breaks: Taxes are based on 40% of the appraised value and there is a $2,000 county homestead exemption. On a home in Clayton valued at $80,000, county property taxes would be $440 (millage rate of .14410). City taxes would be $2,028 (millage rate of 6.5%). Tax Assessor's office is 782-5068.

Medical Care

Both local hospitals are JCAH-accredited and offer basic general care and operate 24-hour emergency room service. Both have excellent reputations for quality care. If there's a need for extreme care, patients can fly by helicopter to Gainesville, Ga. or Atlanta. **Major hospitals and regional medical centers: Ridgecrest**

Hospital is a private facility offering general surgery, radiology services, intensive and coronary care. **Rabun County Memorial Hospital** has physical and respiratory therapy, radiological service, CAT scans, mammograms and cardiac monitoring.

Emergency medical services (EMS): Ambulance service has one unit for trauma, the other as a transporter. Service is available through the Rabun County Emergency Medical Service and Rabun Rescue. Response times vary depending on road conditions, weather, etc.

Physician's referral: Ridgecrest *782-4297* or Rabun Memorial *782-4233*.

Continuing Education

There are no community colleges in town, but some drive to Clarksville (35 miles) and take courses at Clarksville College. Other colleges within an hour drive are Piedmont College (Demorset: 35 miles); Clemson University (Clemson, S.C.: 45 miles); and Western Carolina University (Sylva, N.C.: 44 miles).

Services for Seniors

Silver Eagles is a special retirement organization that serves as a networking center and a focal point for social activities. Many members are "heavy hitters," former corporate presidents, executives and business owners. SCORE and AARP also have local chapters For **SCORE** information contact Howard Aiken *(947-3532)* or Dick Newkirk *(782-5950)*. For **AARP**, call the Chamber *(782-4812)*.

Crime & Safety

The Clayton Police make the Maytag repair man look swamped. When we asked the desk sergeant about crime prevention programs he laughed. There are none because there's no crime to prevent! If you move in, give a call and say hello *(782-3333)*.

Earning a Living

Clayton is not an easy place to find work. Many people own their own businesses and hire themselves, leaving little opportunities for others. That is unless you're in a position to create your own business. The community, growing as it is, has a great need for retail and service businesses. In fact, Georgia Tech did a survey recently and found that what was sorely lacking in Clayton were fine restaurants. Tourism continues to be the backbone of the local economy.

Starting a business: Contact the Rabun County Chamber *(782-4812)* and the Georgia Department of Trade *(656-3586)*.

The job market: See above.

When the Kids Come to Visit

Aside from the wonderful state parks and lakes, people travel to Atlanta for fun: Atlanta Zoo, Fernbank Science Center and Planetarium, The Carter Center Library, Atlanta Botanical Gardens and the Japanese Rose Gardens (115 miles).

Getting Around Town

Roads & interstates: US 441 and 23, US 76, closest interstate is I-85 at Commerce, GA.

Airports & airlines: Atlanta International Airport (115 miles): Delta, USAir, American, Continental, United Northwest, TWA. Also, Greenville/Spartanburg Airport (83 miles) USAir, American, Delta.

Public transportation: No mass transit. Closest rail service is in Cornelia (32 mi.).

Managing without a car: A car is a necessity.

What Residents Already Know

There is such a tremendous variety of wildflowers blooming at any point in the year, you can make some unbelievable centerpieces.•Sometimes in winter it's warm enough to play golf but cold enough to still get in some skiing—all on the same day. Try that in Scottsdale!•Clayton is a very safe, trusting community. Not only do residents keep their homes unlocked, they leave their keys in the car!

For More Information

Chamber Of Commerce Office:
Rabun County Chamber
of Commerce
P.O. Box 761
Clayton, 30525
782-4812

Newspaper:
Clayton Tribune (weekly)
P.O. Box 425
Clayton, 30525
782-3312

Realtor:
Jackie West
Coldwell Banker/
Hal West Realty
P.O. Box 1234
Clayton, 30525
782-2222

21. Maui, Hawaii

Area Snapshot

Nickname: "The Valley Isle"
Area code: 808 **Zip code:** 96708-79
Time zone: Hawaiian time is 2 hrs. behind PST; 5 hrs. behind EST
Local population: 93,000
% of population 65+: 20%
U.S. region: West Pacific/Central Hawaii
Closest metro area: Honolulu, 100 miles by air
Nearby areas to consider: Wailea, Kapalua, Kaanapali, Hana
Median housing price: $268,000
Best reasons to retire here: Scenic beauty, extraordinary tropical climate, wonderful people, fabulous golf, laid-back atmosphere.

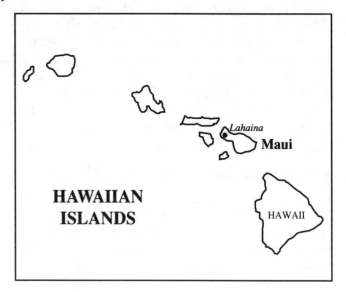

HAWAIIAN ISLANDS

Lahaina

Maui

HAWAII

Fabulous Features

Two words in the English language share the definition: "any place of great beauty and perfection." They are paradise and Maui. Indeed, there is no lovelier place on earth. With the exotic protea flowers, tropical sunshine, gentle trade winds and snowcapped volcanic mountains, your days are blissfully calm. It's the very reason so many CEOs, doctors and entertainers live here. Maui is the second-largest Hawaiian island and the most likely to appeal to the country club set. It's the golf capital of the state, with 30 exciting courses and 365 play days. Windsurfing is an experience and everyone from 8 to 80 is out there trying. Homes range from a simple 3BR arrangement to 11,000 sq. ft. mansions that are the ultimate, opulent hideaways. Cattle ranching in Hana (means work) and tourism (more than 2 million visitors a year) are the economic backbone of the island. Whale watching and biking down the Haleakala volcano (rumor has it that New York City could fit inside the crater) are enjoyable pastimes.

Retirees who are opened-minded to a society of international neighbors (Japanese, Chinese, Hawaiian, Filipinos), and who crave a lifestyle rich in relaxation and warm people, will never regret heading due west. To borrow from the mental health profession, when you live in Hawaii, you live in a dream state.
Possible drawbacks: Bar none, the biggest problem will be visitors who come for a week and stay indefinitely.•Newcomers from the mainland are a minority, the "haoles" (foreigners). If you won't work to earn the acceptance of the natives and learn to converse using some pidgen, adjusting will be difficult.•Paradise doesn't come cheaply. Real estate, food, taxes and entertainment require deep pockets. We spoke to one couple who said "We decided if we could live any place for one year, it would be Hawaii. That was seven years ago and even on a fixed income, we're living comfortably." Where there's a will, there's a way.

"You can quote me on that"

"Maui is paradise and I wouldn't trade it for the world. People told me I would feel isolated, but I lived in Alaska for six years and I found that to be much more so. And, yes, it's expensive to live here, but I don't feel overwhelmed by the costs. I've taken up golf since I moved in and it's how I socialize and spend my day. The thing I love the most is the casual attitude and attire to fit the mood. It was just what I was looking for."—A.P.

Climate

Elevation: sea level to 10,023'	Avg. High/ Low	Avg. Rainfall (Inches)	Avg. # Days Precip.	Avg. % Humidity
Jan.	80/64	3.6	11	74
April	82/66	1.3	11	68
July	86/70	.21	5	63
Oct.	86/69	1.1	7	65
YEAR	83/67	18	-	-
# days 32° or below: 0		# days 90° or above: 0		

Let the Good Times Roll

Recreation: Maui is the golf capital of Hawaii with some of the most exciting and internationally recognized courses. Wailea Resort's Blue and Orange as well as Kapalua are the sites of many classic events. The Plantation Course is one of the longest and most challenging, and the much-awaited Waikapu Golf Course will be the 31st course on the island. For property owners, greens fees are substantially reduced at municipal courses (possibly $10 instead of $60). Maui is also the world's best place for windsurfing. The snorkeling off Maui in the Molokini Crater is another great diversion, along with parasailing, jet skiing, fishing, swimming, sailing, tennis, power boating, bike riding and sunbathing.

Culture: The Maui Symphony plays throughout the year in various locations on the island, and the Maui Community Theater offers performances with promising local talents. Plans calls for the Maui Community Cultural Arts Center to be built in a few years, which will bring ballet, theater, and symphony to the island.

Annual events: The Art Maui Exhibit (March) Lei Day: lei making contests and Queen coronation (May); Lei Festival (June); Annual Up Country Fun Fair (June) Kapalua Jazz Festival (June); Aloha Week (Sept.); Maui Country Fair (Sept.); Halloween in Lahaina: almost as good as the Mardi Gras (Oct.); Makawao Rodeo (July).

Local Real Estate

The whole island of Maui is a retirement community, so you won't find specially designated developments as you would in Florida and Arizona. Limited availability of average-priced homes ($200,000), found in all parts of the island, make Maui a seller's market. Keep in mind that when purchasing property, you'll be asked to make a decision about purchasing the land and the building (a fee-simple purchase) or a leasehold (ownership expires at a certain time), which is less costly. Leaseholds are also better for investment properties, as 100% of it is considered a depreciable asset.

Median price for single family home: $268,000. Mind you, this will buy a small home with basic amenities. Larger, more extravagant homes start at a half million and the sky is the limit.

Median price for 2BR condo: $160,000. The average price is $200,000 for a brand-new 3BR, 2BA (2BR would go for $180,000). The newer models may not come with a pool (a way to keep the cost down to $180,700—the maximum for FHA approval) but most older models will have one as well as a tennis court. The majority are also situated within walking distance to the beaches.

Rental housing market: $800 for a 2BR apartment; $1,200/month plus utilities for a single family house.

Common housing styles & features: Because the climate is so conducive to outdoor living, homes in Hawaii are not as large as on the mainland. The averaged-priced homes (basic wood frame tract) are about 1,000 sq. ft. with 3BR, 2BA, small decks, and possibly garages or carports (no basements). Lots are 7,000 sq. ft.

Amenities in condo developments: For the lower priced units, most complexes have a pool. In the $200,000 price range, tennis and putting greens may also be included.

Nearby areas to consider: Wailea, Kapalua, Kaanapali, Hana.

Unique features of these areas: Wailea and Kapalua are resort areas that have great appeal to retired CEOs and entrepreneurs who have sold their interests. Many have built or bought into estate subdivisions, such as Alexandra and Baldwin's Development. In Kaanapali, the AMFAC development is equally as prestigious. Kapalua (the most exclusive) has two hotels and a Ritz Carlton going up. Lot sizes average 2-7 acres with homes running 11,000 sq. ft. The lots alone are $1.2 to $6 million and they've practically sold out. The town of Hana is owned by the Hana Cattle Ranching family and is a small, idyllic community. There's a lot of tropical vegetation, and it's a desired getaway for millionaires, movie stars, and recording artists. You'll be "neighbors" of Jim Nabors, Carol Burnett and Kris Kristofferson.

What Things Cost

What everyone wants to know is, are living costs any worse than New York or Los Angeles? You betcha. Overall living costs are 30% higher than the national average, but the real killers are housing (43% higher) and personal income tax (66% higher). In fact, it ranks 8th for the highest tax burden per capita. Virtually all necessities (food, clothing and shelter) are imported, contributing significantly to higher purchase prices.

Gas company: Maui Gas Service (liquid petroleum). $1.80 per gallon and $60 to rent tank *(244-2022)*.

Electric company: Maui Electric. If all electric, monthly bills avg. $90. With combined gas/electric, electric portion averages $70/mo.

Water/sewer: *(243-7730)*. Avg. mo. bill is $20.

Phone company: GTE Hawaiian Telephone *(643-3456)*. Basic rate is $16.85/mo. Installation is $45 if home is already wired; new wiring is $95 for the first jack.

Car registration/license: Out-of-state license and plates are valid until they expire. Then, you'll be required to take a vision and written test and possibly a road test. Must provide proof of Social Security number. To use your plates, get a permit sticker within 10 days of arrival (good for a year). Registration requires a lot of paperwork: a Hawaiian safety inspection sticker, shipping receipt with your arrival date, Hawaii no-fault insurance card and certificate of ownership. License: $4.25; tags and title: based on year/make of car. Driver's manual: $4 at any book store. DMV: *(243-7840)*.

The Tax Ax

Sales tax: 4% (no exemptions). **State income tax:** 10%. The Department of Taxation can offer more information *(548-4242)*. **Retirement income:** Federal and Government pensions are not taxed. Private pensions are not taxed if employee contributions are no longer made.

Property taxes & tax breaks: Both homes and property are taxed. These are calculated separately: $3.50 per $1,000 assessed house value; $3.50 per $1,000 assessed property value. Tax breaks applicable only if the owner is the occupant. From ages 55-59, there's a $60,000 maximum exemption. Those 60-64 get an $80,000 maximum exemption and residents 65-69 are entitled to a $100,000 maximum exemption. Property Assessor *(527-5500)*.

Medical Care

Major hospitals/regional medical centers: **Maui Memorial Hospital** is the only one serving the island (in Wailuku). It's a JCAH-accredited facility and specializes in acute care, oncology, radiology, coronary care and general surgery. It also offers 24-hour emergency service. **Emergency medical services (EMS):** Emergency medical service is provided by Internal Life Support, a private ambulance concern. **Physician's referral:** Maui Hospital *244-9056*.

Continuing Education

Maui Community College allows seniors to enroll in most courses for free. It also offers a Senior Network, which teaches computer skills and allows unlimited access to them *(244-9181)*.

Services for Seniors

Kaunoa Senior Center sponsors leisure and nutrition programs, telephone check-ins and friendly visits; Senior Softball League plays all over Hawaii; There are local chapters of **RSVP** *(243-7848)* and **AARP** *(879-8754)*. The Department of Aging publishes a monthly tabloid for seniors, AARP distributes a newsletter and *Maui News* has a special section each month for senior news and events.

Crime & Safety

Considering that it's such a tourist haven, crime is very low. Some attribute it to the honest work ethic and high employment rate of the locals. Others say the climate makes people mellow. The police say that strict sentencing and the inability to escape off the island are the real deterrents. Gambling is illegal, and drugs don't seem to be an issue.

Earning a Living

Current business climate: Tourism, agriculture and building homes are the mainstays of the island. It is estimated that 6,000 new homes will be built by the year 2000. Construction-related businesses fare well in this area. The garment industry has a presence, albeit an unstable one.

Help in starting a business: The Small Business Development Center *(548-7645)* or the Chamber will assist with permits, locations, business plans and advertising *(871-7711)*.

The job market: Unemployment is extremely low. In fact, many residents have 2-3 jobs just to make ends meet. Some companies said they preferred employees who were totally acclimated to the island life (apparently it takes about a year to stop acting as though you're on vacation).

When the Kids Come to Visit

Haleakala Crater: 10,023 feet, many bicycle down this crater of the Haleakala Volcano, the world's largest dormant volcano. Seven Sacred Pools: great diving, swimming, or splashing under the falls created by the cascading pools. "The Road to Hana": magnificent, crooked 30-mile road to the charming town of Hana: 54 bridges, lush vegetation, spectacular views of the ocean, and cute little mountain critters that love Maui chips! Lahaina: old whaling village with beautiful boutiques and art galleries. Whale watching: the grey whales migrate annually past Maui's shores. If you're lucky, you'll spot a mother whale frolicking with her baby (Nov.-April). Iao Valley: natural moss covered rock formation said to resemble JFK.

Getting Around Town

Roads & interstates: 30, 31, 36, 37, 340, 360, 377, 378. **Airports & airlines:** Of three airports on the island, the main one is in the port of Kahului. It is served by Aloha Island Air, Aloha, Hawaiian, Air Molokai, American, Delta and United. Kahului is the island hopping airport and Hana (southeast) is a private airport. Honolulu International Airport is served by all major Hawaiian, American domestic and international carriers *(836-6411)*. **Public transportation:** None (that's exactly how they want it to stay). **Managing without a car:** A car is as essential as sunscreen. Maui takes up 728 sq. miles.

What Residents Already Know

Here are 10 things you won't find in Maui: billboards, snakes, change of seasons, privately owned beaches, daylight savings time, mobile homes, poison ivy, professional sports, fur coats and ordinary sunsets.•There are only a few main roads on the island and most are two lanes. It doesn't take much to back up traffic.•Want to know more about life in Hawaii? Check out these books from the library: *Hawaii* (James Michener), *Fax to Da Max* (a humorous look at Hawaiian statistics by Jerry Hopkins), and *The Pocket Hawaiian Dictionary* (Mary Kawena Pukui).

For More Information

Chamber of Commerce Office:
Maui Chamber of Commerce
P.O. Box 1677
Kahului, Maui 97632
871-7711

Newspaper:
Maui News
100 Mahalani Street
Wailuku, Maui 96793
Have the Friday edition delivered
for 3 months ($12)
800-827-0347

Realtor:
Jim Wagner, CRS
Re/Max Mana Kai Realty
1325 S. Kihei Rd.
Maui, 96753
800-800-8708 or 879-4571

22. Coeur d'Alene, Idaho

Area Snapshot

Nickname: "City by the Lake"
County: Kootenai
Area code: 208 **Zip code:** 83814
Local population: 25,000 **County:** 70,000
% of population 55+: 20%
U.S. region: Northern Idaho
Closest metro areas: Spokane, Wash., 33 miles
Nearby areas to consider: Hayden Lake, Sand-point, Post Falls
Median housing price: $75,000
Best reasons to retire here: Gorgeous lake country, fabulous skiing, year-round recreation, country club communities, affordable housing and taxes, excellent health care, friendly people

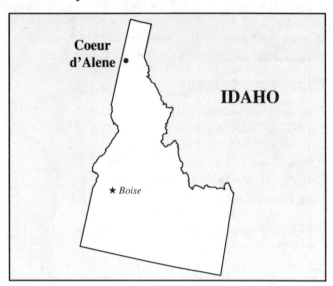

Fabulous Features

When *National Geographic* says that Lake Coeur d'Alene is one of the five most beautiful lakes in the world, you can believe it. And when world-famous Coeur d'Alene Hotel is named the number one mainland resort in the world by Conde Nast's *Traveler*, you start to wonder what else this majestic town of 25,000 offers. The rolling wheat fields, green forests, views of the snowcapped Rocky Mountains, crystal-clear lakes (75 in the region), will absolutely take your breath away. Life in Coeur d'Alene is a never-ending vacation with parasailing, jet skiing, canoeing and fishing (in the most fish-rich lakes). And that's just one season. Golf, cross-country skiing and snowmobiling are waiting the rest of the year. For retirees, even better news is the availability of beautiful new homes in the $100,000 range (lovely, older homes sell for much less). Once dependent on mining, timber and agriculture (the Rathdrum Prairie produces 20 percent of the world's Kentucky Bluegrass

seed), the "City on the Lake" is now viewed as a premier resort community. Tourism, new-comers and new industry are injecting millions of dollars into the economy. Retirees are an important part of the mix with first-rate health care and services to provide for their needs. Coeur d'Alene may have just been discovered by the magazines, but lifelong residents will tell you that the regal vistas and memorable sunsets have been here the whole time.

Possible drawbacks: The winters can be brutally cold, snowy and gray. For months. Every year. Many retirees head out to warm-weather climates. Taxpayers might look longingly over the border at their neighbors in Washington who pay no state income tax (although their sales tax is close to 3% higher). At a maximum rate of 8.2% on taxable income over $43,000, it's got to hurt.

"You can quote me on that"

"I retired here from Washington many years ago and I've seen tremendous changes in the community, mostly good. We have the resorts to thank for giving our economy strength when agriculture, mining and timber have taken on lesser importance. Coeur d'Alene is a wonderful place to retire. People are caring and nice. The only thing I would warn people about is our winters are harsh. We don't get wind, but the snowfall and the cold is tough. Lots of retirees are snowbirds with homes in Florida or Arizona. —Mrs. L.M.J.

Climate

Elevation: 2,333'	Avg. High/ Low	Average Inches		Avg. # Days Precip.	Avg. % Humidity
		Rain	Snow		
Jan.	33/19	1.3	21	17	82
April	60/32	1.4	1	11	59
July	85/50	.8	-	5	46
Oct.	58/32	2.9	.6	9	71
YEAR	58/34	20	58	-	-
# days 32° or below: 140			# days 90° or above: 10		

Let the Good Times Roll

Recreation: Life centers around the Coeur d'Alene Lake and its 123 miles of sandy shoreline. The beaches are dazzling and the sailing and yachting are superb. Within 50 miles are 74 other lakes, including Hayden Lake and Spirit Lake. Fishermen are happy 12 months of the year with plenty of trout, bass and salmon waiting. Tub Hill, the Coeur d'Alene National Forest and other back-country areas are ideal for hiking, biking and camping. There is also hiking and camping along the 45-mile lake at Farragut State Park (former site of a WWII boot camp). The sleepy St. Joe River is the world's highest navigable river, and boating is a favorite pastime. Skiing at the three major resorts in the area is another fabulous diversion. Coeur d'Alene also offers six golf courses, municipal tennis courts, and miles of snowmobile and cross-country ski trails. The town also boasts the world's longest floating boardwalk. It's no wonder that the National Civic league recently designated Coeur d'Alene one of 10 "All American Cities" (the only one in Idaho).

Culture: The city's Performing Arts Alliance Series attracts nationally known performers to the area. And with three college campuses in the city (Lewis-Clark State College, the University of Idaho and North Idaho College), cultural opportunities abound. North Idaho College presents several theater performances and a concert series during the year. Their art gallery is a fine addition to the several in town. The Summer Theater puts on four Broadway musicals each summer, attracting talented performers from all over the region.

Annual events: Art on the Green: one of the top art shows in the Northwest with more than 35,000 spectators (Aug.); Jazz Fest (Aug.); Multiple Sclerosis Ski Challenge (Jan.); North Idaho Fair (Aug.); Coeur d'Alene to Spokane Canoe Marathon (June); 3C's Wine Festival (April).

Local Real Estate

It's been a seller's market for the past two years because of the huge influx of easterners and westerners who have come into the market with big equity payouts. Retirees are grabbing nice 3BR homes for $70,000-$80,000. In the $100,000-$125,000 range, you can get a new 3BR house (2,500-3,000 sq. ft.) with ample custom work, and lots of acreage. Golf course communities near Hayden Lake Country Club, Fairview, Avendale and Highlands are in the $200,000 range and up.

Median price for single family home: $75,000.

Median price for 2BR condo: $50,000.

Rental housing market: Rentals are hard to find because there has been so much in the way of sales activity. When available, a 2BR apartment is $325-$425; a 3BR house ranges from $500-$700/mo.

Common housing styles & features: New construction has been tremendous, with lots of ranches (most have basements), townhouses, condos and patio homes coming in. The lakeside properties on both Lake Coeur d'Alene and Lake Hayden offer wonderful views and are great investments.

Amenities in condo developments: Pool, tennis courts.

Nearby areas to consider: Post Falls, Hayden Lake, Sandpoint. **Unique features of these areas:** Post Falls (9 mi. west) is on the Spokane River and offers less expensive homes. Hayden Lake is exclusive country-club territory with beautiful homes on the fairways. Sandpoint (46 mi. north on Ponderay Lake) has many retirement communities with homes starting in the $70,000.

What Things Cost

Gas company: Washington Water Power *(664-0421).* For a 1,500 sq. ft. home, gas and hot water heating (including electric) runs $953 a year. Gas heat + hot water can be as low as $8/mo. in summer and $48/mo. in winter.

Electric company: Kootenai Electric *(765-1200)* offers a level pay (budget system). A 4BR home will run $48/mo on average (not an all-electric home) and $70/mo. in winter.

Phone company: GTE *(883-0300)*. Basic monthly service including unlimited local calls and touchtone is $19.60. Maintenance service is available for an extra $1.50/mo.

Car registration/license: Registration depends on year of car—lowest is $21, highest: $49; Title fees: $8; Driver's license: $19.50 plus $3 for written test; License plates: included in registration fees.

The Tax Ax

Sales tax: 5% (prescription drugs exempt).

State income tax: Idaho's income tax for those married, filing jointly is on a sliding scale from 2% (for taxable income up to $4,999) up to 8.2% for taxable income over $43,000.

Retirement income: Private pension income is taxed as ordinary income. Social Security is not taxed. There is a $30 food credit for residents 65 and older.

Property taxes & tax breaks: Property is assessed at true market value. The current tax rate in the county is 1.6% of $1,000 of valuation. If you live in the city limits, it's 2.2% There is also a generous 50% exemption off the value of the home up to a maximum $50,000. County Tax Assessor *(769-4400)*.

Medical Care

Major hospitals/regional medical centers: Kootenai Medical Center (JCAH-accredited), is a full-service hospital serving 5 counties in Northern Idaho. It offers every major specialization, including coronary and cancer care, diabetes therapy and education, MRIs, general surgery, physical therapy and radiology, among others. The hospital is widely known for its North Idaho Cancer Center, which offers treatments, support groups and social services. Self-improvement classes and support groups (bereavement, caregivers and numerous others) and even courses on wills and trusts are offered to the community. **Pine Crest Psychiatric Hospital** (JCAH-accredited),

offers a 24-hr. crisis hotline *(800-221-5058)*. **Emergency medical services (EMS):** All firefighters are trained EMTs and work in conjunction with the county paramedics. There are two squad vehicles for EMS and other rescues. Average response time is less than six minutes. **Physician's referral:** Kootenai Medical Center *667-6441*.

Continuing Education

Lewis-Clark State College has a satellite campus in town that offers evening classes open to the community. It also offers special-interest courses such as "History of the Incan Empire." Seniors pay $20 to register plus $5 per credit *(666-1551)*. North Idaho College has a very popular elderhostel program (June), which always features courses on North Idaho's literature, history and geology. They also have an expanding Community Education program, which just started—"Growing Wise," a six-part class studying life past 50 (enrollment: $40). More classes being created for seniors every year *(769-3444)*.

Services for Seniors

The Lake City Senior Center organizes numerous activities including bridge, cribbage, china painting, dance classes and a grandmother's group. The services include income tax and banking assistance, referrals for assistance, a legal aid ombudsman and a monthly newsletter. The local **AARP** chapter also meets here. There is an active club for seniors called the Rambling Rovers (they've gone to Europe, Hawaii, Alaska and other exciting destinations). Call the Senior Center about membership *(667-4628)*. "Senior Review" is a great monthly newspaper *(772-6450)*.

Crime & Safety

The Coeur d'Alene Police Department has a senior ombudsman, and a fraud hotline for seniors to call if they are concerned about phony deals. This has dramatically increased the awareness of scams that had previously been ripping off the elderly. With respect to other crime, auto theft and burglaries are frequently reported although they don't pose a serious threat. Tourist season brings crowds and nuisance arrests. Violent crime is minimal and, when it does occur, it's usually drug-related rather than random.

Earning a Living

Current business climate: For the past two years, the real estate market has been as hot as a pistol and the town has fortified its image as a premier resort community. Lumber, agriculture and mining have waned as a backbone of the economy but still have a presence. In the last four years, more than 20 major companies have relocated, including U.S. Products. **Help in starting a business:** The Panhandle Area Council, affiliated with the Small Business Development Center, is an active organization that provides counseling services. It offers an excellent business incubating program and a loan program for fixed asset financing and working capital. It also provides job counseling, training and placement programs for people of all ages *(772-0584)*. **The job market:** Reports from the front line are that jobs are plentiful and area businesses are not afraid of hiring seniors.

When the Kids Come to Visit

St. Joe River (world's highest navigable river) is great for boating and fishing; Lake Coeur d'Alene has every imaginable water sport; Silverwood (family theme park 15 miles north) is a Victorian village built around an antique aircraft museum with antique air shows, locomotive rides and an amusement park; Silver Mountain has the world's longest gondola rides, which take you up the mountain for your biking excursion or to enjoy the restaurants); Farragut State Park on Lake Ponderay offers campgrounds, hiking, swimming and picnicking.

Getting Around Town

Roads & interstates: I-90, US-95. **Airports & airlines:** Kootenai County Airport has commuter service by Empire Airlines, connecting northern and southern Idaho. Spokane International Airport (33 miles east) is served by Continental, Delta, Horizon, United, Northwest and United Express. **Public transportation:** Panhandle Area Transit covers one route through town and offers no senior discount ($1 one way). It does offer curb-to-curb service for a suggested donation of $1.50. **Managing without a car:** A car is essential.

What Residents Already Know

While she was waiting to have her car repaired, a Chicago woman noticed a wall calandar with a magnificnet picture. She said to herself that wherever that place was, she wanted to go. It was Coeur d'Alene and she retired here last year. Stories like that are a dime a dozen. This is the only city in the world with a golf course that has a floating green (that 14th hole on the lake is a killer, but then so are the $120 greens fees). There's great consternation regarding the 16 days of the year that farmers are allowed to burn the bluegrass seed. The environmentalists are trying to eliminate the method. The farmers (and long-time residents) know it's an integral part of their survival.

For More Information

Chamber of Commerce Office:
Coeur d'Alene Area Chamber
of Commerce
400 Northwest Boulevard
P.O. Box 850
Coeur d'Alene, 83814-0850

Newspaper:
Coeur d'Alene Press (daily)
201 North 2nd Street
Coeur d'Alene, 83814
664-8176

Realtors:
Frank Vernon
Davis Realty
1724 E. Sherman Ave.
Coeur d'Alene, 83814
667-5511

Roger Agte
All Star Realty
1034 North 3rd Street
Coeur d'Alene, 83814
667-1525 or 800-452-5468

23. Bloomington, Indiana

Area Snapshot

Nickname: "The Break Away Town"
County: Monroe
Area code: 812   **Zip code:** 47401, 47404, 47408
Local population: 60,660   **County:** 108,000 (includes student body of 32,000)
% of population 65+: 9.2%
U.S. region: Southern Indiana
Closest metro area: Indianapolis, 50 miles
Nearby areas to consider: Nashville, Brown County
Median housing price: $89,000
Best reasons to retire here: Endless cultural and recreational opportunities, affordable lifestyles, lush rural country setting, "Big Ten" town (home of Indiana University).

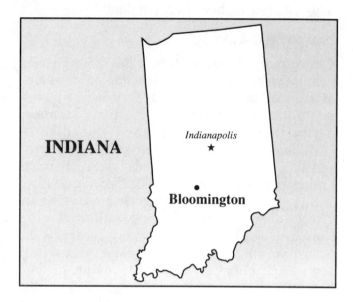

Fabulous Features

"What should we do today?" is not a pertinent question when you've retired to Bloomington. There is more culture, recreation and sports packed into this "Big Ten" town than may be available in some states. Some cities are predominantly outdoor locales, others lean towards great things to do inside. This awe inspiring little town in southern Indiana has both. The lake filled region has rolling hills, a national forest and a temperate climate, adding to the enjoyment of those who are hikers, fishermen, sailors, skiers, and campers. The culture enthusiasts are only minutes away from a world of opera, ballet, symphonies, and some of the most captivating performing arts in the Midwest. Even the architecture is world-famous, with sculpture by Caulder and a theater designed by I.M. Pei. And then there's that famous "Hoosiermania" you hear so much about. Residents cherish their Big Ten football and basketball teams, cramming into Memorial Stadium and Assembly Hall for

another hopeful season. Real estate opportunities in Bloomington and surrounding Brown County are a wonderful assortment of small, large, contemporary, colonial, suburban, country, wooded, lake views, dunes, golf communities, condos and houses. You can shop 'till you drop. What's more, living costs are reasonable, the climate is reasonable and the people are (you guessed it) reasonable. From the town that brought you two NCAA Championships, Bloomington is indeed a winner!

Possible drawbacks: The summer humidity can be uncomfortable but hurry back for the gorgeous fall foliage.•Traffic in town can be a nightmare, so be prepared. It is a challenge finding time to do all that you want.•Medical care is limited, with only one hospital serving the area. Many people spoke of traveling to Indianapolis to visit specialists for certain problems or treatment (although they did have high praises for Bloomington Hospital).

"You can quote me on that"

"Bloomington is truly an all-American city and I'm from Texas. The people are so full of good will and charm and the city offers so much to do, regardless of your tastes and interests. The biggest surprises have been the tremendous growth of the area and the fact that even if it's a college town, the towns people don't feel out of it. The community caters to every interest."—Mrs. S.C.

Climate

Elevation: 851'	Avg. High/ Low	Average Inches		Avg. # Days Precip.	Avg. % Humidity
		Rain	Snow		
Jan.	41/24	3	-	12	75
April	64/42	3.7	-	13	65
July	88/64	3.5	-	9	67
Oct.	69/44	2.5	-	8	71
YEAR	62/43	40	17	-	-
# days 32° or below: 113			# days 90° or above: 27		

Let the Good Times Roll

Recreation: Lake Monroe and Lake Lemon are the places to head for fishing, boating, hunting and trapping (with limits set by the Dept. of Natural resources), picnicking, swimming and hiking. Lake Lemon is also great for bird watching; Griffy Lake has wonderful canoe trails for wildlife observing or just plain fun; Golf, tennis and skiing (Ski World and Paoli Peaks) are ready when you are. The Pointe Golf and Tennis Club on Lake Monroe is a beautiful facility. And IU's own Wildermuth Center has two pools, a running track, and several other indoor sports.

Culture: "Do I hear a waltz?" Yes, and an opera and a symphony and a jazz quartet. It may seem inconceivable that a small college town could be viewed as a cultural mecca of the Midwest, but Bloomington is deserving of the designation. As home to one of the finest music schools in the world, concert-goers are the first to enjoy opera stars, musicians, and stage performers who ultimately achieve international recognition. Residents never tire of going to the MAC (Musical Arts Center) for the opera (has the longest-running season in the western hemisphere) and Broadway productions, the Fine Arts Auditorium for dance and music or top entertainers, and several other local repertory theaters. The museums are no less auspicious, with the Fine Arts Museum (ranks among the finest University Art museums in the country with more than 25,000 works; the building's architect was I.M. Pei) and the Lilly Library with its rare book collection, sheet music and compositions. There are literally hundreds of performances and events during the year

Annual events: Little 500 Bike Race: the legendary bike race as featured in the movie, "Breaking Away" (April); Crappiethon, USA: the fishing tournament where fish are tagged for prizes (May); Bloomington Renaissance Festival (June); Taste of Bloomington (July); 4H Monroe County Fair (Sept.); 10K marathon (Nov.) Canopy of Lights (Dec.); Madrigal Dinners: University presents 16th century food, music and fun and the Nutcracker (Dec.).

Local Real Estate

With a constant flow of faculty moving in and out, there is always a lot of real estate activity. Traditionally, Bloomington and Brown County have been a big second-home market as well. Retirees come looking for ranch-style homes with acreage and wooded surroundings or new condo/golf course communities. Homes will start at $150,000 but many are in the $200,000-$300,000 price range (particularly in the exclusive parts of Brown County). Condos are much less.

Median price for single family home: $89,000
Median price for 2BR condo: $110,000
Rental housing market: 2BR rental apartments: $400-$800/month. Houses: $500-$1,500/month. Single family houses are readily available as many visiting faculty will rent for a year, leave the area and the home vacant.

Common housing styles & features: 3BR, 1-2 baths, garages, basements, very few carports. Look at Lake of the Four Seasons area and The Pointe for golf communities. Meadowood is strictly a retirement development.

Amenities in condo developments: There are many beautiful condo developments in the area but most do not come with outdoor amenities (pools and tennis courts).

Nearby areas to consider: Nashville, Brown County. **Unique features of these areas:** Brown County offers the ultimate in countrified living. Homes range in price from $200,000 to a half million. Smallest available lots are 5 acres. Privacy and exclusivity are what you pay a premium for, and to be within 20 minutes of the center of town. Brown County draws 5 million visitors a year to enjoy Brown County State Park, Yellow Wood Park and Hoosier National Forest. Nashville (pop. 500) is a quaint village in the center of Brown

County. Homes start at $60,000 and go up to $200,000.

What Things Cost

Overall living costs are 1% over the national average with housing, transportation and health care being a fraction under. Only utilities ran as a high as 9% above the rest of the country. In our interviews, however, everyone commented that they thought the cost of living in this area was extremely favorable. Food and entertainment were a fraction of what many had been accustomed to paying.

Gas company: Indiana Gas *(800-666-2853)*. Basic rate: $9.45 per month plus usage. A 3BR home would average $60/mo.

Electric company: Public Service of Indiana *(336-2023)*. Avg. monthly bill for electric is $143 for a 3BR home.

Water/sewer: Bloomington City Utilities *(339-1444)*. Avg. monthly bill is $20-30/mo. $15 fee to reset meter.

Phone company: Indiana Bell *(556-3510)*. Basic monthly service: $25. Connections run $47 with wiring in home ($50 for first jack, $30 each additional).

Car registration/license: Registration, title and tags varies according to make of car, year, transmission. For example, a 1985 standard trans., 4-door sedan would cost $75. License: $6/yr. DMV: *(336-3018)*.

The Tax Ax

Sales tax: 5% (prescription drugs are exempt).

State income tax: 3.4% on adjusted gross income.

Retirement income: $1,000 exemption for residents 65+.

Property taxes & tax breaks: The current millage rate in the city of Bloomington is 9.4323 per $100 of valuation. There is a $1,000 mortgage exemption if the outstanding mortgage exceeds $1,000. Homeowners who occupy their residence are entitled to an additional $1,500 exemption. For more information contact the Tax Assessor's office *(333-3501)*.

Medical Care

Major hospitals/regional medical centers: Bloomington Hospital is the only full service, accredited hospital in the area. It offers cancer care, MRI, laser surgery, cardiac care and rehabilitation, kidney dialysis, and all types of therapy. Next year, they will also do cardiovascular surgery.

Emergency medical services (EMS): 24-hour ambulance response is available throughout the county. Average response time is 6-9 minutes.

Physician's referral: Ask-A-Nurse Referral *336-0471*. Bloomington Hospital *330-5252*.

Continuing Education

Indiana University does not have a continuing education program specifically for seniors, although classes are open to any resident on a non-degree basis for $75 a credit hour. IU does run a very popular Mini-University one week each June where more than 100 professors lecture on various topics. And there's a fabulous Elderhostel each July with at least one American History course taught by the legendary Professor Irving Katz. The cost to commuters is $175 *(855-8995)*.

Services for Seniors

Bloomington's Area Agency on Aging is an excellent source for referrals on seniors services. Aside from providing valuable services, they publish several directories with listings and coupons *(334-3383)*. Many of the national senior organizations have local chapters, including **RSVP** (Retired Senior Volunteers). **AARP:** *(876-5880)*. and **SCORE:** *(336-6381)*. More than 500 people age 55 and older participate in the Senior Games of Indiana (Sept.), competing in over 20 team and individual sports.

Crime & Safety

In spite of the large student body population (35,000), Bloomington is a very safe community. Violent crime is rare and when it occurs, it's not random. Burglaries and thefts are more prevalent but mostly when the campus empties for vacations. The low crime rate is attributed to the stable base of permanent residents, the vast majority who are gainfully employed. The student population may be rowdy but not criminal (their parents would kill them). The police have also gotten the cooperation of the post office. They've implemented a Carrier Alert Program that urges mail carriers to be observant of unusual situations (they'll alert police if mail hasn't been taken in for a while, etc.).

Earning a Living

Current business climate: It's a competitive marketplace with many businesses trying to appeal to students. But the economy is generally healthy, with many affluent professionals and retirees in the area.

Help in starting a business: Anyone starting a business can get help from either SCORE or the Small Business Development Center. Both can be reached by calling the Chamber of Commerce *(336-6381)*.

The job market: With a 3% unemployment rate, minimum wage jobs go begging. There are signs everywhere advertising for help. For help with job training and placement, contact the Agency on Aging *(334-3383)*.

When the Kids Come to Visit

Aside from the multitude of campus activities and sights, kids love the Cyclotron (light shows); Kirkwood Observatory (observe the night sky); Lake Lemon, Lake Monroe and the Hoosier National Forest. There are ample state parks, movie theaters, mini-golf, etc., in the area.

Getting Around Town

Roads & interstates: State Roads 37 and 46. Bloomington is 45 miles west of I-65 and 45 miles south of junction of I-65, I-69, I-70 and I-74.

Airports & airlines: Monroe Airport offers direct flights to and from Chicago and Indianapolis. Indianapolis International Airport (45 minutes) is served by American, Delta, TWA, United, Midway, USAir and other major carriers.

Public transportation: Bloomington Public Transportation covers the city and county. The fare is 50¢ one-way for all. IU has a campus bus system as well.

Managing without a car: Although public transportation is quite good, the nicer residential areas are not on a bus line, so a car is a necessity. Disabled people can arrange for door-to-door transportation through the Office on Aging.

What Residents Already Know

There are more four-way stops and one-way streets per capita than probably even San Francisco or Boston, and it drives the newcomers crazy. •Whenever you walk into a restaurant, you're bound to see someone dressed in a getup (and it's not necessarily a student). •This is southern Indiana and slight southern drawls and expressions are part of the lingo. "You'ns" is their version of "You all," as in "You'ns want to go for a drive?" •There are a lot of wealthy retirees in these parts who love the life but miss the designer boutiques. Are you listening, Mr. Gucci?

For More Information

Chamber Of Commerce Office:
116 West 6th Street
Bloomington, 47401
336-6381

Newspaper:
Herald-Times/
Sunday Herald Times
1900 South Walnut Street
Bloomington, 47401
332-4401

Realtor:
Sandy Castle
Century 21 Peek & Associates
1409 North College
Bloomington, 47404
336-7713

24. Cape Cod, Massachusetts

Area Snapshot

County: Barnstable
Area code: 508   **Zip code:** 02601
Local population: 185,000 (500,000 in summer)
% of population 65+: 25%+
U.S. region: Northeast
Closest metro areas: Boston, 77 miles; Providence, R.I., 77 miles
Nearby areas to consider: Osterville, Centerville, Barnstable, Cotuit, Hyannisport
Average housing price: $135,000 (areas vary)
Best reasons to retire here: Scenic beauty and wildlife, long stretches of beaches; low property taxes, small, laid-back communities with large retirement population, artist's colony.

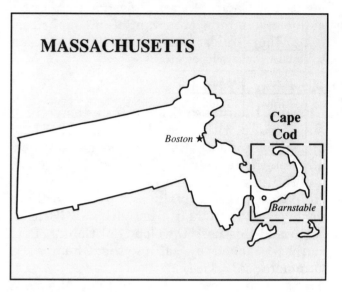

Fabulous Features

Vacationing on the Cape has been a time-honored tradition for easterners, but more and more retirees are discovering its wonderful year-round possibilities as well. The community takes great pride in attracting an eclectic group of writers, artists, corporate executives, and business owners from all over the country—and even the world. It's both a sportsman's paradise as well as an intellectual colony, even the change of seasons is diverse. Indian Summer is a dazzling splash of color, winters are mild, spring and summer are temperate and lush. The appeal of the cape is the natural charm and beauty of the island. It has 300 miles of shoreline, crystal lakes and ponds, pine-scented woods and area wildlife. The Cape Cod peninsula is the southernmost tip of the Commonwealth of Massachusetts. There are 15 towns subdivided into villages. Barnstable, Bourne, Falmouth and Yarmouth are the largest. Real estate is a steal and property is well spaced, adding to the rural feel. Cape Cod has always been a fabulous place to sit a spell. Now it's a place to both unwind and recharge any day of the year. **Possible drawbacks:** The first thing new residents have to get used to is the annual invasion of summer tourists which wreak havoc and congestion, especially in Hyannis. Transportation is limited, so not having a car will mean hardship. If you're counting on a job to support your retirement, you will find equal unemployment opportunities. The Cape Cod Commission has traditionally chosen in favor of preserving the environment vs. commercial development and industry, which limits jobs. The quiet of a well-protected natural paradise—at least during most of the year—is exactly what attracts most of its residents though.

"You can quote me on that"

"We moved here almost 30 years ago and have never regretted a day. It's beautiful, clean, and relaxed. We're big golfers and love being able to play as much as we do. Also the people are so interesting. They come from all walks of life, but what's more, because the community is so small and intimate, you get to meet them all. No one puts on airs. We have lots of CEOs, entertainers, and artists who live here year-round and it just keeps things very interesting. We feel we're living a very healthy lifestyle. The biggest drawback is traffic but that's anywhere you go and we think there are a million times more advantages to the Cape, so it doesn't get to us."— Mrs. M.M., Centerville

Climate

Elevation: 37'	Avg. High/ Low	Average Inches		Avg. # Days Precip.	Avg. % Humidity
Jan.	38/25	2.7	11	13	72
April	53/35	3.8	trace	11	70
July	74/62	2.5	-	9	80
Oct.	62/46	2.3	-	9	72
YEAR	56/42	38	34	-	-
# days 32° or below: 92			# days 90° or above: 4		

Let the Good Times Roll

Recreation: The Heritage Plantation of Sandwich has 76 acres of landscaped grounds, flower beds and nature trails. Nearby waterways allow for deep-sea and freshwater fishing, day trips by ferry to the islands of Nantucket and Martha's Vineyard, and eight clean, white beaches, (including Veterans, Kalmus, Sandy Neck, Craigville, Orrin & Sea Street Beaches). Golf is playable year-round at 30 courses, including Iyanough Hills Golf Course and Tara Hyannis Fiddler's Green Golf Course. Biking, hiking, and bird watching are other activities you can enjoy.

Culture: So the saying goes in Cape Cod, "People may retire their bodies here, but not their minds." Cultural offerings include Cape Cod Symphony Orchestra, Hyannis Ballet Company, Barnstable Comedy Club (for theater productions), Summer Stock Theater (Cape Cod is famous for its productions), Cahoon Museum of American Art (Cotuit), Community College Theater Productions, Academy of Performing Arts, Cape Cod Conservatory of Music and Art, and the Cape Cod Museum of Natural History.

Annual events: Chamber of Commerce Golf Tournament (May); Hyannis Harbor Festival (June); Barnstable County Fair (July); Hyannis Street Festival, Boston Pops By the Sea, and Cape Cod Chili Challenge (Aug.); Italian Fest on Main Street, (Oct.); Hyannis Harbor Lighting and Hyannis Christmas Stroll (Nov.).

Local Real Estate

A buyer's market, most homes are selling under $125,000. In the $150,000 price range

you can land a beautiful 3-4BR cape or ranch priced at $200,000 a few years ago. The second-home market is small.

Median price for single family home: $135,000. $125,000-$150,000 is the average.

Average price for 2BR condo: Low $100,000 range. Belmont in Harwich on the Beach: $200,000 range.

Rental housing market: Rental housing is available, mostly on a weekly basis for tourists. Rents avg. $1,000 in season (mostly houses and condos).

Common housing styles & features: Most are ranches and capes. There is some contemporary construction, but it's limited. Exteriors are wood frame or weathered shingle (no brick).

Amenities in condo developments: Most have pools, more exclusive developments have beaches and golf courses. **Nearby areas to consider:** Osterville, Centerville, West Barnstable, Barnstable, Cotuit, Hyannisport.

Unique features of these areas: Osterville is a small, rural village with boutiques and galleries. The homes are some of the most expensive and elite on Cape Cod, but very special insofar as architecture and class. Centerville is located between Osterville and Hyannis on the south side of the Cape. It's more residential and near the beaches. There are many nice, single family homes available, with close access to the shopping and services in Hyannis. West Barnstable and Barnstable are historic districts, with strict codes on land development to preserve the natural beauty of the area. Cotuit is primarily residential with the warm-water beaches nearby. It's a very pretty, historic area but with recent commercial growth, it's also becoming more self-sufficient. Much needed stores, restaurants and services are coming in. Homes are priced higher in this area. Hyannisport is the most exclusive area because it's right on the water.

What Things Cost

Housing prices and property taxes are so low, there's a phenomenon called the "Cape Cod Windfall." It's the amount of money retired residents can save by living in a less costly home on Cape Cod. Real estate taxes are often 50% less than most areas in the northeast.

Food and utilities are more expensive, but health care is low.

Gas company: Colonial Gas *(394-9851)*. Avg. mo. bill: $70, can go as low as $20 in the summer and as high as $200 in the winter (gas heat drives up the price). No deposit required.

Electric company: ComElectric *(291-0950)*. Avg. mo. bill is $70-75; $100 in the summer. No deposit required.

Phone company: New England Telephone *(778-3300)*. $34.79 to establish residential service. $10/mo. for a measured line (pay for every call); or $20/mo. for unlimited local calling.

Water/sewer: Barnstable Water Co. *(775-0063)*. Residential connection fee with a meter is $8 ($18 for new home). Water rates avg. $16.20/quarter. No deposit required.

Car registration/license: DMV *(775-0591)*. $40 plates; $50 title; $70 license (total fee for written test, road test and issuance). Additional 5% sales tax on auto purchases.

The Tax Ax

Sales tax: 5% (prescription and over-the-counter drugs, food, clothing exempt). **State income tax:** 6.25% on earned income (will roll back to 5.95% in 1/92); 12% on unearned income. **Retirement income:** Residents 65+ filing singly get a $700 exemption. If married filing jointly, both must be 65+ to each take the exemption. **Property taxes & tax breaks:** According to state law, assessments are done every three years. Barnstable's current rate is $7.69. A $100,000 home would then pay $769, plus additional $156 for the fire district. The surrounding villages have their own but similar rates. For residents, 62+, an annual homestead exemption allows you to pay real estate taxes based on 70% of fair market value (opposed to 100%).

Medical Care

Major hospitals/regional medical center: **Cape Cod Hospital** was designated by Medicare as a sole community provider in 1984 and as a regional referral center in 1987. It is an accredited, full-service hospital serving the Cape and all outlying areas. It offers general surgery, two critical care units (ICU and a coronary care unit) and radiation therapy. It has the third highest number of Medicare patients in Massachusetts. The nearest teaching hospital is at Boston University (90 minutes). **MediCenter Five** is a local service for non-emergencies. **Emergency medical services (EMS):** Every town on the Cape has a 24-hour medical emergency service its own fire department. The EMS (Cape and Islands EMS) has stations in each of the 15 villages and on the two islands. Response times vary by district and figures range from 4-6 minutes. All EMS techs are paramedics (highest training). Two private ambulance companies serve the Cape: Cape Cod Ambulance (advanced and basic), and the American Geriatric Emergency Service (AGES) for basic life support. **Physician's referral:** Ask-A-Nurse service at Cape Cod Hospital *771-1800*.

Continuing Education

Cape Cod Community College (Barnstable) runs the Academy of Lifelong Learning for residents 60+, offering day and evening classes. It also offers peer supported study groups (10-14 weeks) where members choose the course of study such as "Great Books," "Cape Cod History," and current affairs: $75 a semester ($125 for two semesters). Membership gives access to college library, gyms, etc. *(362-2131)*. Western New England College opens all courses to residents *(362-4936)*. Cape Cod Conservatory of Music and Arts offers courses in dance, music and art *(362-2772)*.

Services for Seniors

Council On Aging/Senior Center *(790-6365)*; Elder Law Project *(771-7458)*; Elder Services Hotline *(800-922-2275)*; 160 nonprofit organizations on Cape Cod that cover a full range of Philanthropy. Media: Senior Cape Cod Forum (Monthly) 72 Winter Street, Hyannis, 02601 *(778-5042)*. **AARP:** Local chapter #227 (Hyannis) Contact Hilda Culkins *(771-5171)*.

Crime & Safety

Cape Cod is a very safe area but crime rates do increase in the summer. There has also been a surge of drug-related crime and even a homeless population in the outlying areas. Currently, there are no crime prevention or self-defense courses offered to seniors, but the Council on Aging has a program in the works.

Earning a Living

Current business climate: There is virtually no manufacturing on Cape Cod; most businesses are tourist-related or service- and trade-oriented. The area continues to grow, and is open to innovative stores or services that fill a void.

Starting a business: The Small Business Development Center helps with planning and business decisions. Through the Chamber, people can take courses sponsored by the SBA and the Economic Development office *(362-3355)*. The Community College in West Barnstable offers classes. Seasonal minimum wage jobs are the best to hope for.

When the Kids Come to Visit

Aqua Service of Cape Cod (dolphin shows, petting zoos); Marine Aquarium and Zoological Park (W. Yarmouth); Cape Cod Potato Chip Factory; Cape Cod Railroad Tours.

Getting Around Town

Hyannis is the main shopping and commercial district on the Cape and is the gateway to the nearby islands of Martha's Vineyard and Nantucket.

Roads & interstates: Mid Cape Hwy., Rte. 6, Rte. 28, Rte. 132, Rte. 149.

Airports & airlines: The Barnstable Municipal Airport in Hyannis is served by Delta and Continental and offers shuttle service to Boston, with ongoing connections to Washington and New York. Boston is half an hour by air (1 1/2 hrs. by car or bus).

Public transportation: Hyannis Bus Terminal has regular transport to major cities; Full-service marine facilities, ferry and airline services to Martha's Vineyard and Nantucket; 24-hour taxi service; free transportation service for seniors through the Cape Cod Regional Transit Authority "B" Bus.

Managing without a car: Though options are available, living on the Cape without a car is very limiting.

What Residents Already Know

If you're a gardener, prepare for the challenge of your life. With the gusty winds and sandy soil, you'll have to learn how to defy the claim that "You can't grow it on the Cape."•Cape Cod is a bird-lovers paradise with more than 400 species recorded here, (one reason there is great emphasis on land conservation and preservation)..

For More Information

Chamber Of Commerce Office:
Hyannis Area Chamber
Of Commerce
319 Barnstable Road
Hyannis, MA 02601
508-775-2201

Barnstable Newcomers 428-4445

Newspapers:
Cape Cod Times (daily)
319 Main Street
Hyannis, 02601
775-1200

Barnstable Patriot (weekly)
P.O. Box 1208
Hyannis, 02601
771-1427

Realtor:
Mr. John A. Drew
Coldwell Banker
1 Century Plazas
1185 Route 28
Centerville, 02632
775-1404

25. Carson City, Nevada

Area Snapshot

Nickname: "Capital City"
County: Carson City/Douglas Counties
Area code: 702   **Zip code:** 89701
Local population: 40,300   **County:** 74,000
% of population 65+: 15%
U.S. region: Northwest Nevada (borders Lake Tahoe, California)
Closest metro areas: Reno, 30 miles
Nearby areas to consider: Gardnerville, Minden
Median housing price: $115,000
Best reasons to retire here: Four fabulous seasons, a 3-star combination of breathtaking mountains, desert and lakes; low, low taxes, surrounded by Reno and Lake Tahoe, phenomenal skiing, fishing, hunting.

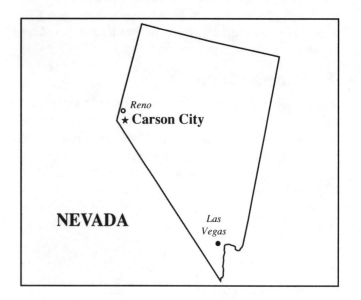

Fabulous Features

Carson City is the perfect retirement spot for people who go into stores and say "I'll take one of those and one of these and that over there." Life in this town is an endless stream of choices and opportunities. Some of the most spectacular skiing in the world is 23 miles west in Lake Tahoe or 50 miles south to famous Squaw Valley. Drive 30 miles north and you're in Reno with the glamorous casinos and first-rate entertainment. Head 30 miles in any direction and you're in "Terrific Trout Territory" (people say that Pyramid River and Walker River are superb). And 20 miles northeast is the desert and historic Virginia City, great fun for exploring old mines and ghost towns. The 72 miles around the Lake Tahoe Shoreline are without a doubt some of the most scenic in the country. Carson City, at the base of the Sierra Nevada Mountains, is heaven on earth. The four moderate seasons bring you snow without blistering cold and desert warmth with suffocating humidity. The homes are small, manageable and affordable. But the best news for retirees is the taxes. Or lack of taxes. It seems the only time you part with your money is at the tables. Take note that Carson City is also the state capital (the smallest one in the U.S.) and brings most of the gainful employment to the area. You'll love this place. It's an old western town with a new lease on life. Growth has been gangbusters and it's understandable why.

Possible drawbacks: The higher altitude (4,600 ft. and climbing) may be a potential health hazard for those with lung and respiratory problems.•Shopping is limited. There are malls, but not the big-city size. There are car dealers, but not many. Be prepared to deal with limited selection and prices. But Reno and other shopping areas are a short drive away.

"You can quote me on that"

"I lived in Southern California for 15 years and then came to Carson City. It was the best move I've ever made in my life. I am only 20-30 miles from some of the most incredible action that exists. The skiing is world-class, there's excellent hunting and fishing, the casinos and entertainment in Reno are fantastic. And this town is just great. I've never seen such a responsive police department before. You call and they're there in three minutes flat. I highly recommend retiring here but don't expect to sit back much. You'll get left behind in the dust."— Mr. D.B.

Climate

Elevation: 4,687'	Avg. High/ Low	Average Inches		Avg. # Days Precip.	Avg. % Humidity
		Rain	Snow		
Jan.	45/18	.6	6	6	75
April	64/30	.3	2	4	50
July	91/47	.3	-	3	38
Oct.	70/31	.4	trace	3	51
YEAR	67/32	4.7	26	-	-
# days 32° or below: 187			# days 90° or above: 47		

Let the Good Times Roll

Recreation: Situated in one of the most spectacular mountain and lake-filled regions in the country, there is non-stop outdoor action. People travel from around the world to ski in the Lake Tahoe Basin (they get 300-500 inches of snow a year, the sun is out 75% of the days and with elevations to 10,000 ft. and a variety of terrains, you've got it made). There are 16 resorts within 60 miles, all with breathtaking vistas on the horizon. The Heavenly Ski Resort is a grand spot for day and night fun. Big game hunters and fishermen are in paradise, with birds, elk, deer, freshwater streams and alpine lakes to challenge you. Trout fishing doesn't get any better than at Pyramid Lake and Walker River. For golfers, Eagle Valley has two challenging 18-hole courses. And in town, there are more than 600 acres of parks (18 in all) for free play as well as organized programs for seniors (come on over and "Aquacize" at the community pool).

Culture: The Brewery Arts Center offers wonderful visual performing arts and as well as a range of arts/crafts classes. The Center is home to the Carson City Chamber Orchestra, Carson City Community Band and Carson City Chamber Singers. There are numerous museums, historic buildings, and mansions depicting the western heritage: Bowers Mansion, Governors Mansion, State Railroad Museum, Stewart Indian Museum, Carson City Fire Museum, and the Nevada State Museum (many exhibits tracing the emergence of the state capital).

Annual events: Early Days Ski-Athalon (on wooden barrel staves) Lake Tahoe (March); Kit Carson Rendezvous, a gathering of mountain men, Indian pow-wow, wagon train and jamboree (June); Capital City Fair (July); Nevada Day Celebration and Parade with a Grand Ball, hard rock drilling contest and more (Oct.). In nearby Virginia City, there are camel races (Sept.) and in Reno the Air Race and the Great Reno Balloon Race (Sept).

Local Real Estate

Half of the new arrivals in Carson City are retirees and they're creating a great demand on housing. Fortunately there's enough to go around. The west end of town has the older homes (10-15 years), most are small 3BRs on 60 x 120 lots. Town homes and duplexes in the southeast section are also popular. Prices range from $95,000-$104,000. New homes are in Dayton (east of town), and start at around $120,000. There are no retirement "ghettos." Seniors buy anywhere they find a nice home.

Median price for single family home: $115,000. New homes average $120,000. Many retirees are also buying commercial and residential properties for income opportunities.

Median price for 2BR condo: $70s-$80s. This is not a condo market, however. Homes provide more space for the same money.

Rental housing market: The vacancy rate has never been this low and rentals don't stay on the market long. A 3BR/2BA home runs $700-$800/mo. A 2BR apartment averages $525-$625/mo.

Common housing styles & features: Most of the older homes are wood-sided, ranch styles with 3BR, 2BA. All have garages but no basements. The newer homes have the 2 x 6 insulation, which is very efficient (really keeps the house cool or warm as needed). Lot sizes outside of town average a half acre to 2 acres.

Amenities in condo developments: 2-3BR, pool, tennis courts, exterior maintenance.

Nearby areas to consider: Gardnerville/ Minden (15 mi. south).

Unique features of these areas: These are small/rural communities that still have that cattle country feel. A lot of retirees move out there for the wide open space. Homes are comparably priced to Carson City but be aware that shopping, medical services and other amenities are limited.

What Things Cost

Overall living costs are 4% above the national average, with utilities running 20% below. Housing is 15% higher and health care 19% above the average (ACCRA, 1st Quarter, 1991).

Gas company: Southwest Gas Corporation *(588-6602)*. Average monthly bill is $41. Winter months can average $95. A $70 deposit may be required.

Electric company: Sierra Pacific Power Company *(541-2040)*. Average monthly bill is $60-$70.

Phone company: Nevada Bell *(333-4811)*. Basic unlimited local calls $13.55/month. Measured rate per local call: $9.80. $45 connection fee. $25 deposit may be waived.

Car registration/license: Registration is based on $4 per $100 of assessed valuation of each vehicle, plus $23. Title cost is $10; plates are $1; inspection is $1; and a driver's license is $10 for a 4 year period (687-5370).

The Tax Ax

Nevada's tax structure is extremely favorable. There is no personal income tax, no death taxes, sales tax has liberal exemptions and property taxes are very low.

Sales tax: 6% tax (prescription drugs, medical services and food for home consumption are exempt).

State income tax: No income tax.

Property taxes & tax breaks: The current rate is $2.73 per $100 of valuation based on 35% of the assessed valuation (it works out to be close to 1% of the appraised value). For example, a home assessed at $115,000 would run approximately $1,098 per year. For current information, contact the tax assessor's office at *(887-2130)*.

Medical Care

Major hospitals & regional medical center: Carson-Tahoe Hospital (JCAH-accredited) just completed an $8 million expansion and renovation. This full-care facility now has a new 7,000 sq. ft. emergency/trauma center, an ambulatory surgery center, medical imaging, a roof-top heliport, cardiac care and most other specialties. Its community programs include wellness and nutrition classes and special help for diabetics. For serious cases, people go to regional medical centers in Reno.

Emergency medical services (EMS): The fire departments's paramedics (2 at each of 3 stations) have been through 6 months of intensive training. Each call is responded to by both an ambulance and fire engine. Response time: 3-4 minutes.

Physician's referral: Carson-Tahoe Hospital *882-1361*.

Continuing Education

Western Nevada Community College (Carson City) has a Community Services division which offers one-day workshops, field trips, and interesting classes like massage therapy, photography, geology and more. Prices vary but seniors are entitled to a 20% discount. They are also eligible to enroll in academic courses for free *(887-3015)*. The University of Nevada at Reno (32 mi.) has one-week elderhostel programs five times a year. Average cost is $300 per person. They also run an ElderCollege, which is a "learning in retirement" institute. They offer both peer and instructor run classes on everything from the History of the Jews to creative writing. Membership is $35 and entitles participants to course discounts. Their aim is to offer both social and academic opportunities *(784-4046)*.

Services for Seniors

Carson City Senior Citizen Center recently opened a beautiful new facility that provides activities and programs for more than 2,000 active adults (60+) including exercise classes, card groups, and AARP's 55/Alive driving class. Their dance band (retired professional musicians) is a huge success. They also distribute a senior discount directory to more than 100 local stores and restaurants *(883-0703)*. The **RSVP** chapter is extremely active, placing senior volunteers in approximately 150 different local agencies. They also provide transportation to Reno twice a week for shopping and medical care *(687-4682)*.

Crime & Safety

The word on the street is you don't mess around with the Carson City police. They're tough, they're on top and they care deeply about the residents and businesses. The police chief regularly orders breakfast for business people and asks for ideas on how the department can improve services. They also respond in 3 minutes flat when you need them. As there are no blighted areas, people feel safe walking anywhere in town. What crime exists is mostly auto theft and burglaries (homicides and violent crime are rare). Of interest to older adults is their "RUOK" (Are You OK?) program where the police check in by phone on a regular basis. Persons convicted of committing crimes against seniors also may face state penalties as well as city.

Earning a Living

Current business climate: Nevada's favorable tax structure allows businesses to flourish rather than choke. It also helps that the recent population growth has stimulated tremendous activity. Numerous businesses have been crossing the border from as far away as San Francisco to get in on the boom. Light manufacturing and tourist-related trade have a very promising future.

Help in starting a business: Contact the Chamber of Commerce's Small Business Development office for assistance *(882-1565)*.

The job market: As the capital, almost 34% of workers are in local and state government jobs. Trade and service employees account for 39%; with the balance in light manufacturing, construction, finance, insurance and real estate. The economy is stable and the outlook for work is great.

When the Kids Come to Visit

Children's Museum (in the Nevada State Museum) with hands-on displays; Railroad Museum (weekend train rides); Stewart Indian Museum (walk through an old Indian schoolhouse); Horseback riding at the Winter's Creek Dude Ranch.

Getting Around Town

Roads & interstates: Highway 395, US 50. **Airports & airlines:** Reno Cannon International Airport (35 mi.) is served by American, Continental, United and Delta. **Public transportation:** None. **Managing without a car:** Impossible.

What Residents Already Know

Would you like to talk to the Governor? Come on in and ask his secretary if he's available? If he's not already speaking to someone else, he'll be happy to chat. Or you can catch him at Sizzler's.•The handyman cometh, only when he's not fishing or chucker hunting. Most people work according to when it suits them.

For More Information

Chamber of Commerce Office:
Carson City Chamber of Commerce
1900 South Carson St., Suite 100
Carson City, 89701
882-1565

Newspaper:
The Nevada Appeal
PO Box 2288
Carson City, 89702
882-2515

Realtors:
Dean Barnett and Donna Zappin
Coldwell Banker/
1st Western Realty
1987 N. Carson St.
Carson City, 89701
883-2300

Mr. John Uhart
Allison Realty
1135 Terminal Way, Suite 205-A
Reno, 89502
329-1446

26. Las Vegas, Nevada

Area Snapshot

Nickname: "Entertainment Capital of the World"
County: Clark
Area code: 702 **Zip codes:** 89101-15
Local population: 773,282 **County:** 807,499
% of population 65+: 25-30%
U.S. region: Southern Nevada
Closest metro areas: Los Angeles, 285 miles; Phoenix, 180 miles
Nearby areas to consider: Henderson, Boulder City
Median housing price: $115,000
Best reasons to retire here: Great entertainment and nightlife, favorable tax structure, affordable housing, dry, desert climate, gateway to most major cities, and everyone will come to visit.

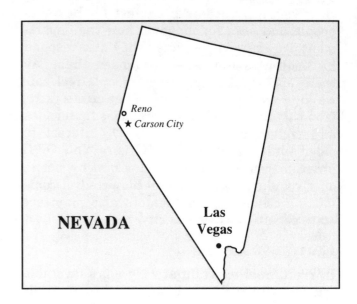

Fabulous Features

Betting on Las Vegas as a retirement spot? Odds are you'll be glad you did! If nothing else about this city appeals to you, you'll love the fact that Nevada residents pay *no* income tax, no inheritance or estate taxes (property taxes are favorable, too), and if you're in business, the tax bite is barely a scratch. The real estate market is as vast as the desert. Every imaginable type of dwelling and price range is here, with new golf communities and condo developments in the southwest section. The varying desert climate is a surprise to many. When it drops into the 30s some January nights, newcomers think it's a fluke (it's not), and the next day brings sunshine and 60. Fall and spring bring constant sunshine and comfortable temperatures in the 60s and 70s. With more than 320 days of sun and low humidity, the outdoor life is unbeatable. Recreation at the nearby national and state parks offers everything from skiing to hiking to canoeing, and golf and tennis are playable all year. There's also a high level of cultural activity, including an exciting Master Series at the Artemus W. Ham Concert Hall (Shanghai Symphony, a Shakespeare Festival production of Twelfth Night, the Vienna Chamber Orchestra, to name a few). Services for seniors, as well as health care, are in abundance and their referral and networking sources are excellent. It's easy to get help. Everyone we spoke to said the same thing, "You may think you know Las Vegas but you don't really know it until you live here."

Possible drawbacks: It gets so hot in July and August, you'll start daydreaming about Alaskan cruises.•There will be days when you wished that gambling was legal but tourists were not.•This is a *big* city and no matter how you cut it, it has its share of traffic, crime, and red tape. Despite its drawbacks, Las Vegas has an ideal mix of flash, dazzle, rest and relaxation to please the retiree who wants the best of both worlds.

"You can quote me on that"

"Our best friends moved here last year and kept raving. They bought a gorgeous home for little money, they made friends, they take trips, they play golf. They sounded like a commercial. We finally sold our house and came down for a few months to rent. Living in Las Vegas is so different than I expected. You're not effected by the strip and the tourists. That part of the city is a different world. Now we just bought a house and we sound like a commercial."—Mr. H. Z.

Climate

Elevation: 2,180	Avg. High/ Low	Average Inches		Avg. # Days Precip.	Avg. % Humidity
		Rain	Snow		
Jan.	56/33	.31	-	3	45
April	78/50	.27	-	2	28
July	104/75	.44	-	3	18
Oct.	81/53	.22	-	2	27
YEAR	79/52	3.8	1.7	-	-
# days 32° or below: 39			# days 90° or above: 140		

Let the Good Times Roll

Recreation: The national and state parks and preserves in southern Nevada will captivate you if you do nothing more than just look. But if you're inclined to camp, hike, ride horses, ski, fish, hunt or windsail, you're going to have an absolute ball. Lake Mead National Recreation Area is 1.4 million acres of wildlife, scenery, and Lake Mohave. Red Rock Canyon Recreation Lands and Toiyabe National Forest are just some of the parks to enjoy year-round. For golfers, there are 18 golf courses (most 18-hole) and opportunities to watch several world cup invitationals during the year. UNLV's Running Rebels, the 1990 NCAA champs, is one of the most exciting college basketball teams in the country. Watch them at the Thomas & Mack Center *(729-3900)*. The Las Vegas Stars (San Diego Padre's Triple A farm team) plays at Cashman Field Center. All those world title boxing matches, PGA golf, auto racing and tennis matches you watched on TV are right down the block. Enjoy, enjoy!

Culture: The "Entertainment Capitol of the World" boasts its own kind of culture: 365 days of round-the-clock nightclub acts, performers, comedians, etc. For more highbrow tastes, the performing arts are equally compelling: The Artemus W. Ham Concert Hall presents an unbelievable Master Series. Other offerings include the Las Vegas Civic Ballet Association; Nevada Dance Theater; Theater Ballet of Las Vegas; Actors Repertory Theater; Clark Community College Drama; Las Vegas Community Theater; Nevada Musical Theater Guild; Nevada Opera Theater; Sierra Wind Quintet; Art galleries; the Arboretum At UNLV; Barrick Museum of Natural History; Desert Demonstration Gardens; and the Las Vegas Art Museum.

Annual events: Hell Dorado (May): parade, rodeos, and competitions.

Local Real Estate

No market is hotter than Las Vegas (and we don't mean the weather). A plentiful inventory of both new and existing houses and condos, in every price range, is available. Prices start at around $68,000 for an older, small house close to the strip (most framed or stucco). The more desirable areas are to the southwest, with home prices ranging from $80,000 to $1 million. The large, luxury homes start closer to $200,000. Most have pools, covered parking, and contemporary designs. In the master planned golf/retirement communities, such as Sun City, townhouses and villas average $150,000 for a 3BR, 2BA (1800 sq. ft.).

Median price for single family home: $115,000. Average price ranges $128,500. Lot sizes are 50 x 100 (older homes may be larger).

Median price for 2BR condo: $72,800

Rental housing market: Wide availability of homes and condos. Houses rent for $800-$1200/ mo. Apartments go for $500-$700/mo.

Common housing styles & features: Frame and stucco , tile roofs, contemporary layouts, pools, 3BR or 2BR with a den, single-story.

Amenities in condo developments: pools, golf courses, security (hotlines for assistance), clubhouse, etc. Some, like Sun City, are age restricted.

Nearby areas to consider: Henderson, Boulder City. **Unique features of these areas:** Henderson (pop. 80,000), halfway between Las Vegas and Lake Mead, is a mixed community of young and old, with scores of new, planned communities and developments. Avg. priced home is $90,000. It has excellent recreation, and it's the "Sweet Tooth Capitol of Nevada"— (Ethel M. Chocolates, Kidd and Company Marshmallows and Gold Bond Ice Cream are made here). Boulder City (pop. 14,000) is a clean, green oasis in the desert, situated near Lake Mead and Hoover Dam. It's small with wide, tree-lined avenues and it's the only city in Nevada that prohibits gambling. It's also a slow-growth area—not much in the way of new shopping or construction. Home costs are comparable to those in Las Vegas.

What Things Cost

According to ACCRA, overall living costs are 8% above the national average. Health care and housing drive up the figures, although utilities are some of the lowest in the country (17% below average). Food is also less costly here; restaurants traditionally are bargains (the casinos didn't want people wasting good money on food when they could be wasting it on the slots). Many offer delicious meals for less than $5, and almost every place has seniors discounts.

Gas company: Southwest Gas *(368-1100)*. Avg. mo. bills: $20, but winter months can avg. $100 (it can get down into the 20s and 30s.)

Electric company: Nevada Power Company *(367-5555)*. Depending on whether you use all electric or combined electric and gas, and how much heat and air conditioning you use, avg. monthly bills can range from $50-$80. Summer months can go up to $100-$120. Deposit of $50-$90 may be required.

Phone company: Cental Cellular *(877-7400)*. Basic mo. service is $10.30 plus 7% tax. Extra services: $5.25/mo. Installations: $18.75 and up. $50 deposit may be required.

Car registration/license: New resident's cars must undergo a smog check by a certified inspection station (new cars exempt) to register. Driver's license: $10 (must surrender your out-of-state license and take a written test and eye exam). Registration varies based on depreciated value of car. Cost includes tags (plates). For example, an '89 Buick Regal costs $225/yr. DMV *(641-0090)*.

The Tax Ax

In Nevada, it's not as much a tax ax as it is a "tax lacks." **Sales tax:** 6% (food is exempt). **State income tax:** None (40% of state revenues come from gaming taxes). **Property taxes & tax breaks:** Nevada's statutory limit is 3.64 per $100 of valuation. The current range of millage rates varys from 2.1783 to 3.1581. To calculate, multiply the value of the home by 35%. That equals your depreciated asset value. Then multiply that figure times the millage rate. For example, in Las Vegas proper, the millage rate is 2.9245 (Boulder is 2.2800). A home valued at $100,000 would run $1,023/yr.

Medical Care

The health care community is expanding. There are 9 major hospitals, and an almost overnight creation of clinics. The Heart Institute of Nevada is just one of the specialty facilities available. **Major hospitals/regional medical centers:** All have 24-hour emergency and are JCAH-accredited. **University Medical Center of Southern Nevada** (UMC), has Nevada's only trauma burn unit. It also has a brain injury unit, cardiac care, oncology, renal dialysis, critical care and lithotripsy equipment for elimination of stones. **Desert Springs Hospital** has cardiac and intensive care, radiology, and full surgical. **Valley Hospital Medical Center** offers open heart surgery, cancer care, and physical therapy. It offers "Flight for Life" emergency transport system. Other hospitals include **Humana Hospital. Emergency medical service (EMS):** Mercy Ambulence, a private company takes EMS calls for most of Clark County. Response time is less than 8 minutes, 90% of the time. All EMTs are trained paramedics or nurses. **Physician's referral:** Valley Medical Hospital *388-4000*.

Continuing Education

University of Nevada, Las Vegas (UNLV) lets residents 62+ attend any fall/spring class *free*. Summer classes are 50% of course tuition *(739-3011)*. Clark County Community College: Seniors pay a one-time registration fee of $5-$10 and classes are free *(643-6060)*.

Services for Seniors

Senior Centers throughout the city and in surrounding communities offer programs and services covering health and wellness, transportation, education, recreation, employment and living assistance. **RSVP** *(385-1328)*; Senior Citizens Information and Referral *(366-1522)*; **AARP** *(386-8661)*; Prime Magazine *(871-6780)*; Senior Spectrum *(792-3963)*; Senior Times-Nevada Senior World *(361-3632)*; Senior

Citizens Protective Services *(455-4291)*; Nevada Senior Olympics *(361-3632)*.

Crime & Safety

Gangs are an unwanted California import. Despite their efforts to create havoc, crime has gone down in the past year. The Southwest area and parts of the southeast are perfectly safe. According to the latest FBI statistics, for every 1,000 people in Las Vegas, 71 people were a victim of some sort of crime (from purse snatching to burglary), ranking it 47 in the country. Compare that to Atlanta or Miami where crimes per 1,000 are close to triple that figure.

Earning a Living

Current business climate: *Inc.* magazine recently rated Nevada first for business growth in the country and the census shows that it's the fastest-growing state (3,000-5,000 residents arrive every month). With the recent construction boom, more than 47,000 new jobs were created last year alone. Add to that the most favorable tax climate (no corporate income tax, personal income tax, franchise tax, or inventory tax) and all signs point to tremendous opportunity in this state of "Aces." **Help in starting a business:** SCORE (Service Core of Retired Executives) has an orientation on business opportunities *(338-6611)*. **The job market:** Jobs are available in every sector. AARP Community Service Employment *(648-3356)*; Nevada Business Services 55+ Program *(385-6100)*; Senior Community Service Employment *(385-5941)*.

When the Kids Come to Visit

Barrick Museum of Natural History; Guinness World of Records Museum; Las Vegas Museum of Natural History; Circus Hotel/Casino; Lied Discovery Children's Museum; Southern Nevada Zoological Park; Wet n' Wild; Ripley's Believe It or Not Odditorium; Nellis Air Force Base (home of the Thunderbirds); Imperial Palace Antique/ Classic Auto Collection; and the Liberace Museum.

Getting Around Town

Roads & interstates: US 93, 95, 466 and Interstate 15. **Airports and airlines:** McCarran International Airport is served by America West, American, Continental, Delta, Hawaiian Air, Midway, Northwest, Southwest, TWA, United, and USAir; Private aviation at McCarran International Airport, North Las Vegas Air Terminal, Sky Harbor Airport. **Public transportation:** Las Vegas Transit System, Sunshine Bus, Las Vegas Trolleys. **Managing without a car:** Las Vegas is so spread out you'd be terribly limited.

What Residents Already Know

The "Sin" capital of the world has more churches per capita than most major cities. Also, with the city growing at an extraordinary pace, water is used up at lightning speed. A proposed $1.95 million pipeline across central Nevada may be the answer, but not before a controversial referendum takes place. It's got the environmentalists pitted against the city.

For More Information

Chamber of Commerce Office:
Las Vegas Area Chamber
of Commerce
2301 E. Sahara Ave.
Las Vegas, NV 89104
457-4664

Newspaper:
Las Vegas Sun
121 S. Martin Luther King Blvd.
Las Vegas, 89106
385-3111

Realtors:
David M. Bryson
RE/MAX
3025 W Sahara Ave. #103
Las Vegas, 89102
800-955-5889

Judy Meunier
Coldwell Banker
1095 E. Sahara Ave.
Las Vegas, 89104
734-7135

27. Ocean County, New Jersey

Area Snapshot

Nickname: "New Jersey's Best Host"
Area code: 908 (new for this area)
Zip codes: 08754 (Toms River), 08701 (Lakewood), 08759 (Manchester, Whiting)
County population: 433,203   **% of pop. 65+:** 33.4%
U.S. region: East Central New Jersey
Closest metro areas: New York, 70 mi.; Atlantic City, 45 mi.; Philadelphia, 60 mi.
Townships to consider: Dover, Lakewood, Manchester, Berkeley, Brick
Median housing price: $140,000
Best reasons to retire here: Small community living, temperate climate, affordable housing, top health care, planned retirement communities (the largest concentration of seniors in the state).

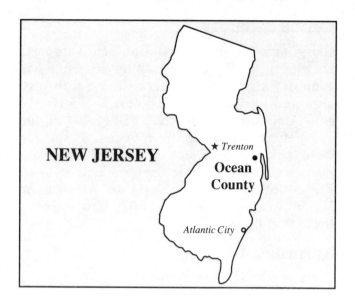

Fabulous Features

Ocean County is New Jersey's second largest in population, and it continues to be the fastest growing. Traditionally it was retirees who came in droves, now it's younger people who come for the good life, too. The Jersey Shore is off the beaten path but within shouting distance from family and friends and big-city life. It is also a major tourist region yet it has sprawling industrial parks, giving it a stable economic base. For retirees, the real appeal is that it's like Florida with winter. It's got the same casual, on-the-ocean lifestyle, huge retirement communities, wonderful culture and recreation, ample health care, endless shopping and the kids *love* to visit. You won't find Florida weather but it's certainly more temperate than New York. Being on the shore means summers are more bearable and winters aren't as fierce. As for real estate options, choices are numerous. You can opt for a planned retirement community or more heterogeneous neighborhoods. If you're active and independent the services for seniors won't be of interest. But if you're in need, there's a support system the likes of which you've never seen. The beauty of Ocean County is that in spite of runaway growth, it has maintained the same great qualities that attracted families back in the '40s and '50s—a rural feel, fresh air, coastal dunes and much to see and do.

Possible drawbacks: As with any tourist area, "in season" means fighting the crowds, the traffic and congestion and higher prices. Another drawback is that Ocean County is so spread out. There are more than 30 different townships and boroughs covering 638 square miles. Finding your special niche will take some legwork.

"You can quote me on that"

"We retired to Florida two years ago and hated the heat. It was also a lot more expensive than we thought. My son said we should just come back to Queens but that wasn't right either. We wanted open space, friends our age and a slower pace. I had a cousin who retired to Lakewood and loved it. We visited him and said this is for us."—G.G., Lakewood Township

"We came here because my husband needed special care but I'm still very active myself. Most of the good retirement communities are perfect for couples like us."—A.H., Whiting Township

Climate

Elevation: 45'	Avg. High/ Low	Average Inches		Avg. # Days Precip.	Avg. % Humidity
		Rain	Snow		
Jan.	42/28	3	6	12	73
April	61/39	3.4	.4	11	70
July	84/67	3.7	-	10	72
Oct.	67/48	3.2	trace	9	71
YEAR	63/45	41	18	-	-
# days 32° or below: 88			# days 90° or above: 18		

Let the Good Times Roll

Recreation: The 45 miles of oceanfront and 150 miles of shoreline are just the beginning of outdoor life in Ocean County. It's possible to visit a different beach every day of the week, including the popular Island Beach State Park (NJ Transit shuttle buses make the trip easy). For fishing and canoeing, head to Toms River and Barnegat Bay. The more adventurous types can try waters a trifle bigger— the Atlantic Ocean. With more than 200 marinas in the county, the boating life is another pleasure. The summers bring daily regattas and power boat racing. Park life is another major asset, especially Ocean County Park in Lakewood (formerly the Rockefeller estate). Facilities for swimming, tennis, and fishing spread over 300 acres. You'll also find the Senior Tennis Clinic, Senior Gold Tournament and Senior Bowling Day (free to residents). The county's public and private golf courses are challenging and enjoyable on lush, rolling greens.

Culture: People come here thinking that for "real culture" they can always run into New York or Philadelphia. But "real" culture has it's place in the sun, too. The Ocean County Cultural Directory needs more than 50 pages to describe all the offerings. Highlights include: the 70-year old Strand Theater (Lakewood), which offers touring Broadway and local productions, the Garden State Philharmonic, and Ocean County College's Fine Arts Center which brings in ballet, films and other enriching programs. The County's Cultural and Heritage Commission coordinates year-round programs in cooperation with theater groups, museums, galleries, and historical site.

Annual events: Lakewood Fair Days (August) Lakewood Renaissance Festival (September), Founder's Day (Dover Township), the Ocean County Fair (Berkeley) and Barnegat Bay Race Week (August).

Local Real Estate

There are 45 senior communities that offer ideal living arrangements. The homes are generally one-story, small and affordable, but well-designed for the most versatile living space. There are also numerous second homes (from small cottages to luxurious estates), most of which are waterfront. Condominiums in and outside retirement villages are in abundance. **Adult communities:** Community Holiday City and Silver Ridge Park, both in Berkeley Township (each have four different communities): Lions Head and Greenbriar I & II in Brick Township; Leisure Village in Lakewood Township; and Crestwood Village in Manchester Township. Some communities offer continuing care; many are non-profit. Others have combined nursing homes with living quarters for independent spouses. It's possible to buy a 2BR condo with garage for between $40,000 to $60,000. A continuing care facility offering medical services might have an entrance fee of $115,000 for a 2BR unit, with monthly maintenance of $2,100. A studio might run $60,000 with a $900 monthly maintenance fee. Services include cleaning, landscaping, repairs, meals, security, bus service, laundry, parking, trips, guest apts., shopping, a clubhouse and library.

Median price for single family home: $140,000. At an adult community: $80,000.

Current median price for 2BR condo: $100,000

Rental housing market: Apartments: $650/ mo. Small houses rent for $700.

Common housing styles & features: There are very few multi-family dwellings.

Amenities in condo developments: Pools, tennis, clubhouse and exterior maintenance.

What Things Cost

Housing costs are some of the most affordable in the state, and living costs overall will be less than in areas closer to the major cities. The effective income and property taxes bring relief to former New York area residents.

Gas company: New Jersey Natural Gas *(938-7977)*. Avg. bill is $30-59/mo. Winter months run $100-120. Deposits not required for homeowners.

Electric company: Jersey Central Power and Light *(531-3277)*. Avg. bill $55.58/mo. Summer: approximately $20 higher. Deposits may not be required.

Phone company: New Jersey Bell *(outside New Jersey 800-755-1078)*. Basic Service is $12-20/mo. with call waiting, touchtone, unlimited local calling, Pay $95 deposit and $42 connection charges.

Car registration/license: $42.90 for plates, registration. Title fee is $5.7% sales tax on new car purchase. $22.50 for 4-year license.

The Tax Ax

Although sales tax has just increased to 7%, the food-clothing-drug exemptions are still in effect. The income tax rate for seniors and property taxes will seem low, particularly if you've been paying them in neighboring New York.

Sales tax: 7% (clothing, prescription drugs, over-the-counter drugs sold for pain and food for immediate consumption are exempt).

State income tax: Ranges from 2-7%.

Retirement income: If married, filing jointly and over age 62, there is a $10,000 state income tax exclusion. The exclusion for singles is $7,500. Private and government pensions exclude the first $7,500. There is no estate taxes over and above federal credit.

Property taxes & tax breaks: Taxes vary considerably by township. An example, using the 1991 effective tax rates for a home valued at $100,000, property taxes would be as follows: Dover: $1,607; Lakewood: $2,119; and Brick: $1,517. There is an added tax for fire districts which vary from an extra 10-16¢ per $100 of valuation. Contact the Ocean County Tax Appraisers office for current rates *(929-2008)*.

Medical Care

Major hospitals/regional medical centers: **Kimball Medical Center** (Lakewood with a satellite facility in Manchester), has the only state-funded, clinically oriented geriatric program in the county. **Community Memorial Hospital** (Toms River), has regional renal dialysis, cancer and cardiac care centers. Visiting Homemaker Services provide physical, speech and occupational therapy. There is also an excellent hospice program with counseling for families. Other hospitals include: **Medical Center of Ocean County** (Brick), **Southern Ocean County Hospital** (Manahawken) and **Garden State Rehabilitation Center** (Toms River).

Emergency medical services (EMS): Lakewood has two advance life support teams operating round the clock. Response time is under 6 minutes. The Community Medical Center also operates a fully staffed EMS division. Ocean county has 6 squads of volunteer EMT personnel.

Physician's/dental referral: *286-6111*; Dental: *370-7562*.

Continuing Education

Ocean County College (Toms River) For $5 per tuition credit, seniors can take courses such as Money Management for Retirees, All About Condominiums, and Wills and Estate Planning. Swimming and fitness programs are also available *(255-0400)*. To be eligible, be able to prove age and residency.

Services for Seniors

There are scores of nutrition and meal programs, seniors centers, and community outreach programs. Write to Ocean County's Office of Public Information for their "Golden Years Guide" listing all available services. (County Administration Building, Hooper Ave, Toms River, 08754). Media: Most villages have their own weekly or monthly papers. Kimball Medical Center publishes "Senior Straight Talk," a free newsletter. The Office for the Aging has a monthly paper, Senior Statesman provides a Senior Citizen Fact Book *(929-2091)*. **AARP:** For chapter information contact Dorothy Ludgate *(899-0533)* or Bert Hock *(693-0383)*. Senior discounts are widely available.

Crime & Safety

Police and fire departments are tuned in to the needs of seniors, maintaining educational programs and Neighborhood Watch efforts. Considering the increased population, crime rates are surprisingly low, particularly in the retirement communities. Extra patrols in the summer help alleviate trouble in beach areas when the crowds soar.

Earning a Living

Current business climate: Due to the population growth, this area has seen comparable growth in retail, wholesale and industrial sectors. Businesses are now cautiously optimistic, although starts and expansions have slowed in the past two years. The downtown areas are losing stores at a fast clip. **Help in starting a business:** New Jersey Employment Services will assist with advertising and recruiting employees for new businesses as well as help with securing loans. **The job market:** Part-time/minimum wage work is readily available because of tourist attractions, restaurants and shops. The Private Industry council can assist in job placement *(240-5995)*.

When the Kids Come to Visit

Six Flags Great Adventure, the largest theme park and drive-through safari in the country, is only 15 minutes by car; Cattus Island Park and Nature Center hosts free boat rides (Toms River); Barnegat Lighthouse State Park, Seaside Parks Beach and Boardwalk, Ocean County College Planetarium (Toms River).

Getting Around Town

Roads & interstates: Garden State Parkway (exit 82) and U.S. Highway 9 (the more leisurely route) bring you right in. Route 70 is the east-west link to Philadelphia. Route 35 is the scenic route to the beaches. All state and national highways link up to the Garden State Parkway.

Airports: Robert J. Miller Airpark (between Berkeley and Dover townships) offers flights to Atlantic City, Trenton, New York and both major airports: Newark Airport and Philadelphia International Airport. From the northern part of the county, Newark is an hour. From the southern part, it's an hour to the Philadelphia airport.

Public transportation: Ocean County operates a mass transit bus system with services to the beaches, major shopping, and sightseeing. Many retirement communities offer their own private bus service. County provides seniors with free transportation to doctors, shopping, recreational and government offices.

Managing without a car: A car is a plus but not an absolute necessity.

What Residents Already Know

The best buys in town are seafood and cranberries.•Hate to eat home? You could dine out every day of the year and not hit the same place twice.•The beaches are the perfect combination of clean, safe and close. For excellent German Deli food, try Lehr's.

For More Information

Chamber Of Commerce Office:

Ocean County Chamber
Of Commerce
611 Main St. Suite 2,
Toms River, 08753
349-0220

Newspapers:

Asbury Park Press
500 West Water St.
Toms River, 08754
349-7000

Ocean County Observer
8 Robins St.
Toms River, 08754
349-3000

Realtor:

Sherry Finn
Weichert Realty
1322 Hooper Ave.
Toms River, 08754
240-0500

28. Las Cruces, New Mexico

Area Snapshot

Nickname: "Crossroads of the Southwest"
County: Dona Ana
Area code: 505   **Zip code:** 88004
Local population: 62,000   **County:** 140,000
% of population 65+: 11%
U.S. region: South Central New Mexico
Closest metro areas: El Paso, TX, 45 miles
Nearby areas to consider: Deming
Median housing price: $80,000
Best reasons to retire here: The retirement population is booming because of low taxes and housing costs, temperate but not humid climate, ample recreation, healthy environment, and a nice, slow pace.

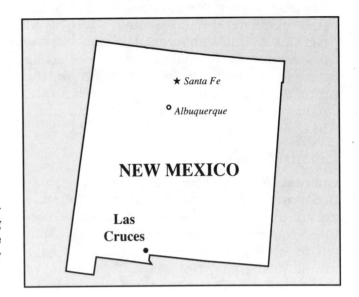

Fabulous Features

Las Cruces is the second-largest city in New Mexico, and one with a colorful history, rich with Indian and Spanish lore. Located in the Mesilla Valley, you'll never forget the first time you lay eyes on the Rio Grande River and the Organ Mountains. They're as awesome as the blue skies and fiery sunsets. Although the city has developed into a small metropolitan area, it has the feel of a great hometown—the kind you dream about returning to. Could be the mild winters, the dry air or the 350 days of sunshine. The presence of New Mexico State University bring culture and vivacity to what might otherwise be just another small town. For retirees, the best news is the low cost of living but not at the expense of a great lifestyle. Taxes are low, but services are surprisingly abundant. The Handbook of City Services lists more than 100 phone numbers. Additionally, between the fabulous assortment of parks, recreation and cultural attractions in or near Las Cruces, one retiree told us he had been so busy he needed to take a restful vacation.

Possible drawbacks: Some feel that a small-town, small-mind mentality prevails, stifling economic development and efficient planning for the future.•This is the land of "mañana." The pace is slow and nobody ever seems to be in a hurry. If you're a fast-moving Easterner, it could be culture shock.•Watch out for severe dust storms in the spring. Strong winds gust over the fields, picking up dirt and momentum. But overall, the climate and lifestyle are wonderful.

"You can quote me on that"

"Our home was San Fernando, California, but for retirement we wanted lower living costs and a relaxed lifestyle. We wrote letters to Chamber of Commerces all over the Southwest and settled here. We really love it. The people are great, the economy is expanding and the weather is hot but not humid. Come and compare."—M.P.F.

Climate

Elevation: 3,896'	Avg. High/ Low	Average Inches		Avg. # Days Precip.	Avg. % Humidity
		Rain	Snow		
Jan.	57/30	.3	-	4	50
April	79/49	.2	-	2	30
July	95/70	1.5	-	8	48
Oct.	79/50	.08	-	4	48
YEAR	77/49	7	4	-	-
# days 32° or below: 66			# days 90° or above:101		

Let the Good Times Roll

Recreation: Within driving distance are some of the most magnificent state and national parks including Caballo Lake, City of Rocks, Elephante Butte, Pancho Villa, Rock Hound and Smokey Bear. Federal lands include: Gila National Forest; Gila Cliff Dwellings; Lincoln National Forest; White Sands National Monument; Aguirre Springs Recreation Area and the Organ Mountain Preserve. There are also 57 full-service city parks, 5 public pools, a roller rink, an auto race track, a shooting range, 18 tennis courts, and 3 golf courses (one private). The Sunland Park racetrack (40 minutes south) is open from October through May. Las Cruces also has free tours of Binns Vineyards and Winery and La Vina Winery.

Culture: As the hometown of New Mexico State University, the cultural opportunities abound. Las Cruces hosts one of the largest arts councils in the state. It also has its own symphony and lyric opera company, a ballet company and a community theater group. The American Southwest Theater Company uses the university as its home base. For those interested in crafts, there are weavers and potters guilds among the 35 smaller arts organizations in the arts council. Las Cruces also has a museum system including the Brannigan Cultural Center, the Las Cruces Museum of Natural History and the Bicentennial Log Cabin Museum.

Local Real Estate

Local realtors have been very busy the past few years and the market remains active. Interest rates are low, retirees are settling in by the hundreds. Availabilities are good and the price is right.

Median price for single family home: $80,000
Median price for 2BR condo: $60,000
Rental housing market: 3BR house $425-$900/ mo.; 2BR apt. $300-$900/mo.
Common housing styles & features: The most popular styles are the Santa Fe look, which is a more artistic version of an adobe style house (framed stucco); the Territorial Style, a more traditional style, and simple Spanish-influenced style with red tile roofs. Houses do not have basements.
Amenities in condo developments: Although there are a few developments, condos are not a popular choice. People prefer home ownership because of the desire for the beautiful southwest landscaping. It's all natural vegetation requiring minimum maintenance. There is plenty of land available and given the choice, most people opt for property and a private home.
Nearby community to consider: Deming (55 mi. west). **Unique features of this area:** Deming (pop. 12,000) is evolving into a very popular retirement town because housing prices are extremely low (the average costs $45,000) and it's much smaller than Las Cruces. It is most famous for its pure air and water and the fact that it was the first place in New Mexico to hold an annual Great American Duck Race. It's a real "quack-up."

What Things Cost

According to ACCRA, living costs are approximately 2.5% below the national average. Housing costs are 8% below, and utilities and health care are also less than the average American city.
Gas company: City of Las Cruces Water, Sewer and Gas *(526-0246)*. Average monthly gas bill is $21.12. Winter prices are double.
Electric company: El Paso Electric *(526-5551)*. Average monthly bill is $60-100 for a three bedroom house with air conditioning.
Phone company: U.S. West Communications *(245-6800)*. Basic monthly service is $17.17 with unlimited local calls and touchtone service. Measured service is $9.04 a month, with additional charges for each local call.

Car registration/license: Registration varies by weight and year of car. The fee includes title transfer, sticker and plates. For example, a 1990 car weighing 3,500 lbs. would run $37.80. Driver's license: $10 (good for 4 years). There is also a 3% excise tax on new vehicle purchases *(827-2255)*.

The Tax Ax

Sales tax: There is a 5%-6.8% Gross Receipts Tax which varies by region.

State income tax: The current rates are as follows if married filing jointly: $24,000-$36,000—$883; $36,000-48,000—$1,591; 48,000-$54,000—$2,420, and $54,000 or more is $2,874.

Retirement income: If over 65 and married filing jointly with an income under $30,000, residents can deduct $8,000 off taxable income. With incomes between $31,000 and 51,000, seniors pay between $1,000 to $7,000 (the higher the income the smaller the deduction). Income of $51,000 has no deductions. Estate taxes: There is no inheritance tax and the estate tax is a "pick up tax" from the federal government (whatever the feds take satisfies the state).

Property taxes & tax breaks: Real estate tax is equal to $20.73 per each $1,000 of assessed value. Homes are assessed at 33 1/3% of market value. A $60,000 home would run $414/yr. A 160,000 home would cost $1,104/yr. Residents deduct a $2,000 household exemption before calculating taxes.

Medical Care

There is only one general hospital in town and although emergency room waits are getting longer, most people feel the care is good. Also, in the past few years, numerous specialists have moved to the area, giving people choices as to whom they want to see.

Major hospitals & regional medical centers: Memorial Medical Center has a trauma unit, cardiology, oncology and outpatient care programs. An ambulatory care center is under construction as are facilities for open heart surgery. The nearest teaching hospital is **R E Thomason General Hospital** in El Paso (30 mi.). **Emergency medical services (EMS):** Eleven paramedics and 30 EMT's. Average response time within city is 6.5 minutes. EMS has a full advanced life support service with state-of-the-art equipment.

Physician's referral: Memorial Medical Center *522-8641*.

Continuing Education

Dona Ana Community College has an extensive continuing education program for all ages. Classes include writing and publishing, computers, real estate, crafts, dance, and language. The cost is $26 per credit. New Mexico State offers a continuing education program that allows adults to enroll in undergrad classes. The cost is $56.50 per credit.

Services for Seniors

The **Munson Senior Center** is a wonderful place for people 50 and up. It offers a full range of programs, classes, dances and many other activities and services *(526-2492)*. There is also the **Rio Grande Retired Senior Volunteer Program** which coordinates volunteer placements at hospitals, schools and more. Seniors can get a membership card from the **Munson Center** which entitles them to merchant discounts. **AARP:** contact Walter Baker *(525-3990)*.

Crime & Safety

Auto thefts have traditionally been a problem, although in these economic times, burglaries are becoming the greater concern. But believe it or not, the police report that the biggest threat to seniors is fraudulent crime. The police get calls all the time from older people who have realized they've given bank information over the phone or bought a phony product from a convincing salesperson. **Advice from the police:** Never give any personal or credit information over the phone and join a Neighborhood Watch Program.

Earning a Living

Current business climate: During the 1980s, Las Cruces was the eighth fastest-growing area in the country, leading to a great expansion in the service sector. Even now, the Chamber receives 200-300 inquiries a month from people interested in relocating, reflecting opportunities for continued growth. Also, a new port of entry from Mexico is being developed in the southern part of the county, which many believe will further stimulate employment.

Help in starting a business: SCORE (Service Corp. of Retired Executives) has a local chapter of former executives who provide free consulting to local businesses and entrepreneurs *(523-5627).*

The job market: The outlook for seniors is good because of numerous service industries seeking part-time workers. White Sands Missile Range and New Mexico State University are the largest employers. JTPA (Job Training Placement Act) runs a program for those 55 and older, placing them in a variety of businesses for a four-month basis with full pay. The program also runs training classes in vocational skills *(524-6250).*

When the Kids Come to Visit

The Rio Grande River is a fabulous recreation site in most seasons. La Mesilla is an historical colonial village; Carlsbad Caverns National Park (3 hrs.) has incredible caverns; the Living Desert, Zoological and Botanical Garden State Park; White Sands National Monument and Park holds the largest inland placement of white sand dunes in the U.S.; Silver City (2 hrs.) is home of Billy the Kid; Gila National Forest (in Silver City) is great for camping and fishing. Ruidoso is a ski resort town in the Sierra Blanca Mountains (2 hrs.).

Getting Around Town

Roads & interstates: US Highway 70; Interstates 10, 25.

Airports & airlines: Las Cruces International: 8 mi. Mesa Airlines (offering 3 daily shuttles to Albuquerque); El Paso International Airport (47 miles); American Airlines, America West, Delta & Southwest Airlines.

Public transportation: Roadrunner Transit is a brand new city bus company which has already won awards for promptness and service. One way for seniors is 25¢. For the physically impaired there is a $1 charge for door-to-door delivery.

Managing without a car: It's possible.

What Residents Already Know

There's a great opportunity for bargain hunting in nearby Juarez, Mexico (50 miles south). Shoppers flock there for leather goods, pottery and clothes. Juarez is also fun for bullfighting. • The food at Memorial Medical Center is good enough that business people actually go to their cafeteria for lunch.

For More Information

Chamber Of Commerce Offices:

Las Cruces Chamber
Drawer 519
Las Cruces, 88004
524-1968

Deming-Luna County Chamber
P.O. Box 8
Deming, 88031
546-2674

Newspapers:

Las Cruces Sun-News (daily)
P.O. Box 1749
Las Cruces, 88004
523-4581

Sam Lopez
P.O. Box 881
Deming, 88031
546-2611

Realtor:

Patricia Kirkpatrick
Sunstate Realty
1240 S. Telshor Blvd.
Las Cruces, 88001
521-3252

29. Santa Fe, New Mexico

Area Snapshot

Nickname: "The City Different"
County: Santa Fe
Area code: 505   **Zip code:** 87504
Local population: 55,859
County population: 98,928
% of population 65+: 12.8%
U.S. region: North Central New Mexico
Closest metro areas: Albuquerque, 60 miles
Nearby areas to consider: El Dorado and Pecos
Median housing price: $128,000
Best reasons to retire here: Impressive art center and cultural opportunities, fabulous ski country, diverse ethnic backgrounds, low taxes, even lower humidity.

Fabulous Features

Nestled in the foothills of the Rocky Mountains, Santa Fe is indeed a different city. It is not only the oldest capital city in the country, it's at the highest elevation (6,500 feet and counting). With its blend of Spanish, Indian and Anglo cultures, some have likened it to living in a foreign land where people blend together in almost harmonic conversion. Without a doubt, Santa Fe is both an art lover's and sports enthusiast's paradise. Skiing (yes, skiing) in Santa Fe and nearby Taos is considered the best adventure in the Southwest. At elevations of 10,000-12,000 feet and over 225 inches of annual snowfall, there is no finer powder skiing (and you thought New Mexico was only sand and desert). For the art lover, not only are there close to 200 galleries, but the ancient ruins and historical landmarks are fascinating. And so is the growing list of celebrities who know a great city when they see one. Robert Redford, Ted Danson, Jane Fonda, and Brian Dennehy, are just a few who are building *mucho grande* homes. The finishing touch is the wonderfully dry climate. Relative humidity averages a very comfortable 45% and the sun shines at least 300 days a year. Winters are chilly but not frigid, allowing for outdoor activities year-round. One retiree from California told us, "If someone comes here and is bored, there's no place that would excite them!"

Possible drawbacks: In spite of the down market, real estate is still some of the most expensive in the state. Retiring here can be costly, with food and health care taking a bigger bite than in many other parts of the country. There is no public transportation, so count on having a car.

"You can quote me on that"

"We've lived in Florida, California, Nebraska and other states and nothing compares to Santa Fe. It's very colorful, beautiful and different. We love the different cultures (Spanish, Anglo and Indian). When you talk to someone on the street, you never know which language they'll speak. The Spanish and Indian markets sell beautiful jewelry and all kinds of artifacts. We're trying native New Mexican food, too, which is wonderful. Santa Fe is growing so fast, people are trying hard to preserve the local customs."—L.M.

Climate

Elevation: 6989'	Avg. High/ Low	Average Inches		Avg. # Days Precip.	Avg. % Humidity
		Rain	Snow		
Jan.	42/15	.4	6	6	60
April	60/30	1.1	1	6	45
July	83/51	2.4	-	10	60
Oct.	70/32	1.1	.5	6	55
YEAR	63/32	14	29	-	-
# days 32° or below: 157			# days 90° or above: 33		

Let the Good Times Roll

Recreation: They call this the Land of Enchantment and when you breathe the air, take in the mountains and race down the rivers, you'll understand why. Recreational opportunities in this small city are extensive, with 53 city parks, swimming pools and tennis courts. There are three challenging golf courses. Santa Fe Downs is a popular race horse track. Some of the outdoor highlights include: Santa Fe State Park (at an altitude of 7,000 feet, the lakes and forests are captivating; The Santa Fe National Forest offers fishing, camping, and boating; Cochiti Lake is great for sailing and motorboats; and Humphries State Wildlife Area (9,000-acres of natural habitat...enter by horse or foot. Elk hunting is permitted). If you ski or are willing to try, your experience will be daunting anytime from Thanksgiving through Easter. The Sangre de Cristo Mountains offer exciting trails, sunshine and warm desert air.

Culture: Santa Fe has been recognized as one of the cultural centers of the Southwest given its vast art galleries, the opera, museums and historical sites. Some of the more intriguing museums include the Laboratory of Anthropology; the Museum of Fine Arts; the Museum of International Folk Art, The Wheelwright Museum of the American Indian; and the Palace of the Governors (built in 1610, it's the oldest used public building in the country). The Santa Fe Opera is an internationally famous outdoor auditorium that was founded in 1957. At last count, there were close to 200 galleries city-wide, including the Wadle Gallery for Western art and the Janus Gallery for contemporary sculpture.

Annual events: March of Dimes Celebrity Ski Classic (March); Santa Fe Pow Wow (May): Indian drum groups from U.S. and Canada; Santa Fe Art & Crafts Benefit (June); Rodeo de Santa Fe (Sept.); Winter Market (Dec.): The Spanish market, storytelling, food festival.

Local Real Estate

Santa Fe's real estate market is very soft, with prices coming way down, mortgage money very tight and people acting very cautiously. Still, the brokers have seen the cycle before and remain optimistic. Many retirees who come to the market rent for six months. Nearly 90% will buy or build within the first year. New construction is more alive than resale activity. It's also a strong second-home market.

Median price for single family home: $128,000. Average prices range between $133,500 to $185,000.

Median price for 2BR condos: $128,500. Townhouses start at $117,000. New luxury units avg. $191,000.

Rental housing market: Avg. rental for 3BR house is $1,000/mo. 2BR apts. are $500/mo. The rental market has remained strong, which has driven up prices in the past few years, but at least there is no shortage of homes and condos to rent.

Common housing styles & features: Strict architectural controls require that exteriors be pueblo (red clay) or Spanish territorial. Preservation of historic buildings is widespread and strict zoning codes are in effect.

Amenities in condo developments: Most offer pools and tennis courts. Many developments have 9-hole golf courses.

Nearby areas to consider: El Dorado, Pecos.

Unique features of these areas: El Dorado is a new, small, bedroom community with more rural surroundings. Lot sizes are larger than Santa Fe (around 1 acre) and landowners join the local association, which entitles them to community facilities (tennis, pool, stables). Housing prices range from $90,000 to $300,000. Pecos (25 minutes outside Santa Fe) is situated in a beautiful, natural setting on the Pecos River (it's a lot greener than Santa Fe), allowing for great summer recreation. The town is small and rural and property is not nearly as expensive as in Santa Fe.

What Things Cost

Food, real estate and health care costs are above average, yet property taxes and utilities are quite low. State income tax is also favorable for seniors.

Gas company: Gas Company of New Mexico *(438-6900)*. Rates vary widely by season. In the summer, avg. bill is $13-14/mo. Winter months, bills average $60.

Electric company: Public Service of New Mexico *(473-1600)*. Avg. bill is $40-$50/mo. Summer can be higher with air conditioning. A $50 deposit may be required.

Phone company: U.S. West Communications *(765-6800)*. Basic budget service is $18/mo. (includes touch tone).

Car registration/license: New residents must apply for a New Mexico license within 30 days. Registration varies by weight and year of car. The fee includes title transfer, sticker and plates. For example, a 1990 car weighing 3,500 lbs. would run $37.80. Driver's license: $10 (good for 4 years). There is also a 3% excise tax on new vehicle purchases *(827-2255)*.

The Tax Ax

Sales tax: There is a 5.87% gross receipts tax.

State income tax: The current rates are as follows if married filing jointly: $24,000-$36,000: $883; $36,000-$48,000: $1,591; $48,000-$54,000: $2,420; and $54,000 or more is $2,874.

Retirement income: If over 65 and married filing jointly with an income under $30,000, residents can deduct $8,000 off taxable income. With incomes between $31,000 and 51,000, seniors pay between $1,000 to $7,000 (the higher the income, the smaller the deduction). Income of $51,000 has no deductions. Estate taxes: There is no inheritance tax and the estate tax is a "pick up tax" from the federal government (whatever the feds take satisfies the state).

Property taxes & tax breaks: Real estate tax is equal to $18.05 per each $1,000 of assessed value. Homes are assessed at 33 1/3% of market value. An $80,000 home would run $469/yr. A 135,000 home would cost $776/yr. Residents deduct a $2,000 household exemption before calculating taxes. Call the Santa Fe Tax Assessor for more information *(984-6551)*.

Medical Care

Major hospitals/regional medical centers: St. Vincent's Hospital is the only general full-service facility in the northern New Mexico. It is JCAH-accredited and expanding rapidly. It has recently opened its inpatient and outpatient rehabilitation centers, expanded its emergency room services and is working to enlarge its cancer care center (the new linear accelerator which can replace chemo therapy will be available here soon). It currently offers free screening for skin and prostate cancer. Other specialties include cardiac care and rehabilitation, diabetes treatment, MRI, home health services, arthritis treatment and radiology. The hospital is highly respected for its community wellness programs, including a popular mall walking program at Villa Linda Mall and the Santa Fe Century, a 25-50 mile bike ride. **Emergency medical services (EMS):** The Fire Department's EMS Team has more than 80 technicians, paramedics and specialists and 6 ambulances, which are available on a 24-hour basis. They claim to have the best response rates in the state, averaging 5-7 minutes. **Physician's referral:** *986-8888*.

Continuing Education

Santa Fe Community College has a Community Services Division, which offers an exciting Lifelong Learning program. The workshops and non-credit courses are very popular with retirees. Enrollment ranges in price from $20 to $85 per semester. Course offerings include "Women and Money," "The Marriage of Food and Wine," and "Tracing Your Family Genealogy." *(471-8200 ext. 251)*.

Services for Seniors

The Mary Esther Gonzales Senior Center is one of the most active and influential in state, with numerous activities including transportation, meals, entertainment, companions and a Foster Grandparent Program, which offers attention to school-age children with special needs. There is also an active **RSVP**

Chapter, with several hundred volunteers working in the community. **AARP:** The local chapter is affiliated with the Albuquerque chapter. Contact the Senior Center for more information *(984-6735)*.

Crime & Safety

In the past few years, the Santa Fe Police Department has been very proactive in reducing crime; rates in all major categories dropped in the past two years. The Department urges newcomers to get involved in Neighborhood Watch to continue the fight. It recently purchased a training video on crime against the elderly, which will be incorporated into its existing programs.

Earning a Living

Current business climate: Santa Fe has not felt the effects of the recession as deeply as many other parts of the country. Because it is the state capital, the state and federal governments are the largest employers (unemployment: 3.9%, well below the national avg.). With population growth, there is every reason to be optimistic about opportunities in Santa Fe. **Help in starting a business:** The Small Business Administration offers workshops for entrepreneurs at Santa Fe Community College. **The job market:** Beyond the minimum wage jobs, the outlook for seniors is not very promising. With little industry and a growing population, it's very competitive.

When the Kids Come to Visit

Taos Pueblo (Taos) is one of the oldest occupied settlements where the Pueblo Indians live the same way as their ancestors; Randall Davey Audubon Center: nature trails, art museum and historic buildings; Santa Fe National Forest: boating, hiking, picnicking, fishing and camping; Rio Grande Wild and Scenic River (35 mi. north of Taos): camping, fishing and hiking; Santa Fe Children's Museum: a "hands on" museum; El Rancho De Las Golondrinas: preserved Spanish village; Bandelier National Monument: hiking, cliff dweller's ruins and a 12th-century pueblo.

Getting Around Town

Roads & interstates: I-25; US 64, 285
Airports & airlines: Santa Fe's municipal airport is served by Mesa Airlines, a commuter line. Albuquerque International is the closest commercial airport (60 miles).
Public transportation: Taxis are available, but there is currently no mass transit system (one is in the proposal stage).
Managing without a car: A car is a necessity.

What Residents Already Know

The most popular book among residents is "Death Comes for the Archbishop," Willa Cather's tale of the French Priest who came to Santa Fe in the early 1800s and changed it forever.•Shop till you drop with more than 450 stores (downtown alone), 200 art galleries (one of the largest art centers in the country), farmer's markets and several malls.•Santa Fe is fabulous ski country, with the Sandia Peak Tramway: the world's longest aerial tram that soars to over 10,000 ft. in minutes.

For More Information

Chamber Of Commerce Office:
Santa Fe Chamber of Commerce
P.O. Box 1928
Santa Fe, 87504-1928
983-7317

Newspapers:
The New Mexican (Santa Fe)
P.O. Box 2048, Santa Fe, 87504
983-3303 or 800-873-3372

Santa Fe Reporter (weekly)
P.O. Box 2306
Santa Fe, 87504
988-5541

Realtors:
Mr. David Barker, **Barker Realty**
222 E. Marcy
Santa Fe, 87504
983-2400

Ms. Barbara Clay, **Clay Properties**
P.O. Box 86-3
Santa Fe, 87504
983-8599

30. Sullivan County, New York

Area Snapshot

Nickname: "Borscht Belt" (old name), "Gateway to the Catskills" (new name)
County: Sullivan County
Area code: 914   **Zip code:** 12701
County population: 69,277
% of population 65+: 15.8%
U.S. region: Catskill Mountains, Upstate NY
Closest metro areas: NYC, 90 mi.; Phila., 160 mi.
Nearby areas to consider: Liberty, Rock Hill
Median housing price: $83,000
Best reasons to retire here: A beautifully lush rural area within driving distance to New York City, excellent recreational opportunities, affordable real estate, great entertainment.

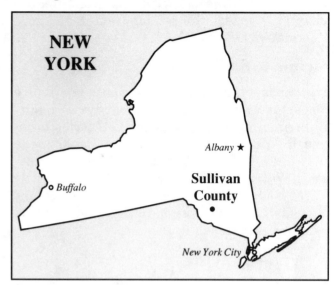

Fabulous Features

For generations, the scenic Catskill Mountains and Sullivan County have been a retreat for city folk who needed a weekend in the country. Now those same people, retired and in need of clean air, wide open space and affordable homes, are coming to stay. Interestingly, a large percentage of Sullivan County natives who leave as young adults eventually come back to buy second homes and/or retire. It's no wonder that the U.S. Agriculture Department designated it as one of the three "rural retirement" counties in New York state. What's the draw? For starters, if there is something you enjoy doing outdoors, it's here and it's unbeatable. The skiing, fishing, boating, hunting, golfing, horseback riding, hiking, and camping are some of the best on the East coast. Real estate and taxes are less costly than all the surrounding urban areas and people especially appreciate the quiet, country ambiance. And let's not forget the top-rated entertainment

brought in by the area resorts like the Concord and Browns Hotel. Medical care is efficient and very much in tune with the needs of seniors. As one retiree so aptly put it, "The air is clean, the water is pure and the people are lovely."

Possible drawbacks: Statistically, Sullivan County has the third highest crime rate in New York state. Everyone attributes it to the transient workers hired by the hotels to fill minimum wage jobs. Read between the lines and you find that most of the crime is on themselves. Unfortunately, it's a real blemish for an otherwise idyllic place.•There is no public transforation and the region is spread out, so a car is a must.•There's no relief from winter in these parts. The county theme song is "Let it snow, let it snow, let it snow"—to the tune of 86 inches a year. However, if you're in the mindset to settle in for the winter, it's a beautiful place to be.

"You can quote me on that"

"My husband was born and raised in Sullivan County and had family here. We liked to visit and figured it was just as good a place to retire as any. We liked the idea of living in a small, rural community but having lots of things to do. Also, we're still close enough to New York to drive in whenever we get lonely for our grandchildren. I highly recommend this area for active retirees like us."—J.H., Monticello

Climate

Elevation: 3000'	Avg. High/ Low	Average Inches		Avg. # Days Precip.	Avg. % Humidity
		Rain	Snow		
Jan.	32/15	.8	20	14	72
April	52/32	2.8	5	14	69
July	80/58	4.2	-	12	71
Oct.	61/38	3.3	-	11	73
YEAR	56/35	32	-	-	-
# days 32° or below: 153			# days 90° or above: 7		

Let the Good Times Roll

Recreation: Fishing: What more can be said about a place that introduced fly-fishing and fly-casting to the country? With hundreds of lakes and streams, it's a fisherman's holiday. Junction Pool is "Trout Town USA." Rivers and reservoirs are stocked annually by the State. **Golf:** More than 40 courses, many PGA approved. Greens fees are moderate, even at 18-hole championship courses (most also open to public). **Skiing:** Great downhill and cross-country skiing including Hunter Mountain (Ulster county). The Catskills is horse country with stables, riding academies and famous Monticello Raceway: the fastest half-mile harness track. Walnut Mountain Park: hiking, cross-country skiing and baseball. State recreation includes Basherkill Wildlife Management, Beaverkill State Campsite, and Crystal Lake State Reservation.

Culture: Theater: Catskill Actors Theater, Forestburg Playhouse (a 120-year-old barn for summer stock shows), Tusten Theater and Seelig Theater. Museums: Roscoe and W. Railway Museum, Catskill Fly Fishing Center, Sullivan County Museum and the Art and Cultural Center. Delaware Valley Arts Association sponsors community art programs. Sullivan County Community College has an exciting senior summer cultural series. Sullivan County also has a Historical Society, Dramatic Workshop and the Catskills Arts Society.

Annual events: Annual Ice Carnival (Jan.); Winter Carnival (Mar.); Senior Artists Spring Show Exhibit (May-June); Arts and Crafts Fair (Aug.); Metropolitan PGA Pro Golf Tournament (Sept.); Fight Night in the Catskills, Browns Hotel (Sept.).

Local Real Estate

The real estate market is a depressed one and homes are selling well under market value. The choices of second homes, condominiums, town houses, estates and farms are fabulous. There is something new and exciting in the works. Harris Village (Harris), the nation's first luxury housing development, is being built adjacent to a full-service community hospital for seniors. Aside from access to sophisticated medical care, the development will offer recreational facilities, shopping, transportation and security. Prices start at $137,500 plus a $1,055 monthly service fee (housekeeping, chores, real estate taxes, repairs and many extras). Call *(800-242-7879)*.

Median price for single family home: $83,000. $115,000 new.

Median price for 2BR condos: $90,000-$100,000

Rental housing market: 3BR house: $400-$850/mo.; 2BR house $350-$750/mo. Seasonal rentals were always a mainstay, now year-round rentals are popular as a way to offset inflated prices during peak summer months.

Common housing styles & features: Large country kitchens, large acreage, stone fireplaces, sprawling ranches, lakefront property, wrap-around decks.

Amenities in condo developments: Tennis courts, pools.

Nearby areas to consider: Monticello, Callicoon. **Unique features of these areas:** Monticello is one of the largest townships and offers the most in shopping and services and a wide variety of homes (all price ranges). Callicoon is one of the most rural areas with farms and mountains. It's a good 20 minutes from major services, but housing costs are some of the lowest in the county ($85,000-$95,000).

What Things Cost

Living costs in general are much lower than the urban and suburban areas that retirees migrate from. Food, housing, utilities and property taxes enable people to live on a fixed income comfortably. **Gas company:** There is no natural gas in Sullivan county. Purchase oil or gas from private companies. Currently gas is cheaper (install a furnace and monthly consumption avgs. $1 per gallon). Avg. is $100/mo. Call Sullivan County Gas *(794-8484)*. **Electric company:** New York State Electric and Gas *(800-541-2014)*. Avg. monthly electric bill is $55 (billed bimonthly). **Phone company:** New York Telephone *(890-8030)*. Basic monthly service starts at $10.10. Unlimited calling starts at $22.86 month. Touchtone and other services are extra. **Car registration & license:** Title fee: $5; Registration based on weight: small $30-$40; med $40-$50; lg. $50-$80.; Driver's license: $17.50 (good for 4 years); License plates: $8.

The Tax Ax

Sales tax: 7% (food and prescription drugs are exempt).

State income tax: Net taxable income for married persons filing jointly is taxed at the following rates: $12,000 or below: 4.3%; $12,000-$18,000: 5.3%; $18,000-$24,000: 7.3%; $24,000-$28,000: 7.3%; $28,000+: 7.7%. The standard deduction is $10,200.

Retirement income: After age 59, the first $20,000 of pension income (including IRA's) is exempt from New York State income tax. Estate taxes: On a $600,000 estate, state tax would equal $20,000.

Property taxes & tax breaks: If new county budget is passed, 1991 taxes will be based on 100% of market value or approximately $15 per $1,000 of valuation. Thus, homes valued at $100,000 would pay $1,500/yr. Taxes vary widely among the townships. County Tax Appraisers office *(794-3000 ext. 5014)*. There is no homestead exemption, although eligible seniors who meet residency requirements can get a 50% reduction in town, county and school taxes.

Medical Care

Major hospitals & regional medical centers: Community General Hospital (Harris), is a full-service hospital with one of the best geriatric care facilities in the country. It has specialists in all fields including cardiology, endocrinology, urology and in/out patient

rehabilitation. In addition, it offers WISE (Wellness Independent Senior Experience): a preventive self-care program for seniors. A diabetes and arthritis center are planned. **Grover M. Hermann** (Callicoon), is an extension of Community General Hospital and provides similar services on a smaller scale. Two hours from New York and Philadelphia gives people the option to go to the large teaching hospitals. **Emergency medical services (EMS):** The county offers 22 volunteer ambulance corps and rescue squads. Avg. response time: 12-20 minutes (it's a rural area and all are volunteers). A special emergency control service dispatches units throughout the county (Monticello and Liberty have their own system). **Physician's/dental referral:** *794-3300 ext. 2157* (Community Hospital's Medical Board Office makes referrals).

Services for Seniors

Office for the Aging provides transportation, meal service, income and property tax assistance. **EISEP** (Expanded In-Home Services For Elderly Persons): provides non-medical, in-home support to seniors not eligible for help through medicaid *(794-3000 ext. 5000)*. **RSVP** (Retired Senior Volunteer Program): places seniors in non-profit organizations throughout the county. There is no local **AARP** Chapter in Sullivan County.

Continuing Education

Sullivan County Community College provides non-credit continuing education courses (many in summer) such as tap dancing, Jewish songs, bridge and EMT instruction. Fees range from $20-$50. A Performing Arts series is also part of the program *(434-5750)*. Catskills Arts Society provides a variety of non-credit arts and crafts classes. They have their own gallery and organize bus trips to museums, shows, etc. as well as a summer celebration series. Sullivan County BOCES (run by the school district) offers evening vocational and academic courses.

Crime & Safety

The first thing the Sullivan County Sheriff's Department wanted us to know was that it's really a safe place to live. Statistics say it has the third highest crime rate in New York (per capita). They say it's because the transient hotel workers commit crimes against each other. There are property crimes, but assaults and homicides are low, particularly in outlying townships like Callicoon. Liberty, Thompson and Fallsburg is where most of the crime occurs. Liberty and Monticello have police departments, the rest of the county is patrolled by the Sheriff's Department and each township has its own constables. Given that most of the law enforcement personnel live and work here, there's a vested interest in public safety.

Earning a Living

Current business climate: Sullivan County is experiencing growth in the service sector and the health care industry. When the depressed real estate market turns around, it will only enhance the outlook. Tourism and agriculture (poultry production) are the backbone of the economy. **Help in starting a business:** Contact the Chamber of Commerce for information on local business development centers and the revolving loan funds available for business expansion *(292-2070)*. **The job market:** With many nursing homes and facilities for the elderly, health care delivery has a strong employment picture that continues to grow.

When the Kids Come to Visit

Upper Delaware Scenic and Recreational River was designated as part of the National Wild and Scenic River System in 1978. Includes Skinners Falls, canoeing, fishing and camping. Catskill Fun Lane (amusement park with miniature golf and pony rides). Howe Caverns (caverns to explore). Hunter Mountain (skiing in winter, ethnic fests in the summer). New York State Forest Preserve of fishing, camping, nature trails. Apple Pond Farming Center (Callicoon): educational farming center. Historic Sites and Districts: Minisink Battleground Memorial Park, Fort Delaware, Grahamsville and Liberty Historic Districts.

Getting Around Town

Roads & interstates: Rt. 17 ("The Quickway"), Rt. 17B, Rt. 42. **Airports & airlines:** Stewart International Airport (Newburgh: 45 min.) direct air service via American Airlines. Sullivan County International Airport and Monticello Airport have charter service and private aircraft. **Public transportation:** No public transportation available. However, the Sullivan County Office of Aging offers transportation to shopping for $2 (roundtrip) once a week in each township *(794-3000 ext. 5000)*. **Managing without a car:** Impossible.

What Residents Already Know

Sullivan County's Office of Public Information is a tremendous resource *(794-3000 or 800-882-CATS)*. • You can pick up some fabulous real estate buys now, but new property taxes rates will go into effect this year and that's going to mean big increases in many townships.

For More Information

Chamber Of Commerce Offices:
Sullivan County Chamber
P.O. Box 6, Liberty, 12754
292-2070

Monticello Chamber of Commerce
26 Landfield
Monticello, 12701
794-2212

Newspaper:
Times Herald Record
P.O. Box 2046
Middletown, 10940
343-2181

Realtors:
Bill Reiber
Reiber Realty
188 Broadway
Monticello, 12701
794-0211

Vivian Jacoby
Vivian Jacoby Realty
P.O. Box 571
Rock Hill, 12775
794-5957

31. Asheville, North Carolina

Area Snapshot

Nicknames: "Land of the Sky" or "Paris of the South"
County: Buncombe
Area code: 704   **Zip codes:** 28801-16
Local population: 61,456   **County:** 174,436
% of population 65+: 25.8%
U.S. region: S.E. U.S. Western North Carolina
Closest metro areas: Greenville, S.C., 70 mi.; Charlotte, 125 mi.
Nearby areas to consider: Hendersonville
Median housing price: $88,000
Best reasons to retire here: Fabulous year-round climate, mountainous region, much to see and do and a lifestyle/programs for seniors unsurpassed by any city this size.

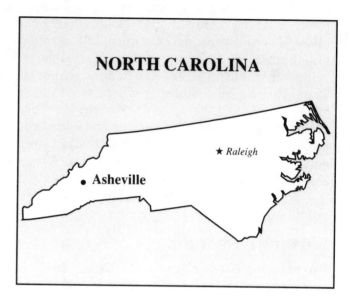

Fabulous Features

The term "quality of life" has become a catch phrase for so many different cities today that it has lost meaning. But if ever there was a place that was worthy of owning up to the expression, it's Asheville. Located on a plateau divided by the French Broad River and surrounded by mountains, Asheville draws many a vacationer who comes back for good. Residents enjoy the sophisticated city life knowing that a million acres of natural wilderness is within shouting distance. The year-round climate is unbeatable—not too hot or cold. The culture, recreation and amenities for a city this size are remarkable, and the quality of health care gets raves. The appeal to retirees is that the city is big enough not to be stifling, but not so large that it loses its small-town friendliness. Or its small-town crime rates. Public safety is essentially a non-issue. Ultimately, the retirees who flock here are off their rockers, morning, noon and night if they are so inclined. It's no wonder Asheville is consistently ranked and rated as a fabulous place to live. **Possible drawbacks:** In the past few years there has been a serious water supply shortage although the town fathers are on the verge of making a decision about new resources.•People are surprised that it gets as hot as it does in the summer. But unlike parts of Florida, at least the evenings cool off considerably.•The rental market is as tight as a drum. If your intent is to come down for a few months, give yourself ample lead time to find a place.•The 7% income tax (with very few exemptions) has some people keeping one eye on Florida.

"You can quote me on that"

"We absolutely love it here. The area is beautiful, the climate is perfect. We love the art and culture. Come and enjoy."—M.A.

"Our home is Chicago and we wanted to retire to a place that had mountains but not too much snow. We also dreamt of cool summers. Asheville has it all. People are so honest. You can pay everything by check, nobody asks questions. There's almost a spiritual aspect to the people. The only bad part is the high income tax."—J.H.

Climate

Elevation: 2,175'	Avg. High/ Low	Average Inches		Avg. # Days Precip.	Avg. % Humidity
		Rain	Snow		
Jan.	48/27	2.9	-	11	70
April	69/42	3.5	-	9	58
July	84/63	4.9	-	12	74
Oct.	69/45	3.3	-	8	69
YEAR	67/44	38	18	-	-
# days 32° or below: 104			# days 90° or above: 7		

Let the Good Times Roll

Recreation: Asheville is bliss for outdoor enthusiasts. With an invigorating, temperate climate, you can sail and fly fish on Beaver Lake, go white-water rafting on the Nantahala or ski at Cataloochee. The lakes, rivers and mountains call you to action year-round. If golf is your game, you could play a different course every day for two weeks in and around Asheville. The public and private courses have reputations for being beautiful, challenging and uncrowded 10 months a year (the mountain golf is splendid). Hikers have hundreds of miles of trails to cover. Sports: Asheville is home to the Houston Astros Farm Team and UNC's basketball team; There's also the new Asheville Speedway for short track stock car racing. The North Carolina Horse Show Complex hosts some of the top shows in the Southeast. National and state parks: Mount Mitchell State Park (the highest mountain east of the Rockies at 6,684 ft.); Pisgah National Forest, The Great Smoky Mountains (the most visited of all national parks) plus 233 mountain peaks over 5,000 ft. in elevation.

Culture: Pack Place, a $14 million education, arts and science center (opening in late 1991) will be a cultural magnet for the entire region. It's the icing on the cake for an area this size that has its own symphony, ballet (Baryshnikov danced here with the ballet after spending a week fly-fishing), museums, repertory theater, 50 arts organizations and the world-renowned Brevard Music Center of Performing Arts (25 mi.).

Annual events: Mountain Dance & Folk Festival and Shindig On The Green are two of the most popular tourist events in the region, bringing dancing and traditional folk music to town. Highland Handcraft Guild Fair (one of the oldest in the country), Bele Chere, Goombay and Riverfest are special festivals. Discovery Day, which draws 2,000 students, enjoys a salute to local heritage.

Local Real Estate

The market is well-balanced for both buyers and sellers. With low interest rates and fairly good inventory, both sides are doing well.
Median price for single family home: $88,000.
Median price for 2BR condo: $65,000-80,000 (the well appointed units start at $100,000).
Rental housing market: Year-round rentals are practically non-existent. Seasonal rentals may be easier with enough lead time. 2BR apartment averages $350/mo.; a 3BR house rents for $400/mo.
Common housing styles & features: Many traditional 2-story homes and contemporary ranches with basements.
Amenities in condo developments: Many 2-story townhouses and 1-story apartments. Some of the more expensive units have access to golf. All have pools and tennis.
Nearby area to consider: Hendersonville.
Unique features of this area: Hendersonville is a small town (pop. 12,000) approximately 18 miles south that attracts a very large percentage of retirees. There's considerably more condo construction there, and prices are somewhat lower.

What Things Cost

Cost of living is approx. 5% below the national avg., mostly in housing, utilities and health care. Construction: lowest in the country.
Gas company: Public Service Co. *(253-1821).* Avg. bill: $50/mo., with summer as low as $15, winter up to $75. Homeowners pay no deposit.
Electric company: Carolina Power & Light *(258-1010).* Avg. monthly bill is $126.
Phone company: Southern Bell *(378-6000).* Basic service is $11.66/mo including unlimited local calls. Average monthly bill is $20-$25.
Car registration/license: Registration: $10; Title: $35 + 3% tax on car's current value; Plates: $20; Driver's license: $16.

The Tax Ax

North Carolina claims its taxes are 30% below the U.S. average, although income tax takes quite a bite.

Sales tax: 6% (prescription drugs, eye glasses and some medical supplies and services are exempt).

State income tax: 6-7%, with $2,000 personal exemptions allowed. If married filing jointly with taxable income over $21,250, taxes will be $1,275, plus 7% on any income over $21,250.

Retirement income: Up to $2,000 in retirement benefits is excluded (or $4,000 of government retirement benefits). Inheritance taxes: none for surviving spouse.

Property taxes & tax breaks: 1991 tax rate in Asheville proper is $1.49 per $100 of valuation. A home valued at $100,000 would have annual property taxes of $1,495. There is no homestead exemption. Personal property (cars, boats, mobile homes, etc.) are charged at the same rate.

Medical Care

Major hospitals/regional medical centers: Asheville is western North Carolina's regional health care center, with more than 300 physicians covering every specialty. This is unheard of in other comparable-sized cities. The major hospitals include: **Memorial Mission,** which specializes in total cardiac care, laser angioplasty and comprehensive cancer care. They have the only air ambulance in the region and have one of the few hand/upper body reconstruction centers in the country. **St. Joseph's** is strong in rehabilitative care and also offers an "Ask-A-Nurse" referral service. There are also several specialty hospitals including **Thomas Rehabilitative** for spinal cord and head injuries and for stroke and pain victims.

Emergency medical services (EMS): 8 ambulances, 75 paramedics. Response time is 6 minutes. **Physician's referral:** *800-321-6877* ("Ask-A-Nurse" Referral Program). Information on dentists also.

Continuing Education

UNCA's Center for Creative Retirement (see below) offers a "College for Seniors." Take undergraduate courses or special classes (drama, ceramics, economics). 8-week program is $80, $140 per couple *(251-6140)*. Elderhostel program also available *(251-6600)*. Center for Creative Retirement has numerous other classes and programs *(251-6140)*.

Services for Seniors

The University of North Carolina Asheville has developed a Center for Creative Retirement, the only one of its kind in the country. Recently, President Bush named this center as one his "1,000 Points of Light." It was designed to encourage leadership, volunteerism, technology transfer, retirement planning, health promotion and peer learning/teaching. They offer seminars, a Retirement Wellness Center and a College for Seniors, among numerous other programs. It costs $25 to become an associate and it's certifiably the most innovative and important organization for seniors we've ever heard of. Write to the Center at UNCA, Asheville, 28804-3299 *(251-6140)*. Carolina Senior Citizen—a monthly paper. Subscription $12/yr. *(251-5881)*. **AARP:** For membership, contact Rick or Betty Davis *(665-2860)*.

Crime & Safety

Asheville is a "wet" city amongst adjacent "dry" counties. It also has several major interstates running through the outskirts of town. Given these circumstances, an average of 150,000 outsiders come to and through Asheville every day. In spite of this, crime is extraordinarily low. Compared to other cities its size, the number of serious offenses would seem trivial if you are coming from a major metropolitan area. The Police Department attributes the area's safety record to the high level of involved citizens who are not afraid to report crime or testify. If you commit a crime in Asheville, you will very likely get caught. Burglaries are the most common crime. When you start looking at real estate, call the police and they will tell you if a certain neighborhood or even a block is prone to break-ins. **Advice from the police:** Please call if you suspect anything at all or want assurances about personal safety.

Earning a Living

Current business climate: Asheville is a regional hub for manufacturing, health care, banking and tourism, giving it a diverse and stable economy. It's not a feast-or-famine market, which makes it conducive for small businesses to have time to grow. More than 50 percent of the local businesses have only 1 to 3 employees, indicating that the entrepreneurial spirit is alive, and the community is receptive to services that meet needs.

The job market: Many retirees have come here and started successful second careers in real estate and insurance. Or, they have turned volunteer work into a job or business. As for part-time employment, the unemployment rate is below the state average—which, in turn, is below the national average. If you are inclined to work, getting an interesting job should not be a problem.

When the Kids Come to Visit

Farmer's Market (36-acres of fresh produce and wonderful crafts); Biltmore House: a 255-room French Renaissance Chateau belonging to the late George Vanderbilt; The Health Adventure Children's Museum; Asheville Antique Row (downtown); and The Asheville Nature Center (native animals in their natural habitats).

Getting Around Town

Roads & Interstates: I-40 and I-26 (the largest interchange in the southeast, US Highways 19, 23, 25 , 70 & 74; Blue Ridge Parkway (a 470-mile road skirting town exclusively for leisure travel and recreational use).

Airports & airlines: Asheville Regional Airport serviced by USAir, Delta and several commuter airlines. Charlotte International Airport (125 mi.) is served by all major carriers.

Public transportation: The City Transit Authority has more than 400 daily scheduled stops within the city limits. Private lines cover the suburbs and rural areas. **Managing without a car:** Possible, but not very convenient

What Residents Already Know

In 1990, Asheville aligned with a sister city, Vladikavkaz, Russia. The two mountain cities hope to exchange cultural and educational experiences.•Asheville is great literary colony having been home to Thomas Wolfe, Carl Sandburg and F. Scott Fitzgerald. Today the thriving Writer's Workshop attracts 1,000 participants as do the numerous continuing education classes for creative writers.•If this city is good enough for Richard Boyer (the co-author of *Places Rated Almanac*), why, it's got to be special!

For More Information

Chamber Of Commerce Office:
Asheville Chamber
of Commerce
P.O. Box 1010
Asheville, 28802
258-3858

Newspaper:
Asheville Citizen Times
P.O. Box 2090
Asheville, 28802
252-5611

Realtors:
Betty Arnold
Beverly Hanks & Assoc.
300 Executive Park
Asheville, 28801
254-7221

Mr. Lee Adams
Four Seasons Realty
1340 I Patton Ave.
Asheville, 28806
253-3309

32. Brevard, North Carolina

Area Snapshot

Nickname: "Land of Waterfalls"
County: Transylvania
Area code: 704 **Zip code:** 28712
Local population: 5,388 **County:** 25,500
% of population 65+: 10%
U.S. region: Western North Carolina (New Appalachia)
Closest metro area: Asheville, 25 miles
Nearby area to consider: Hendersonville
Median housing price: $85,000
Best reasons to retire here: Small town in the Blue Ridge Mountains, beautiful rural setting, peaceful environment, outdoor beauty, affordable, friendly people!

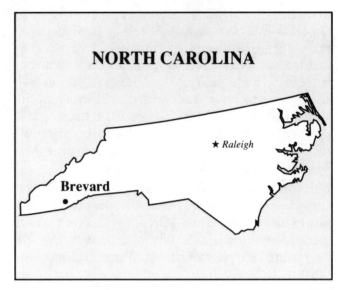

Fabulous Features

Brevard is the little town that could. It's a rural respite in the Appalachias where the fresh mountain air, invigorating climate and relaxed pace are your ticket to healthy living. It's a tiny dot on the map but a tremendous find for retirees who are looking for a certain way of life. The kind of life where activities revolve around your neighbors, nature's amenities and your own hobbies and interests. What's unique to this countrified town is that it has a genteel sophistication about it. The famous Brevard Music Center and Brevard College contribute culture and enrichment. The Pisgah National Forest and the majestic Blue Ridge Mountains offer the most basic gifts of nature to soak up. Days are slow-paced, quiet times to pursue what interests you. The city is well-managed, with new water and sewer facilities, award-winning recycling programs and a good infrastructure. Housing is affordable, the people are educated and friendly, and there is a feeling that you are very much a part a community. In this environment, you will rediscover a quality of life that you may have thought you lost along the way.

Possible drawbacks: There are no "twelve-plex" movie theaters, no gourmet restaurants, no two-tiered shopping malls. What you see is what you get. Many "horn-blowers" come from the big city and try to change all that. They're frustrated with the lack of "big city doings," to which natives ask, "Isn't that why you left?" Caveat Emptor—Brevard is a small town and built to stay that way.

"You can quote me on that"

"Believe it or not, we came from Honolulu. We wanted a very different way of life for retirement but were still concerned about being bored. Would you believe I don't have enough time in the day to do all that I want? I've gotten so involved doing volunteer work, and I'm intrigued with the ruby and sapphire mines in the area. It's a wonderful life and the people are very friendly. My advice is if people are going to settle here they have to relax to enjoy."—Mrs. J.C.

"We're from Madison, N.J., and discovered this area on a couple of camping trips. We couldn't wait to retire here and say goodbye to high taxes and the miserable winters. We visited several times before buying just to make sure we would be comfortable. Now we absolutely love it. I wouldn't live anywhere else. The people make it wonderful. My advice is to just slow down a little. It's good for you."—Mrs. E.H.

Climate

Elevation: 2,230'	Avg. High/ Low	Average Inches		Avg. # Days Precip.	Avg. % Humidity
		Rain	Snow		
Jan.	48/27	2.9	-	11	70
April	69/42	3.5	-	9	58
July	84/63	4.9	-	12	74
Oct.	69/45	3.3	-	8	69
YEAR	67/44	38	18	-	-
# days 32° or below: 104			# days 90° or above: 7		

Let the Good Times Roll

Recreation: Brevard is an outdoor enthusiast's paradise. Just five minutes from downtown is the entrance to the Pisgah National Forest (its breathtaking beauty covers 35 percent of the county), and its two most noted attractions, the Cradle of Forestry and Looking Glass Falls. There, you can hike, rock-climb, and fish the day away. The U.S. Forest Service Museum offers a special introduction to the woodlands, identifying the plants and animals that inhabit the forest. Fishing enthusiasts head to the French Broad River and the Davidson River for unsuspecting trout. The Great Smoky Mountains area gateway to outdoor recreational opportunities. There are 223 mountain peaks in Western North Carolina alone for exploration year-round. Come out of the woods long enough for a football game, though. Remember how good it felt to root for the home team? Get your loudest cheer ready for the Brevard High School Blue Devils, where the fall ritual is to pack the stadium.

Culture: The Brevard Music Center attracts internationally known musicians. Residents can look forward to visiting the opera, the symphony and touring Broadway shows. Brevard College (dating back to 1800s) is one of the top Junior colleges in the country, and features the Little Theater, with four enjoyable performances a year. The Brevard Chamber Orchestra performs year-round.

Annual events: Festival of the Arts Week (July); Jazz at Brevard (August); Halloween-fest (October); Christmas Parade (with tree-lighting and horse-drawn carriage rides).

Local Real Estate

Demand has picked up significantly in the past year, leading to higher prices but still a strong and varied inventory. With almost half the property in the county national forest, government owned or uninhabitable because of the topography, land is at a premium. Most homes are resales (there is very little new construction in Brevard). Between $150,000-$200,000 can buy you a 2,500-3,000 square foot home with a large lot in a golf-course community such as Conneste Falls (5 1/2 miles from Brevard) with five lakes, a pool and a clubhouse. Glenn Cannon Country Club is another golf-course community with many 3-bedroom single family homes. There are some new homes to choose from around in Deer Lake, where lots range from $20,000-$65,000, and gorgeous new homes start at $150,000. The second-home market is very big and smaller, older homes sell to retirees in the mid $80s. These homes tend to be in town and convenietly close to shopping.

Median price for single family home: $85,000

Median price for 2BR condo: $74,000 (condos are a very popular option and there are many to choose from).

Rental housing market: 2BR apartments are available for $450 a month, houses rent for $550 a month plus utilities.

Common housing styles & features: Many are 3BR/2BA two-story colonials with brick exteriors.

Amenities in condo developments: Pools, some golf course communities.

Nearby area to consider: Hendersonville (18 miles). **Unique features of this area:** Hendersonville, with a population of 20,000 in the greater area, will give you access to the same natural beauty. But it's a bigger town and the shopping and amenities, while not vast, will be more costly than in Brevard. The housing prices are comparable. The percentage of the retired population is very high here as well.

What Things Cost

Except for the sticker shock of land prices, living costs in this county are comfortably moderate. You certainly won't pay any more for the basics than where you're coming from.

Gas company: Public Service of North Carolina *(883-8201)*. There is neither a connection charge nor a deposit required for homeowners. The average monthly bill for a 2,000 sq ft. home is $80-$100. Budget billing is available.

Electric company: Duke Power *(883-8255)*. Average monthly bill is $90-$110. No connection charge or deposit required with a good payment history.

Water/sewer: The average monthly bill is $12-$15.

Phone company: Citizens Telephone Company *(884-9011)*. Basic monthly charge is $17.

Car registration/license: You'll need to bring your title, proof of insurance and mileage. New plates: $20; title fee: $35; notary fee: $3; Driver's license is $10 for four years. You are required to take a written test.

The Tax Ax

North Carolina claims its taxes are 30% below the national average, although income tax can certainly take a healthy bite.

Sales tax: 6% (prescription drugs, eye glasses and some medical supplies and services are exempt).

State income tax: 6-7%, with $2,000 personal exemptions allowed. If married filing jointly with taxable income over $21,250, taxes will be $1,275, plus 7% on any income over the $21,250.

Retirement income: Up to $2,000 in retirement benefits is excluded (or $4,000 of government retirement benefits). Inheritance taxes: none for surviving spouse.

Property taxes & tax breaks: The combined city and county millage rate is $1.05 per $100 of valuation. Thus, a $150,000 home would run $1,575 a year.

Medical Care

Major hospitals & regional medical centers: Transylvania Community Hospital in Brevard is a 64-bed hospital used primarily for stabilizing and diagnostics. General surgery is available here and the hospital offers a good coronary ICU. Helicopter transport is available to **Memorial Mission** and **St. Joseph Medical Center** in Asheville, N.C.

Emergency medical services (EMS): EMS is county owned and operated, with a volunteer corp in Brevard handling the first response. The local 911 also has a computer locater to automatically provide an address and location to the dispatcher (it is essential to register with the police when you move in so they know to include your home in their file). Response time is 5 to 8 minutes, with the EMS vehicles stationed in Brevard.

Physician's referral: Transylvania Community Hospital *884-9111*.

Continuing Education

Brevard College has developed an excellent series of courses for seniors, including water aerobics as well as local interests such as gem mining. The college also offers a unique course for residents and newcomers called "Leadership Transylvania," which introduces attendees to the leaders in the community, as well as to human services, health care, local government, etc. Brevard is also host to a special Seniorhostel program five times a year. Nearby Blue Ridge Community College offers courses to seniors, gratis.

Services for Seniors

Brevard's seniors get involved in all aspects of community life, particularly as volunteers. Through the combined efforts of 32 churches and senior volunteers, the Sharing House provides clothing, crisis counseling, and other services to the needy. Contact the chamber for their directory called "Volunteer Opportunities." They can also provide information on **AARP** memberships and various local clubs *(800-648-4523)*.

Crime & Safety

Crime only seems to be what you read about in the paper. There are no particular crime prevention programs for seniors because this is a very safe and secure city. In this caring community, you'll find neighbors take responsibility for each other's welfare. This is of great importance to retirees who travel frequently or return north for months on end. Residents can leave with confidence knowing their property will be secure.

Earning a Living

Current business climate: There is a growing demand for certain retail and service businesses because currently, most major shopping has to be done in Hendersonville and Asheville. Residents would welcome the opportunity to support local entrepreneurs.

Help in starting a business: Contact SCORE for free counseling with business plans, loan applications, and other needs *(883-8456)*. Blue Ridge Community College and Western North Carolina University offer free guidance as well.

The job market: Employment opportunities in Brevard are very limited.

When the Kids Come to Visit

Sliding Rock Glacial Rock has a natural slide. Hike in the forest and see more than 200 waterfalls, wade in the creeks, enjoy a picnic, or go bike riding.

Getting Around Town

Roads & interstates: US 64 and US 276.
Airports & airlines: Asheville Regional Airport (25 miles) is served by Delta and USAir.
Public transportation: There is no public transit system, just taxis.
Managing without a car: It's not advisable.

What Residents Already Know

Getting parts for your car can take a while, especially for foreign makes.•Two new shopping areas are going up in Brevard, and the whole town is ready to celebrate.•If you're a former college professor, college president, professional or Ph.D., you'll find yourself in good company. Brevard is a "smart" place to be.•The community thrives on seniors who volunteer their time. They welcome newcomers who dig in.

For More Information

Chamber Of Commerce Office:
Brevard Chamber of Commerce:
P.O. Box 589
Brevard, N.C. 28712
800-648-4523

Newspaper:
Transylvania Times
P.O. Box 32
Brevard, 28712
883-8156

Realtor:
Allen Winterhaller
Coldwell Banker/Melton Co.
226 S. Caldwell St.
Brevard, 28712
884-4300

33. Chapel Hill, North Carolina

Area Snapshot

Nickname: "Southern Part of Heaven"
County: Orange
Area code: 919 **Zip codes:** 27514-27516
Local population: 40,000 **County:** 92,000
% of population 65+: 13%
U.S. region: South East
Closest metro areas: Durham, 8 miles; Raleigh, 25 miles
Nearby areas to consider: Hillsborough, Pittsboro, Farrington
Median housing price: $138,000
Best reasons to retire here: Colonial beauty, wonderful climate, small but cosmopolitan area, outstanding health care, UNC is a cultural magnet.

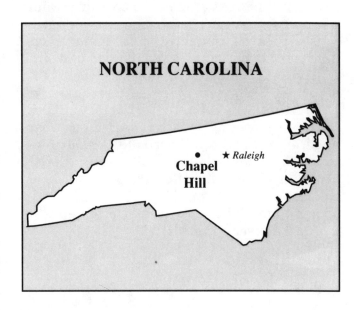

Fabulous Features

When people say Chapel Hill is a smart place to retire, they're not kidding. With the influence of the University of North Carolina (student enrollment of 25,000), the world renowned Research Triangle Park (largest planned research park in the country employing 33,000 people) and two major teaching hospitals, there are more educated residents than perhaps anywhere in the world. Their intelligence is confirmed by having chosen to live in a fabulous town like Chapel Hill. Its history and colonial beauty set the stage for some of the most beautiful homes and neighborhoods in the South. Culture, recreation, shopping and antiquing are the official pastimes, with an abundance of places to enjoy all. Even the climate cooperates. Winters are short, fall and spring are breathtaking. Health care is outstanding (the doctor-to-patient ratio is 5 times the national average) with Duke University Medical Center and UNC Hospital in your backyard. Finally, we discovered that the quality of life is really special. Chapel Hill is a small, charming and accessible community with a very involved citizen groups and a warm welcome for newcomers. One resident said she'd lived all over the country and had never experienced the genuine friendliness she found here.

Possible drawbacks: Living costs are higher than in most other areas of the state (real estate can be very pricey).•Any place this fast-growing and desirable will have growing pains. You'll learn all about transportation needs, waste disposal problems.•There's a very popular new bumper sticker that reads, "Helms Happens." Senator Jesse is not too popular in these parts.

"You can quote me on that"

"We moved from Dayton and fell in love with the weather. It's wonderful living here. There's always something to do. I suggest other people rent first. There are so many beautiful areas and you can't really know what you're buying until you live here awhile. The thing that surprised us was the shortage of nursing homes."—M.V.

"What attracted us to Chapel Hill was the University. We're very happy but there are days we wish were closer to a large city. We came from San Francisco and aren't used to feeling boxed in. The biggest surprise was how sophisticated and friendly the town is. If you make an effort, you won't be lonely here."—S.J.

Climate

Elevation: 487'	Avg. High/ Low	Average Inches		Avg. # Days Precip.	Avg. % Humidity
		Rain	Snow		
Jan.	51/30	2.9	-	10	73
April	72/47	3	-	9	65
July	88/67	5	-	11	75
Oct.	72/48	2.8	-	7	74
YEAR	70/48	41	7.8	-	-
# days 32° or below: 83			# days 90° or above: 48		

Let the Good Times Roll

Recreation: Chapel Hill has nine public parks, 21 tennis courts, two swimming pools and four athletic fields. There are three golf courses (one private). University Lake is great for boating. With five exciting teams to watch, bring your seat cushions with you! In basketball and football, there are three Division I powerhouses including UNC's Tar Heels (is the next Michael Jordan playing?) and Duke's Blue Devils. Remember "Bull Durham?" The movie was based on the real Durham Bulls, the Atlanta Braves Class-A minor league team. Residents love the team as much as their field (Durham Athletic Park has such old-fashioned charm).

Culture: They squeeze more cultural arts into this tiny town than you can believe. UNC offers concerts, plays, movies and numerous other events (many are free or require a nominal fee). A favorite is the Playmakers Repertory Company, which produced professional shows every month. The newly renovated Ackland Art Museum has collections ranging from Egyptian artifacts to present day works. As for music, visit the North Carolina Symphony and Chapel Hill Arts Center for great jazz concerts and dances. There are more than 100 different listings in "Where to Find the Arts in Orange County." Call 967-9251 ext. 2669 for more information.

Annual events: Apple Chill Street Fair (April), Historical Homes and Gardens Tour, Raleigh Springs Arts Festival (May), and the Raleigh Jazz Festival (October); Festifall Street Fair (October) and the North Carolina State Fair (October).

Local Real Estate

Chapel Hill is a seller's market, with many newcomers grabbing up homes much less costly than where they're from (California, Toronto, Long Island). The appeal is that housing prices were flat for the past three years so the buys are very desirable.
Median price for single family homes: $138,000 (avg. price is $170,000).
Median price for 2BR condos: $80,000-$90,000.
Rental housing market: Rentals are tough in any college town and Chapel Hill is no exception. The bulk of apartment complexes are on campus and home rentals are scarce (they start at $600/mo. plus utilities).
Common housing styles & features: The "transitional" look is very popular. Traditional on the outside, contemporary on the inside (lots of glass, hard wood floors, light airy rooms, etc.). Construction is mostly wood siding (no vinyl) and virtually all are two-story. If you want a ranch style, it will have to be custom built. Lot sizes on the new homes are 1/3 acre. Many older homes sit on one acre lots. There are no basements.
Amenities in condo developments: There are two new retirement golf communities in town, which are attracting buyers who don't even play golf. The social activities and amenities are the big draw.
Nearby areas to consider: Hillsborough, Farrington and Pittsboro. **Unique features of these areas:** Farrington is an up and coming area, attracting many retirees. It's smaller and more rural, with houses ranging from $150,000 to $200,000. Hillsborough (8 miles north) has housing that pre-dates the revolution and is practically a living museum of the American Revolution (taxes are somewhat lower, too). Pittsboro (Chatham County) is a very small town with much lower taxes.

What Things Cost

According to ACCRA, living expenses are 10% higher than the national average, with housing and goods & services driving up the costs. Utilities are about 4%-5% lower than the national average.
Gas company: Public Service Co. *(942-5104).* Avg. monthly bill is $11-$14. Bills are highest

in December and January No deposit required for homeowners ($50 for rentals).

Electric company: Duke Power Company *(967-8231)*. Avg. monthly bill $25-$40 with hot water heat; $70 all electric. Bills higher May-Sept. Deposit not required with good credit history.

Phone company: Southern Bell *(832-3377)*. Basic monthly service is $20 (includes touch-tone, long distance access); installation: $42.75 if home was previously wired ($99 for new installs). No deposit required with good credit history.

Car registration/license: Registration :$35; new plates: $20; Driver's license: $10 (cash only).

The Tax Ax

Sales tax: 5%. (prescription drugs, eyeglasses, certain medical supplies are exempt).

State income tax: 6-7%, with $2,000 personal exemptions allowed. If married filing jointly with taxable income over $21,250, taxes will be $1,275, plus 7% on any income over the $21,250.

Retirement income: Up to $2,000 in retirement benefits is excluded (or $4,000 of government retirement benefits). Inheritance taxes: none for surviving spouse.

Property taxes: Assessed at $1.56 for every $1,000 of valuation. Thus a $100,000 home would pay $1,560/yr. There are no homestead exemptions.

Medical Care

Major hospitals & regional medical centers: University of North Carolina Hospital is a teaching hospital known for its cardiology and state-of-the-art facilities with new radiation and oncology centers. Prides itself for the **Jaycees Burn Center,** which provides critical care and rehab for burn victims. There is also an Arthritis Center. **Duke University Medical Center** (Durham-12 miles), is a teaching hospital. **Durham City General Hospital** is a major center as well.

Emergency medical services (EMS): South Orange Rescue Squad. Every police officer is EMT trained. They are the first to respond. Response time: 3-4 minutes. 45 Chapel Hill police are Public Safety Officers. They are cross-trained for all police, fire and EMT duties.

Physician's referral: Durham County Hospital Corporation *800-433-7511.*

Continuing Education

The University of North Carolina has a wonderful program for seniors over 65. They can register for any course at no cost (on a seat-available basis). The university also offers elderhostel programs. Duke University (Durham: 12 miles), offers the Diller School of Continuing Education. For $90, seniors can take as many courses as they want (on a seat-available basis). Chapel Hill schools offers additional programs including Saturday School for Seniors. Take gourmet cooking, language and computer training. Peer Learning Group and Shared Learning Group have seniors sharing their skills and expertise with other seniors.

Services for Seniors

Chapel Hill takes great prides in offering a variety of services and programs for active seniors. There are already two senior recreational centers, and because of the high demand, a third is under construction. There is an active **RSVP** chapter, which coordinates volunteer efforts among seniors. There is also a **SCORE** chapter for retired executives. Media: Orange County Department of Aging publishes "Senior Times." Call the Senior Center for information *(968-4478)*. **AARP:** The Orange County chapter meets in Hillsborough (8 mi.). Call Lucy Hays *(732-3089)*. Discount cards available for statewide savings.

Crime & Safety

For a university town, crime rates are low, with most offenses being against property, not persons. If Sergeant Frick is any indication of how caring the police department is, Chapel Hill residents are in excellent hands. Frick, who conveyed a sincere interest in the safety of Chapel Hill seniors, is in charge of the crime prevention programs for them and is especially interested in helping people preserve their "collectibles." He encourages newcomers to drop in and introduce themselves.

Earning a Living

Current business climate: Chapel Hill is a very progressive community and also environmentally sensitive. Zoning restrictions are complex, with an emphasis on preventing water shortages. **Help in starting a business:** Economic Development Commission *(967-9251)* and UNC's Small Business Technology and Development Center (Raleigh) *(733-4643)*.
The job market: Part-time work is readily available in all sectors (retail, restaurants, services, health care, etc.).

When the Kids Come to Visit

Morehead Planetarium; Museum of Science in Durham ("hands-on" children's program); Beaches and mountains are approx. 2 1/2 to 3 hours away for wonderful day trips.

Getting Around Town

Roads & interstates: I-40; I-85; US-15; US-501; State 54 and 86.

Airports & airlines: Raleigh/Durham International Airport is the major hub for American. Also serviced by United, Delta, TWA and USAir.
Public transportation: Local bus service from Chapel Hill Transit System.
Managing without a car: It's possible.

What Residents Already Know

Everyone takes the 1 1/2 hour drive to High Point for furniture shopping. Prices don't get any better than going direct to the source. •The famous Research Triangle Park has attracted more Ph.Ds per capita than anywhere else in the country. Makes you feel smart for just knowing that.•Once the academic year starts, everyone in town looks so young you may want to run to a nursing home to make sure there are still people in town who are older than you.

For More Information

Chamber Of Commerce Office:
Chapel Hill/ Carrboro Chamber
of Commerce
104 South Estes Drive
Chapel Hill, 27515
967-7075

Newspapers:
Chapel Hill Herald (Daily)
106 Mallette Street
Chapel Hill, 27516
967-6581

Chapel Hill Newspaper (Daily)
505 W. Franklin St.
Chapel Hill, 27516
967-7045

Realtors:
Sally Jesse
Marin Properties
312 W. Franklin St.
Chapel Hill, 27514
929-1355

Ms. Pat Briegs
RE/MAX Triangle Realty
1506 E. Franklin St.
Chapel Hill, 27514
968-1901

34. Outer Banks, North Carolina

Area Snapshot

Nickname: "The Natural Choice"
County: Dare
Area code: 919   **Zip code:** 27948-59
Local/county population: 23,000
% of population 55+: 25%
U.S. region: Southeastern North Carolina (coastal region)
Closest metro area: Norfolk, 90 miles
Nearby areas to consider: Currituck County
Median housing price: $126,000
Best reasons to retire here: Remote resort destination, four mild seasons, intriguing historic landmarks, excellent recreation, very casual lifestyles.

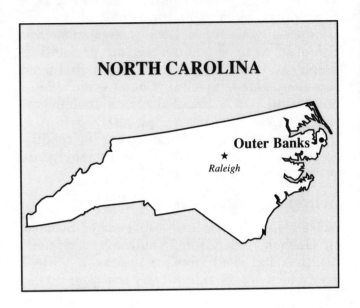

Fabulous Features

Do you know the feeling when everyone tries to squeeze into a tiny elevator before the doors close? That's what's happening in tranquil Dare County, the Outer Banks of North Carolina. This small, remote island has been a cherished vacation haven, rich in history and natural, nautical beauty. But in the past decade, more than 9,000 retirees have unpacked and stayed. Yearning for months of pristine beaches rather than weeks, for mild, sunny seasons instead of snowdrifts, rugged seniors are plunking down old equity dollars for a piece of the lofty seas. They care not about the ballet, but bluefish. A day on the dunes beats two weeks at Disney World. Although living in a village where some stretches are less than a mile across is limiting, it is paradise for those who can be left to their own devices. Homes are small and manageable (but, of course you can spend millions on a mansion). The outdoor opportunities are immense and retirees are the main import. If you are tempted by a life on the Ocean but refuse to set foot in Florida, "dare" to be different. But, hurry. With 85% of it marshland, this elevator will soon reach capacity.

Possible drawbacks: Medical care is limited to the eight clinics in the county (one finally offers 24-hour service). Small hospitals are an hour by car, with more serious emergencies airlifted to Norfolk (unless grounded by bad weather). Retirees with conditions that require frequent medical attention would be advised to visit here but live somewhere else.•Culture is a lost art in the Outer Banks. Thinking of the White Marlin Open as a source of entertainment takes some getting used to.•Worried about hurricanes? Living on a barrier island with its high winds and flooding poses a threat of evacuation in severe weather.

"You can quote me on that"

"I'm retired from the Air Force and have lived in most of the country. I love the Outer Banks because I feel like I'm on vacation every single day. I don't find it to be as expensive as everyone told me it would be. Produce is higher but that's about it. My advice to other people? Please don't come (little joke). No really, it's great, but not for everyone."—R.B., Nags Head

Climate

Elevation: 7'	Avg. High/ Low	Average Inches		Avg. # Days Precip.	Avg. % Humidity
		Rain	Snow		
Jan.	52/38	4.2	-	11	81
April	66/52	3.1	-	8	74
July	84/72	5.9	-	12	81
Oct.	71/59	4.8	-	9	80
YEAR	68/55	55	2.1	-	-
# days 32° or below: 34			# days 90° or above: 1		

Let the Good Times Roll

Recreation: The Cape Hatteras National Sea-shore, extending 70 miles, was the first water recreation area operated by the National Parks Service. It was a hard act to follow. In short, the Outer Banks is blessed with an abundance of outdoor recreation including fishing, sailing, boating, windsurfing, jet skiing, surfing, skin diving, tennis, horseback riding, hang gliding and golf. Nags Head Golf Links is an 18-hole Scottish-style course and Sea Scape Golf Course is a scenic 18-hole course that winds over the dunes. Fishing is "beyond great," says one angler. The "big blues" and "red drum" (channel bass) are here in fall and spring (when fishing gets serious). Head out to Oregon Inlet or Albemarle Sound and take your best shot.

Culture: There are several art galleries on the Outer Banks, which include original works of Picasso, Rembrandt and Renoir. From June through August, the Waterside Theater presents "The Lost Colony," an outdoor drama reflecting the life of the early settlers. However, if you crave a steady diet of symphony, ballet or theater, you'll be traveling to Norfolk.

Annual events: There are literally dozens of annual festivals and events in Dare County including Old Christmas Rodanthe (old-fashioned Christmas on Hatteras Island); Easter Windsurfing Regatta & Dash for Cash (March); Annual "Red Drum" Fishing Classic (May); Annual Hang Gliding Spectacular (May); Nags Head Woods 5K Run (May); Kitty Hawk Kites Triathalon of Wind Sports (June); Outer Banks Celebrity Tournament (June); Rogallo Kite Festival (June); Wright Brothers Fly In At Kitty Hawk (June); Seafood Festival and Blessing of the Fleet (July). Fishing tournaments throughout the year.

Local Real Estate

It's been a buyer's market for the past two years, primarily because of the soft housing market in the East. People unable to sell their homes in the New York area (where many retirees are from) are reluctant to commit to a new house. Most homes in the area are on one-half acre and are new (less than 10 yrs. old), averaging $126,000. Although many are between the sound and the ocean, waterfront property will not necessarily be more expensive. We found a 4BR, 2BA oceanfront single family house in Kill Devil Hills for $124,900. Other waterfront properties will go for $1 million. There are no retirement "ghettos" as such; the idea is to buy a location and they'll throw in the house.

Median price for 2BR condo: $65,000. Condos on the water are priced more like homes. A 3BR, 2BA townhouse on the oceanside in Duck is asking $150,000.

Rental housing market: As a resort area, rentals are widely available. The short-term rentals (weekly) are mostly on the east side. The oceanside homes start renting at $450/week. The oceanfront homes rent for $750 to $3,000/week. Owners count on $20,000-$30,000 from summer rentals alone and they get it! Long-term rentals (yearly) are mostly on the sound (west side) and go for $500/mo., plus utilities. Don't come looking for highrise condos—nothing here is higher than five stories.

Common housing styles & features: Most homes have wood exteriors and one or more decks. The average lot size is 80 x 100 (new houses are 100 x 200) for 3BR, 2BA (approx. 1,400 sq. ft.) with fully furnished kitchens. Houses are built on pilings, so don't look for basements.

Amenities in condo developments: Pools and tennis courts.

Nearby area to consider: Currituck County.

Unique features: The Currituck mainland is an up-and-coming location with larger subdivisions, more property, and bigger homes for your money. Most homes have 3/4 to one acre. The average home is 1,600 sq. ft, 5-10 years old and has 3BR, 2BA (no basement). The average price is $75,000. The county's claim to fame is that there are no stop lights. On the Outer Banks (beach side) there are homes for people who want a remote location. They're an hour from civilization and a half hour from paved roads. Still, people are scooping them up as investments or for a place to hide.

What Things Cost

Overall living costs were 14% above the national average, with housing 50% above. As with many remote island locales, the cost of "importing" food, produce, goods and services drives prices up while limited supply/outlets sustains the higher mark-ups.

Gas company: No natural gas service (bottled gas available).

Electric company: North Carolina Power *(473-2161)*. Avg. bill: $75/mo. Connection charge is $23.74. Deposits not required with good credit history.

Water/sewer: Dare City Water Department *(473-1101)*. Connection is $90; average bill for 3 months is $45.

Phone company: Carolina Telephone & Telegraph Company *(338-9811)*. Basic monthly service is $20. Installation with existing wiring is $23.26. New installs are $71 per jack. Deposit may not be required.

Car registration & license: Registration: $10; Title: $35 + 3% tax on car's current value; Plates: $20; Driver's license: $16.

The Tax Ax

Sales tax: 6% (prescription drugs, eye glasses and some medical supplies and services are exempt). There's an additional 3% occupancy tax (rentals, motels, etc.)

State income tax: 6-7%, with $2,000 personal exemptions allowed. If married filing jointly with taxable income over $21,250, taxes will be $1,275 plus 7% on any income over the $21,250.

Retirement income: Up to $2,000 in retirement benefits is excluded (or $4,000 of government retirement benefits). Inheritance taxes: none for surviving spouse.

Property taxes & tax breaks: Dare County has a current millage rate of 51¢ per $100 of val-uation (includes fire and sanitation assessment). That is added to the millage rates if you own a home in the following townships: Kill Devil Hills-44¢; Kitty Hawk-45¢; Manteo-35¢; Nags Head-34¢; Currituck-56¢. When combined, the average tax rate is $1 per $100. Thus, a home assessed at $129,000 would run $1,290/yr. The town millage rates will be reduced during the 1992 tax year.

Medical Care

Medical care is the one serious deficiency in the Outer Banks although even at its present state, it has vastly improved from only a few years ago. The problem is that the closest hospital is in Elizabeth City (1 hour).

Major hospitals & regional medical centers: There are eight medical centers in the county and the newest, **Regional Medical Center** in Kitty Hawk, is providing ambulatory and diagnostic services (a first). It also offers cardiology services, pulmonary, dialysis, general and orthopedic outpatient surgery, radiology, and gastroenterology. **Albermarle Hospital** in Elizabeth City and **Chesapeake General** are both an hour's drive. Emergency patients are transported by air to **Depaul Medical Center** in Norfolk (weather permitting). **Emergency medical services (EMS):** Eight ambulances and one helicopter are available for medical emergencies. Response time varies widely depending on locale. **Physician's referral:** *261-9000*.

Continuing Education

The Chamber provides educational seminars at minimal cost to members *(441-8144)*. College of the Albermarle in Manteo *(473-2264)* and the Dare City Center allow seniors to enroll in many courses for free on a space-available basis. They must also be state residents for 6 months or more.

Services for Seniors

The Thomas A. Baum Center offers a lot of different programs for seniors including the Senior Games, seminars, the 55/Alive Defensive Drive Course (**AARP**) as well as health programs. The Senior Center's newsletter,

"Senior Media," will help keep you informed of activities and events *(441-1181)*.

Crime & Safety

This is a perfectly safe place to live evidenced by the number of open cars that have keys in the ignition. Crime is very low and although there are burglaries, basic precautions would cut it down even further. There is a separate police department in each town and all have safety awareness programs.

Earning a Living

Current business climate: Limited land available for commercial zoning has slowed business growth. And while the population has skyrocketed (70% in the past 10 years), nobody promised the area would be immune to the recession and seasonal traffic. **Help in starting a business:** There is a desperate need for large, discount stores. There is an over-saturation of restaurants, boutiques and tourist shops, and only the innovators survive. There is a local SCORE chapter for help *(441-8144)*. **The job market:** For every well-paying job, there are 300 applications. Part-time tourist-related jobs are available. For help, write to: Employment Security Commission, 422 McArthur Drive, Elizabeth City, 27909 *(335-5426)*.

When the Kids Come to Visit

Jockey's Ridge: a state park with the largest sand dunes on the east coast; North Carolina Aquarium (Manteo); Elizabeth II: tours of working ships with people dressed in 16th-century attire (Manteo); Elizabeth Gardens: 16th century gardens, period furniture, art works; Aurora Fossil Museum (come find your own); Belhaven Memorial Museum (like spending a day in grandma's attic); Early American artifacts in Elizabeth City; Wright Brothers Memorial: replica of Kitty Hawk, (original is at the Smithsonian).

Getting Around Town

Roads & interstates: Routes 12 and 158. **Airports & airlines:** Dare County Regional Airport for charter and commuter service; Norfolk International Airport (90 mi.) is served by most major carriers. **Public transportation:** None. **Managing without a car:** Impossible. People come here to get away from it all, and that's where the Outer Banks is—away from it all!

What Residents Already Know

People run to the post office when they know the new L.L. Bean and Land's End catalogs have arrived. With limited shopping, mail order is big business. •Don't expect southern accents. Second and third generation residents speak "Elizabethan," as in "Good Noight, sleep toight."•Summertime can mean battening down the hatches. It's when tourists (and maybe a hurricane) take over by storm. Residents sing "See you in September."

For More Information

Chamber Of Commerce Office:
Outer Banks Chamber
of Commerce
P.O. Box 1757
Kill Devil Hills, 27948
441-8144

Newspaper:
Coastland Times
1500 N. Croatan Highway
Kill Devil Hills, 27948
441-2223

Realtors:
Greg Cremia
Kitty Dunes Realty
P.O. Box 275
Kitty Hawk, 27949
261-2171

Carla Hardison
The D.A.R.E. Company
P.O. Box 2598
Kill Devil Hills, 27948
441-1521

35. Eugene, Oregon

Area Snapshot

Nickname: "Green Eugene"
County: Lane
Area code: 503   **Zip code:** 97440
Local population: 109,785
County population: 280,000
% of population 65+: 12.7%
U.S. region: Western Oregon
Closest metro area: Portland, 110 miles
Nearby area to consider: Florence
Median housing price: $69,700
Best reasons to retire here: Blue skies and clean air, university influence, laid-back lifestyle, great recreation and continuing education, drive to the ocean or mountains.

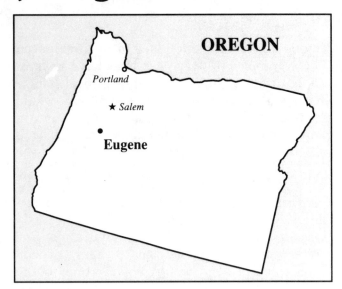

Fabulous Features

House-rich Californians have been scooping up property in Eugene for years. More and more retirees are discovering that this Oregon oasis and sister city Springfield are a delightful place to hang your hat. The community is safe, it's clean and the town prides itself on its very laid-back approach to living. Some attribute this to the large counter culture of 30- and 40-year olds who left the big bad world and came for a high quality of life. Others say that the moderate year-round climate (annual temp is 63 degrees) and sumptuous surroundings would "de-hyper" anyone. The Pacific Ocean is an hour to the west, the Cascade Mountains an hour to the east. People speak of the healthy mind/healthy body attitude that prevails. Young and old are out on the trails and in the classroom. They thrive on recreation (river rafting, hiking, fishing) and educational pursuits (the University of Oregon and Lane Community College have terrific continuing education programs). With over 40 inches of rain each year, the area is green, lush and wooded. Homesites are spectacular, particularly those on the gentle Willamette River. Sacred Heart General Hospital and EMS have earned national recognition (this is one of 10 best cities in which to get sick). Eugene is a find.

Possible drawbacks: The business base is not very diversified. The area is dependent on the timber industry and the economy is currently sluggish. There's no sales tax in Oregon, so state-operating revenue comes from income and property taxes. Medical costs are fairly high, but facilities are excellent and well staffed.

"You can quote me on that"

"We knew we wanted to leave the Los Angeles area so we researched every square inch of California and Oregon to find the perfect retirement spot. We found the crown jewel here. Our quality of life zoomed from 50% to 99%. You can breathe the air, see the natural beauty and smell the pine scented breezes. We have total peace and contentment here."—Mr. W.E., Springfield

"We're from southern California and moved to this area because we wanted a change of lifestyle but still be on the Pacific ocean. Eugene is wonderful because it's a small town that thinks like a large city. Its beautiful and peaceful but it's also a well-run metropolis. It's a free thinking city with a lot of integrity."—H. and S. W., Fall Creek

Climate

Elevation: 366'	Avg. High/ Low	Average Inches Rain	Snow	Avg. # Days Precip.	Avg. % Humidity
Jan.	46/33	7.1	-	18	90
April	61/39	2.3	-	13	78
July	83/51	.3	-	2	80
Oct.	64/42	4	-	11	85
YEAR	63/42	41	7.1	-	-
# days 32° or below: 54			# days 90° or above: 15		

Let the Good Times Roll

Recreation: Fisherman don't have to travel far for their catches. The calm Willamette River, which runs through the center of the city, is a final resting place for trout. White-water rafting is on the McKenzie River and there are lakes and streams for boating, water sports and fishing. The area is also known for its 40 developed parks covering 1,600 acres, which provides for picnicking, jogging and biking. The natural forested areas are great for hiking and camping. Pools, athletic fields, lighted tennis courts and an outdoor amphitheater provide year-round access for fun. A professionally supervised staff from the Parks Department runs programs for seniors. Autzen Stadium at the University is the site of many exciting sporting events such as UO's Football team, the fighting Yellow Ducks (Donald is their mascot).

Culture: The Hult Center for the Performing Arts (a 2,500-seat concert hall) is home to the Eugene Sym-phony, the Eugene Ballet Company, and the Eugene Opera Company. The University of Oregon campus has McArthur Court, which hosts concerts, sporting and cultural events. The Lane County Fairgrounds brings enter-tainment, equestrian events, ice skating, and hockey to town and eight historical, science and art museums add to the enrichment.

Annual events: Oregon Beach Festival (June); Coburg Golden Days (July); Art and the Vineyard (4th of July) Eugene Festival of Musical Theater (July); Coburg Art Fair (Sept.); Eugene Oktoberfest; Doll & Toy Festival (Nov.).

Local Real Estate

Median price for single family home: $69,700. Average price of a 3BR house runs between $90,000-$105,000; resales average $77,500. Breeden Bros. (the area's largest home builder) have beautiful "first class" homes for $90,000-$130,000.

Median price for 2BR condo: Some are as low as $40,000, but most will be priced between $50,000-$80,000. The newer models are asking around $115,000 (3BR).

Rental housing market: The rental market is very tight, with less than a 1% occupancy rate (college towns are famous for this). New apartment house construction of late may open things up a bit. Decent single-family houses are scarce; duplexes and multifamily complexes have a greater availability.

Common housing styles & features: Most homes are frame construction and two-story (one-story is available but less in demand). Both traditional and contemporary designs are available with new homes featuring skylights, vaulted ceilings and master suites with jacuzzis.

Amenities in condo developments: Most are townhouse style (two-story), some have pools. Most are small developments. Colony Oakes is a planned condo community with gorgeous views and jacuzzis. 2-3BR are selling for $110,000-135,000.

Nearby areas to consider: Springfield (3 miles east of Eugene across the Willamette River). Florence (Coastal city). **Unique features of these areas:** Springfield is a similarly nice community but not as large, and without the university. Its appeal is that it's an hour from the ocean, an hour from skiing. Florence (50 mileq west) is a charming little coastal town attracting a lot of retirees. Waterfront property is at a premium but inland prices are similar to Eugene.

What Things Cost

Overall living costs are 4% above the national average with housing and health costs driving the price up (housing is 19% health care 25% above the average). Utilities are 33% below average (ACCRA, 1st quarter, 1991).

Gas company: Northwest Natural Gas Co. *(342-3661)*. Avg. monthly bill is $35-$40 for gas heat and range.

Electric company: The Eugene Water & Electric Board *(484-2411)* says their rates are only 1/3 the national average. Avg. monthly bill for all electric is $84/mo (not including air conditioning). No deposit is required.

Phone company: U.S. West Communications *(484-7770)*. Monthly base rate is $18.16. Initial hook-ups range from $12-25. No deposit is required.

Car registration/license: Plates are $45.50 per passenger vehicle; Driver's license is $25. A written test is required.

The Tax Ax

Sales tax: None

State income tax: Income over $10,000/yr is taxed at a rate of 9%. The standard deduction for persons 65 and older who are married and filing jointly is $4,000.

Retirement income: A new Retirement Income credit was just passed which allows for up to a 9% credit on pension income if total income does not exceed $45,000. At least one spouse must be 58 or older.

Property taxes & tax breaks: Oregon just passed Ballot Measure #5 to reduce the effective property tax rate every year for the next five. This won't, however, automatically lower taxes because homes will still be appraised at market value, which continues to increase. In 1991, the maximum tax rate in Lane County is $27.50 per $1,000 of valuation. Thus, a $70,000 home would cost $1,925/yr. There is a senior property tax deferral for those 65 and older whose income does not exceed $24,000. Contact the County Assessor's office for more information *(687-4321)*.

Medical Care

Major hospitals/regional medical centers: Sacred Heart General Hospital is the largest hospital in the area. It's a JCAH-accredited teaching hospital known for its advances in research. It has the best trauma/emergency team in the region and is a major referral center (patients come from Sacramento and Portland). It is the regional expert on cardiovascular and cardiac care (their Heart Center earns national recognition). Other specializations include cancer care and rehabilitation and physical therapy. It offers a number of outreach programs for seniors as well. **McKenzie Willamette Hospital** is a smaller, full service hospital in Springfield.

Emergency medical services (EMS): In 1985, the Eugene/Springfield EMS team was named best in the nation by the Paramedic's Association (a city can't receive the honor more than once) and *Fortune* magazine identified the area as one of the 10 best places to have a heart attack. Response time is under 4 minutes and all fire trucks are equipped with automatic heart monitors.

Physician's referral: Sacred Heart *686-6962*.

Continuing Education

University of Oregon has an excellent elderhostel program for two weeks each summer *(346-3111)* as well as a continuing education program for seniors 65 and older. Many classes can be audited for free. Lane Community College has a great Continuing Education Department with close to 400 different courses, many directed to seniors. Those who are 62-plus get a 50% discount off an already low tuition. Some classes are $10-$40 for 30 weeks and include woodworking and outdoor recreation *(726-2252)*.

Services for Seniors

The Parks and Recreations Department oversees the Trudy Kauffman Senior Center and the Campbell Senior Center, which offers a tremendous variety of programs. These include river rafting, legal aid, summer socials, health classes and a night at the ballet. It also runs classes for adults whose parents are aging, as well as outreach programs to help with shopping and other needed services. Membership is free to those 55-plus (they claim that people can't wait to be old enough to participate).

Crime & Safety

Hard core crime is practically non-existent (there was one homicide in 1990), but property crime (car break-ins) is more predominant.

Still, overall crime is so low because the area's demographics are solid. The percentage of the population that is older and college-educated is pretty high for a town this size. People feel very safe and many speak of leaving their doors unlocked all day. It's one of the prime reasons the area is growing so rapidly.

Earning a Living

Current business climate: The University is one of the largest employers in the area and mail order, publishing and computer firms play a part in the growing service trade. However, being dependent on the timber industry has hurt Eugene's economy, which is depressed. Unemployment is 6% (was 4% for many years).

Help in starting a business: Contact SCORE *(484-5485)* and the Small Business Development Center at Lane Community College for help with business ideas. They run seminars on advertising and marketing and other topics *(726-2255)*. The Eugene/Springfield Metropolitan Partnership, Inc. is also interested in speaking to prospective business owners *(686-2741)*.

The job market: Part-time work is very hard to come by so many people have turned to running services from their homes.

When the Kids Come to Visit

Lively Park/Splash (the only "Wave Technology" pool in the northwest); Fifth Street Public Market; University of Oregon Art Museum; scenic drives up the McKinsey River.

Getting Around Town

Roads & interstates: I-5, State Highways 58, 99, 126.

Airports & airlines: Mahlon Sweet Airport (9 miles out of Eugene) just completed a $20 million expansion, which improved service tremendously. The airport is served by five national/regional carriers with direct service to San Francisco, San Jose, Los Angeles, Denver and Portland.

Public transportation: The Lane Transit District provides an an excellent city bus service for the Eugene/Springfield Metropolitan area.

Managing without a car: Yes it's possible. The bus system works well and there are services to provide transportation to seniors when none other is available.

What Residents Already Know

Wearing jeans to the opera or a fine restaurant is no big deal. With a large mix of hippies, yuppies, "dinks" (dual income, no kids) and retirees, being laid back is a law. People are just glad you came. What you wear is your call. • The town offers the "cadillac" of services, the city genuinely provides for all. • Watch out for the "weekend warriors"—all the joggers, bikers, and athletes who take over the town to stay in shape.

For More Information

Chamber Of Commerce Office:
Eugene Area Chamber of Commerce
P.O. Box 1107
Eugene, 97440-1107
484-1314

Newspaper:
The Register-Guard
P.O. Box 10188
Eugene, 97440-2188
485-1234

Realtors:
David C. McJunkin
Breedon Bros Homes
366 Donald Street
Eugene, 97405
729-2923

Susan Rasmussen
Keystone Real Estate
1501 N. 18th Street, Suite 100
Springfield, 97477
746-1233

36. Lincoln City, Oregon

Area Snapshot

Nickname: "Kite Capital of the World"
County: Lincoln
Area code: 503   **Zip code:** 97367
Local population: 6,340   **County:** 39,000
% of population 65+: 28%
U.S. region: Central Oregon Coast
Closest metro areas: Portland, 90 miles
Nearby areas to consider: Gleneden Beach, Coronado Shores
Median housing price: $85,000
Best reasons to retire here: Small coastal town on the Pacific Ocean, invigorating but mild climate, clean air, excellent recreational opportunities, affordable real estate.

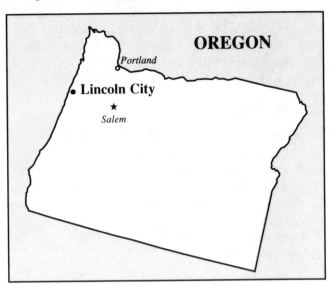

Fabulous Features

Imagine Malibu without the crowds, the expense and the movie stars, and you've got a picture of this wonderful coastal community. Lincoln City has a number of advantages up on that private enclave to the rich. The climate is more moderate, the air is cleaner and the views more breathtaking. Situated between seven glorious miles of sandy beaches and Devils Lake (680 acres of natural formation), Lincoln City is bordered by the Pacific Ocean and the Coast Range Mountains. And there's one other big difference. You can buy five homes in Lincoln City for the price of one in Malibu. The average sale price last quarter was $72,000. Year-round recreation is unbeatable with excellent power boating (some say the best in the world); fishing, hiking, snorkeling and more. The retirement community is the fastest-growing segment of the population and they happen to be getting younger every year. The seniors who settle in the area are busy, involved and anxious to take advantage of all the natural resources. They're also downright nice people. As one former Californian said, "I always wanted to live in a place where I liked all my neighbors and I finally found it." Wonder if they can say that in Malibu?

Possible drawbacks: Medical services have improved vastly in the past few years but they're still limited. Acute cases and major emergencies have to be airlifted to Portland. Not unlike many small towns, services are limited (the only public transportation is a Greyhound bus that travels down Highway 101) entertainment is limited and shopping is limited (get the picture?)

"You can quote me on that"

"My sister and I drove here from Colorado to visit a childhood friend. I called my husband and said, "Sell everything. I'm never going home." This weather is invigorating. Chilly and windy all the time. I love the beaches and I've learned to fly a kite. Let me tell you that's great exercise. We bought a small home inland for very little money and now I've got friends coming to visit and they're looking around and they understand why we left."—Mrs. G.Z.

"We didn't live far from here already (Salem) and we had bought a home years ago in Coronado Shores. Living on the ocean is great for your outlook on life. We like the people here very much. Everyone is nice and the atmosphere is laid-back. We highly recommend that other retirees come here to look."—Mr. and Mrs. W. W.

Climate

Elevation: 32'	Avg. High/ Low	Average Inches		Avg. # Days Precip.	Avg. % Humidity
		Rain	Snow		
Jan.	47/35	9.5	-	23	85
April	56/40	4.6	-	18	83
July	64/49	.96	-	7	82
Oct.	61/45	6.8	-	16	85
YEAR	58/43	63	5.7	-	-
# days 32° or below: 39			# days 90° or above: 3		

Let the Good Times Roll

Recreation: High prevailing winds make Lincoln City a fabulous place for flying and watching kites at "D" River Wayside State Park in the heart of town. As a coastal community on the Pacific Ocean, you can jump right in for fishing, boating, swimming, waterskiing, wind surfing, canoeing, sailing and speedboat racing (for six weeks in summer the water temperature is a delightful 70°). The Cascade Head Scenic Research area (5 mi. north) with 12,000 sq. mi. of federally protected estuaries and experimental forest land, has trails for hiking, and breathtaking views of the Salmon River flowing into the Pacific. Drop your line at Devils Lake. There are nine types of freshwater fish as well as exciting speedboat racing (the American Power Boat Association says it has the best length, depth and location for racing in the world). Surrounded by natural marshes and timberland Devil's Lake is also a haven for bird watching. Six local golf courses, public tennis courts, 13 parks, and a beautiful rec center with an indoor pool are among the local recreation outlets available.

Culture: There are more art galleries per capita in the Lincoln City area than in any other town in Oregon. The Oregon Coast Council for the Arts sponsors year-round shows and performances. The Performing Arts Center in nearby Newport brings in musical entertainment and theater. The Sitka Center for Art and Ecology at Cascade Head offers classes and performances combining visual and performing arts with nature. The Cascade Head Festival features summer weekends of jazz and classical music. Theater West (a local repertory company that are very impressive) performs throughout the year and the Lincoln City Historical Museum offers residents and visitors a nostalgic trip through the past.

Annual events: Salishan Lodge hosts the Lincoln City Music Festival (includes a visit from the Portland Symphony); Two-day International Kite Festivals (spring and fall) with celebrities, seminars and even a kite hospital; Sandcastle building contest (Taft beach with 200 contestants each August); Blues and Jazz festivals (Sept.); Wine Festival (March).

Local Real Estate

It's been a seller's market for the past few years. Demand has been tremendous, with many retirees in the state looking for a place close to home. The vast majority come from Salem and Portland, others from California. The effect has been devastating to the locals, as housing prices and taxes are rising more rapidly than the tide.

Median price for single family home: $85,000. Oceanfront properties range from $100,000-$500,000; ocean views go for $75,000-$200,000; lake fronts are $75,000-$190,000; small inland homes range from $25,000-$55,000. Larger houses start at $80,000 and sell up to $300,000. The average sale price is $101,000.

Median price for 2BR condo: $90,000. The range is from $70,000-$200,000 depending on the view and location. Most retirees are opting for houses instead because the price is the same and they prefer their own front door.

Rental housing market: There is such a serious shortage of short-term housing that at many times of the year you couldn't rent a tent. Houses will rent for $500-$1,000/month, apartments are less but are like mirages. You know they're there, you just can't touch them.

Common housing styles & features: Wood siding is the most popular exteriors. Homes are neither traditional nor contemporary, they're almost a hybrid of both. Many of them are beach cottages that have been expanded. Of late, there's been more new construction.

Amenities in condo developments: To ease the shortage of rentals condo units are being converted to rental pools, almost like hotels, rented weekly and monthly. This is a great option for retirees who are "testing the waters."

Nearby areas to consider: Coronado Shores, Gleneden Beach (at the southern tip of the city).

Unique features of these areas: Coronado Beach is a popular area for second homes. Most homes are one-story priced from $65,000-$150,000. Gleneden Beach is located near the Salishan Resort Hotel which offers 5-star dining and championship golf. Condo developments are in the $140,000-$220,000 range. Homes start at $169,000 and go up to a half million.

What Things Cost

Gas company: Northwest Natural Gas *(994-2111)*. For a 3,000 sq. ft. home with gas heat, the avg. is $55/mo. and could go as high as $100 in winter. No deposit required.

Electric company: Pacific Power & Light *(994-2144)*. Avg. bill for an all electric 1,780 sq. ft. home would be $70. With only partial electric, the avg. bill could be half that. The highest month is Jan., when it could cost $110.

Water/sewer: City of Lincoln City *(996-2151)*. Within city limits, the avg. bill is $33.38 for 2 months (plus $15 name change for the first bill). No deposit required for new customers.

Phone company: United Telephone Co. *(800-877-1125 in Oregon)*. Avg. monthly base rate is $10.10 and a $25 set up charge. Calling features cost $2/ea. per month. Deposit may not be required.

Car registration/license: Registration: $45.50; driver's license: $25. Written test, proof of residency and surrendering of old license are required.

The Tax Ax

Sales tax: None

State income tax: Income over $10,000/yr. is taxed at a rate of 9%. The standard deduction for persons 65+ and who are married filing jointly is $4,000.

Retirement income: A new retirement income credit was just passed, which allows for up to a 9% credit on pension income if total income does not exceed $45,000. At least one spouse must be 58+.

Property taxes & tax breaks: Oregon just passed Ballot Measure 5 to reduce the effective property tax rate every year for the next five. This won't, however, automatically lower taxes because homes will still be appraised at market value, which continues to increase. In 1990, in Coronado Shoes, for example, a $100,000 home would run $1,899 a year. In Gleneden Beach, and Lincoln city proper taxes were a little higher. Contact the Tax Assessor's office for current information *(765-2177)*.

Medical Care

Major hospitals/regional medical centers: North Lincoln Hospital is a small general hospital (50 rooms, 4-bed ICU) with 24-hour emergency care. The hospital participates in the Heart Emergency Network run by the Providence Heart Center (Portland) and "Life Flight" for emergency air service to two trauma centers in Portland. The Surgical Suite was recently renovated and is now equipped for surgery, intensive/coronary care, respiratory therapy and radiology. The hospital offers numerous classes to the community as well as free health screening clinics.

Emergency medical services (EMS): Lincoln City Ambulance operates round-the-clock with a full crew of paramedics and EMT's. Response time during the day is 1 minute; at night it's 3 minutes.

Physician's referral: North Lincoln Hospital will send you a list of area doctors *994-3661*.

Continuing Education

Oregon Coast Community College allows seniors to enroll in either credit or non-credit courses for 50% off the tuition (must be 62+). As the community is very artistic, popular classes are painting and creative writing. It also runs an elderhostel the first two weeks of December ($285). Courses are of local interest such as ecology and coastal marine life.

Services for Seniors

AARP's local chapter offers a tax aid service as well as the 55/Alive Mature Driving Class *(265-9617)*; The Council on Aging's Senior Center offers year-round activities, day trips, classes, crafts, astrology and a very popular quilting class that raises money for the center (most of it is city-subsidized). Programs are also coordinated with the local recreation center for aerobics and swimming *(994-2722)*.

Crime & Safety

For a tourist area, crime is very low. What criminal activity does exist is alcohol related/domestic violence among locals residents. There has also been more of a drug presence lately but a narcotics reporting line (you can call in with anonymous tips) is helping to stem the tide. For the most part safety is not an issue. Person-to-person crimes are rare and people are out day and night with nary a worry fortheir safety.

Earning a Living

Current business climate: Tourism is the backbone of this community and 60% of the population is employed by the 250 services businesses that cater to visitors. According to the Small Business Development Center there is a tremendous need for small services such as home and appliance repair, and shopping services. Lack of public transportation, creates a great need for taxi service between Newport (25 mi.) and Lincoln City. A courier service for businesses would be an instant success. What they don't need are more gift shops and crafts stores. The tourist season is not long enough to make a living year-round.

Help in starting a business: The Small Business Development Center (Oregon Coast Community College) is available for business counseling, management and employee training, etc. A full-time director based in Lincoln City will work with entrepreneurs at no cost *(994-4166)*.

The job market: Minimum-wage work at restaurants and resorts is available in season.

When the Kids Come to Visit

Kite flying and viewing at "D" River Wayside State Park; bumper boats on the lake, mini-golf, tidepooling (when the tide goes out, the kids come in and look for seashells, crabs and loose change).

Getting Around Town

Roads & interstates: State Highway 101

Airports & airlines: Portland International Airport (90 mi. northeast of Lincoln City) is served by most major carriers; Salem Airport (60 mi. east) is served by Horizon Air for commuter flights.

Public transportation: None available.

Managing without a car: Impossible.

What Residents Already Know

Long-time residents would do anything to stop the flow of "Equity Immigrants" from California. They have created such demand for property that assessed values and taxes are skyrocketing.•There was more traffic on Highway 101 this summer than in the past 30 years. The word is out about the Oregon coast. •There are more motels here than between San Francisco and Seattle.

For More Information

Chamber Of Commerce Office:
Lincoln City Area Chamber of
Commerce
P.O. Box 787
Lincoln City, 97367
994-3070

Newspaper:
The News Guard (weekly)
930 NE Hwy 101
Lincoln City, 97367
994-2178

Realtors:
Barbara Christian
**Century 21 Pacific Shores
Property**
1831 SW Hwy 101
Lincoln City, 97367
800-733-2873

Mr. Blanchard Smith
Coldwell Banker/Gesik Realty
1815 NW Highway 101
Lincoln City, 97367
994-7760

37. Medford, Oregon

Area Snapshot

Nickname: "The Pear City"
County: Jackson
Area code: 503   **Zip code:** 97501
Local population: 46,324   **County:** 145,690
% of population 65+: 30%
U.S. region: Rogue River Valley (Southern Oregon)
Closest metro areas: Eugene, 166 mi. (27 mi. north of California border).
Nearby areas to consider: Applegate Valley
Median housing price: $95,000
Best reasons to retire here: Scenic river valley, great real estate buys, ample recreation and culture, friendly small town.

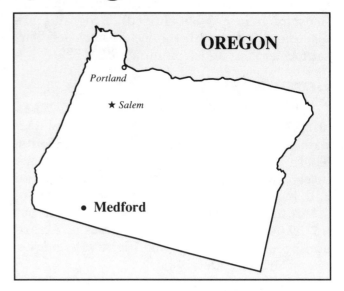

Fabulous Features

House hunting in Medford is a fantasy-come-true. What's your wish? Pine trees? Mountain views? Farmland? City living? Unincorporated towns? Riverfront homes? It's all here, and at prices that are affordable, considering the amount of house and property you get. No wonder Californians are crossing the border in caravans. Medford is a very liveable town. The rural environment has been laid out for ease of getting around and thanks to long-range planning, the residential and business areas are spacious and uncongested. Situated in the heart of the enchanting Rogue River Valley, you'll find four delightful seasons (none overbearing). There's no more rain than in San Francisco (average annual is 19"). In fact, you'll have so many opportunities to be outside, you may begin to wonder why you bought such a lovely home. Spend your days skiing, golfing, fishing, hiking, taking a ride to the mountains or the beautiful Oregon coast. Culture abounds with annual Shakespeare Festivals and classical music under the stars. This is also a fruit lover's paradise—75% of the nation's Bosc pear crop grows here (this is the home of Harry & David). Medford is indeed a sweet place to be.

Possible drawbacks: Don't come looking for tumult and commotion. Medford is small, laid-back and the loudest noises come from buzz saws. • Compared to other parts of Oregon, the average prices of houses are higher, but values have been holding steady.

"You can quote me on that"

"I may be 27 miles from my home state of California, but I'm a million miles away because my life is so different. What I paid for my 20-acre ranch overlooking the city wouldn't have gotten me a two-bedroom condominium in Sacramento. I look out at the mountains, I go fishing or play golf any day I want. And the people are so sweet. I keep waiting for the novelty to wear off but it hasn't."—Mr. E.D.

"We bought a beautiful new house for $125,000 that looks like it was in a magazine. I said to my husband, after all these years you finally got me something I wanted. It's like a dream. The people are so nice, we enjoy our activities and we're starting to make some friends. I'll tell you, I didn't expect to see so many retirees like us. There are so many who live here."—Mrs. B.G.

Climate

Elevation: 1,380'	Avg. High/ Low	Average Inches Rain	Average Inches Snow	Avg. # Days Precip.	Avg. % Humidity
Jan.	44/29	3.2	-	14	88
April	64/37	.98	-	9	70
July	90/54	.25	-	5	63
Oct.	67/39	2.1	-	8	74
YEAR	66/40	20	8.1	-	-
# days 32° or below: 91			# days 90° or above: 48		

Let the Good Times Roll

Recreation: Camping, fishing, hunting, river rafting, snow and water skiing—it's all here. The Bear Creek Bike and Nature Trail offers a three-mile path for cyclists and hikers. Rogue River (one of the most remote river courses in the U.S. protected by the Wild and Scenic Rivers Act, is ideal for fishing and boating. Nearby Mt. Ashland, dominating the Siskiyou Mountain Range, is ideal for skiing Thanksgiving through April. In town are 100 city parks, a quarter-mile stock car race track and the Southern Oregon A's (minor league baseball team).

Culture: The Tony Award-winning Oregon Shakespeare Festival in Ashland (12 mi.) stages lively, often bawdy, dramatizations of the Bard's greatest works, with elaborate sets and costumes. The Outdoor Theater was patterned after the Fortune Theater of 16th-century London. The Angus Bowmer and Black Swan theaters, next-door hold performances from February through October; The Peter Britt Musical Festival in nearby Jacksonville offers classical music under the stars. Medford also boasts a symphony, a chorale and two community theaters.

Annual events: Oregon Shakespeare Festival in nearby Ashland (Feb.-Oct.); Peter Britt Musical Festival in Jacksonville (classical concerts all summer); Oktoberfest and Jazz Jubilee (Oct.); Jackson County Fair (July).

Local Real Estate

There is a tremendous interest in the Medford area because of its proximity to the mountains and to California. Relocation package requests at the Chamber were up 20 percent this year over last. Right now, it's neither a buyer's nor seller's market. The most exciting news in home construction here is the "Super Good Sense" house: the most energy-efficient vapor-locked house ever built. This house, available in a wide range of prices, takes a major wallop out of utility costs. (How would you like to have a home twice the size of your last one, but with half the heating costs?) Retirees are buying them like they're going out of style.

Median price for single family home: $95,000. In town, new homes sell for an average $99,000; resales for $90,000. In the country, new homes are in the $150,000 range; resales can be found for approximately $120,000.

Median price for 2BR condo: Nobody buys condos because big, beautiful houses are available for essentially the same price.

Rental housing market: Apartment rentals are much easier to find than house rentals. Apartments range from $275 to $500 a month. Houses when available rent from $500 to $700 a month. Condos are not available for the most part.

Common housing styles & features: Exteriors are wood-sided with brick fronts. For $130,000, you can get a new 2,300 square foot house with oaks floors, french doors, bay windows, a huge living room/dining room, and so on. For land lovers, you can buy on a mountain for $200,000 and be in the city within 15 minutes.

Nearby area to consider: Applegate Valley.

Unique features of this area: Applegate Valley, between Medford and Grants Pass on Highway 238, is a lovely, small rural town at an elevation of 1,400 feet. The grass is green all year (no snow in winter), and retirees who want a true retreat will find it here.

What Things Cost

Gas company: CP National *(772-5281)*. Winter bills average $45 a month No deposit required.

Electric company: Pacific Power *(776-5420)*. No deposit is required. The average monthly bill for a 1,780 sq. ft. home is $61. The highest month is January, when it could cost as much as $176 a month. Low months run between $39 and $49.

Water/sewer: Medford Water Commission *(770-4511)*. Average monthly bill is $15-$20. A $30 deposit may be required.

Phone company: U.S. West Communications *(779-6116)*. Basic budget rate is $10.65 plus 5¢ per minute. Initial service fee runs between $12 and $24. No deposit is required.

Car registration/license: Registration: $45.50; driver's license is $25. Written test, proof of residency and surrendering of old license are required.

The Tax Ax

Sales tax: None

State income tax: Income over $10,000 a year is taxed at a rate of 9%. The standard deduction for persons 65 and older and who are married filing jointly is $4,000.

Retirement income: A new retirement income credit was just passed, which allows for up to a 9% credit on pension income if total income does not exceed $45,000. At least one spouse must be 58 or older.

Property taxes & tax breaks: Oregon just passed Ballot Measure 5 to reduce the effective property tax rate every year for the next five years. This won't, however, automatically lower taxes, because homes will still be appraised at market value, which continues to increase. In 1991, the maximum tax rate in Jackson County ranges from $18 to $24 per $1,000 of valuation. Thus, a $90,000 home might run from $1,620 to $2,160 a year. There is a senior property tax deferral for those 65 and older whose income does not exceed $24,000. Contact the County Assessor's office for more information *(776-7061)*.

Medical Care

Major hospitals/regional medical centers: Both are JCAH-accredited and offer 24-hour emergency. **Providence Hospital** (owned by the Sisters of Providence), has general surgical and rehabilitative services, an intensive care unit, coronary care unit and diagnostic imaging. Nursing students from several local colleges train here. Seniors can take advantage of Providence 55 plus, a free association offering emotional support, referrals, and personal assistance with Medicare *(773-6611)*. **Rogue Valley Medical Center** has an alcohol and drug abuse treatment program, cancer care, cardiovascular services, digital angio-graphy, and dialysis. The hospital provides clinical experience for local medical students. Its Senior Source Advantage program is an excellent referral service *(773-6281)*.

Emergency medical services (EMS): Firefighters and ambulance drivers are EMT trained for basic life support. The average response time is 2 to 3 minutes in the city, and 5 to 8 minutes in the outlying areas.

Physician's referral: Jackson County Medical Society *772-7511*.

Continuing Education

Southern Oregon State College offers two interesting programs for seniors. "Senior Ventures" is a cooperative effort with four other colleges for residents 50 and older. Enrollment ranges from $115 to $375, depending on the course. The college also runs an elderhostel, which offers classes for one to two weeks and includes 5 courses and meals. Cost is $100/per week. Both programs are available year-round *(552-7672)*.

Services for Seniors

Rogue Valley Medical Center offers "Senior Source Advantage," an excellent referral network for information on needed health services, screenings, help with insurance and Medicare, and any type of special services in the area *(773-6281)*.

Crime & Safety

Crime was up 15% last year according to the Medford Police Department. The reason? There were 132 cases of holiday shoplifting (a lot more than the previous year). Overall crime has been level, with most arrests having nothing to do with violence. Medford is a very safe area. One program worth noting is the Alzheimer Alert System. Afflicted persons can be registered with them, and should they ever wander off, can easily be returned to their families because the police will be familiar with them.

Earning a Living

Current business climate: This area is one of the fastest growing in the state and it's not feeling the impact of the recession or the depressed logging industry as many other Oregon towns are. Many new businesses are establishing themselves and there's enough activity to be optimistic.

Help in starting a business: Contact the Chamber of Commerce's Economic Development Department for information about business opportunities *(779-4847)*.

The job market: Employment is good. Harry & David, the huge fruit mail-order house and Cosco stores continually hire part-time workers. People who want work will find it.

When the Kids Come to Visit

Jacksonville, a National Historic Landmark Town (5 mi.); Children's Festival in Jacksonville (every July); The Bear Creek Bike and Nature Trail; Oregon Caves (the "Marble Halls of Oregon"); Crater Lake National Park (the deepest lake in the U.S. and Oregon's only national park) is 80 miles northeast.

Getting Around Town

Roads & interstates: I-5
Airports & airlines: Medford/Jackson County

Airport (10 minutes from downtown) is served by United Air Lines, Horizon Air, United Express.

Public transportation: Rogue Valley Transit is the local bus company. Seniors pay half price: 35¢ one-way, or with a monthly pass ($12.75-$18.75).

Managing without a car: Impossible. Because of budget cuts, bus service is limited to weekdays and the Medford area is too spread out to walk most anywhere.

What Residents Already Know

You can't go too far in this town without "spotting" a bumper sticker or T-shirt that says, "Save a logger, eat an owl"—a grassroots rebellion against the conservationists who are making a case for spotted owls.•An unbelievable five-star restaurant is here. The Jacksonville Inn is the second highest rated "dinner house" in Oregon (they have 700 of the world's finest wines).•You've got to like a place where the motto is "We hug our visitors!"

For More Information

Chamber of Commerce Office:
The Chamber of Medford/
Jackson County
304 S. Central
Medford, 97501
772-6293

Newspaper:
The Medford Mail Tribune
P.O. Box 1108
Medford, 97501
776-4455

Realtors:
Mr. Clare L. Stevens
Re/Max Ramsay Realty
7604 Hwy 238
Jacksonville, 97530
899-1184

Mr. Doug Morse
Coldwell Banker/Pro West
150 Crater Lake Ave. # L
Medford, 97504
773-6864

38. Charleston, South Carolina

Area Snapshot

Nickname: "The Holy City"
County: Charleston (The Trident Area)
Area code: 803   **Zip code:** 29401-29413
Local population: 73,757
% of population 65+: 18.1%
U.S. region: South Central coast of South Carolina (on the Atlantic Ocean)
Closest metro area: Savannah, Ga., 105 miles
Nearby areas to consider: Kiawah, Seabrook, Mt. Pleasant, Summerville, Isle of Palms
Median housing price: $79,000
Best reasons to retire here: Great climate, culture and graciousness of Old South, Atlantic coast is your backyard, luxurious retirement and resort areas.

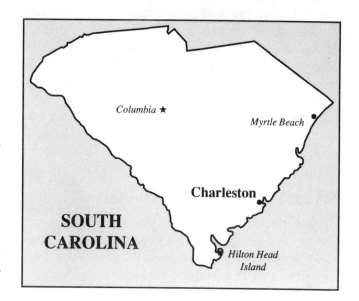

Fabulous Features

Charleston is one of the most charming and picturesque coastal cities in the south. Originally the state capital, it has the feel of a 17th-century European town. Historic areas lure residents and visitors alike with the promise of a stroll into the past. Quaint, narrow streets, stately antebellum homes and an air of gentility hint at the opportunities for comfort—Southern style—in Charleston. And with 90 miles of Atlantic beaches, it's an ideal year-round spot to soak up the great outdoors. To cool off in the summer, people go to the ocean in the morning, get in the car and within hours are enjoying the cool mountain air of the beautiful Blues (Blue Ridge Mountains). For the upscale buyer, the barrier coastal developments of Wild Dunes, Kiawah and Seabrook are gorgeous resort communities with fabulous amenities. Many retired CEOs winter here. As for taxing your pocketbook, South Carolina offers welcome relief. Nationally it was ranked 41st for states with the lowest per capita tax rates (combined state and local taxes), which contributes to the low cost of living. We spoke to people who talked of nothing but friendliness, history, natural resources and the best master-planned golfing communities around.

Possible drawbacks: You know what they say about low-lying areas on the ocean. It's only a matter of time before you're battening down the hatches. Residents take it in stride, but Hurricane Hugo was a reminder of the cruelty of Mother Nature.•Typical of a resort community, public transportation is limited. •The high humidity in the summer takes more than a mint julep to cool off.

"You can quote me on that"

"We moved here from Long Island because of the climate and lower property taxes. We're very happy with our decision. The biggest surprise was how friendly everyone was. It's not like New York."—E.D.

Climate

Elevation: 46'	Avg. High/ Low	Avg. Rainfall (Inches)	Avg. # Days Precip.	Avg. % Humidity
Jan.	60/37	3	10	75
April	76/53	3	7	70
July	89/71	8.2	14	80
Oct.	77/55	4	6	79
YEAR	75/54	50	-	-
# days 32° or below: 39		# days 90° or above: 51		

Let the Good Times Roll

Recreation: The many waterways and barrier islands off Charleston make it ideal for water sports. Sailing is popular, and freshwater fishing on Lakes Marion & Moultrie (Berkeley County) are excellent. There are 15 major parks in Trident county including; Cypress Gardens, James Island County Park, Magnolia Plantation Gardens (America's oldest-founded in 1685) and Palmetto Island County Park. The Charleston area is also a golfer's paradise with hundreds of local courses, including The Wild Dunes in Isle of Palms, ranked 34th best course in the world by *Golf Magazine*.

Culture: The Charleston Museum (founded in 1773, is oldest museum in North America) Other museums include the Citadel, Confederate, Gibbes Museum of Art and Patriot's Point, the worlds largest maritime & naval museum. Charleston has its own symphony orchestra, a community repertory theater, ballet, and recital groups.

Annual events: Lowcountry Oyster Festival (February), Southeastern Wildlife Exposition; (February), Spoleto International Arts Festival U.S.A. (May-June), House & Garden Candlelight Tours (September-October: Get an inside look at some of the beautiful privately-owned homes in historic district); Plantation Days (November: visit magnificent pre-Civil War plantations).

Local Real Estate

The housing market is stable, with neither plunging values nor rampant increases. Property taxes have definitely increased but are not out of line. One of the loveliest but most expensive areas in town is the historic district. Many retirees also look to the barrier islands of Seabrook and Kiawah. Avid golfers settle in the Wild Dunes community.

Median price for single family home: New homes average $79,000, with resales averaging $70,000. The luxury home market starts at $100,000 and goes as high as $1 million. Average lot size is 100 x 120.

Median price for 2BR condo: $80,000. The luxurious units go for $150,000-$200,000.

Rental housing market: Rental 2BR apartments average $550 a month. They can run more with fireplace, vaulted ceilings, or if located on marsh area. Houses average $700-$1,000 a month. Hurricane Hugo hurt the rental market, but it's finally opening up again. Private homes are not as readily available as apartments.

Common housing styles & features: The most common style in this area is the Charleston single house. These narrow houses are one-room wide and several stories high, with piazzas (side porches).

Amenities in condo developments: Most have pools and gardens. Some even have private docks and marinas.

Nearby areas to consider: Kiawah, Seabrook, Mt. Pleasant, Summerville, Isle of Palms.

Unique features of these areas: These areas tend to be small, close-knit upscale communities on the beach, ideal for casual lifestyles. People gravitate there for the golf, tennis and boating. Housing prices start at $175,000 and continue to climb.

What Things Cost

ACCRA shows that living costs in this area are 1% below the national average. Groceries, utilities and health care costs are more than 5 percent below average. Housing and transportation are on par with the rest of the country.

Gas & electric: South Carolina Gas & Electric *(554-7234)*. Average monthly bill is $50. Peak months (June-September) averages $58. Gas average is $48 a month and is slightly higher in July and August. A $100 deposit may be required.

Phone company: Southern Bell *(733-6445)*. Basic service with unlimited local calls is $16.90 a month. Low-use service is $8.45 a month. Discounts for using Southern Bell as long distance carrier are available.

Car registration/license: Registration: $12; License plates: $5; Driving tests: $2; Permits and licenses: $10.

The Tax Ax

Sales tax: 5% (prescription drugs exempt).

State income tax: Your state tax liability is based on the amount of federal taxable income. Any income higher than $10,000 is taxed at a rate of 7%. Long term capital gains are taxed at a lower rate than earned income. In South Carolina, there is no intangible tax as in Florida, Georgia and North Carolina.

Retirement income: There is no tax on Social Security or pensions (public or private). South Carolina offers a choice of deducting $3,000/year of federal taxable income for life, or waiting until 65 and deducting $10,000 a year for life. Estate taxes: 6%-8% except for property passing to a spouse. The first $320,000 is exempt.

Property taxes & tax breaks: Real estate taxes are based on millage rates (which vary by district). To estimate taxes, multiply price of home by the millage rate, then multiply that by either 4% (if you own and occupy home) or 6% (if you own home and rent it out). For example, a $100,000 home in the historic district would run $2,055/year (1990 millage rate of .3426). For residents who are 65 and older, there is an annual $20,000 homestead exemption.

Medical Care

Major hospitals/regional medical centers: The major JCAH hospitals are within an eight block radius in downtown Charleston. **MUSC Medical Center** is the state's largest teaching center and has an aggressive heart and kidney transplant program. It is the only tertiary care (advanced medicine) and Level I trauma center in the area. They also offer the only helicopter transport system. **Trident Regional Medical Center** is a private (JCAH) hospital. It has recently expanded its services and specializes in coronary care and renal dialysis. Overall, medical costs across the state are some of the lowest in the United States.

Other hospitals include **St. Francis Xavier, Roper Hospital** and **Charleston Memorial.**

Emergency medical services (EMS): There are 10 medical units with 2 paramedics, with 5-6 min. response time. South Carolina also has a statewide network of emergency vehicles and helicopters.

Physician's referral: Physician Finder *797-3463.*

Continuing Education

Charleston College: This school offers continuing education programs for all. Seniors pay just $25, and can take any class(es) they choose, if space is available. Popular classes include "History of the South," "Charleston Architecture" and "Art Appreciation." **Trident Technical:** Seniors are invited to register in any undergraduate class. It's free if you register the same day classes begin. There is an elderhostel program through St. Christopher Center in Seabrook. Classes are $25 each for ten weeks and cover a wide range of subjects.

Services for Seniors

The Trident Area Agency on Aging offers numerous services for the elderly *(745-1710).* Two Senior Centers offer activities, home health care referrals, etc. If interested in **AARP,** call *(744-8021).*

Crime & Safety

Charleston is as safe a place to live as any city this size. In fact, there's less crime now than 20 years ago because the city has made public safety its top priority. Charleston has the highest ratio of police for every 10,000 citizens than anywhere in the United States as well as an Elderly Support Program, which gives any senior who calls, the name of a specific individual who will serve as their liaison. **Most common crime against seniors:** If they're affected by anything, it's property crimes. And yet the retirement communities and island resort areas are very safe.

Advice from the police: "Get actively involved in your Neighborhood Watch Program. It's the best way to protect you and your home."

Earning a Living

Current business climate: Hurricane Hugo had a very disastrous effect on the local community. Tourism was way off, leading to slowdowns in construction and so on. It has just recently started to turn around. At one time, *Inc.* magazine ranked Charleston seventh as a "Hot Spot" for business locations.

Programs to help you get started: Contact George Hanlin at SCORE for assistance *(724-4778)*. There is also a Small Business Development Center in town.

The job market: Part-time jobs are readily available, although seniors who settle here are more likely to get involved in volunteer work. AARP can assist with job placement *(744-8021)*.

When the Kids Come to Visit

Where to begin? Treat your family to a birds-eye view of Charleston. Eagle Balloons features hot-air balloon tours of the city or relive the Civil War on the water. Take a yacht tour of Fort Sumter, the site of the beginning of the war. At Cypress Gardens, enjoy flower gardens, hiking and boat rides through the Freshwater Preserve. Or treat the kids to a canoe ride on Palmetto Osle Country Park's mile-long canoe trail. Charleston is within easy driving distance to two of the southeastern Seaboard's most popular resort areas—Myrtle Beach (lots to do for the kids) and Hilton Head Island, a golfer's dream. If you choose to settle in Charleston, you'll never want for visitors.

Getting Around Town

Roads & interstates: I-26, I-95, I-526, US Highway 17, US 52, US 78, US 178

Airports & airlines: The Charleston International Airport serves the entire trident area. The major carriers are United, American, Delta, and USAir.

Public transportation: None.

Managing without a car: Virtually impossible.

What Residents Already Know

Bring your green thumb to South Carolina. The mild 4 seasons is ideal for perennials, annuals and edibles.•The whole Palmetto state is horse country In Charleston, the Plantation at Stono Ferry has steeplechasing and polo.•Those 65 and older get into state parks for free. After 1 year of residency, fishing and hunting licenses are also free.

For More Information

Chamber Of Commerce Office:
Charleston/Trident Chamber
P.O. Box 975
Charleston, 29402
577-2510

Newspaper:
The Post & Courier
134 Columbus St.
Charleston, 29403
577-7111

Realtor:
Ms. Betty Carter
Hamrick-Carter, Inc.
1118 Savannah Highway
Charleston, 29407
571-1655

39. Hilton Head Island, South Carolina

Area Snapshot

Nickname: "The Play Hard, Rest Easy Island"
County: Beaufort
Area code: 803 **Zip code:** 29925-6, 29928, 29938
Local population: 24,000 **County:** 86,400
% of population 65+: 20.5%
U.S. region: Southeastern Seaboard
Closest metro areas: Savannah, 40 miles; Charleston, 90 miles
Nearby area to consider: Beaufort, 35 miles
Median housing price: $216,000
Best reasons to retire here: Fabulous year-round climate, golfer's paradise, resort setting on the ocean, environmental preservation, great recreation and services.

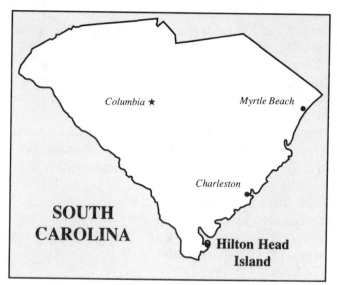

Fabulous Features

To urban achievers, Hilton Head has always been a coveted sanctuary; a place to unwind, rejuvenate and head home for the next stretch in the fast lane. Now, for many retirees, it has become their home away from home. The mild winter climates (50s-60s), surrounded by flawless fall and spring seasons allow for an outdoor life. The driving force, no doubt, is golf. Not just your average 18-holes, but relaxed, unpressured games on championship courses (Hilton Head is ranked #1 for having more courses on the "World's Best List"). With a 12-mile stretch of Atlantic Ocean beaches at your doorstep features boating, fishing, biking, clamming and swimming are on the day's agenda. Housing prices are stable and the market offers a full range of beautiful homes. In spite of the growth in tourism and population, Hilton Head has remained steadfast about environmental preservation of natural marsh settings and wildlife refuges. This treasured barrier island shall remain a sanctuary for the soul.

Possible drawbacks: There is a universal sigh of relief around Labor Day when the tourists depart and normal traffic patterns resume. Residents claim tourists don't bother them because they know where and when to avoid them, but that also means avoiding the best restaurants. When you enjoy your resort home so much, finding enjoyable vacation spots can be a challenge.

"You can quote me on that"

"Our home was Cleveland, but our hearts belonged to Hilton Head. We vacationed here for years and felt we knew the island well. It's everything we wanted for our retirement, but it may not be for everyone. The pace is slow and most people socialize through golf and tennis. I recommend that people rent for a while before buying, and, come at different times of the year. Summers are humid and crowded. The off season when the island is at its best."—K.G.

"We moved from Cincinnati and every day I wake up here and feel like I've died and gone to heaven. We vacationed here for 26 years and never tire of it. The people are vibrant and have a wide diversity of interests. The big adjustment at first was the high price of food shopping, but now there's more competition and the prices are better."—B.C.

Climate

Elevation: 8'	Avg. High/ Low	Avg. Rainfall (Inches)	Avg. # Days Precip.	Avg. % Humidity
Jan.	60/40	2.9	9	75
April	77/55	2.9	7	70
July	90/72	7.9	14	80
Oct.	77/57	2.8	6	79
YEAR	76/56	51	-	-
# days 32° or below: 22		# days 90° or above: 64		

Let the Good Times Roll

Recreation: Hilton Head's 25 golf courses are some of the best-designed in the world. Jack Nicklaus, George and Tom Fazio and Robert Trent Jones are just a few of the architects behind the sprawling airways, wide rolling greens and daring water hazards. Harbour Town Golf Links at Sea Pines Plantation is considered one of the most challenging and distinctive (it's home of the prestigious MCI Heritage Golf Classic) but there are numerous courses for all levels of play. There are also more than 200 tennis courts. Having such temperate climate enables residents to be thoroughly active all year to bike, boat, fish, ride horses, play polo, go crabbing, windsurf and explore. There are 12 beautiful miles of white sandy beaches!

Culture: Fundraising has begun and land has been donated for a brand-new cultural arts center, which will be a tremendous asset to the island. There is a Cultural Council which promotes year-round events from member organizations. These include the Hilton Head Orchestra, Jazz Society, Choral Society, Dance Theater, Playhouse, Art League, Institute for the Arts and Friends of the Library, to name a few. The Hilton Head Playhouse offers musical, comedies, and dramatic performances during the year. The Overlook Cabaret is known for its enjoyable dinner theater. The Museum of Hilton Head offers a great perspective of the island's history and environment.

Annual events: The MCI Heritage Golf Classic (part of the PGA tour) and the Family Circle Tennis Tournament are major events each April. Springfest is a month-long festival with music and dance and arts and crafts (March).

Local Real Estate

The real estate market is very active, with lots of beautiful homes to choose from. Depending on the amenities, a nice 3BR, 2-3BA 10-year old home is selling for $175,000-$275,000. Size-wise they'll be 1,500-2,500 sq. ft. on a 110 x 150 lot. A fair number are one-story, low-maintenance homes, ideal for retirees. If you plan to build, be aware of the strict architectural reviews that will be enforced if trees have to be cut down (the island is meticulously maintained). Many retirees head to the golf communities of Sea Pines Plantation (south) and Hilton Head Plantation (north). There are also some lovely older homes (30 yrs.) but don't come looking for handyman specials.

Median price for single family home: $216,000 (although you can still find a nice house for around $120,000).

Median price for 2BR condo: $100,000

Rental housing market: Houses: $900/mo.+ utilities; 2BR apartment: $600/mo.

Common housing styles & features: Many homes are one-story, well-laid-out contemporaries. Exterior is cypress or cedar siding (stucco and brick are rare). Most homes are 3-4BR and 2-3BA.

Amenities in condo developments: Plantations such as Sea Pines and Hilton Head have fabulous amenities including golf, tennis, health club, bike trails, and more.

Nearby area to consider: Beaufort.

Unique features of this area: Beaufort is an old Civil War town with Victorian homes, charming shops and many traditions.

What Things Cost

Gas company: No natural gas on the island. Most heat their homes with electric.

Electric company: Palmetto Electric (681-5551). Basic monthly service is $6.65 plus 7¢ per kwh. Avg. monthly bill would can be in the $150 range. Jan. and Feb. (heating) bills can be as high as July and August (air conditioning). Deposits are not required for homeowners.

Water/sewer: There are 10 private companies on the island. Hilton Head Utilities says that avg. monthly bills are $30-$40 *(681-8292)*. No deposit is required.

Phone company: Hargray Telephone Company *(785-2166)*. Basic monthly service is $14.31. Installation is $22 per line. A $100 deposit is required for rentals.

Car registration/license: Registration: $12; license plates: $5; driving tests: $2; permits and licenses: $10.

The Tax Ax

Sales tax: 5% (prescription drugs exempt)

State income tax: Income over $10,000 is taxed at a rate of 7%. Long-term capital gains are taxed at a lower rate than earned income. There is no intangible tax as in Florida, Georgia and North Carolina.

Retirement income: No tax on pensions (public or private). South Carolina offers an option of deducting $3,000/yr. of federal return for life or waiting until 65 and deducting $10,000 year for life. Estate taxes: 6%-8% except for property passing to spouse. The first $320,000 is exempt.

Property taxes & tax breaks: Beaufort County assesses market values every five years. To calculate estimated property taxes, multiply the current assessed value by either 4% (permanent legal residents) or 6% (second home or vacant home). That assessed amount is then multiplied by the current millage rates. In Hilton Head, it's .1901. Thus, a $250,000 home owned by a permanent resident would run $1,901. For residents 65+, there is an annual $20,000 homestead exemption. For the home valued at $250,000, your property taxes would be reduced to $1,748. Call the Beaufort County Assessor's office for more information *(525-7295)*.

Medical Care

Major hospitals/regional medical centers: Hilton Head Hospital is a private, not-for-profit JCAH-accredited facility with 80 beds and 24-hour emergency care. Services provided include cardiology (not surgery), physical therapy, radiology and oncology, laser and general surgery. There are also two family medical centers to handle routine procedures.

Emergency medical services (EMS): Hilton Head Rescue, a private volunteer company with 5 ambulences. They respond to 1,600 calls a year. Response time is less than five minutes for ambulances.

Physician's referral: Call the hospital for assistance *681-6122*.

Continuing Education

University of South Carolina/Hilton Head Campus offers a wonderful arrangement for Continuing Education students who are 60 and over. Courses are free of charge, even if taken for credit. You must be a property owner and show proof of age. There is a one-time fee of $15 for undergraduate courses; $25 for graduate courses. The University is in the process of developing a creative program strictly for seniors, modeled after the fabulous Center at the University of North Carolina in Asheville. In the past, USC has participated in elderhostel programs *(785-3995)*.

Services for Seniors

S.H.A.R.E. is the island's Senior Citizens Center. It coordinates programs and activities year-round and distributes a free newsletter. It also offers a senior jobs bank and a volunteer action center. **SCORE** and **AARP** also have local chapters. Call the Senior Center for the current presidents *(785-6444)*.

Crime & Safety

What crime? People feel a high degree of safety because the community is small and very protective. Many said they do not lock their cars or homes. Women said they feel safe walking on the beach at night or early morning. To guard against problems, each plantation has its own private security efforts. The Police Department has a number of awareness programs to keep people assured. Apparently it works. Another deterrent is the high conviction rate of reprimanded suspects.

Earning a Living

Current business climate: Hilton Head has a fertile business environment with a growing diversity stimulated by the island's growth.

Help in starting a business: To find out about the needs of the community, contact the Chamber of Commerce *(785-3673)* as well as the local SCORE chapter out of the Technical College of Lowcountry. For information on SCORE, call the Senior Center *(785-6444)*.

The job market: As is the case with many resort islands, part-time jobs are available in season. Fulltime positions related to tourism are in great demand with pay scales being low. For a solid, steady income, one has to "buy" a job, either by starting a business or getting a real estate license, etc.

When the Kids Come to Visit

Rent bikes and explore the North and South Forest Beach Drives, or take the William Hilton Parkway to the Palmetto Dunes; The Island Rec center offers activities for all ages; Head for the beaches and go sailing, canoeing, windsurfing and horseback riding. All are open to the public. In case it rains, there are nine movie theaters in town.

Getting Around Town

Roads & interstates: State 278 (I-95 is 40 miles).

Airports & airlines: Hilton Head Airport served by USAir Express; Savannah International Airport served by USAir, American, Delta and United.

Public transportation: None.

Managing without a car: The only place a car is not absolutely necessary is Seabrook Plantation, which provides transportation and is accessible to shopping.

What Residents Already Know

The golf is great but the prices are steep at the public courses. A cart and greens fees can average $40 to $90 a day.•The best beaches are in Sea Pines-Forest Beach (southern section of the island).•The town government is small and the retirees very vocal. Every month one reads about another petition they're circulating to get changes implemented. They're the not-so-silent caretakers of the island.

For More Information

Chamber Of Commerce Office:
Hilton Head Chamber
P.O. Box 5647
Hilton Head, South Carolina 29938
785-3673

Newspapers:
The Island Packet
P.O. Box 5727
Hilton Head, 29938
785-4293

The Hilton Head News
P.O. Box 5466
Hilton Head, 29938
785-5255

Realtors:
Julie Toon Pawley
**Coldwell Banker/
Toon Pawley Real Estate**
P.O. Box 5250
Hilton Head, 29938
800-845-3520

James Wedgeworth
Charter 1 Realty
P.O. Box 6125
Hilton Head, 29938
785-4460

40. Myrtle Beach, South Carolina

Area Snapshot

Nickname: "America's Favorite Sun"
County: Horry County
Area code: 803   **Zip code:** 29572-7; 29578 (PO Boxes)
Local population: 27,890   **County:** 156,800
% of population 50+: 23.2%
U.S. region: South/Central East Coast
Closest metro area: Charleston, 94 miles
Nearby areas to consider: Murrell's Inlet, Surfside, North Myrtle Beach.
Median housing price: $90,000
Best reasons to retire here: Lowcountry beach resort with big city amenities, low taxes and living costs, temperate climate, ideal setting on the central east coast (it's a day's drive to Florida or New York).

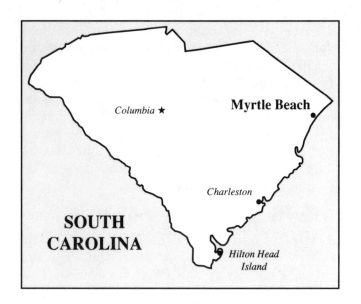

Fabulous Features

South Carolina's Grand Strand Area provides the perfect recipe for a joyous retirement. Start with the delightfully pleasant year-round climate. With the sun shining brightly more than 200 days a year, one mild season is more gorgeous than the next. Add beautiful oceanfront condominiums, tastefully designed residential developments or vacation cottages that are affordable and you're on your way. For good measure, throw in world-class golf and tennis facilities, white sandy beaches, ample recreation and culture, low crime, exciting continuing education programs and fine medical care. The icing on the cake is the reasonable cost of living. Mix it all together and you'll have an enviable lifestyle. And that's no half-baked idea!

Possible drawbacks: Tourism is a double-edged sword (it's the most visited area in the state). It's the area's economic base, but it also brings it's share of congestion and crime in peak seasons.•The Myrtle Beach Air Force Base, another boon to the economy, will probably be closed within the next few years, eliminating jobs and medical facilities for the military.•Can hurricanes strike twice? Residents swear they'd hate to be around for another Hugo, but no one seems to be moving away from this leisure-minded coastal community.

"You can quote me on that"

"We're absolutely happy with our decision to retire here. What's great is that everyone is a transplant, which is your common bond. And everyone is so friendly and laid back. I highly recommend the area, just come and rent for six months and look in every direction before you buy. Each section is a little different."—M.C., Surfside

"We retired from Brigantine, N.J., and wanted a place that was warmer, but not hot like Florida. I researched areas that were affordable, had good weather and nice homes. That's Myrtle Beach in a nutshell. We thought the houses were some of the nicest we'd ever seen for the price. They're new, one floor, with the latest windows and appliances. We also love being this close to the ocean. Myrtle Beach is beautiful, clean and friendly... Before you buy or build, decide what's more important...being on the ocean or on a golf course."—A.G. and I.G.

Climate

Elevation: 33'	Avg. High/ Low	Average Inches		Avg. # Days Precip.	Avg. % Humidity
		Rain	Snow		
Jan.	60/39	2.8	-	9	75
April	74/52	3.3	-	7	71
July	88/72	4.3	-	13	80
Oct.	76/56	2.3	-	7	78
YEAR	74/55	46	1	-	-
# days 32° or below: 28			# days 90° or above: 48		

Let the Good Times Roll

Recreation: Myrtle Beach is the center of the Grand Strand area, where the agreeable climate allows for 12 months of outdoor and ocean activity. Horry County stretches over 60 miles of gorgeous, clean Atlantic Ocean beachfront that's minutes from residential areas. Boating and fishing are favorite pastimes (12 marinas and piers). Come try your luck surfcasting, deep-sea fishing and pier fishing. For golfers, the Grand Strand is the Seaside Golf Capital of the World (Myrtle Beach National Golf Club is the only course with Arnold Palmer's Seal of Approval)! With more than 70 different 18-hole courses, you could literally play a different one for two months and still have others to try. The area is also a camper's delight. There are more than 7,000 individual sites for settling in (12 locations for motor homes). Watch the Myrtle Beach Blue Jays at Coastal Carolina Stadium (the Class A Farm Team of the Toronto Jays).

Culture: Brookgreen Gardens (Murrell's Inlet): the world's largest outdoor collection (500 pieces) of American Sculpture in a garden setting surrounded by wildlife. Georgetown offers tours of the historic district and the Rice Museum (by tram, boat, or foot depending on the season). Coastal Carolina College Theater features local productions. Long Bay Symphony Orchestra and the Carolina Opry (surfside); country music and a Dixie Jubilee.

Annual events: Senior Games (April): athletic olympic style events for residents 55+. Annual Sun Fun Festival (June): kicks off the summer season with parades, celebrities, beach games, music. Annual Doll Show (Spring) Murrells Inlet Seafood Festival (Spring). Annual Canadian-American Days Festival (March). The Annual Grand Stand Fishing Rodeo (April thru October); Art In The Park (Summer).

Local Real Estate

Most people choose homes or condominiums between one and 10 miles from the beaches. 90% of new residents are relocating permanently rather than as snowbirds. Retirees are buying the small, energy-efficient homes with low maintenance.

Median price for single family home: $90,000. (many homes priced in the $150,000 range). Small 3BR homes start at $60,000.

Median price for 2BR condo: $125,000 (Oceanfront 2BR). Prices drop as you move inland.

Rental housing market: Avg. house is $650/ mo. although scarce. Townhouse and condo rentals run $550/mo. on a month-to-month or annual lease.

Common housing styles & features: Brick homes are most economical. Average lot sizes for new homes are 85 x 125. Custom builts are everywhere.

Amenities in condo developments: Indoor and outdoor pools, workout rooms.

Nearby areas to consider: Murrell's Inlet, Surfside, North Myrtle Beach. **Unique features of these areas:** Murrell's Inlet has been called the Seafood Capital of the World (the fish really bite here). It looks like plantation country with salt marshes and live oak trees. Surfside is more of a traditional, old small southern town. The streets are built around the old oak trees and it's much less touristy. North Myrtle Beach is a collection of small seaside villages that consolidated in the '60s. All are connected to Myrtle Beach along Hwy. 17.

What Things Cost

Overall living costs run 8% below the national average, with utilities averaging 35% below the average. Health care and food are also less costly here than in other parts of the country.

Gas company: South Carolina Electric and Gas Co. *(236-6413)*. A 3,500 sq. ft. home avgs. $100/mo. (highest consumption-Jan.) $100 deposit is not required with good credit history.

Electric company: Santee Cooper Electric *(448-2411)*. Avg.: $40/mo. Dec., Jan. and July are $70-$80. $100 deposit may be required.

Phone company: GTE Phone Company *(800-532-2311)*. Basic Service is $20-$30/mo. Deposit not required with good credit history.

Water/sewer: Avg.: $15/mo. in Myrtle Beach; $30 outside the city. A deposit of $30-$120 is required; varies based on rental or ownership, in or out of the city (Myrtle Beach pays less).

Car registration/license: Registration and plates: $17. Permits and licenses are $10. Driving tests: $2, DMV *(626-9183)*.

The Tax Ax

Sales tax: 5% (prescription drugs exempt).
State income tax: Income over $10,000 is taxed at 7%. Long-term capital gains are taxed at a lower rate than earned income. There is no intangible tax as in Florida, Georgia and North Carolina.
Retirement income: No tax on pensions (public or private). South Carolina offers an option of deducting $3,000/yr. of federal return for life or waiting until 65 and deducting $10,000/yr. for life. Estate Taxes: 6%-8% except for property passing to spouse. The first $320,000 is exempt.
Property taxes & tax breaks: In Myrtle Beach, property taxes are calculated at a rate of 4% (must be legal resident for one year) or 6% (new resident or residents whose legal address is elsewhere). That figure is multiplied by the millage rate of .2134. Residents 65+ are eligible for a $20,000 homestead exemption. For a home valued at $100,000, the property tax would run $2,845 for the first year. For a 4% exemption (after one year), you must apply at the county tax assessor's office *(626-1361)*.

Medical Care

Major hospitals/regional medical centers: Grand Strand General Hospital is a JCAH facility with mammography service, cardiac care (has the only 3 cardiologists and the first cardiac rehab center in the county) nuclear medicine and emergency care (7 board-certified emergency specialists on staff); cancer care (surgery and chemo on site; radiation therapy at another facility in the area). **Conway Hospital** is a JCAH-accredited general medical and surgical facility. The nearest teaching hospitals are at Duke University in Durham and Medical University in Charleston.

Emergency medical services (EMS): 5 stations in the Grand Strand from North Myrtle Beach to Garden City. Average response time: 4 minutes.

Physician's referral: *497-2128*, or call "Ask-A-Nurse;" a free 24-hour information service including physician referral *347-8199*.

Continuing Education

USC Coastal Carolina College (10 mi. west) offers an exciting program for seniors 55+ called "The Third Quarter" (academic exercise for the older adult). Pay a membership fee of $85 for six classes ($135 per couple) or $25 per class. Take "Aging and the Brain," "A Magical Tour of Historic Britain" and other stimulating classes *(448-1481)*. Horry Georgetown Technical College offers on-site industrial training, retraining, running your own business and management training. Seniors/residents can attend any class for $10 *(448-8506)*.

Services for Seniors

The Myrtle Beach Senior Center operates from TEC College. Fundraising is in progress for a separate center, which will offer recreation, education and social functions. Seven other centers in the county run programs and services. Horry County Council on Aging (HCCOA) provides needed services to the community *(449-7402)*. **AARP** meets the first Monday of the month (September-June) at St. Philips Lutheran Church *(449-9547)*.

Crime & Safety

Violent crimes are minimal; minor violations and property crimes make up most criminal activity. Tourist and summer season brings the crowds, and subsequently, the rise in the need for police involvement. Residents told us they felt it was a very safe area. They wouldn't be aware of crime if not for stories in the paper. The police urge seniors to take extra precautions at the height of the season to avoid purse snatchings, pickpockets, etc. Also, it pays to become active in their Citizen Watch Neighborhood System, which educates residents about home safety. There's an excellent rapport between the police and the community.

Earning a Living

Current business climate: Businesses that cater to tourism or specialize in health care stand good chances of developing. Unemployment is very low now (3.5%) but most residents are concerned that the closing of the Air Force base will have a negative impact on the economy, jobs, and real estate. It's the area's largest employer (4,000 people).

Starting a business: The Chamber has a consultant available to discuss business opportunities *(626-7444)*. Georgetown Technical College offers continuing education programs on starting and expanding businesses *(448-8506)*.

The job market: As with most tourist areas, part-time and minimum wage jobs are the most readily available.

When the Kids Come to Visit

Wild Water & Wheels; Myrtle Beach Pavilion and Amusement Park; North Myrtle Beach Amusement Park; Sun Fun Amusements; Surfside Pavilion and Amusement Park; Brookgreen Gardens; South Carolina Hall of Fame.

Getting Around Town

Roads & interstates: US Route 17 (the major highway), 501, and Interstates 95, 20.

Airports & airlines: Myrtle Beach Air Force Base houses the local jetport. Service provided by USAir, American, and Eastern Metro Express (commuter flights).

Public transportation: Coastal Rapid Transit (CRTA) provides convenient local bus service. Also, Myrtle Beach runs a trolley service during the summer.

Managing without a car: Because the area is so spread out, most residents find it necessary to have cars.

What Residents Already Know

With Hurricane Hugo still a vivid memory, many areas are designated as official flood zones. Flood insurance is a requirement. There are no policies to buy for peace of mind. Hurricanes are a real threat in these parts. Less threatening but just as spooky, several shipwrecks off the South Carolina coast offer exciting adventure for scuba divers. Ghost stories are legend in the Grand Strand. Ask about the Grey Man and Alice.

For More Information

Chamber Of Commerce Offices:
Myrtle Beach Area Chamber
of Commerce
P.O. Box 2115
Myrtle Beach, 29578
626-7444 or 800-356-3016

North Myrtle Beach: 249-3519
South Strand Office: 651-1010
Grand Strand Welcome Center:
626-6619

Newspapers:
The Sun News (Daily)
P.O. Box 406
Myrtle Beach, 29578
626-8555

The Journal (weekly)
P.O. Drawer 8309
Myrtle Beach, 29578
236-3602

Realtor:
Fred Frye
Coldwell Banker
Frye Realty, Inc.
315 Highway 17, N.
Surfside Beach, 29575
238-1238

41. Austin, Texas

Area Snapshot

Nickname: "The Capital City"
County: Travis
Area code: 512   **Zip code:** 78767, 78701
Local population: 480,022   **County:** 576,407
% of population 65+: 11.3%
U.S. region: Hill Country; Central Texas on the Colorado River
Closest metro area: San Antonio, 75 miles
Nearby areas to consider: Lakeway
Median housing price: $92,000
Best reasons to retire here: Mild winters, excellent services and opportunities for outdoor recreation, affordable housing, retired military, university influence.

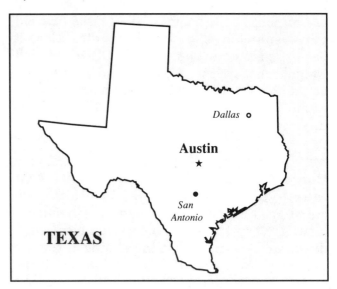

Fabulous Features

To live deep in the heart of Texas Hill Country is to have the privilege of nature's grandeur at your doorstep. The first thing that strikes newcomers is the sparkling lakes and sloping terrain. Austin has never needed to spruce up its image with a man-made skyline. And yet it is as much a corporate, political and educational arena as the largest cities in the country. As the Texas state capital and the home of the University of Texas, there is more "intelligence" here than at the CIA. People spoke of the progressive attitudes and cutting-edge technology but also of the innate ability to get back to basics. A high quality of life is first and foremost. For retirees, the great appeal is the great outdoors—12 months of waterfront fun, hiking, and fishing. The great indoors isn't so bad either with the University having so much to share with the community. Services for seniors are good (take a free ride on the bus any time), housing is abundant and affordable, the health care facilities are most impressive and, compared to many other big cities, living costs are within reason. The extra bonus is there is no personal income tax. Austin is indeed a "capital" city.

Possible drawbacks: If being surrounded by college kids, politicians and high-tech types will unnerve you, you may want to look elsewhere.•You'll need relief from the dreadfully hot summers. Just head for the hills—the Hill Country, that is, where lakes and rivers offer cool respite from the Texas heat.

"You can quote me on that"

"My husband is retired from the military and he knew Austin well. We came here because of the living costs and how much there is to do. The University adds a lot. It attracts a retiree who is active, and likes culture—thinking people. I don't like the heat and humidity, but I do like the hilly terrain on one side of town and the flatlands on the other. The Air Force base offers us a lot, too. Good medical, activities and so on. We're very happy here."—Mrs. B.S.

"We've always loved Texas Hill Country and visited many times. We also found the price of houses and utilities fairer than most other big cities. But what we've come to really love are the people. They're friendly, intelligent and they have our kind of attitude. "If I can't do it today, I'll do it tomorrow.""—Mr. and Mrs. K.R.

Climate

Elevation: 634'	Avg. High/ Low	Avg. Rainfall (Inches)	Avg. # Days Precip.	Avg. % Humidity
Jan.	60/50	1.8	8	71
April	79/69	3.5	7	65
July	95/85	1.9	5	62
Oct.	81/70	3	6	65
YEAR	79/68	32	-	-
# days 32° or below: 24 # days 90° or above: 116				

Let the Good Times Roll

Recreation: Situated on the banks of the Colorado River, city outdoor recreation facilities are vast, with more than 11,000 acres of parkland and waterfront to enjoy. A favorite spot is Zilker Park with its spring-fed swimming pool, Barton Springs (always at a cool 68 degrees). Sail on Lake Travis, go rafting on the Guadalupe River, watch the annual "Liberty Mutual Legends of Golf" seniors tournament, take off at the Town Lake Hike and Bike trail, or sit a spell and enjoy the magnificent wildflowers at Zilker Gardens. There are more than 20 private and public golf courses (wait until you see the rolling greens and waterfalls), and more than 200 tennis courts (all the "Grand Slam" surfaces are here.)

Culture: If you're coming from a metro area and fear a small city will leave you culturally deprived, don't worry. The Austin Symphony Orchestra, Ballet Austin, Austin Lyric Opera, the Paramount Theater for Performing Arts, and Zachary Scott Theater are just some of the offerings. The University of Texas Performing Arts Complex has other wonderful presentations at Bass Concert Hall, the Bates Recital Hall, the Opera Lab Theater and the B. Iden Payne Theater. Museums include: Lyndon B. Johnson Library and Presidential Museum, Laguna Gloria Art Museum; Elizabeth Ney Museum & Sculpture Conservatory, the Texas Memorial Museum and the home of O. Henry.

Annual events: Exciting annual sports tournaments and events are a local pastime including the PBA Columbia 300 Open (bowling); the Capitol 10,000 (the largest 10k race in the U.S.); The Liberty Mutual Legends of Golf (PGA Tour); the Austin Rowing Club Regatta; Austin/Travis County Livestock Show and Rodeo; and the Austin Triathalon (runner's marathon). Austin's Aquafest draws crowds each August to tap their toes to music, and sample Southwestern cuisine.

Local Real Estate

The real estate market has picked up tremendously in the past year and prices are up 11%. It's turning into a seller's market because inventory is decreasing but there is still a lot to show. Most neighborhoods are very well-maintained (we hear owners are very conscientious). Most retirees buy to stay. Austin is not a big second-home market.

Median price for single family home: $92,000. New custom builts average $130,000 (2,000 sq. ft.) Existing homes average in the mid-80s.

Median price for 2BR condo: $100,000 (less costly, smaller, closer to campus).

Rental housing market: Houses (1,600-1,800 sq. ft.) are $650-$800/mo.; 2BR apts. are $475-$525/mo. Currently, the rental market is very tight due to the lack of new construction. Apartments seem to be creeping up in price the most. Homes are widely available to rent.

Common housing styles & features: Typically homes are ranch style (one-story) with no basements or attached garage. 3BR, 2BA with fireplace are very popular.

Amenities in condo developments: Retirees come here looking for one-story units but there are none to show. Most condo developments sell two-story townhouses. All have pools and clubhouses.

Nearby area to consider: Lakeway. **Unique features:** Lakeway is a beautiful golf course community 15 minutes outside of Austin. Situated on three golf courses and a lake, it offers luxurious 2,300 sq. ft. homes ranging from $150,000-$200,000. Interiors have 3-4BRs, 2 1/2 BA. Construction is stone and brick (very little siding).

What Things Cost

ACCRA (1st quarter, 1991) places Austin at a fraction under the national average in overall costs. Utilities and goods and services come in 9% higher than average, but housing and health care are just under 10% below average.

Gas company: Southern Union Gas Company *(477-6461)*. Avg. monthly bill is $20-$24. January avg. bill: $70. $50 deposit is required.
Electric company: Electric Utility Dept. *(322-6300)*. Avg. monthly bill in summer is $125-$150. In winter, electric can run $150-$200/mo.
Phone company: Southwestern Bell Telephone Co. *(870-5150)*. Basic monthly service: $13.85. Installation plus first month paid in advance.
Car registration/license: New residents must get a Texas driver's license within 30 days of establishing residency. License tags are based on year of car: 1989-92: $58.80: 1986-88: $50.80: 1985 and older: $40.80. Title fee: $10. Road and bridge fee: $5. New residents impact fee: $15. Driver's license: $16 for 4 years.

The Tax Ax

Sales tax: 8% (Prescription drugs/food not for immediate consumption are exempt)
State income tax: None.
Property taxes & tax breaks: Current property taxes are assessed at $2.29 per $100 value. There is an annual state homestead exemption of $5,000 if one spouse is 65+. Additionally, there is an exemption for seniors of $25,000 off appraised value. Tax on a $90,000 home would run $2,061 without any exemptions.

Medical Care

Have you heard the expression, "Ask two Texans an opinion and you'll get three answers?" That was the response we received concerning the quality of health care in Austin. There was a contingency that said for serious medical problems they'd head to Houston. The second group said they thought that the level of care at area hospitals was second to none and a third group who said health care was so expensive here, the least they could do is cure you.
Major hospitals/regional medical centers: There are 12 hospitals in Travis county including the following: **Brackenridge Hospital** is a JCAH-accredited regional teaching hospital and referral center. It has the only trauma center in Central Texas, as well as an excellent heart and orthopedic center. Brackenridge Lab has recently received a two-year

accreditation from the College of American Pathologists (one of 4,000 in the country.). **St. David's Health Care System** specializes in open heart surgery, cardiac catheterization, acute care and physical therapy. **Seton Medical Center** is the home of the Central Texas Heart Institute (transplants) oncology, orthopedics, general medical/surgical and seniors programs. **South Austin Medical Center** is known for its Texas Regional Kidney Stone Center, laser eye treatment, and post mastectomy support programs. **Emergency medical services (EMS):** Austin's EMS system was named first in the nation by the National Association of Emergency Medical Technicians. Their operation includes Star Flight (an emergency helicopter service for outlying areas) and 15 vehicles with either basic or advanced life support. Overall, the average response time is 6.7 minutes. **Physician's referral:** Travis City Medical Society *458-1121*.

Continuing Education

University of Texas has 300 different classes in their continuing education program alone. Enrollment varies, but can range from $17-$165. Lifetime Learning Institute (Concordia Lutheran College) offers eight-week courses on creative writing, law and many academics: $12/course. The teaching staff includes retirees, professors and local professionals *(452-7661)*. There are also continuing education classes at the Austin Community College *(997-8800)*, as well as an elderhostel at St. Edward's University *(448-8649)*.

Services for Seniors

The **Information and Referral Network for Older Adults** is an excellent source for learning about eldercare and other needs *(451-0106)*. **AGE** (Austin Groups for The Elderly) is a consortium of 12 non-profit agencies that provide services to seniors *(451-4611)*. The **Adult Services Council** publishes a monthly newsletter, "The Advocate" *(451-7433)*. **AARP** has a local chapter *(255-8952)*.

Crime & Safety

Austin was recently ranked 14th highest in the U.S. for crimes per 1,000 people. But the motto is if you don't go looking for trouble, it won't find you. Common sense dictates that you avoid areas where crime is more rampant. The Austin Police Department has 20 community awareness programs, free home security checks and advice on preventing break-ins.

Earning a Living

Current business climate: The current climate for new business starts is excellent. *INC.* magazine recently named Austin the number-one city for entrepreneurs. With a 3%-4% annual growth rate, projections for the next few years are optimistic. Between the university and the state government, the city is crawling with professionals, executives and legislators. They need services, restaurants, bars, word processing, and more.
Programs to help you get started: Contact the Small Business Development Center *(482-5288)* and SCORE *(482-5111)* for help.
The job market: Many seniors find part-time work within the university system, however, they compete with the college kids for openings. For help with job placement, call Green Thumb, Inc. through AGE *(451-4611)*. The IRS is the largest part-time employer with more than 4,200 workers. The state and local government also hire part-time help.

When the Kids Come to Visit

The Rotunda at the State Capital; University of Texas; LBJ Library; Barton's Spring (great swimming); Johnson City (home of LBJ); Austin's Children's Museum; Nature's Wilderness Trail at the Wild Basin Preserve; The Alamo in San Antonio (75 mi.); McKinney Falls State Park.

Getting Around Town

Roads & interstates: I-35, US-290, US-183, Texas-71. **Airports & airlines:** Robert Mueller Municipal Airport is served by American, America West, Delta, Continental, Northwest, Southwest, United, TWA, USAir and Conquest Airlines (commuter flights). **Public transportation:** Capital Metro operates daily with more than 300 vehicles, express routes, and park and ride service. Bus service is free to seniors at any time. The Delo Downtown Green Trolley is free to any resident. Capital Metro also offers Tele-Ride: door-to-door service for seniors (2-hours notice) for 50¢ one-way. Standard reservations are available if service is used at least 3 times a week. **Managing without a car:** Absolutely. Public transportation is good.

What Residents Already Know

The Texas State Racing Commission approved the first parimutuel license in the state, making way for a $50 million Sam Houston Race Track to be built in Harris County.•Plans are underway for a $700 million airport to be built northeast of the city, ready for operation in February, 1995. It will have the same capacity as Chicago's O'Hare Field.•Austin residents love their tennis and are proud of the recent USTA appointment for having one of four regional training centers in the U.S.

For More Information

Chamber Of Commerce Office:
The Greater Austin Chamber
Of Commerce
P.O. Box 1967
Austin, 78767
322-5694

Newspaper:
The Austin American-Statesman
166 East Riverside Drive
Austin, 78767
445-3500

Realtor:
Ms. Noveleen Parker
**Coldwell Banker/
Richard Smith Realty**
5000 Bee Caves Rd. Suite 200
Austin, 78746
328-0828

42. Brownsville, Texas

Area Snapshot

Nickname: "On the Border By The Sea"
County: Cameron
Area code: 512   **Zip code:** 78520-2
Local population: 109,000   **County:** 260,120
% of population 65+: 10% (50% in the winter)
U.S. region: Southernmost city in Texas (25 mi. inland from the Gulf)
Closest metro areas: Corpus Christi, 100 miles
Nearby areas to consider: McAllen/Mission
Median housing price: $55,000
Best reasons to retire here: Very scenic, large winter retirement haven, very affordable ("a poor man's Florida"), perpetual summer, square dancer's paradise.

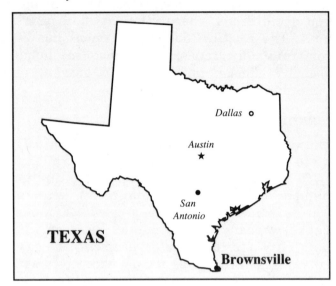

Fabulous Features

With the swaying palm trees, fragrant citrus groves, tropical flowers and wide, modern avenues as the backdrop, it's easy to get a sense of déjà vu. Why, Brownsville looks just like Florida! But make no mistake, The Rio Grande Valley is distinctive in its own right. When you see 10,000 seniors do-si-do-ing down by the resacas (winding rivers), you know it isn't Miami. For decades, Brownsville has been the home base of Winter Texans—approximately 200,000 seniors who migrate from the Midwest in their RVs to whoop it up for a few months. But in the past five years, tens of thousands of people have made the area their year-round home because you can't beat Brownsville for low living costs. Real estate and property taxes are dirt cheap, there's no personal income tax, the sub-tropical climate is a welcome retreat from wind chill factors and—as far as diversions go—this joint is jumpin'! The hot spot is neighboring Mexico, where you can literally walk across the border and into Reynosa's "Pink Zone" for food, fun and dollar-stretching shopping. The fishing and hunting are superb and the unspoiled beaches and gentle trade winds on South Padre Island invite you to every imaginable water sport. What's more, this is the square dancing capital of the world. Grabbing your partner is as natural as breathing. Everywhere you "turn" are fun-loving seniors who know they've found the secret of youth: the good life in Brownsville.

Possible drawbacks: There's a reason you don't hear about "Summer Texans"—it gets hot, hot, hot. June through August are in the 90s with 75% humidity.•Bordering Mexico brings its share of crime, most prevalent of which is auto theft. Yet surprisingly, few people spend the money to park in the guarded garages.•The crowds and the traffic come with this territory. Claustrophobics beware.

"You can quote me on that"

"Brownsville is a far cry from Carmel, Indiana, where we're from. But we'd been coming here on vacation for 14 years and finally bought a place. That was four years ago and we love it. We're crazy about the weather and the people. Everyone is so friendly, evel kids hold the door open for you. Everyone is nice to Winter Texans, too, because they help the economy so much. If you don't mind hot weather and you're kind of carefree about things, you'll love Brownsville."—Mrs. I.B.

Climate

Elevation: 23'	Avg. High/ Low	Avg. Rainfall (Inches)	Avg. # Days Precip.	Avg. % Humidity
Jan.	70/51	1.4	7	77
April	83/67	1.3	4	73
July	93/76	1.1	5	73
Oct.	85/67	3.3	7	73
YEAR	82/65	26	-	-
# days 32° or below: 3		# days 90° or above: 117		

Let the Good Times Roll

Recreation: There are 12 city parks, including the Dean Porter Park with an indoor/outdoor pavilion, 3 pools, tennis and more. Several golf courses are within a 30-minute drive. Because of the climate, hunting and fishing are some of the best in the West. Big and small game are found here and across the border (Texas has extended the season and bag limits are liberal). You can also charter a boat off Port Isabel or South Padre Island for some serious deep-sea fishing (the tarpon and mackerel are typical offshore catches). South Padre's long stretch of clean, unspoiled beaches are perfect for waterskiing, surfing and boating.

Culture: As with much of Texas, Brownsville is quite a historic area (the Mexican War was fought here and it's the sight of the oldest U.S. Army Post). The Confederate Air Force Museum and the Fort Brown area are interesting. Art museums reflecting the rich, colorful landscape of the Rio Grande Valley are here, including the Brownsville Art League Museum. The Brownsville Community Concert Association brings great concerts to town and the Texas Southmost College's Patron of the Arts sponsor musical and dramatic performances in season.

Annual events: Charro Days (a pre-Lenten celebration of mixed cultures); Confederate Air Show (a recreation of WWII air power); Riofest (Harlingen arts festival); Rio Grand Music Festival; Fishing Tournaments (South Padre Island).

Local Real Estate

The real estate market was comatose last year but is being resuscitated slightly. The average priced home is still between $50,000-$60,000. Larger homes (1,900-2,100 sq. ft.) with 3BR 2BA, a 2-car garage and a large yard will run $85,000. However, Winter Texans and other retirees don't come down here to buy what they just got rid of. They all head for the mobile and modular homes. The RV parks are where all the action takes place! It's estimated that there are more than 500 parks in the Brownsville/Harlingen/McAllen area.

Median price for single family home: $55,000 (Many homes sell in the $30s and $40s.)

Median price for 2BR condo: $60,000 (more desirable models at places like the Rancho Villa Country Club sell in the $80s).

Rental housing market: The rental market in winter is tight as a drum, but when they become available, tenants pay an average of $600-$700 a month for a fair sized house and $350 plus for a 2BR apartment. Off season you name the price.

Common housing styles & features: One-story ranches without basements are very popular.

Amenities in condo developments: Some golf course communities, most other developments offer pools and maintenance.

Nearby areas to consider: McAllen, Mission (Hidalgo County).

Unique features of these areas: These areas are not vastly different—there's just more of it. More RV parks, more people, more restaurants, more churches.

What Things Cost

When you're this close to Mexico, lower prices become contagious. Overall living costs are 11% below the national average, with housing, utilities and health care being extremely affordable. Real estate and rentals are more than 30% below the national average. Groceries are 5% higher than the average city, but that is offset by the fact that most food items are tax-exempt. There is also no personal income tax and property taxes are very low.

Gas company: Rio Grande Valley Gas (542-3531). The average monthly bill is $22 (the highest consumption occurs in January with an average bill of $49). A $50 non-refundable deposit may be required. There is a $9 charge for a connection. Each utility charges $25 to turn on a meter (gas, electric, water).

Electric company: Public Utility Board *(544-3970)*. The average monthly bill is $40 to $50 (the highest usage occurs in August and September when costs average $120-$200 for an all-electric home). Deposit may not be required.

Phone company: Southwestern Bell *(542-7481)*. Basic monthly service is $12.30 for unlimited local calls. Economy plan is $7.90 (25 local calls); installation starts at $38.35.

Car registration/license: New residents must get a Texas driver's license within 30 days of establishing residency. License tags are based on year of car: 1989-92: $58.80; 1986-88: $50.80; 1985 and older: $40.80. Title fee: $10. Road and bridge fee: $5. New residents impact fee: $15. Driver's license: $16 for 4 years.

The Tax Ax

Sales tax: 8% (Prescription drugs and food not for immediate consumption are exempt).

State income tax: None.

Property taxes & tax breaks: Current property taxes are assessed at $2.29 per $100 value. There is an annual state homestead exemption of $5,000 if one spouse is 65 or older. There is also an exemption for seniors of $25,000 off appraised value. Tax on a $55,000 home would run $1,259 without any exemptions.

Medical Care

Major hospitals/regional medical centers: Both are full accredited facilities with 24-hour emergency care. Neither hospital has a burn center (the closest is Galveston). **Brownsville Medical Center** offers radiology, mammography, and an intensive coronary care unit. For residents, they put on health fairs for free screenings, blood pressure, cholesterol, and glaucoma tests. They encourage registration as a way to keep files on record in the event of an emergency. **HCA Valley Regional Medical Center** is an acute care hospital with a coronary Care ICU, a physical rehabilitation unit, a women's center, and a medical/surgical unit. Open heart patients are sent to **Valley Baptist** in Harlingen (25 miles) or to the outstanding **Texas Medical Center** in Houston (50 minutes by air).

Emergency medical services (EMS): The Fire Department oversees the EMS team and reports an average response time of 8 minutes within the city (11-12 minutes within the county).

Physician's referral: Brownsville Medical Center *544-1511*; HCA Valley Medical *831-9611*.

Continuing Education

Texas Southmost College offers both an elderhostel and an Elder Institute. The hostel runs in fall and winter for 30 consecutive weeks. Participants can stay in a the beautiful old Fort Brown Hotel and Resort. One-week sessions run $300 *(544-8200)*. The Elder Institute is for area residents and offers a variety of classes including floral design, computers, Spanish, etc. For $55-$75, you can take up to three courses. At the University of Texas at Brownsville, residents can audit classes for $20 *(982-0100)*.

Services for Seniors

The Brownsville Senior Citizens Center is in the process of a bond referendum to build a new center. In the meantime, it is a good source of information on services and programs available to the elder community *(544-2767)*. **AARP** has a local chapter. Call *(544-5300)* for the name of the current officers.

Crime & Safety

Drug trafficking and drug-related crime are rampant and, although they don't appear to be a direct personal threat to the average citizen, there's no point in wearing blinders. The police urge caution and parking in guarded parking lots because the residual affect of living in Brownsville is that auto theft is as common as a siesta. Everyone knows someone who's had at least one car stolen. In fact, car insurance premiums could be higher than your mortgage! Conversely, we heard numerous stories showing acts of kindness and a sense of trust. It's important to remember that, by and large, the area is safe to live and walk. The majority of people are law-abiding.

Earning a Living

Current business climate: It is currently an economically depressed area, with businesses holding their breath until the recession ends. Unemployment is at an all-time high (16%) and there is little part-time work available. In the past, businesses that catered to agriculture and tourism were strongholds. Local leaders talk of seeing some breakthroughs, but it's like turning the ship around while it's docked.

Help in starting a business: For those who want to persevere, the Brownsville Economic Development Council is eager to assist new business owners and will work with them to find the right location, make contacts, etc. The University of Texas/Pan American at Edinburg has a Center for Entrepreneurial Development where business students and specialists counsel prospective business owners. Call Nick Soto at *(541-1183)* or contact the school directly *(381-3361)*.

The job market: Cameron County's Private Industry Council has a state-funded Job Training Placement Agency and on-the-job training programs *(542-4351)*.

When the Kids Come to Visit

Gladys Porter Zoo; Stillman House Museum; Historic Brownsville Museum; Historic Fort Brown Area; Palo Alto Battlefield; Port of Brownsville; Laguna Atascosa Wildlife Refuge; Confederate Air Force Museum; Port Isabel Lighthouse; South Padre Island; Boca Chica Beach.

Getting Around Town

Roads & interstates: I-77, I-83, I-281
Airports & airlines: Brownsville/South Padre Island International Airport is served by Southwest, American, Continental, and Aero Monterrey. Many flights heading north require a change of planes in Houston or Dallas.
Public transportation: Brownsville Urban Mass Transit allow seniors to travel at half fare (15¢) or 20 rides for $3. The routes cover most of the city.
Managing without a car: No one recommended it.

What Residents Already Know

Prescription drugs can be gotten for a song across the border. The *farmacias* are stocked with many of the same medications found in the U.S. at a fraction of the cost. • Even Winter Texans have clout. After 30 days in residence they can become legal voters and are known to be a not-so-silent majority when politician propose something not in their best interest. • American currency is a *"muy"* welcome commodity in Old Mexico. Bring all you want. They'll take more.

For More Information

Chamber Of Commerce Office:
Brownsville Chamber of Commerce
P.O. Box 752
Brownsville, 78522
542-4341

Newspaper:
The Brownsville Herald
P. O. Box 351
Brownsville, 78520
542-4301

Realtor:
Isabel Brege
Century 21/Echols Group
2035 Price Rd. Suite C
Brownsville, 78521
541-9161

43. Kerrville, Texas

Area Snapshot

Nickname: "Palm Springs of Texas"
County: Kerr
Area code: 512   **Zip code:** 78028
Local population: 18,500   **County:** 36,000
% of population 65+: 25% to 30%
U.S. region: In the heart of Texas Hill country on the Guadalupe River.
Closest metro areas: San Antonio, 62 miles, Austin, 96 miles
Nearby areas to consider: Fredericksburg
Median housing price: $65,000
Best reasons to retire here: Large retirement population, excellent services, small rural area (but close to big city), low crime, affordable, wonderful climate.

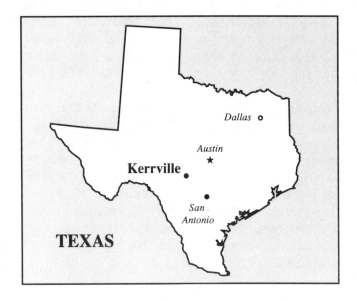

Fabulous Features

Kerrville is a picture-perfect retirement community. Nestled in the rugged terrain on the Guadalupe River, the panoramic views don't get any better than this from atop the rolling hills. People think everything in Texas is big, but Kerrville is a pleasant contradiction. It's very small, very friendly, and the whole city is geared to providing services and activities for seniors. The 3 C's of a great retirement—climate, crime and cost of living are at almost idyllic levels. The climate is warm to hot with comfortable humidity. Crime is low (there are so many different law enforcement officers around, you wouldn't dare get in trouble) and living costs are low. What makes Kerrville really special, though, is how helpful and interested people are. Everyone took the time to talk to us (we always take that as a good sign), and many people also spoke of having the best of both worlds—the benefits of living in a quiet, rural community but being within an hour of San Antonio for culture, medical and air travel.

Possible drawbacks: There is no local bus service so a car is a necessity.•Local shopping is limited, and in some cases, more costly than San Antonio.•Although Kerrville offers quality medical care for a town this size, it is still somewhat limited. Residents go to San Antonio for some needs, which may be a hardship on the spouse who has to travel to the hospital frequently.

"You can quote me on that"

"I'm from Waterloo, Iowa and I love it here. I came to Kerrville a year ago and think it has everything. The climate is perfect, there's hardly any crime, and there's a good ethnic mix, too. Kerrville is small, but there's so much to do. I have friends from all over the country come visit and I can entertain them for the whole time. Kerrville is also convenient to the airport and medical care in San Antonio."—L.D.

"We've lived in Texas our whole life and thought we'd retire somewhere else. But the best place for us was our own backyard. The town is tiny but not boring. Also it doesn't cost as much to live here. And we've made good friends. The kids said they weren't going to visit because there would be nothing to do. Well we showed them such a good time, they're coming too much."—R.F.

Climate

Elevation: 2,000'	Avg. High/ Low	Average Inches		Avg. # Days Precip.	Avg. % Humidity
		Rain	Snow		
Jan.	62/35	1.5	-	8	51
April	78/54	2.4	-	8	60
July	97/73	1.9	-	4	59
Oct.	79/54	2.9	-	6	65
YEAR	79/54	27	1	-	-
# days 32° or below: 23			# days 90° or above: 123		

Let the Good Times Roll

Recreation: Kerrville State Park (500-acres) is the area's premier spot for camping, swimming, fishing and nature studies. There is one private and one public golf course in town, but the claim to fame here is that there are more playable days than in Palm Springs. There are many other courses within driving distance. There are also 25 tennis courts and many seniors look forward to the scheduled tournaments for retirees. This is also game hunting country-deer hunting is big business. And don't forget to bring your cameras. Photo safaris in the Hill Country are common because it boasts the largest collection of natural roaming exotic game in the Western Hemisphere.

Culture: Kerrville has evolved into a small artist's colony, with more than 40 resident artists. Their works are displayed at local galleries and boutiques; Hill Country Arts Foundation offers year-round art and drama classes; The Pointe Theater has outdoor summer performances on the banks of the Guadalupe; The Kerrville Performing Arts Society brings in shows, concerts and other live performances; There are three museums, including The Cowboy Artists of America (the only one in the U.S. to feature works by living western artists).

Annual events: Hill Country District Jr. Livestock Show (Jan.), Texas Wildlife Exposition (Mar.), Kerrville Easter Festival and Chili Classic, Cowboy Artists of America Museum Anniversary (April); Texas State Arts and Crafts Fair (May); Crider's Rodeo and Dance (Aug.); Heart O' The Hills Golf Tournament (Aug.); Kerrville Folk Festival Too (Labor Day); Kerr County Fair (Oct.).

Local Real Estate

The whole state of Texas is a buyer's market and Kerrville is no exception. Homes are widely available in all price ranges and there are some beauties in the bunch.

Median price for single family homes: $65,000. New: $90,000 (1,800 sq. ft.).

Median price for 2BR condo: None available (the only condo development in town sat empty for so long the bank turned into a rental unit).

Rental housing market: The rental market is tight, with only a 1%-4% vacancy. Houses are even more scarce. Apartments range from $250-$500/mo.

Common housing styles & features: There is no tract housing and none of the houses have basements. The 1-story split plan is very popular with retirees, with the master bedroom on one side, 2 guest rooms on the other. Most layouts are casual and informal.

Nearby area to consider: Fredericksburg.

Unique features of this area: Fredericksburg is a small but beautiful rural town with a large German population. There are many retirees who find it quaint, others who say that after living there for 10 years, you'll still be considered a newcomer. It is an area steeped in tradition and family lines.

What Things Cost

Recent surveys show that living costs are 2-4% below the national average, with utilities, food and housing being very affordable in comparison. With no state income tax, retirees on a fixed income should be able to live comfortably.

Gas company: Lone Star Gas Company (257-4033). Avg. monthly bill is $5.50 (for delivery) plus a little more than 5¢ per measured cubic feet. That can add an average of $52/mo. to the bill for a 3BR home. The highest gas consumption is in Dec./Jan. Deposits may not be required. Connection fee: $25.

Electric company: Kerrville Public Utility Board (257-3050). Avg. monthly bill is $66-$74. Bills in January (the highest) can avg. $112.

The deposit is twice the cost of the average estimated consumption.

Phone company: Kerrville Telephone Company *(257-1111)*. Basic monthly service runs $6.80 (no charge for touchtone service). Deposit may not be required. Installation starts at $14.88.

Car registration/license: New residents must get a Texas Driver's license within 30 days of establishing residency. License tags are based on year of car: 1989-92: $58.80; 1986-88: $50.80; 1985 and older: $40.80. Title fee: $10. Road and bridge fee: $5. New residents impact fee: $15. Driver's license: $16 for 4 years.

The Tax Ax

Sales tax: 7.75% (prescription drugs and groceries are exempt).

State income tax: None. Estate taxes: None over and above the federal credit.

Property taxes: Property tax for Kerrville residents includes a city tax, a county tax and a school tax. At age 65+, the school tax is frozen (you'll never pay any higher than that) and you become eligible for a $15,000 homestead exemption off the school tax ($5,000 exemption if you're under 65). At age 65, you're also eligible for a $3,000 county homestead exemption. A home valued at $50,000 home would pay $816.30; taxes on a $100,000 home would be $1,632.60. County Tax Assessor's office *(896-1414)*.

Medical Care

Kerrville is considered the regional medical and diagnostic center in the area, although sometimes it is necessary to drive to San Antonio for certain types of care, such as open heart surgery or neurosurgery.

Major hospitals/regional medical centers: All three major hospitals are JCAH-accredited and offer specialties. **Sid Peterson Memorial Hospital** is a private, nonprofit facility. In addition to its general services, it runs a program for seniors called, "Caring Card." Participation is free, as are the quarterly health screenings and newsletters. **Kerrville State Hospital** offers geriatric care, alcohol rehab and psychiatric care. Veterans Administration Hospital offers an excellent wellness

program and support groups for eligible families. **Kerrville Kidney Disease and Dialysis Center** is a ten-station free-standing dialysis center. **Kerrville Radiation Therapy Center** has an Oncologist on staff to provide therapy for cancer patients. **Heart of the Hills Cardiac Rehab Center** provides individualized exercise programs for heart patients.

Emergency medical services (EMS): Three ambulances Response time within city limits is four minutes; within county: 8-11.5 minutes. There is also emergency helicopter service to San Antonio.

Physician's & dental referral: *257-0630*.

Continuing Education

The Kerrville Independent School District's Adult and Continuing Education offers many interesting classes including rockwork, languages, computer and vocational courses. Enrollment fees range from $1-$5 per hour, with computer classes averaging $50-$75 a course *(257-2218)*.

Services for Seniors

Dietert Claim Senior Citizen's Center (named for the family that donated the land) is a learning and social activity facility offering numerous activities and programs, including "Meals On Wheels," in-home health care and transportation *(257-6228)*. **AARP:** Guadalupe Chapter meets at Dietert Claim. Other organizations for retirees include the Exxon and Shell Annuitants, Retired Teachers Association and **SCORE** (Service Corps of Retired Executives). Senior discounts are widely available.

Crime & Safety

For one small town, there's sure a lot of law enforcement coverage. There's the city police, the county sheriff's department, the state highway patrol, the Texas Rangers and a regional drug task force office—all in Kerrville. It's no wonder the police department says Kerrville has one of the nation's lowest crime rates. If you commit a crime here, you're probably going to get caught! When there are burglaries, it's generally because of public complacency—homeowners leave their doors unlocked while they're gone, etc. The police department runs numerous programs on crime prevention for seniors including protection for the physically impaired and home safety. Two other excellent programs are "Courtesy Calling," where they'll make daily phone calls to the homebound to check on their status, and HEAT (Help Eliminate Auto Theft). If you have a HEAT decal on your car window and the car is on the road between 1 and 5 AM, the police will stop the driver and ask for identification.

Earning a Living

Current business climate: Many of the shopkeepers have been in business for decades and have a "buy it or leave it" attitude. They can do that because modern retailing hasn't found its way here yet. Residents are very anxious for discount outlets and stores with large inventory so they don't have to drive to San Antonio for major purchases. With the constant flood of newcomers, the local economy can support businesses that come in and fill a much needed void.

Help in starting a business: None available.

The job market: The employment market is very tight, with mostly minimum-wage jobs being the available.

When the Kids Come to Visit

The Cowboy Artists of America Museum, Y.O. Ranch (a native and exotic game ranch), Crider's Rodeo and Dance Hall, Rockbed River, Dude Ranches, Tour of a Zoo Breeding Facility. Nearby San Antonio and limitless outdoor activity in the heart of Texas Hill Country will keep your family coming back to visit.

Getting Around Town

Roads & interstates: IH-10, Highways 16 and 27.

Airports & airlines: San Antonio International Airport (62 miles); Eleven major airlines including American, America West, Delta, Continental, Northwest.

Public transportation: There is no local bus service in Kerrville. Transportation can be arranged through taxi service and the Dietert Claim Senior Center *(257-6228)*. Dietert Claim has weekly transportation for seniors to San Antonio, doctors and shopping.

Managing without a car: Impossible.

What Residents Already Know

This is no ordinary Texas dustbowl. Kerrville is at a high elevation, it's got hills and it's quite cosmopolitan. It's also a real melting pot—80% of the residents came from someplace else, either big Texas cities or from anywhere in the U.S. Newcomers don't take well to many of the local merchants who have "bad" attitudes and would be very open to businesses that discounted, had good service and treated people right.

For More Information

Chamber Of Commerce Office:
Kerrville Chamber of Commerce
Retirement Committee
1200 Sidney Baker
Kerrville, 78028
896-1155

Newspaper:
Kerrville Daily Times
429 Jefferson Street
Kerrville, 78028
896-7000

Realtors:
Mr. Greg Bitkower
Bitkower Mangement
433 Water St., Suite B
Kerrville, 78028
257-6592

Mr. Ben Peek
Coldwell Banker
2123 Sidney Baker
Kerrville, 78028
896-5500

44. San Antonio, Texas

Area Snapshot

Nickname: "The Alamo City"
County: Bexar County (pronounced bear)
Area code: 512 **Zip code:** 78240—97
Local population: 935,900 **County:** 1,185,000
% of population 65+: 10%
U.S. region: South Central Texas at the edge of the Gulf Coastal Plains
Closest metro areas: Austin, 70 miles
Nearby areas to consider: Kerrville and New Braunfels
Median housing price: $65,000
Best reasons to retire here: A city rich in history, mild winters, low cost of living, affordable housing, top-notch health care, strongly favored by retired military, excellent public transportation.

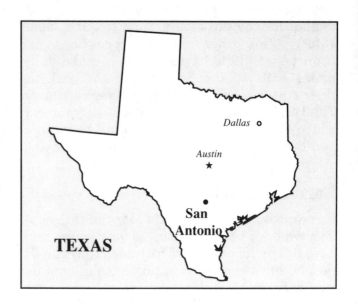

Fabulous Features

There is so much to love about this charming, modern city that has clung to its old-world ambience. The San Antonio River winds through the downtown area, a perfect compliment to the contemporary office buildings, hotels and galleries. Retired military are not the only ones who have strong attachments to the city. Seniors from all over the U.S. settle here to enjoy the mostly pleasant climate, the endless action and affordable real estate. In fact, when recently compared to 23 other urban areas with a million or more people, San Antonio had the lowest overall living costs. "The Alamo City" is also widely known for excellent medical care and research. Special preventive programs for seniors at Humana Hospital and Santa Rosa Health Care are fabulous. Retirees pride themselves in blending in with the crowd. You don't find large retirement communities here, just nice neighborhoods for all.

Possible drawbacks: If you've been dreaming of small-town living, skip San Antonio. It's a metropolitan city with matching red tape. Of all the areas we researched, it was ranked #1 for difficulty in gathering information, particularly when we asked about crime. No one wants to tarnish this city's outstanding image, but being close to the Mexican border has made it convenient for drug traffickers. Both property and violent crime are up, yet people we asked said they had no fears. Also look out for the summer heat. Some days feel like 120 in the shade. Without precautions, heatstroke and sunstroke are possible. The good news is, nearby lakes and rivers provide relief from the heat and the city pace.

"You can quote me on that"

"We moved here from Montgomery, Ala., but being with the military, we've lived all over the country. We love it here. The medical care is excellent, there are many volunteer opportunities, the pace is delightful and we can enjoy the rodeo one day and opera the next."—D.C.

"We were most surprised by the relaxed friendliness of the people—race and culture mean nothing. Everyone is welcome."—M.L.

Climate

Elevation: 812'	Avg. High/ Low	Avg. Rainfall (Inches)	Avg. # Days Precip.	Avg. % Humidity
Jan.	62/40	1.7	8	68
April	80/59	2.5	8	64
July	96/74	1.7	4	61
Oct.	82/59	2.8	6	66
YEAR	80/58	27	-	-
# days 32° or below: 24		# days 90° or above: 115		

Let the Good Times Roll

San Antonio is the home of the NBA Spurs, the Missions (LA Dodgers Farm Team) and the Texas Open (PGA Tour).

Recreation: Residents enjoy the 340-acre Brackenridge Park (adjacent to the fabulous San Antonio Zoo), Friedrich Wilderness Park (a wildlife sanctuary) and McAllister Park (make reservations for overnight camping). Call Parks and Recreation for information on public pools, tennis courts and golf courses *(821-3000)*. Head out to Canyon Lake for sailing and windsurfing and to Calavera and Braunig Lakes for freshwater fishing.

Culture: This city has it all—from classical music to Dixieland, from fine art treasures to live theater. There's the San Antonio Ballet Company, Little Theater, Performing Arts Association, San Antonio Symphony, McNay Art Institute, San Antonio Museum of Art, Carver Community Cultural Center, and Chamber Arts Ensemble. Senior Citizen discounts are widely available.

Annual events: Fiesta San Antonio, a week long festival celebrated every April began as a memorial to the heroes of the Alamo. Other events: San Antonio Festival (14 days of music, drama and dance), Armed Forces Week (May), Fun-Tier Nights (July), Nissan Grand Prix of San Antonio (Sept.), Oktoberfest (Oct.).

Local Real Estate

Not unlike other former "boom towns" in Texas, the residential market has spiraled downward for the past few years, making it a legitimate buyer's market. And although property taxes have gone up, they are still proportionately lower compared to other major cities across the country.

Median price for single family home: $65,000. New: $90,360 (1,800 sq. ft.). It's a buyer's market.

Median price for 2BR condo: Range from $32,000-$70,000

Rental housing market: Market is very limited now. But when available, houses go for $700 to $900/month (1,600-1,800 sq. ft.) 2BR Apt.: $450.00/month

Common housing styles & features: From old world charm to ultra modern. Mostly 2-story with attached garage and fireplace, central air. No basements.

Amenities in condo developments: Washer/ dryer connections, central air, patios, electric kitchens, pools, tennis courts, jogging trails, etc.

Nearby communities to consider: New Braunfels (30 mi. northeast); Kerrville (65 mi. northwest). **Unique features of these areas:** They're part of scenic Texas Hill Country. The towns, originally inhabited by Germans, are clean, small, rural areas with homes starting in the $60s.

What Things Cost

ACCRA (1st Quarter, 1991) shows that living costs are 5.1% below the national average. Housing costs run close to 15% below and utilities run more than 20% below the national average.

Gas company: City Public Service *(225-2541)*. Average monthly bill is $21.80. The highest gas consumption occurs in January with an average bill of $49.83.

Electric company: City Public Service *(225-2541)*. Average monthly bill $65.25. The highest electric consumption occurs in August with an average cost of $90.47.

Water/sewer: Water bills avg. $12-$15/month. Sewer charges average $13-$16/month.

Phone company: Southwestern Bell Telephone Co. *(229-7171)*. Basic monthly service runs $8.45. Installations start at $60.

Car registration/license: New residents must have a Texas driver's license within 30 days of establishing residency. License tags (Title fees) are based on year of car: '89-91: $68.80; '86-88: $60.80; '85 and older: $50.80. A $10 road and bridge fee is included. New Residents Impact Fee: $15; Driver's license: $16 for 4 years. With a valid license, no driver's test is required.

The Tax Ax

Sales tax: 8.25%. (Prescription drugs and food and are exempt).

State income tax: None.

Retirement income: Estate taxes—None. No inheritance taxes.

Property taxes & tax breaks: Property taxes are assessed at $1.94 to $2.37 per $100 of value within city limits. Taxes for a $65,000 home might run $1,300. Outside the city, property taxes range from $1.46 to $1.96 per $100 valuation. There is an annual $8,000 homestead exemption if the retiree is living in the residence by January 1.

Medical Care

Major hospitals/regional medical centers: The 33 general hospitals, including two U.S. Dept. of Defense hospitals, one V.A. and two Texas State hospitals, provide outstanding care and research facilities. **Wilford Hall Medical Center** (Lackland Air Force Base) is the largest U.S. Air Force Hospital. The **Brooke-Army Medical Center's** world-famous burn center is also here. The JCAH-accredited hospitals include: **Santa Rosa Health Care Corp.**, operating 5 hospitals in the city. Seniors rave about "Santa Rosa for Seniors" a club that offers education, screenings, referral services, fitness and exercise, a monthly newsletter and even hospital discounts. Membership is free *(228-2805)*. **Humana Hospital** operates 4 JCAH-accredited hospitals. They specialize in diabetes, cardiovascular care, transplants. It's a regional cancer center and by spring, 1992, they'll have completed a Heart Institute. Their Humana Seniors Association offers a full range of programs and services for $15/yr. Members who depend solely on Medicare don't pay hospital deductibles *(692-8224)*. **Medical Center Hospital** (a teaching hospital) has the only civilian Level-I trauma center in Bexar county. **South Texas Medical Center** is a 700-acre medical complex with 8 hospitals, numerous clinics, labs and more. It is widely known for cancer research and therapy.

Emergency medical services (EMS): 21 emergency vehicles—all advanced life support. 262 paramedics. Response time: 5.2 minutes within the city; 6.4 minutes outside the city.

Physician's referral: Bexar County Medical Society *734-6691*. Dental: San Antonio District Dental Society *732-1264*.

Continuing Education

Our Lady of the Lake University *(437-6711)*: Continuing education classes in fall and spring. Subjects include computers, genealogy, language and sailing. Enrollment fees vary from $40 to $300 per course. **San Antonio College** *(733-2000)*: Courses include computers, real estate, floral design, insurance and law enforcement. Enrollment fees: $1.25/hr. **St. Mary's** *(436-3321)*: Classes include interior design, history and fashion design. 10 month programs (Aug.-June) cost $95 per month. These courses are geared toward employment opportunity. **San Antonio Public Schools** also offer continuing education classes.

Services for Seniors

The Senior Citizen Council is a wonderful source for information and referrals. They have Nutrition Centers located in almost every neighborhood. Senior housing information also available *(222-1845)*. Media: The Senior Sentinel is a monthly newspaper. Subscriptions are $5. Call the Senior Citizen Council *(222-1845)*. **AARP:** For local chapter information, contact Joe Slattery, P.O. Box 64, San Antonio, 78291 *(655-2287)*.

Crime & Safety

San Antonio is near the Mexican border, which creates its share of drug-trafficking problems. This is presumably the cause of the recent increase in violent and property crimes. Statistically, the rate of burglaries per 1,000 households makes it the 4th mostly likely city in the U.S. in which to be a victim. In real terms, 55 homes per 1,000 were burglarized. The safest area to live seems to be the north side of town. The downtown area is also quite safe due to extra patrols. **Advice from the**

police: Seniors are urged to participate in crime prevention programs for seniors, including personal safety and home security.

Earning a Living

Current business climate: San Antonio was recently ranked 18th best city in the U.S. to locate a business (Cushman & Wakefield Real Estate). The National League of Cities ranked it one of the three most innovative U.S. cities for economic development.

Programs to help you get started: The One Stop Business Information Center answers legal, planning and licensing questions *(554-7120)*. There are also state and local assistance programs. Contact: Mr. Trini Lara, Business Information Center, P.O. Box 83996, San Antonio, 78283.

The job market: The job outlook for seniors is not promising, mostly due to military and corporate cuts in spending. However, there is a Job Training Partnership Program that helps with placement and training *(554-7140)*.

When the Kids Come to Visit

The Alamo, Fort Sam Houston, The Spanish Missions, The River Walk, the San Antonio Zoo, Japanese Tea Gardens, Sea World (See Shamu the Killer Whale). Nearby towns nestled in the rolling landscape of the Texas Mill Country promise sightseeing and leisure opportunities. One picturesque village, New Braunfels, features a lazy, tree-lined river that offers hours of tubing and floating fun.

Getting Around Town:

Downtown is no more than 30 minutes from anywhere in the county because of the excellent road system.

Roads & interstates: IH-35, IH-10, IH-37, US-90, US-281, LOOP-410, LOOP-1604 (Loops circle the city).

Airports & airlines: San Antonio International Airport: Eleven major airlines including American, America West, Delta, Continental, Northwest, United, TWA, USAir, and two commuter airlines.

Public transportation: The Metropolitan Transit Authority operates VIA, 590 buses with daily service downtown, across and around town. Seniors fare is 20¢. Streetcars operate shuttles downtown. VIA Trans has special shuttle services for the handicapped, elderly and organizations *(227-5050)*. Residents can manage easily without a car.

What Residents Already Know

With 5 major U.S. Military Installations, Air Force personnel and retirees have a presence felt like nowhere else. It's their town.•People can't wait for the $160 million Alamodome, a multi-use sports and convention center coming in early 1993.•Fire ants bite and they're everywhere, so don't disturb.

For More Information

Chamber Of Commerce Office:

The Greater San Antonio
Chamber of Commerce
P.O. Box 1628
San Antonio, 78296
229-2100

Newspapers:

San Antonio Express News
Avenue E and Third Street
San Antonio, 78297
225-7411

San Antonio Light
420 Broadway
San Antonio, 78205
271-2700

Realtor:

Ms. Luci Cockrell
Apartment Finders, Inc.
(Home Sales/Rentals)
8744 Wurzbach Rd.
San Antonio, 78240
800-922-8440

45. St. George, Utah

Area Snapshot

Nickname: Utah's Dixie
County: Washington
Area code: 801   **Zip code:** 84770
Local population: 26,000   **County:** 45,000
% of population 50: 25%
U.S. region: Southwestern Utah
Closest metro areas: Las Vegas, 125 mi.; Salt Lake City, 304 mi.
Nearby areas to consider: Bloomington Hills, Santa Clara
Median housing price: $95,000
Best reasons to retire here: Spectacular scenery, endless sunshine and dry air, unbelievable skiing and golfing; large retirement population, affordable housing and property taxes.

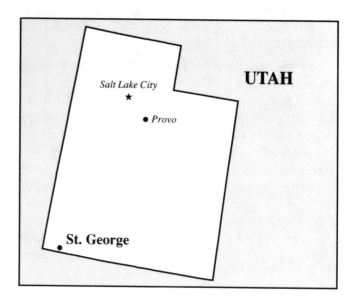

Fabulous Features

Actor/director Robert Redford, Utah's adopted son, says "My fondness for the St. George area almost approaches a sacred degree. I feel something quite spiritually prehistoric about it. I don't know of many places more beautiful." Truly, there is no other region more bountiful in natural wonders. St. George is at the epicenter of some of the earth's most varied landscapes and colors: gold-streaked cliffs and canyons, brilliant red mountains, turquoise lakes, and lush green forests. (They wouldn't shoot a John Wayne movie here because people would think the sets were fake.) Day-to-day life is no less impressive. Beautiful new communities with golf courses, Southwestern-style homes and services are waiting. Housing is affordable with most new models selling between $80,000 and $100,000. There are highs and lows to match the terrain: Culture and continuing education are high; property taxes and crime are low. The climate is as contrasting as the colors—there's dry desert air, palm trees and snow. Just as farmers came in covered wagons in the 1800s, so come caravans of retirees—in Dodge Caravans, station wagons, RVs, and Cadillacs. 72% of the population growth in the past decade were people in their 50s and 60s. As one so aptly stated, "I've come here to live, not to die." And that's not whistling dixie.

Possible drawbacks: Transportation is like a mirage in the desert. The closest major airport is in Las Vegas (2 hrs.). The only way to travel locally is to walk, drive your own car or call one of the two cab companies. It's a small, small town. Driving from one end to the other takes five minutes and now there are "Golden Arches" on both ends. •The desert heat takes some getting used to, although many people commented that they thought it would be worse (it's generally 10 degrees cooler than in Las Vegas).

"You can quote me on that"

"I'm a big golfer so this place is paradise. You can play almost every day of the year and the courses are great (it's also dirt cheap). There are lots of activities for us seniors, really anything you could want is here. It's calm and laid-back. I can't honestly think of anything I don't like. It's nice knowing that people are streaming in from all over the country to enjoy their retirement. We deserve it."—Mr. G.B.O.

Climate

Elevation: 2,880'	Avg. High/ Low	Average Inches		Avg. # Days Precip.	Avg. % Humidity
		Rain	Snow		
Jan.	50/20	.7	-	6	60
April	70/40	.7	-	6	36
July	98/58	.9	-	6	38
Oct.	75/40	.7	-	5	42
YEAR	66/42	8	18	-	-
# days 32° or below: 149			# days 90° or above: 80		

Let the Good Times Roll

Recreation: Recreation in St. George is practically an art form. When you are surrounded by the world's most awe-inspiring scenery, activities can almost be a religious experience. You've golfed before but have you ever seen fairways run down ravines, greens sit on islands in the sky and a course covered with lakes and waterfalls, and lava capped mountains behind you? Welcome to golfing in St. George (Sunbrook). There are seven other exciting courses to challenge you. Tennis buffs turn to the Green Valley area for one of the largest tennis centers in the West. Downhill skiers head to Brian Head and Elk Meadows (same snow depths as Northern Utah) and to Bryce Canyon for cross-country skiing. On many days, the climate accommodates both skiing and golf. For a glimpse at "color country," head for the national parks with camping, boating, swimming, fishing and hiking. These include Zion National Park, Bryce Canyon, Grand Canyon (in Arizona), Capitol Reef, Great Basin, Lake Powell National Recreation Area, Cedar Breaks National Monument. State Parks include Snow Canyon and Kodachrome Canyon, among others.

Culture: Dixie College brings wonderful concerts and performances to the area. Dixie Center is home to the Southwest Symphony, Celebrity Concert Series, art exhibits, the Dixie College Theater, Pioneer Players, College Concert and Chamber Choirs, and the Annual Dixie Invitational Art Show. In summer, the Grand Circle Multimedia Sound and Light Show is presented nightly at the entrance to Zion National Park. The Southern Utah Folklife Festival at Zion (Sept.) is another unique experience.

Annual events: Lions Dixie Roundup: one of the regions largest rodeos (Sept.). St. George Marathon: "biggest little marathon in America" (Oct.). World Senior Games (fall). St. George Art Festival (Easter Weekend). Dixie Week: parades, festivals on the Dixie College campus.

Local Real Estate

St. George is now second to Las Vegas in new housing starts. Gorgeous new golf-course communities and housing developments are springing up in Bloomington Hills and Santa Clara.

Median price for single family home: $95,000. A new 3BR house sells for between $80,000-$100,000. There is also a large inventory of older homes priced $10,000-$15,000 below that.

Median price for 2BR condo: With a pool and tennis courts, prices range from $75,000 to $95,000; no amenities average $55,000-$70,000.

Rental housing market: The winter market was always tight, but now fall and spring are in the same position: tight and driving rentals up. People secure condos a year in advance. Furnished apartments are $450-$650; unfurnished: $375-$550; 2-3BR house: $450-$850.

Common housing styles & features: Stucco exteriors with tile roofs. Popular one-level homes: Mediterranean or contemporary Spanish. Most have grand views (you're not moving here to see your neighbor's backyard).

Amenities in condo developments: Pools and tennis courts.

Nearby areas to consider: Bloomington Hills, Santa Clara. **Unique features of these areas:** Bloomington Hills is part of St. George but is the country club section, which is ideal for golfers. Santa Clara is a smaller, more rural area that is very picturesque (it lies in the red cliff area with an unbelievable view of the snow canyons. Housing prices are $5,000 to $10,000 lower than St. George.

What Things Cost

Overall living costs are 1.5% below the national average while utilities are 20% below. Housing, health care and food are average.

Gas company: Mountain Fuel Supply Co. *(673-7514)*. Gas heat: 2-3BR townhouse (1,300-1,500 sq. ft): as high as $100/mo. (winter) and as low as $7.50/mo. (summer). Most months the average is $20.

Electric company: Dixie Escalante *(637-3297)*. With an electric heat pump, avg. month is $80; with ground-source heat pump; avg. is $60. $100 deposit is required.

Phone company: U.S. West Communications *(801-237-5511)*. Basic service: $15/month with unlimited local calling and touchtone. Or, $12/mo. and get 25 local calls plus 8¢ for each additional call.

Car registration/license: $22 fee includes plates, title and registration fees. License: $10 (includes cost of written test for new residents). For more information call DMV: *(538-8300)*.

The Tax Ax

Sales tax: 6% (prescription drugs exempt).
State income tax: For married filing joint returns, state taxable income over $7,500 is $330.75, plus 7.2% of the excess over $7,500. A personal exemption of $1,500 is allowed.
Retirement income: Utah does not exempt state, federal or private pension income or give an elderly income credit. It follows the federal government in taxing social security income. There is a retirement income exemption for taxpayers 65+ of up to $7,500 per person (regardless of the source). Taxpayers under 65 with qualifying retirement income can deduct up to $4,800 per person. Above certain incomes, these exemptions phase out (reduced by 50¢ for each $1 of adjusted gross income that exceeds 32,000 (for married filing jointly). **Property taxes & tax breaks:** The rule of thumb is that you'll pay 8/10 of 1% of the market value (and rarely over 1%). This takes into account Utah's "primary residential exemption." The taxable value of locally assessed property of a primary residence is reduced to 66.74% of its market value. Tax Assessor: *530-6088*.

Medical Care

Major hospitals/regional medical centers: **Dixie Medical Center** (JCAH-accredited) is the major regional medical center serving southern Utah, northwestern Arizona, and southeastern Nevada. Undergoing a $5 million renovation and expansion, it has an exceptional cancer center (state-of-the-art screening, treatment, research and support center). Services include an air ambulance. dialysis, oncology, radiology/MRI, cardiac care, and a women's center. It also offers a specialty clinic with allergists, neurologists, gastroenterologists, rheumatologists and others. **Emergency medical services (EMS):** St. George's Fire Department has six trained EMTs but only responds to fire calls. Average response time: 3-5 min. Dixie Ambulance Service has intermediate level EMTs (almost paramedic level) that handle medical emergencies. Average response time: 2-4 min. A 911 service is scheduled to start in Dec., 1991, which will streamline the emergency medical service. **Physician's referral:** Dixie Hospital *628-6688*.

Continuing Education

Dixie College offers a continuing education program for seniors. Developed and directed by retirees, the Institute for Continued Learning charges $25 a year and members take as many courses as they want. Classes meet every other week for an afternoon (20 courses in all). Its elder-hostel program runs every week (except in July) and includes golf lessons, geology, pioneers and writing personal histories. A field trip to Zion park is included *(673-4811 ext. 289)*.

Services for Seniors

The St. George Senior Citizen's Center offers exercise classes, dances, recreational trips, health fairs, busing and volunteer drivers, medical claims assistance, legal advice and numerous services. It publishes a monthly newsletter. There is also **AARP** chapter 207, and an **Association for Retired Citizens**—its annual Senior Olympics is now vying for international competition *(634-5716)*.

Crime & Safety

Crime in St. George is mostly misdemeanor thefts and alcohol violations by kids. We kept hearing about golf clubs getting stolen when garage doors were left open at certain condominium complexes. In response, Neighborhood Watch programs are starting up. Everyone senses that crime is coming, but it's not a major concern right now.

Earning a Living

Current business climate: The area is currently experiencing explosive growth (population increased 40% in 5 years) with projections for more of the same through the year 2000. The recession never hit as is evidenced by the vast number of new business starts. **Help in starting a business:** The Chamber of Commerce will try to match up businesses with state assistance programs, and offer free consultations *(628-1658)*. **The job market:** The best way for seniors to find a job is to "buy a job" by bringing your business with you (as so many escaped Californians are now doing). The largest employers are the school district, Dixie College and Dixie Hospital. Tourist trade is also significant.

When the Kids Come to Visit

Grand Canyon's North Rim (160 miles). Zion National Park (42 miles): known for it's steep sandstone walls, canyons and rich colors, it offers hiking, horseback riding, guided tram tours, a nature center for children, and campgrounds. Dixie National Forest (Utah's largest with 2 million acres). Bryce Canyon National Park (125 miles): spectacular red spires shoot up from the bottom. It offers hiking, horseback riding and camping. Ghost Town: deserted remnants of the Wild West pioneer days nearby. Snow Canyon State Park (8 miles). Hike to Johnson's Arch (named for a pioneer), with lava caves and a volcano. Lake Powell (154 miles): huge man-made lake, incredible scenery, boating, fishing, water-skiing, Indian cliff dwellings, marinas, camping. Las Vegas (120 miles).

Getting Around Town

Roads & interstates: I-15. **Airports & airlines:** St. George Municipal Airport provides commuter service to Salt Lake City and Las Vegas. McCarran International Airport, Las Vegas (less than 2 hours) is served by Delta, American, TWA, American West, Midway, Northwest, United, USAir, and other major carriers. **Public transportation:** None. **Managing without a car:** Impossible.

What Residents Already Know

Have you ever heard a southern Utah accent? Short O's sound like Ah's. Oregon is Ahragon.•Donny Osmond, Bruce Hurst (San Diego Padres) and Jay Dawn Blake (the golf pro) could be your neighbors. Long-time residents can tell who the newcomers are. They're the ones who flinch when greeted by strangers (they look as if they're about to be mugged instead of welcomed).•50% of new residents are not of the Mormon faith and most every major religion is represented. All are welcome.

For More Information

Chamber Of Commerce Office:
St. George Area Chamber
of Commerce
97 East St. George Blvd.
St. George, 84770, 628-1658

Washington County Travel
and Convention Bureau
425 South 700 East,
St. George, 84770
800-869-6635

Newspaper:
Daily Spectrum
275 E. Tabernacle
St. George, 84770
673-3511

Realtors:
Claudia Ashby
Bloomington Realty
151 Brigham Road
St. George, 84770
673-6184

Kent Frei
Jerry Jensen Realty
590 E. St. George Blvd.
St. George, 84770
628-1677

46. Charlottesville, Virginia

Area Snapshot

Nickname: "Home of Thomas Jefferson's University"
County: Albemarle
Area code: 804 **Zip code:** 22906
Local population: 40,341 **County:** 68,040
% of population 65+: 12.2%
U.S. region: Central Virginia
Closest metro areas: Richmond, 70 miles; Washington, D.C., 110 miles
Nearby areas to consider: Lake Monticello, Wintergreen
Median housing price: $ 160,000
Best reasons to retire here: Moderate climate, rural area close to major cities, college town, historic area, scenic beauty and culture.

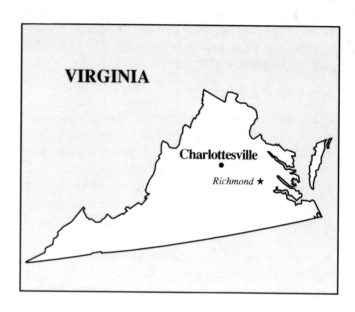

Fabulous Features

Suburban dwellers who are looking for a complete change of scenery will warm to Charlottesville immediately. This pretty city to the east of the Blue Ridge Mountains is a perfect setting for retirement. Sharing its home with the University of Virginia (one of the most beautiful college campuses in the country), there is endless intellectual, cultural and recreational activities to choose from year-round. The modified continental climate offers very mild winters and warm but humid summers. Spring and autumn are the perfect blend of sun and rain and foliage so breathtaking you'll have to drag yourself indoors. With the largest health care providers affiliated with the university, the medical facilities and research are state-of-the-art. But perhaps the most compelling draw is the people. You can hear the friendliness and the sincerity across the wires; we heard stories of kindness and generosity from residents who had nothing to gain by talking. It seems the locals are a sophisticated, diverse group of young and old, with many nationalities represented. They all savor the leisurely lifestyle conducive to a southern town, but are delighted that their lives are rich with friends, activities and community involvement.

Possible drawbacks: The humidity in July is enough to make you want to visit relatives you don't even like.•The rural character is beautiful, but it's not without its expense. Local residents feel the real estate costs are inflated because of all the retirees who move in, in addition to the new professors and univeristy staff who come in every few years.•If you're used to big-city living, you could go through culture shock. Charlottesville is cosmopolitan but small.

"You can quote me on that"

"We relocated from Wallingford, Pa., although my husband is a native Virginian. We love it here. The people are nice, it's quaint, there's so much to do, and it's wonderful being so close to the ocean and the mountains. We've also taken a lot of day trips, like to Washington. And we don't feel alone even though we didn't know anyone. It seems the whole east coast is moving south. I especially like how beautiful the area is. When you drive along the expressway, the medians are filled with flowers."—Mrs. W.M.B.

Climate

Elevation: 644'	Avg. High/ Low	Average Inches		Avg. # Days Precip.	Avg. % Humidity
		Rain	Snow		
Jan.	46/26	3	6	12	67
April	66/41	3.5	.2	10	69
July	86/66	5	-	11	70
Oct.	71/44	3	.1	8	67
YEAR	67/45	43	19	-	-
# days 32° or below: 79			# days 90° or above: 29		

Let the Good Times Roll

Recreation: Any place so perfectly situated between mountains and lakes with a mild year-round climate is bound to keep you active. There are 10 municipal and private golf courses in the vicinty, including the exclusive Farmington and Green Croft country clubs. Chris Green Lake and Mint Springs Lake offer boating and fishing. Shenandoah National Park has hiking, picnicking and mountain climbing. Within the city there are 20 parks, 4 swimming pools (two indoor), tennis courts, and ball parks. The best spectator sport in town is the annual Foxfield Races—steeplechase horse races that wouldn't be the same without tailgate parties, complete with candelabras (even Liz Taylor came one year).

Culture: The Piedmont Council of the Arts is a consortium of local cultural organizations that distributes a monthly calendar of events. Watch for new exhibits at the Bayley Art Museum, a resident artist's gallery. Other activities include: evening concerts, university theater performances, visiting dance troupes, Broadway road tours, the Virginia Festival of American film, the Heritage Repertory Company, and the Ashlawn-Highland Summer Opera Festival. Whenever the mood strikes, you can be at the Kennedy Center in a little over an hour.

Annual events: The Dogwood Festival (April); Historic Garden Week (April); Foxfield (Steeplechase) Races (April and Fall); Virginia Festival of American Film (Fall); Wine Festival (Oct.); First Night/Virginia (a New Year's Eve celebration downtown).

Local Real Estate

It's neither a buyer's nor seller's market. Retired executives and military officers have always been steady customers, as are people affiliated with UVA. It all adds up to a stable market not terribly affected by the recession. Many parents buy ahead and have their children occupy for four years while attending school. Colonial homes are predominant, although much of the new construction is often contemporary. No retirement developments, all who come here are active, independent adults who plan to commingle with students and the rest of the community.

Median price for single family home: $160,000 (new $180,000, resales start at $118,000). A home selling for $160,000 will generally be a 2-story brick with 3BR, 2BA (2,000 sq. ft.), a carport (no garage or basement) on 2 acres.

Median price for 2BR condo: $80,000

Rental housing market: House: $900-$1,000/ mo.; 2BR apt.: $550/mo. As with most university towns, the rental market is very tight. Houses are more readily available, but the high cost can be prohibitive.

Common housing styles & features: Traditional 2-story colonial homes. Most have fireplaces. Larger homes have basements and garages. About 35% are ranch styles.

Amenities in condo developments: Most offer microwaves and major appliances, tennis courts, pools, and clubhouse. Many smaller condo developments have arrangements with larger complexes where owners can pay an annual membership fee for use of facilities.

Nearby areas to consider: Lake Monticello (Fluvanna Cty.), Wintergreen (Nelson Cty.).

Unique features of these areas: Avg. housing prices range from $90,000-130,000. Lake Monticello Lake (15 mi. east) is a gorgeous 360-acre luxury lake development with tennis, pools, six beaches, its own police, fire and private 24-hr. security. Wintergreen, a beautiful winter resort (30 min.), is ideal for the outdoorsman; skiing and horseback riding in your backyard (don't come looking for fishing holes here).

What Things Cost

Virginia has never been an inexpensive place to live, particularly when it comes to real estate and taxes. A recent study by UVA's business school found Charlottesville's living costs slightly above the average in Virginia county. Medical care was the one area with lower-than-average costs.

Gas company: City of Charlottesville *(971-3211)*. Avg. mo. bill: $7.35 + $6.92 per 1,000-3,000 cu. ft. The highest gas consumption occurs in Jan. Deposit: $50 with gas, otherwise $20.

Electric company: Virginia Power *(295-6115)*. Avg. mo. bill: $77.40. Highest electric use: Aug.; avg. cost: $83. Deposit two times highest electric bill for previous year.

Phone company: Central Telephone Company of Virginia *(977-0550)*. Basic monthly service: $12.62. Installation starts at $23.85. Deposit not required with good credit.

Car registration/license: New residents must obtain a Virginia driver's license and change vehicle registration and license plates immediately. Title fee: new car: $10 + 3% sales tax; used: $10 (no tax); License plates: $26 for cars under 4,000 lbs., $31 over 4,000 lbs. $10 for vanity plates. Driver's license: $2.40 (3-7 years). Eye test required when valid license turned in. $12 renewal for 5-year period. Renewals required in the year when the person's age is divisible by 5. Auto Decals $20 per passenger vehicle.

The Tax Ax

Sales tax: 4.5% (prescription drugs-exempt).
State income tax: Taxable income over $15,000 is taxed at a rate of 5 3/4% plus $620.
Retirement income: Virginia offers an elderly income credit of $6,000 for those 62-64 who are not receiving Social Security. For those 65+ it's a $12,000 credit. Double exemptions after age 65 ($800 per person). Estate and inheritance taxes: None.
Property taxes & tax breaks: $1.11 per $100 of assessed value (if you live in the city, or 72¢ if you live in the county), payable twice a year (Dec. 5, June 5). Personal property tax (cars, boats, commercial machinery): $4.20 per $100 of assessed value, payable at same time. There is only a homestead exemption if you are 65 and older (or totally disabled) and have an income of $20,000 or less.

Medical Care

Major hospitals/regional medical centers: **University Hospital** (JCAH-accredited), located on the UVA campus, opened in 1989. Its research facilities are nationally recognized. The hospital is equipped to handle surgical and catastrophic needs, including organ transplants. It also has an excellent burn unit and a Level-I trauma center. University Hospital is also affiliated with **Blue Ridge Hospital**, a special rehabilitation, geriatric and psychiatric facility. **Martha Jefferson Hospital** (JCAH-accredited) is a smaller full-service facility with emergency and critical care units, offering screening and wellness programs for seniors. **Emergency medical services (EMS):** The county has 2 first-response teams, 6 ambulances, 3 medic trucks with a cardiac tray, and a heavy squad vehicle (Jaws of Life). Avg. response time: 4-8 minutes (could be longer in certain parts of the county). **Physician's referral:** *800-552-3723* (24 hrs.).

Continuing Education

With the **University of Virginia** as your neighbor, you can't help but want to continue your education with non-credit evening and day classes on such diverse subjects as manuscript editing, Russian, and literature. Enrollment ranges from $65 to $95 *(924-7114)*. **Piedmont Virginia Community College** has an interesting offer for Virginia seniors who have been residents for a year: Take a class (non-credit) for free, such as Personal Safety. Other classes have enrollment fees of $30-$88. Subjects include "Writing Children's Books," ceramics, and computer skills *(977-3900)*.

Services for Seniors

The **Jefferson Board of Aging** is an advocacy center for seniors with numerous services including nutrition programs, adult day care, home safety, and wellness programs. The **Senior Center** offers recreational and educational programs to adults 55+. Day trips are very popular. Membership is $20 *(978-3644)*. Volunteer work is available through the local **RSVP** (Retired Senior Volunteer Program). **AARP** *(295-5839)*.

Crime & Safety

Charlottesville is a small city with usual crime problems, but everyone conveyed the same messages, 1) it's not pervasive; 2) people feel safe and 3) it's nothing like Richmond and definitely not like D.C. Recent statistics point to very few violent crimes, mostly property. Burglaries are up 8%, no doubt related to the economy. Most people lock their doors and take precautions, nothing more. Crime rates outside the city are considerably less. The Charlottesville Police Department has several crime prevention programs for seniors.

Earning a Living

Current business climate: Of the city's labor force, 25% is professional (engineer, teacher, lawyer) and over half are white collar. Although manufacturing has grown, it still represents a small part of the economy and there isn't much anticipation of sudden growth. **Starting a business:** The local SCORE chapter provides free consultation to small business owners and entrepreneurs *(295-3141)*. A Small Business Development Center affiliated with UVA also provides assistance *(295-8198)*. **The job market:** There is currently low unemployment (3 1/2 %) and job competition is heavy, given the large student body (17,000) that go after service jobs. A surprising number of international banking/brokerage firms are in town as well as medical and legal services where opportunities may be available.

When the Kids Come to Visit

Monticello, "The Little Home of Thomas Jefferson" has been completely restored and furnished; Ashlawn (James Monroe's home) hosts music festivals and summer concerts; Michie Tavern and Virginia Wine Museums (many internationally recognized vintages are in the area); Virginia Discovery Museum.

Getting Around Town

Roads & interstates: US Highways 29, 250, I-66 I-64 connecting with I-81 & I-95. **Airports & airlines:** Charlottesville-Albemarle County Airport is serviced by USAir, United Express, TWExpress with flights to New York, Charlotte, Pittsburgh, Washington, D.C., and Baltimore. **Public transportation:** Transit service operates daily bus service. Seniors who apply ride for half price (30¢ one-way). **Managing without a car:** Extremely limiting.

What Residents Already Know

There aren't any tours of star's homes yet, but Lee Majors, Kate Jackson, Muhammad Ali, Tim Reid, Sissy Spacek and Jessica Lange (with husband Sam Shepard) all have homes in the area. •With the vast rural settings and busy city life, you can still get to one end of town to the other in 20 minutes. One millionairess exclaimed, "The world is my playground, but Charlottesville is my home."

For More Information

Chamber Of Commerce Office:
Charlottesville/Albemarle County
Chamber
P.O. Box 1564
Fifth and Market
Charlottesville, 22906
295-3141

Newspaper:
The Daily Progress
P.O. Box 9030
Charlottesville, 22906
978-7201

Realtors:
Ms. Donna Marshall
Coldwell Banker/Bailey Realty
P.O. Box 6700
Charlottesville, 22906
973-9555

Ms. Ginny Edwards
Real Estate III
P.O. Box 8186
Charlottesville, 22906
973-8333

47. Hampton, Virginia

Area Snapshot

Nickname: "America's First"
County: Hampton
Area code: 804 **Zip code:** 23661-23669
Local population: 134,000 **County:** Same
% of population 65+: 10%
U.S. region: Southeastern Coast (the Virginia peninsula) also called the Hampton Roads area.
Closest metro areas: Norfolk, 10 miles
Nearby areas to consider: Newport News, York County and Poquoson
Median housing price: $82,000
Best reasons to retire here: Beautiful historic waterfront area, laid-back atmosphere, endless activities, temperate climate (except summers), ideal for retired military and outdoor enthusiasts.

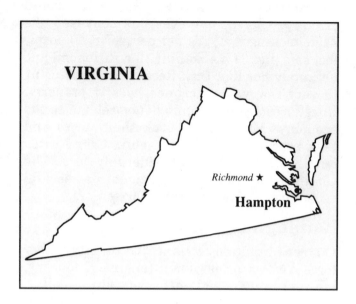

Fabulous Features

In this competitive world, a city that claims to be "first" better be able to back it up. Hampton does indeed. It was the first English-speaking colony, first home to the Navy, and opened the first free schools. The area is so steeped in America's past that it's pure heaven for history and nautical buffs and especially retired military. (One of 9 cities that comprise the Hampton Roads area, Hampton is near other historic areas including Williamsburg, Norfolk, Chesapeake, Portsmouth and Suffolk.) With 7 U.S. installations in the vicinity, it has the largest concentration of military personnel and facilities in the country. Surrounded by the Atlantic Ocean and the Chesapeake Bay, it's also the delight of anyone who hankers for a lifestyle on the water. Then there's an endless stream of culture, recreation, events, classes and attractions to occupy anyone. As for the climate, it's ideal for those

who like the best of both worlds. It's halfway between the sunbelt and snowbelt—not as hot as Florida or as cold as New York. Add to that the beautiful homes and developments, the booming high-tech industry, residents from all over the world, and Hampton is truly a first-class city.

Possible drawbacks: The high humidity is oppressive, the tourist season drives prices up and traffic makes it unpleasant to be near the Hampton Roads Bridge Tunnel—the main access to Norfolk and Virginia Beach. Another thorny issue is local sales tax. Residents pay extra for everything from Cable TV to personal property. For such a historic region, don't they remember the Boston Tea Party? Yet, for those who love its historic setting, water activities and relaxing atmosphere, Hampton's inconveniences may be easily tolerated.

"You can quote me on that"

"I spent my military career in Korea and always dreamed of retiring here. I'm an outdoorsman. I love fishing, boating, the mountains and the seacoast. It's all here plus the warm weather is great. The services and hospitals for retired military are excellent, too."—H.G.

Climate

Elevation: 20'	Avg. High/ Low	Average Inches		Avg. # Days Precip.	Avg. % Humidity
		Rain	Snow		
Jan.	49/32	3	-	11	79
April	68/48	2.7	-	10	70
July	87/70	5.7	-	11	79
Oct.	70/53	3.1	-	8	79
YEAR	68/51	44	8.5	-	-
# days 32° or below: 57			# days 90° or above: 32		

Let the Good Times Roll

Baseball fans catch the Tidewater Tides (NY Mets top-farm club in Norfolk) and Hampton's Peninsula Pilots. The new hockey team, the Norfolk Scope, is always a sellout, and for golfers, two major tournaments come to town, including the Anheuser-Busch PGA Classic.

Recreation: Weekly regattas, fishing tournaments, windsurfing contests, and power boat races are just a few water activities. Air Power Park: An aviation museum with indoor and outdoor exhibits and a space-age playground. Gosnold's Hope Park: Hampton's largest-developed park with campsites, boating, and more. Mill Point Park: A 300-plus seat amphitheater on the river offers free concerts. There's a full range of public and private facilities. Hampton Golf & Tennis has an 18-hole course and tennis stadium seating for 1,000. The Hamptons Golf Course has a 200-acre course including 9 holes of a "links layout" and a traditional 18-hole course. Ten other courses are open to the public. The military bases offer recreational facilities to personnel and families.

Culture: Hampton Roads has been dubbed the "cultural corridor of the Southeast." Museums: NASA Visitor Center (a new Air and Space Center is to open in 1992), Hampton Roads Naval Museum (Norfolk), The Mariners Museum (Newport News), Portsmouth Naval Shipyard Museum, and many more. Art museums: Abby Aldrich Rockefeller Folk Art Center (Colonial Williamsburg), Chrysler Museum (Norfolk), Muscarelle Museum of Art (Williamsburg), among others. Theater: Virginia Stage Company (Norfolk), William And Mary Theater. Dance: Hampton Roads Civic Ballet (Hampton/Newport News), Odu Ballet (Norfolk/Va. Beach). Music: Feldman Chamber Music Society (Norfolk), Virginia Beach Pops-Pavilion Theater, Virginia Choral Society, Virginia Opera (Norfolk) and Virginia Symphony.

Annual events: Hampton Jazz Festival: 3 days of jazz and blues artists. Country Comebacks (May): celebration of the area's rural heritage. Hampton Cup International Championship (Aug.): nation's largest hydroplane powerboat race. Hampton Bays Days (Sept.) a huge 3-day event celebrating the Chesapeake Bay.

Local Real Estate

In the 1980s, builders couldn't put up homes fast enough. Now, with the slow economy and houses wanting for buyers, Hampton Roads is a buyer's market. Waterfront condos and homes can range from $100,000 to $1 million (a *big* dip from a few years ago).

Median price for single family home: $82,000. New (1,500-1,600 sq ft): $111,950. Avg. resale, $91,795. You can also spend $275,000-$550,000. Homes on the water avg. $188,000.

Median price for 2BR condo: $75,000-$95,000 (both new and resales). On the high end, you can spend $195,000-$238,000. Many condos on the water for under $100,000.

Rental housing market: Rentals are readily available May-Sept. 2BR/2BA apt.: $525/mo. avg. 3BR condo on Chesapeake Bay: $650/mo. New single family homes: $750/mo. for 4BR/ 2BA, central air, garage, all amenities.

Common housing styles & features: Victorian, Colonial and contemporary. Most include central air, 2-4BR, 2 1/2 baths, LR, DR, den, fireplace, pools.

Amenities in condo developments: Olympic-size pools, lakes, tennis, security, cable.

Nearby communities to consider: Salt Pond on the Bay, Riverdale, Newport News, Poquoson and York County. **Unique features of these areas:** Exclusive, offering custom built homes, marinas and numerous amenities. Poquoson is the wealthiest city in Hampton Roads.

What Things Cost

According to ACCRA, the Virginia Peninsula has a low cost of living. Housing, health care, and goods and services are approximately 5% below the national average, with only utilities 14% above the average. Unfortunately, taxes don't enter into this equation. As you'll see, Virginians ante up more than most.

Gas company: Virginia Natural Gas *(873-1322)*. Avg. costs depend on usage: Cooking only: $10/mo., Gas heat/hot water: $20-25/mo. Peak usage from Nov.-Feb. 3BR houses avg. $93/mo. Connection charge is $15.75 and a $160 deposit may be required.

Electric company: Virginia Power *(928-2000)*. Basic service: $6.25/mo. If all electric: $127/mo. $90-$180 deposit may be required.

Phone company: Chesapeake & Potomac *(727-8100)*. All service taxed, 20% local/3% federal. Flat rate: $16.14/mo plus message rate of $11.84 (up to 50 calls). Economy service: $8.50 plus 9.6¢ a call. Connection: $38.50, $95 deposit. Advance payment may be required.

Car registration/license: Title fee new car: $10 plus 3% sales tax; used car: $10 (no tax); License plates: $26 for cars under 4,000 lbs., $31 over 4,000 lbs. $10 extra for vanity plates. Driver's license: $2.40 new license, 3-7-year period. Eye test required when valid license from other state turned in. $12 renewal for 5-year period. Renewals required in year when owner age is divisible by 5. Auto decals $20 per passenger vehicles.

The Tax Ax

Sales tax: You name it—it's taxed. Local sales tax is 4.5% (prescription drugs exempt). 17.5% gas tax, 7% tax on cable TV, 3% title tax on cars and 4% tax on restaurant food.

State income tax: Income over $17,000 is taxed at a rate of 5 3/4%.

Retirement income: Virginia offers an elderly income credit, for those 62-64, of $6,000 if not receiving Social Security yet. For those 65+ it's a $12,000 credit. There are also double exemptions after age 65 ($800 per person). Estate and inheritance taxes: None.

Property taxes & tax breaks: $1.20 per $100 of assessed value, payable twice a year (Dec. 5, June 5). Personal Property Tax (cars, boats, commercial machinery): $4.40 per $100 of assessed value, payable at same time. There is only a homestead exemption if you are 65 (or totally disabled) and have an income of $20,000 or less. For a house valued at $130,000, taxes are $1,500 a year. A house valued at $230,000 would require $2,760 in property taxes.

Medical Care

There are 33 hospitals (16 general, 4 military, 3 specialty and 10 psychiatric) in the region. The health care community is widely known for its use of state-of-the-art techniques, its strong volunteer sector and its ties to Eastern Virginia Medical School, which links the hospitals by training new physicians. Rarely do residents have to travel for treatment.

Major hospitals/regional medical centers: The largest health care provider is Norfolk-based **Sentara Health System**, which operates 4 non-profit hospitals. **Sentara Norfolk General** has the region's best trauma level emergency room and offers heart transplants and laser surgery. **Specialties offered by local health care facilities:** reconstructive urological surgery, plastic surgery, cardiac care, kidney dialysis, home health care and geriatrics.

Emergency medical services (EMS): Ten stations (4 equipped with advanced life support). Response time: 5-6 min. Six equipped with basic life support. Response: 3-4 min. All career firefighters are EMT-trained.

Physician's referral: Referral Service *727-7573* and Physician Find (24 hrs.) *874-0123*. Dental: *873-8861* Peninsula Dental Society.

Continuing Education

Hampton is home to some outstanding schools, including the College of William and Mary, Old Dominion University and a satellite campus of George Washington University. Many offer continuing education programs for seniors ranging from dream interpretation to buying real estate. Hampton University home to an annual elderhostel.

Services for Seniors

The Peninsula Agency on Aging (PAA) acts as a liaison for helping seniors find companions, home health aides, respite for caregivers and many other services. PAA has a job club that helps with resumes and training. The **Senior Recreation Services** (part of the Parks and Recreation Dept.) offers weight-loss programs, picnics, trips, and more. **Media:** PAA publishes a monthly newspaper; seniors also subscribe to Senior Times (Landmark Publication). **AARP:** meets every third Thursday *(722-1442)*. Note: Businesses that have PAA Logo in the window offer a 5%-15% discount to seniors.

Crime & Safety

Residents feel Hampton is a very safe place to live. In a recent survey of 26 city services, police protection was ranked 4th best. (Fire, libraries and EMS were 1 to 3 respectively). Although crime is higher in Norfolk, the waterways that divide the cites deter crime in Hampton.

Advice from the police: Get involved in Operation ID, Neighborhood Watch, and the PD's Home Security Program.

Earning a Living

Current business climate: After growth in the '80s, employment and construction have been in neutral for two years. Although some parts of the country envy the stable economy, businesses are definitely taking a wait-and-see attitude.

Programs to help you get started: Contact Virginia's Economic Development office for labor market information and help in recruiting, training personnel *(727-6392)*.

The job market: The outlook for retirees is good, especially retired military. Unemployment (4.5%) is slightly lower than the national average. Largest employers: the government, NASA/Langley Research and Tenneco's Shipyards.

When the Kids Come to Visit

The area's military bases include Langley Air Force Base, Norfolk Naval Base and the Naval Air Station in Oceana. Other attractions are in Williamsburg (24 mi.), including Busch Gardens, Colonial Williamsburg, and Water Country USA. Kids also love Wild Water Rapids (Virginia Beach: 24 mi.) and the Virginia Zoo (Norfolk: 10 mi). There's also Colonial National Historical Park at Yorktown (the scene of the British surrender). Our nation's capital is only a 170-mile drive.

Getting Around Town

Roads & Interstates: I-64 and I-664 provide access to the entire Hampton Roads area as do US 60, 258, 17 and Route 13.

Airports & airlines: Newport News/Williamsburg International Airport is served by Piedmont and USAir. (20 min.). Norfolk International Airport is served by Delta, United, and USAir (20-30 min.).

Public transportation: Pentran is the local bus company. Service is limited.

Managing without a car: Very difficult.

What Residents Already Know

Hampton Roads is the second most populous area in Virginia. Although the climate is mild most of the year, there are freakish weather occurrences like droughts, downpours, heat waves, ice storms, and forsythias blooming in February. • There are close to 150,000 military personnel and 50,000 civilians on the Department of Defense payroll in Hampton Roads, contributing to the over $5 billion going into the local economy.

For More Information

Chamber Of Commerce Office:

Virginia Peninsula Chamber
of Commerce
6 Manhattan Square
Hampton, 23666
766-2000

Newspaper:

Daily Press and Times Herald
7505 Warwick Blvd.
Newport News, VA 23607
247-4700

Realtor:

Ms. Ann Pane
Allied Brokers, Inc.
1004 W. Mercury Blvd.
Hampton, 23666
826-0100

48. Olympia, Washington

Area Snapshot

Nickname: "The City on the Sound"
County: Thurston
Area code: 206   **Zip code:** 98501-7
Local population: 31,000   **County:** 155,000
% of population 65+: 10%
U.S. region: Pacific Northwest (Puget Sound)
Closest metro areas: Tacoma, 30 miles; Seattle, 60 miles
Nearby areas to consider: Tumwater, Lacey
Median housing price: $110,000
Best reasons to retire here: Spectacular scenery, low living costs (no income tax), great college town *and* state capital, wonderful culture and recreation, excellent services.

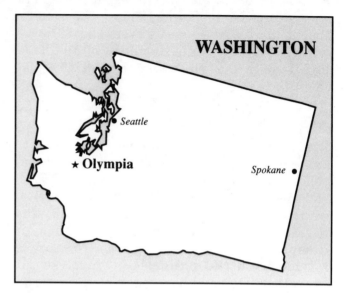

Fabulous Features

Olympia takes a lot of heat for the amount of rainfall that blankets the area year-round, but residents get the last laugh. Yes there are bouts of gray skies and daily drizzles, but it's all taken in stride. Despite the weather, this city on the Sound is the "Camelot" of the West. Surrounded by endless lakes and rivers with Mount Rainier's snow-capped peaks on the horizon, Olympia is a wondrous place to look out on every day. For an economy-sized city, there are giant-sized amenities. Culture, recreation, transportation and services for seniors are so extensive, new residents should be given an orientation session. One thing is immediately evident, however. The hassles, congestion and crime associated with city life don't exist here. As both a college town and the state capital, there is a unique mix of business and basics. People are educated and ambitious but not at the expense of settling for a lesser quality of life. The single most-asked question is about the climate. Does the sun ever shine? Certainly, on average about 40% of each month is clear and bright with the summer season even better—mild (avg. 70) and dry. The health care is excellent, there's no state income tax, and the city is clean and affordable. With our pardons to Lerner and Loewe, "In short, there's simply not a more congenial spot for happ'ly ever aftering than here in Olympia!"

Possible drawbacks: Did you say you wanted a dry, hot climate? Turn the page, Olympia is not for you.

"You can quote me on that"

"My ex-daughter-in-law got remarried and came to Olympia from California with my two only grandchildren. I couldn't stand to be apart from them so I came to visit a month after she moved. I had never been to Washington state and thought it was the most beautiful place I'd ever seen. And when I looked in the paper and saw real estate prices I made two calls. One to a realtor in my neighborhood to put my house up for sale, the other to a realtor in Olympia to find me a house. That was four years ago and I'm happier here than anyplace I've ever lived. I've made wonderful friends and we have a grand time. My ex-daughter-in-law got divorced again and I told her to stay put. I can't keep following her around the country."—Mrs. R.A.

Climate

Elevation: 205'	Avg. High/ Low	Average Inches		Avg. # Days Precip.	Avg. % Humidity
		Rain	Snow		
Jan.	44/30	7.4	-	20	90
April	60/37	3.1	-	15	80
July	72/46	.7	-	9	70
Oct.	61/40	5.3	-	14	84
YEAR	61/39	48	19	-	-
# days 32° or below: 89			# days 90° or above: 7		

Let the Good Times Roll

Recreation: Olympia has 10 city parks that offer activities such as tennis, picnicking, jogging, boating, and hiking on nature trails (the Japanese garden is beautiful). Parks and marinas line the downtown area and there are more than 100 lakes and streams—both freshwater and saltwater fishing opportunities here (bass and trout are plentiful). Puget Sound is an ideal recreation spot, especially for sailing. Mount Ranier is the perfect backdrop and offers excellent camping, fishing, and hiking facilities, as do the nearby Cascade Mountains. For the more adventurous, Mount St. Helens is 120 miles south. Take a fabulous day trip to the rain forest in Olympic National Park. Seven golf courses are within a 20-mile radius. There are also eight ski areas (with cross-country trails) within a few hours' drive. Seattle (60 mi.) is home to the Seahawks (NFL) and the Supersonics (NBA).

Culture: The Olympia Arts Commission, a consortium of cultural organization, does a fine job of promoting the arts. At the Washington Center for the Performing Arts, residents enjoy theater, ballet, symphony, and jazz concerts. Olympia also has its own symphony orchestra as well as numerous museums, galleries and film societies. Three local colleges bring an infusion of culture into the community.

Annual events: Wooden Boats Fair: (May); Super Saturday at Evergreen State College: arts/crafts, music and more (June); Capital Lake Fair (July); Harbor Days: waterfront festival with tugboat races (Sept.); Christmas Island (November); Parade of Lighted Ships (Dec.).

Local Real Estate

Realtors classify Olympia as a buyer's market for homes priced at $140,000 and above and a seller's market for houses $85,000 and below. Anything in the $100,000 and under range (especially resales) is grabbed by retirees. So are new homes, because of built-in warranties and minimum maintenance. Condos are just starting to find a market. For incredible buys, go 30 miles west to Aberdeen, Montesano and Elma. These communities have been hard-hit by the demise in the timber industry, leaving $300,000 homes begging for $60,000-$80,000.

Median price for single family home: $110,000. New homes avg. $115,000; resales avg. $95,000.

Average price for 2BR condo: $80,000-$90,000

Rental housing market: Apartment vacancy rate has been 3%-5%. It is very difficult to find a single-family house. 3BR houses range from $650-$700. 2BR apts. rent for $400.

Common housing styles & features: Colonial, ranch style northwest contemporary. Views of Mount Rainier, lakes, Puget sound, Olympic mountain range, or rolling hills offered.

Amenities in condo developments: Pools, views, exterior maintenance.

Nearby areas to consider: Lacy, Tumwater.

Unique features: Lacey has the major shopping mall and an established retirement community (Panorama City), one of the most highly recognized in the Northwest. Tumwater is the smallest of the tri-cities. It's a very quaint and historic area and home to the Olympia Brewery company. A gorgeous park with waterfalls surrounds the factory to preserve the beauty of the area. Housing prices in both cities similar to Olympia.

What Things Cost

Overall living costs fall within the national average. Utilities run about 12% below, but health care averages almost 40% higher. Housing costs are 4% below average.

Gas company: Washington Natural Gas (357-5571). Avg. 2-person household: as little as $10/mo. in summer and $70/mo. in the winter.

Electric company: Puget Sound Power and Light (357-9333). A 1,500 sq. ft. home avgs. $117/mo. Summer months are lower.

Phone company: U.S. West Communications *(754-3531)*. $13.25 flat rate service: unlimited local calls plus touchtone service. $8.10/mo. measured service (charge per call) includes touchtone service.

Car registration/license: New residents must obtain a Washington license and registration within 30 days. Driver's license test: $7; license and photo: $14. Must have vehicle inspected by Washington State Patrol: $15. Basic registration fee: $27.85 plus $8 for plates and filing fee. State then charges an excise tax of 2.454% of the car's fair market value, which goes to pay for the ferry system.

The Tax Ax

Sales tax: 7.8% (food and prescription drugs are exempt).

State income tax: None (the last Governor who tried to enact one got voted out of office).

Property taxes & tax breaks: Property taxes average 1.8% of assessed value (true market value). A home assessed at $110,000 pays $1,980 a year. County Treasurer *(786-5548)*.

Medical Care

Thurston County ranks first in Washington for the number of physicians, dentists and nurses per capita.

Major hospitals/regional medical centers: St. Peter Hospital is the JCAH regional medical center for the Olympia area. Services include cataract and laser surgery, cancer treatment, kidney dialysis, cardiac rehab., diabetes care, and imaging services. An ambulatory services center and cardiac surgery program are coming soon. St. Peter also organizes a tremendous number of free programs including health screenings, helping the hard of hearing, and even tai-chi classes to get your energy in harmony. Another source of medical care is **The Capital Regional Medical Center.**

Emergency medical services (EMS): Thurston County was first in the country to have a countywide paramedic service. Each fire station serves as a first response team. Firefighters are EMT-trained. Average response time: 4-5 minutes. **Physician's referral:** St. Peter Hospital *491-9480.*

Continuing Education

The Evergreen State College has weekend and evening classes for seniors including writing, languages, and the fine arts, among others. Enrollment is discounted and course costs vary *(866-6000)*. South Puget Sound Community College, in cooperation with the Senior Center, offers classes such as music appreciation, history, the National Park system, dancercise, Hawaiian dance, psychology, computer and golf. Registration is $5 per quarter plus a $5 to $10 fee per class *(754-7711)*. There is also a Senior Intern Program in the Legislature for retirees (55 and older) who want to do research, communication or provide office skills for a small stipend. Contact the Senior Center for more information *(943-6181)*.

Services for Seniors

There is so much in the way of activities and programs for seniors, it takes a 24-page monthly newspaper ("Thurston Manson Seniors News") to report it all. Senior Services for South Sound coordinates various services in Thurston County and operates the Olympia Senior Center. There's also an information and assistance program (offering lists of doctors that take Medicare assignment), case management (to assess for special needs), and a unique family counseling service, which reports on the welfare of older parents to their grown children who live out of the area *(943-6181)*.

Crime & Safety

The Olympia Police Department's conviction rate is well above the national average and the amount of crime is well below the national average. Theft and larceny are the most frequent occurrences and the police have stepped up Neighborhood Watch programs and crime prevention classes. They put on workshops at the Senior Citizens Center several times a year to discuss auto safety, telephone scams, and techniques for preventing your home from being a target.

Earning a Living

Current business climate: Thurston is the fastest-growing county in Washington state and it's stimulating new business starts. Although it's never been a particularly diversified economy, there are signs of growth in the aerospace and health care fields (Boeing is building a new plant in the next county. A word of caution for businesses that infringe on the environment: getting permits and zoning will take forever. **Help in starting a business:** Contact the Small Business Development Center for help with permits, business plans, etc. *(753-5616).* **The job market:** Close to half of the city's employees are government workers, resulting in a stable job market. And, in fact, unemployment is almost nil. Prospects for seniors are excellent because mature people with experience are a welcome sight. In fact, the Thurston County Economic Development started "Jobs After 50" to help with placement *(754-6320).*

When the Kids Come to Visit

Wolf Haven (weekend "howl-ins" at a real wolf sanctuary); Nisqually Reach Nature Center and National Wildlife Refuge (museum, nature trails, guided raft trips); Olympia Farmers Market (Washington's 2nd largest produce market); Capitol Campus and Governor's Mansion (spring cherry blossoms and the Trivoli fountain): see the legislative chambers; Historical tours and museums, including the old capitol building and the Olympia Brewing Company. Mount Ranier (81 mi.) for hiking, camping. Mt. St. Helens Volcanic Monument (120 mi.).

Getting Around Town

Roads & interstates: Interstate-5; US-101; State 8, 121, 510
Airports & airlines: Olympia Airport (the Port of Olympia facility in Tumwater) offers commuter flights and charters; Seattle-Tacoma International Airport (46 mi.) is served by more than 20 carriers, including Delta, American West and TWA. **Public transportation:** Interstate Transit operates an excellent city bus service. Its 16 routes cover 91 sq. miles. Free shuttle service between downtown and the Capitol Campus and a Dial-A-Ride Service are available for the elderly. There is also Custom Bus Service in the evenings and Sundays to areas where regular bus routes don't run. Senior fares: 10¢ a trip or 20¢ for a one-day pass. **Managing without a car:** No problem.

What Residents Already Know

Compared to traffic in Tacoma and Seattle, Olympia has it easy. Here the after work traffic is called "the rush minute."•If you want to plan ahead for a vacation, pick January to go away. With an average of 9 inches of snow and 7 1/2 inches of rain, Arizona looks real good.•People don't tan here, they rust. •The international ties are strong with three sister cities: Olympia, Greece; Yashiro, Japan; and Samarkand, Soviet Union.

For More Information

Chamber of Commerce Offices:
Olympia/Thurston Chamber
of Commerce
1000 Plum S.E., P.O. Box 1427
Olympia, 98501
357-3362

Lacey Area Chamber of Commerce
#7 South Sound Center
Lacey, 98503
491-4141

Newspapers:
The Olympian
1268 E. 4th Avenue, P.O. Box 407
Olympia, 98507
754-5400

Thurston Manson Senior News (free)
529 West 4th Avenue
Olympia, 98501
786-559)

Realtor:
Chuck Gourley
Olympia Real Estate, Inc.
1808 State Avenue
Olympia, 98506
943-6550

49. Sequim, Washington

Area Snapshot

Nickname: The Banana Belt of the Northwest, (pilots call it "The Blue Hole")
County: Clallam
Area code: 206   **Zip code:** 98382
Local population: 3,616   **County:** 56,464
% of population 65+: 50%
U.S. region: Northwest Washington State
Closest metro areas: Seattle, 70 mi.; Olympia, 103 mi.; Victoria, Canada, 12 mi. (by ferry).
Nearby areas to consider: Port Angeles, Port Townsend
Average housing price: $96,000
Best reasons to retire here: Small-town living, high percentage of retirees, invigorating year-round weather, recreation, beautiful, affordable.

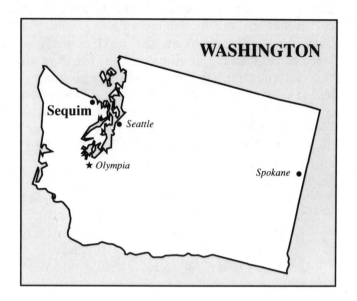

Fabulous Features

As the saying goes, "Sequim is part miracle, part myth." The miracle lies in its idyllic setting. It's not only surrounded by breathtaking views in the Pacific Northwest, it is immediately under the lip of the Olympic Mountains, drastically reducing the amount of rainfall it gets (an average of 16 inches compared to Seattle's 39 inches). The myth is that it's a Northwest version of San Diego (it's not because the temperature rarely exceeds 70). Sequim (pronounced "skwim") has evolved into one of the most talked-about retirement locales in the country. Why have thousands of active, educated, healthy seniors found their way here? Some will tell you that the invigorating year-round climate keeps them young. Others will rave about the majestic beauty of the Olympic Mountains, the clean air and the gorgeous views of Victoria across the peninsula. All will tell you how rich their lives are. It doesn't matter that the town is neither quaint nor cute, it offers more in the way of community involvement, recreation and pleasant days than any other place they could find. It's also extremely affordable, with low property taxes and no income tax! So many of them spoke of having retired elsewhere, then reading about Sequim and shouting, "That's what we were looking for!" Or as one recent retiree said, "No place is utopia. But this place is awfully close."

Possible drawbacks: Highway 101 is the main road through town and the only one heading to Olympic National Park. In the summer, traffic jams and congestion are the norm. State money to build a bypass has no real hope.•There's a fine balance between environmental concerns and beauty. With the growing population, wells and septic tanks dot the landscape. But most residents are quick to overlook Sequim's problems when weighed against the surrounding beauty, crisp climate and leisure opportunities offered.

"You can quote me on that"

"We left San Diego because it was too hot for us there. We love Sequim. It's more rural than we expected, but we have everything we need so there's no reason to travel. There are so many activities, like golf and fishing derbies and we couldn't believe how many campsites they have. The temperature is moderate too. You can go out in shirt sleeves most of the year. And when it rains, it's not a downpour, just a drizzle."—J. & E. I

Climate

Elevation: 180'	Avg. High/ Low	Avg. Rainfall (Inches)	Avg. # Days Precip.	Avg. % Humidity
Jan.	45/32	2.1	8	80
April	56/39	1.1	5	80
July	72/51	.49	3	80
Oct.	59/42	1.3	7	75
YEAR	58/41	16	-	-
# days 32° or below: 2		# days 90° or above: 0		

Let the Good Times Roll

Recreation: Sequim sits in the shadow of the Olympic Mountains and Olympic National Park with all its glorious acres for camping, hiking and fishing (we hear there's plenty of trout, salmon, halibut and cod in the Peninsula). There are a number of fabulous state parks to enjoy including the Dungeness Spit National Wildlife Refuge and Sequim State Park. Spend the day horseback riding, hiking, scuba driving and bird watching. In town is a municipal marina, two 18-hole golf courses, an Aquatic Recreation Center (their hydrotherapy pool is wonderful), a brand-new swimming complex and the John Wayne Marina and Yacht Club, which sponsors special events year-round. Skiing is a one-hour drive to Hurricane Ridge. City parks and ballfields are all over town.

Culture: The Sequim Dungeness Museum and the Natural History Museum are great places to learn the local folklore. The Peninsula Cultural Arts Center sponsors many events and classes throughout the year. Sequim also has a few national historic sites including the Old Dungeness School and the McAlmond house.

Annual events: Sequim Irrigation Festival (May): the oldest event in Washington State. Began as a picnic and program to celebrate the completion of the first irrigation ditch and is now a town festival. Strawberry Festival (July). Fourth of July Celebration: town picnic and fireworks.

Local Real Estate

The real estate market has gone berserk. At Sunland, a 28-year old golf community, there were 80 lots for sale for the longest time. Now a year later, there are two left. Even with the tremendous surge of newcomers, homes for under $100,000 are still available. There is also a wide selection of beautiful, large homes selling for $200,000-$250,000. Let the buyer beware. Once you express interest in Sequim, your mailbox will be filled with great sales letters, brochures and invitations.

Median price for single family home: $96,000 (Avg. prices are $112,000 for new homes, $80,000 for resales).

Median price for 2BR condo: $100,000

Rental housing market: Very tight "take what you can get" basis due to Coast Guard Base and Community College population. Cost for a 3BR house is $300-$600+ and a 2BR apartment is $225-$400/month.

Common housing styles & features: Most homes for retirees are single story.

Amenities in condo developments: Security guards and clubhouses.

Nearby areas to consider: Port Angeles, Port Townsend. **Unique features of these areas:** To start with, they are much larger. Port Angeles is the closest shopping and business district, there's a community college and more cultural activities. Housing is comparably priced. Port Townsend is a charming old seaside town, with Victorian-style houses and great ambiance. Real estate prices are also comparable.

What Things Cost

You can hold onto your pocketbooks here. The tax bite doesn't hurt a bit, shopping is limited so sprees have to be well-planned, housing is affordable and health care costs are well under the national average.

Gas company: There is no supply of natural gas to Sequim. Many people use oil or wood to heat their homes.

Electric company: Public Utility District of Clallam County *(683-4101)*. Typical bill averaged over the entire year is $65-$70 (electric heat).

Water/sewer/garbage: A minimum of $34.99 a month.

Phone company: U.S. West Communications *(373-4468)*. Basic Budget Service is $8.10/month with a 2 cent minimum charge for each local call. Includes touchtone service. Unlimited monthly service is $13.25/month.

Car registration/license: New residents must obtain a Washington license and registration within 30 days. Driver's license/photo: $14; test: $7. Must have vehicle inspected by Washington State Patrol: $15. Basic registration fee: $27.85 plus $8 for plates and filing fee. The state then charges an excise tax of 2.45% of the car's fair market value, which goes to pay for the ferry system.

The Tax Ax

Sales tax: 7.8% (food exempt).

State income tax: None (the last Governor who tried to enact one got voted out of office).

Property taxes & tax breaks: Based on 100% assessed value, amounting to $12.28 per $1,000 of valuation. Residents 62 and older who have lived here for 3 years and have limited income are eligible for exemptions. A $100,000 home would run $1,228/yr.

Medical Care

Major hospitals/regional medical centers: Sequim has an excellent medical clinic and a Radiation Oncology Center (complete cancer care without traveling to a large metro area) but no hospital. The closest, **Olympic Memorial Hospital**, is located in Port Angeles (approx. 16 miles) and happens to be recognized as one of the best hospitals in the country outside of a major metropolitan area. The Olympic Peninsula has attracted top physicians from across the country and also boasts the lowest health care costs in the State of Washington. Residents are fortunate to be one of the few rural areas in the State that has access to both an Oncology and a Kidney Dialysis Center and an outstanding hospital nearby. Olympic Memorial is in the process of adding on a $10 million wing, which will significantly improve its emergency room facilities and other departments as well.

Emergency medical services (EMS): Sequim Fire Department *(683-4242)* has 7 paramedics it sends out with EMTs and firefighters. Olympic Ambulance provides emergency transportation. Average response time is 2 to 5 minutes.

Physician's referral: Call the Sequim Senior Citizen's Center *683-6806* or Information Services *452-3221*.

Continuing Education

Peninsula College (Port Angeles) offers a wide variety of classes geared specifically to seniors. Many classes are conveniently held at the Cultural Arts Center in town, including painting, ceramics, music, photography, languages, writing, Indian Studies, body conditioning, sculpture and writing. Enrollment is generally $12 ($6 per credit). After the second week of school, seniors can take almost any class on campus for $5, on a space-available basis *(452-9277)*. Sequim High School also offers a few Continuing Education courses during the school year.

Services for Seniors

Considering how small the town is, Sequim has a vast number of services and programs. It certainly makes a big difference when half of the residents are in the same demographic boat. Local organizations and clubs include **AARP**, Golden Agers, Grandmother's Club, Retired Teachers, Retired Officers Association and a Retired Senior Volunteer Program (**RSVP**). The Senior Center is very active and provides important services such as hearing tests, hospice care, help with medical coverage and Medicare, transportation and support groups for bereavement, alzheimer's, etc. Currently, volunteers are raising money to expand the facilities (2-acres of land were donated and if enough funds are raised, a new building will be erected *(452-3221)*.

Crime & Safety

Sequim has very few violent crimes. There are occasional break-ins. When asked about crime prevention or public awareness programs, the Police Department couldn't recall ever having one. Obviously there's not much call, which is just how you'd want it.

Earning a Living

Current business climate: With the tremendous population boom, there's been 5% annual increase in new businesses each year for the past five years. As the town has no industry, all of the growth has been in the service and retail sectors.

Help in starting a business: The Port Angeles Economic Development Council can help advise small businesses *(457-7793)*. There is also a local SCORE chapter for personal consultations.

The job market: You can come here looking for anything but work. The market is limited in a good year, let alone tight times. If employment is a necessity, greater opportunities are in Port Angeles.

When the Kids Come to Visit

Olympic Game Farm: 56 species of animals, some exotic. Many used in movies and television commercials. Victoria British Colombia, Canada: a ferry ride away. One of Canada's most beautiful cities with lots to do. Dungeness Recreation Area: one of the longest natural sandpits in the world and still growing; marine and mountain view. Olympic National Park: offers hiking, fishing, camping and spectacular views. Ferry Rides: public ferries run to various cities along the strait of San Juan de Fuca: great for sightseeing. Sequim Bay State Park: hiking, clamming, camping, scuba diving, picnicking and boating. Dungeness Lighthouse: oldest beacon north of the Colombia River. Can hike there and back in a day.

Getting Around Town

Roads & interstates: US 101. **Airports & airlines:** Fairchild International Airport (Port Angeles) is served by Horizon Air. Sequim Valley Airport has shuttle service to Seattle. **Public transportation:** Clallam County Transit is the bus system serving the county. Buses run every hour and seniors 65+ ride free (those 62-64 pay 25¢). There is also a free shuttle bus to downtown. Washington State Ferry Service runs between nearby Port Townsend and Keystone, across the Strait of Juan de Fuca 13 times a day. Fares are $5.55 for an auto and driver, half-off for seniors over 65. There is also ferry service to British Colombia from Port Angeles through Black Ball Transport. **Managing without a car:** It is possible to survive without a car, but very limiting.

What Residents Already Know

Sequim is a gardener's paradise. Flowers, fruits, vegetables, berries and Christmas trees produce bumper crops, thanks to the temperate marine climate and moderate rainfall.•How many places do you know where the "summer rules" for golf games are still posted in late October? In Sequim, golfers play by those rules all year-round.•Mitsubishi Corp. holds an option on land to build a resort near neighboring Discovery Bay. It could mean the best of times or worst of times. No one knows.

For More Information

Chamber Of Commerce Office:
Sequim-Dungeness Chamber
of Commerce
P.O. Box 907
1192 East Washington
Sequim, 98382
683-6197

Newspapers:
The Sequim Gazette
P.O. Box 1750
Sequim, 98382
683-3205

The Peninsula Daily News
P.O. Box 1330
Port Angeles, 98362
452-2345

Realtors:
Brice Flynn
Americus Realty
502-A West Washington
Sequim, 98382
683-3334

Isabelle Dunlop
Dunlop Realty
168 E. Bell St.
Sequim, 98382
683-9691

50. Door County, Wisconsin

Area Snapshot

Nickname: "Thumbs Up," "Door's Open," call it anything but the "Cape Cod of the Midwest"

Area code: 414 **Zip codes:** 54234-9

% of population 65+: 33%

U.S. region: Northeast Wisconsin (the "thumb")

Closest metro areas: Green Bay, 40 miles; Milwaukee, 150 miles.

Nearby areas to consider: Fish Creek, Egg Harbor, Ephraim, Sister Bay

Median housing price: $75,000

Best reasons to retire here: Fabulous year-round recreation (water and winter sports), artists colony, affordable housing, environmentally sound, low crime.

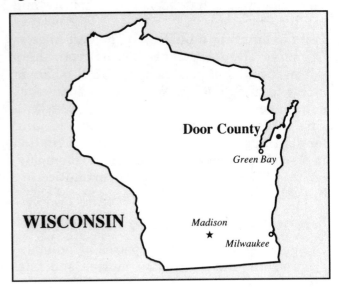

Fabulous Features

Siskel and Ebert would definitely give a "thumbs up" to Door County. Aside from the region offering culture and recreation that's a rise above the rest, it's formation juts out of Wisconsin like a giant thumb. Surrounded by Lake Michigan and Green Bay, the peninsula has more shoreline (250 miles), more lighthouses (12) and more state parks (5) than any county in the country. That's an open "door" to some of the best freshwater fishing and outdoor diversions you've ever experienced. Those enamored of record books also like people to know that the town of Jacksonport is exactly midway between the equator and the North Pole. And in the midst of all the seaworthy are the artists, craftsmen and musicians whose shops and galleries embody the natural splendor of limestone bluffs, snow-laden forests and sandstone cliffs. The famous cherry pie isn't so bad, either (fruit orchards are plentiful). Retired midwesterners are turning to their beloved vacation retreat because it's as comfortable as a worn shoe. The housing is very affordable, the neighbors are friendly, the air and water are free of pollutants, and there is something wonderful to do or explore all year-round: hiking, biking, horseback riding, cross-country skiing, snowmobiling, golf and more. It's all tucked away in the cozy confines of the Great Lakes. Door County stands out, not like a sore thumb, but an outstretched hand welcoming all. Don't bother knocking. Just come in.

Possible drawbacks: No man is an island, except here. There's no public transportation and the closest airport is 45 miles away. The good news is that it contributes to the remoteness of the area and the low crime rate.•You have to pick your home turf carefully. There are lots of great choices but each village has its own unique nuances—some are inland, others on the water, some are quiet, others see heavy tourist traffic, property taxes vary and so on.

"You can quote me on that"

"We'd been coming to Door County with the kids for years but it never occurred to us to retire here. Why would we want to live where there were so many tourists? But after some friends bought a place, they kept begging us to look at the house next door, which was an unbelievable occurance since there's not that many places for sale. Anyway, we bought it two years ago and although we don't use it year-round, we have a grand time when we come. We like the slow pace, the clean air, everything is so relaxed."—Mrs. Z.G., Fish Creek

Climate

Elevation: 588'	Avg. High/ Low	Average Inches		Avg. # Days Precip.	Avg. % Humidity
		Rain	Snow		
Jan.	23/9	-	-	12	78
April	53/36	2.4	-	12	70
July	80/60	3.1	-	11	73
Oct.	59/41	1.9	-	10	75
YEAR	53/36	27	60	-	-
# days 32° or below: 148			# days 90° or above: 3		

Let the Good Times Roll

Recreation: With 250 miles of big-water shoreline and towns named Sturgeon Bay and Fish Creek, you know that anglers have to be happy in Door County. Lake Michigan, Green Bay and nine inland lakes promise catches of enormous chinook, trout and salmon. The Chamber offers a 24-hour fishing hotline *(743-7046)* to keep sportsmen apprised. Five state parks include Potawatomi, 1,200-acres with miles of Green Bay Shoreline; Peninsula State Park (the largest and most popular) with 3,700-acres of forest, limestone bluffs, biking and hiking, an old lighthouse, protected beaches and Whitefish Dunes with the highest dunes in the Great Lakes). The shoreline is 10 minutes from any point for boating, sailboarding and scuba diving. For great golfing, seven courses include Cherry Hills Golf and Country Club and the Alpine Resort and Country Club.

Culture: Although residents deplore the comparison to Cape Cod, one similarity is that they're both artist colonies (you can't help but be inspired by the colors of the seasons). Art shows and festivals are as big as fishing tournaments (well, almost). Cultural opportunities include: Birch Creek Music Center Summerfest Concerts; American Folklore Theater; a chamber music festival every June); The Clearing (founded by landscape architect, Jens Jensen), with year-round painting, sculpting, and writing classes and cabins to stay at; Peninsula Players (the oldest resident professional theater in the country); Red Rooster Playhouse; wildlife sanctuary and nature classes at Baileys Harbor; the Nautical Museum; Door Miller Arts Center (permanent and revolving collection of art).

Annual events: Brown Trout Fishing Derby (May); Door County Art League Showcase (May-Oct.); Mayfest 10K Run, 50K bike race, antiques, (May); Newport Village Day: Celebration of the Pioneer Heritage (June); Egg Scramble (Egg Harbor in June); Art on the Quiet Side (July); Door County Folk Festival (July); Door County Fair (Aug.).

Local Real Estate

Door County has traditionally been a seller's market with limited construction (most people hang on to their homes for decades). When one becomes available, it makes the papers. Rentals, however, are in abundance and most people who come to the area go that route. Prices vary depending on proximity to the water. Waterfront homes can run over $200,000, and houses inland run between $85,000-$100,000. Whether renting or buying, you can choose your favorite setting—near golf, a quiet lakefront site, or in an active tourist area.

Median price for single family home: $75,000. New single family housing and condos start at $100,000, although selection is limited. Resales average $85,000.

Median price for 2BR condo: $100,000.

Rental housing market: Seasonal rentals are widely available for $500 week. Annual rentals are not much more by the month and there's generally a good inventory. Sturgeon Bay has the widest variety of choices because it's inland. But for retirees, the most desirable areas are waterfront villages.

Common housing styles & features: The coves and villages on the Green Bay side are "cape cod" styles, other areas have western or log cabin styles.

Amenities in condo developments: Many area developments have pools and a tennis court.

Nearby areas to consider: In addition to Sturgeon Bay (pop. 9,000), there are 18 small rural towns and villages. Fish Creek (Gibraltar) has gorgeous beaches, cool forests, a bay and harbor and it's the up-beat, high energy part of Door County. Most of the music, entertainment and theater events are here along with great festivals and vintage architecture. Egg Harbor is more rustic, with long, winding roads. The town is shielded from northern winds by towering bluffs. It has a small-town ambience but "with it" looking businesses. Large apple and fruit orchards are north of town. In town are Harbor View Park and the Alpine Golf Course. Sister Bay has natural scenic wonders and is a year-round vacation village. There are two large shopping centers, marinas and docking facilities along the shore and easy access to Peninsula State Park, Ellison Bay Country Club, and Washington Island.

What Things Cost

Overall living costs are not measured, but housing is reasonable (the median is $75,000), property taxes are low (under $1,200 for a $90,000 home not including a state credit), income tax is not unbearable (the maximum rate is 6.93% on taxable income and there are several credits). And, as you'll see, utilities will not bankrupt you.

Gas company: Most people own their own tanks and buy liquid propane.

Electric company: Sturgeon Bay Utilities *(743-5542)*. Wisconsin Public Service Corp. *(743-9666)* serves the villages. Avg. bill for a 2-person household in Sturgeon Bay: $25/mo., winter months avg. $90-$110. Deposits are not generally required. Avg. cost in the villages for a 3BR home (1,500 sq. ft.): $34.50, winter months run in the $120 range.

Phone company: Wisconsin Bell *(800-924-2000* or, out-of-state, *800-523-1428)* serves all but the northern end (GTE North at *800-232-2544)*. New service start-up: $33.05. Monthly basic service: $9.75 plus 6¢ a call (first 60 calls). Call waiting: $2.75/mo. To connect to a new site: $60.90; if wiring exists: $25.90.

Car registration/license: Registration and license plates: $40 plus $5 for title. New resident's license: $15 (plus $4 if you also want a cycle/scooter approval). First license in Wisconsin is valid for 3 years. By presenting a valid out-of-state license, written and driving tests are waived (unless an obvious physical limitation warrants a driving test). A vision test is required. DMV *(743-7151)*.

The Tax Ax

Sales tax: 5.5%. **State income tax:** Married, filing jointly, pay 4.9% for income up to the first $10,000 of taxable income, 6.55% for income between $10,000-$20,000 and 6.93% for income over $20,000. The standard deduction varies by income, but if you're married filing jointly, with income of $35,000, your tax credit is $3,906 (the higher the income, the smaller the credit). **Retirement income:** Pension income is taxed as ordinary income (unless a retired federal worker) and there is a $25 credit for each spouse 65 or older. **Property taxes & tax breaks:** Property taxes are assessed at 95% (on average) of the home's appraised value. Tax rates are per $1,000 of valuation and vary by town: Egg Harbor ranges from $14-$24; Ephraim: $12-$15; Fish Creek: $12-$14; Sturgeon Bay is the highest at $29.75. The state allows a 10% property tax credit off the top.

Medical Care

Major hospital/regional medical center: Door County Memorial Hospital (JCAH-accredited) in Sturgeon Bay is the only in-patient facility in the county. It offers 24-hour emergency services, in- and out-patient surgery, neurology and a new, 1.5 million diagnostic imaging center affiliated with Bellin Memorial Hospital's (Green Bay) cardiac care network. **Emergency medical services (EMS):** Door County operates a dual system of EMTs (first responders) and paramedics. It was the first rural county to develop such a system back in 1979. The EMTs operate from 3 stations in Sister Bay, Sturgeon Bay and Brussels. They're trained at basic life support, and answer more than 2,000 calls a year. Average response time is 5 min. **Physician's referral:** Door County Hospital *743-5566*.

Continuing Education

The University of Wisconsin at Green Bay (1 hr. south) offers four elderhostels a year (avg. price is $300), as well as a new "Learning in Retirement" program. For a $50 membership, you can attend as many classes as you like. Seniors can also enroll in evening classes (non-credit) for half price *(743-5511)*. Northeast Technical College has campuses in both

Sturgeon Bay and Green Bay. All classes are open to the public and some of the non-credit courses cost as little as $3 *(743-2207)*.

Services for Seniors

The Door County Senior Center in Sturgeon Bay offers a variety of services and programs including classes, day trips, social events, nutrition and transportation. It's also the site of the Peninsula Promenader's square dancing, the Golden Agers (card games) and the Retired Person's Activity Club hosting overnight trips *(743-3083)*.

Crime & Safety

From the perspective of the criminal mind, the worst place to do your dirty work is on a peninsula surrounded by water on all sides where the only escape routes are two bridges. That's Door County, and the reason that crime is extremely low. When there is trouble, the sheriff's department has a huge clearance rate (the percent of crimes for which a perpetrator is convicted). There are burglaries during the winter, mostly because the snowbirds leave vacant homes. But on a year-round basis, the "doors" are secure.

Earning a Living

Current business climate: The area has remained a vacation stronghold of the Midwest and the local economy doesn't ebb and tide. The only variables are seasonal, with the summer months attracting tourism (population swells to 200,000). **Help in starting a business:** Contact the Chamber of Commerce for information on business locations, economic factors, etc. *(743-4456)*. The Door County Economic Development Corp may also be of some help *(743-3113)*. **The job market:** A recent

edition of the local paper had several pages of help-wanted ads (both classified and display). Employers were promising free housing, bonuses and other incentives to get qualified people to respond. The signs don't get any better than that.

When the Kids Come to Visit

Death's Door (how inviting!): Take a ferry trip between Washington Island and the straits to see where French Explorer ships didn't make it; Cave Point (scenic county park off Lake Michigan with carved out caves); Thumb Fun Amusement Park in Fish Creek; The Farm (farm recreation) in Sturgeon Bay; Pirate's Cove mini golf (Sister Bay); "Run Wild" at Potawatomi State Park (Smokey the Bear Fun Run each Oct.); The Thresheree (Antique machinery demonstrations, tractor pull, mud pig wrestling each August).

Getting Around Town

Roads & interstates: I-94 to I-43, State Highways 42, 57. **Airports & airlines:** The Austin Straubel airport in Green Bay (45 mi.) is served by Northwest, United Express, American Eagle, Midway Connection. **Public transportation:** None (the only cab service has 1 car). **Managing without a car:** Impossible.

What Residents Already Know

If you come a half-hour early to Pelletier's Restaurant in Fish Creek, you can watch the traditional Scandinavian fish boil over huge open fires (complimentary cherry pie is part of the deal). Or watch the goats grazing on the roof at Al Johnson's Swedish restaurant in Sister Bay. Not your ordinary dining experiences. The new slogan is "Cape Cod: The Door County of the East."

For More Information

Chamber Of Commerce Office:
Door County Chamber
of Commerce
P.O. Box 406
Sturgeon Bay, WI 54235
743-4456

Newspapers:
Door County Advocate (3x week)
P.O. Box 130
Surgeon Bay, WI 54235
743-3321

Realtor:
Mr. Corky Hellyer and
Chris Demaris
Door County Realty
4027 Main Street
Fish Creek, WI 54212
868-2111

Fast Facts

Location	Local Population	Median Housing*	Climate	Best Reasons to Retire Here
Asheville, N.C. (pp. 172-175)	61,456	$88,000	Temperate climate, 4 mild seasons	Beautiful mountains, great programs &services, mild climate
Austin, Texas (pp. 212-215)	480,022	$92,000	Hot summer, storms, mild winters	Services, activity, affordable homes, university, mild winter
Bloomington, Ind. (pp. 140-143)	60,660	$89,000	4 seasons, nice spring, fall, hot summer	Culture, recreation, affordable lifestyle, rural, college town
Boca Raton, Fla. (pp. 88-91)	74,000	$106,400	Warm, sunny yr-round, hot, humid summers	Exclusive, recreation, culture, low crime, scenic, beach
Brevard, N.C. (pp. 176-179)	5,388	$85,000	Mild summers, cold winters, some snow	Beautiful mountain setting, small town, affordable, friendly
Brownsville, Texas (pp. 216-219)	109,000	$55,000	Very hot summer, warm winter	Scenic, ocean, affordable, retirement pop., perpetual summer
Brunswick, Ga. (pp. 124-127)	18,000	$140,000	Mild, warm all year, hot, humid summers	Mild climate, great recreation, scenery & beaches, safe
Cape Cod, Mass. (pp. 144-147)	185,000	$135,000+ avg.	4 seasons, mild winters, glorious fall and spring	Scenic, beaches, low property taxes, art colony, casual, retirement pop.
Carson City, Nev. (pp. 148-151)	40,300	$115,000	4 seasons, no extremes, great ski climate	Mountains, lakes, desert, skiing, fishing, 4 seasons, low taxes
Charleston, S.C. (pp. 200-203)	73,757	$79,000	Temperate, sunny, avg. daily 65 degrees	Southern culture, Atlantic Ocean, retirement & resort area
Charlottesville, Va. (pp. 232-235)	40,341	$118,000	Mild winter, hot, humid summer. Rain and snow	Moderate climate, rural, near cities, college, historic, scenic, culture
Chapel Hill, N.C. (pp. 180-183)	40,000	$138,000	Mild yr-round, some snow	Colonial beauty, mild climate, health care, university

Location	Local Population	Median Housing*	Climate	Best Reasons to Retire Here
Clayton, Ga. (pp. 128-131)	1,700	$75,000	4 mild seasons, rainy summers	Quiet, scenic, yr-round recreation, safe, affordable, friendly
Coeur d'Alene, Idaho (pp. 136-139)	25,000	$75,000	Delightful 4 seasons, warm-weather skiing	Lakes, skiing, affordable homes, taxes & health care, yr-round activity
Colorado Springs, Colo. (pp. 80-83)	290,000	$90,000	Mild, sunny yr-round, little rain	Scenic, climate, outdoor activity, affordable, retired military
Daytona Beach, Fla. (pp. 92-95)	62,000	$86,000	Hot, sunny all yr, rainy, humid summers	Casual lifestyle, ocean, near attractions, low housing, living
Door County, Wis. (pp. 248-251)	n/a	$75,000	Snow, rain in season, temps range from 20-80	Water/winter sports, art colony, affordable homes, low crime, clean
Eugene, Ore. (pp. 188-191)	109,785	$69,700	Cool, 40-60 degrees yr-round, no extremes	Clean air, university, ocean, mountains, recreation
Fayetteville, Ark. (pp. 64-67)	42,000	$79,000	4 mild seasons, rain well-distributed	University, scenic, clean, affordable, outdoor activities
Ft. Collins , Colo. (pp. 84-87)	93,600	$90,000	Dry yr-round, sunny, 50" annual snow	Senior services, culture, recreation, affordable, dry climate
Fort Myers, Fla. (pp. 96-99)	40,000	$82,500	Hot, sunny all yr, rainy, humid summers	Great beaches, casual living, varied real estate, subtropical climate
Gainesville, Fla. (pp. 100-103)	90,000	$68,800	4 mild seasons, no extremes	College, small but cosmopolitan, 4 seasons, afford-able, good medical
Hampton, Va. (pp. 236-239)	134,000	$82,000	Moderate all year, Avg. 59 degrees, 45" rain	Historic water-front, casual, retired military, recreation
Hilton Head Island, S.C. (pp. 204-207)	24,000	$216,000	Temperate, summers 70-80, nice fall	Golf, ocean, resort setting, services, environment-conscious
Hot Springs Village, Ark. (pp. 68-71)	8,500	$90,000	4 mild seasons, long summers, rain yr-round	4 seasons, low taxes, vast recrea-tion, lg retirement pop., great views

Location	Local Population	Median Housing*	Climate	Best Reasons to Retire Here
Kerrville, Texas (pp. 220-223)	18,500	$65,000	Hot, low humidity, Temp range 40-90	Retirement pop., services, rural, low crime, affordable, nice climate
Las Cruces, N.M. (pp. 160-163)	62,000	$80,000	Hot, humid summer, sunny, mild winter	Retired pop., low taxes/housing, dry, recreation, slow
Las Vegas, Nev. (pp. 152-155)	773,282	$115,000	Desert, hot sun all year	Nightlife, entertainment, low taxes, affordable homes, desert
Lincoln City, Ore. (pp. 192-195)	6,340	$85,000	Cool winter (not frigid), pleasant 3 seasons	Pacific Ocean, mild climate, affordable homes, recreation
Maui, Hawaii (pp. 132-135)	93,000	$268,000	Delightful yr-round 80 degrees	Scenic beauty, golf, friendly, tropical climate, casual lifestyle
Melbourne, Fla. (pp. 104-107)	60,000	$71,300	Hot, humid yr-round, ocean breezes	Small city, low living costs, casual life, great family town
Medford, Ore. (pp. 196-199)	46,324	$95,000	Hot summer, mild winter, long spring	Scenic river valley, affordable homes, recreation, culture, friendly
Myrtle Beach, S.C. (pp. 208-211)	27,890	$60,000 ($150,000 on/near beach)	Mild to hot yr-round, warm winter	Low taxes/living costs, beach, resort area, good amenities, friendly
Naples, Fla. (pp. 108-111)	21,000	$137,500	Subtropical, hot, sunny all year	Small, exclusive, amenities, good medical, beaches, subtropical
Ocean County, N.J. (pp. 156-159)	433,203	$80,000 to $140,000	Mild winter, pleasant seasons	Affordable homes, great medical & services, close to cities
Olympia, Wash. (pp. 240-243)	31,000	$110,000	Cool, rainy yr-round, Avg. 46 degrees	Scenic, low costs (no income tax), college, culture, services, activity
Outer Banks, N.C. (pp. 184-187)	23,000	$126,000	4 mild seasons, violent storms	Remote resort area, historic, recreation, casual lifestyle
Palm Springs, Calif. (pp. 72-75)	40,600	$150,000	Desert temps yr-round, very hot summer	Leisure life, dry climate, great golf, tennis, shops, good medical

Location	Local Population	Median Housing*	Climate	Best Reasons to Retire Here
Prescott, Ariz. (pp. 52-55)	30,000	$112,500	4 mild seasons, low humidity	Nice climate, outdoor activity, scenic, low prop. taxes, college
St. George, Utah (pp. 228-231)	26,000	$95,000	Very hot summer, avg. daily temp 50	Sun, dry air, golf, skiing, scenic, affordable homes, low property tax
St. Petersburg, Fla. (pp. 112-115)	250,000	$69,000	Sunny, hot all year, gulf breezes	Sunshine, outdoor activity, affordable homes, taxes, senior programs
San Antonio, Texas (pp. 224-227)	935,900	$65,000	Warm, pleasant mostly, hot, humid summer	Historic, affordable homes, good health care and transportation
San Diego, Calif. (pp. 76-79)	1,200,000	$186,600	Warm, sunny yr-round	Ideal climate, good health care, senior services, culture, recreation
Santa Fe, N. M. (pp. 164-167)	55,859	$128,000	Snow, rain, no extremes, high elevation	Art, culture, ski country, low taxes, low humidity, diversity
Sarasota, Fla. (pp. 116-119)	52,288	$92,075	Subtropical, hot, sunny all year	Culture, real estate affordable, subtropical, lovely beaches
Scottsdale, Ariz. (pp. 56-59)	135,000	$125,000	Dry, desert climate all year	Good medical, dry, lg. retired pop., recreation & service, real estate
Sequim, Wash. (pp. 244-247)	3,616	$96,000	Sunny, mild, little rain	Small, recreation, retired pop., mild weather, affordable, scenic
Sullivan County, N.Y. (pp. 168-171)	69,277	$83,000	Cool breezes, hot summer, cold winter	Rural, affordable homes, near NYC, entertainment, activities
Tucson, Ariz. (pp. 60-63)	405,700	$100,000	Hot, dry all year, cool evenings	Culture, activity, affordable homes, desert climate, medical, college
Winter Haven, Fla. (pp. 120-123)	25,000	$63,400	Pleasant winter, humid summer	Lakes, active retirees, culture, near attractions, small city

* All figures refer to median housing price except where indicated. (See page 51 for definition of median housing price.)

About the Authors

Who is better qualified to write a book about retirement places than a man who has "retired" nearly 700 times? During his 17 years in private practice, Lee Rosenberg, certified financial planner, has successfully guided hundreds of his clients through the retirement process.

Mr. Rosenberg has shared his expertise in the areas of investments, estate and retirement planning with audiences on Fox 5's "Good Day New York," WABC TV's "Eyewitness News," and a host of radio talk shows and financial programs, including "Money Talk," on WGBB Radio on Long Island.

Co-founder of ARS Financial Services, Inc., Mr. Rosenberg has served as chairman of the Long Island Society of the Institute of Certified Financial Planners and is listed in *Who's Who of Financial Planning* (1989-1991). He is also a member of the International Association of Financial Planners and the International Association of Registered Financial Planners, and a registered representative of Cadaret Grant, Inc., member firm of the National Association of Securities Dealers.

Mr. Rosenberg, a graduate of Brooklyn College and the College for Financial Planning, is a well-known speaker and guest lecturer, conducting financial planning seminars at local colleges, libraries, banks and Fortune 500 companies.

Saralee H. Rosenberg is a former sales and marketing executive with more than 12 years of corporate communications experience. She has previously been published in *The New York Times* and numerous other trade publications. Ms. Rosenberg holds a degree in telecommunications from Indiana University, Bloomington, and is a Chicago native.

50 Fabulous Places To Retire In America is the Rosenbergs' second book. They are also the authors of *Destination Florida: The Guide to a Successful Relocation*.

The Rosenbergs live in Baldwin Harbor, N.Y., with their three children. If you would like to get in touch with the Rosenbergs, write to them at 125 Franklin Ave., Suite 6, Valley Stream, N.Y. 11580.